Russia Looks at America
The View to 1917

by Robert V. Allen

Library of Congress

Washington

1988

Library of Congress Cataloging-in-Publication Data

Allen, Robert V.
    Russia looks at America: the view to 1917

    Bibliography: p.

    Includes index.
        1. United States—Foreign public opinion, Russian.
    2. Public opinion—Soviet Union—History. I. Title.
E183.8.S65A544   1988   973   88–600001
                ISBN 0-8444-0593-0

The five phrases in Cyrillic that recur in the background of the title page were selected from the great range of Russian expressions about the United States before 1917. Here is what they mean and where they may be found in the text:

Forty commissars in Chicago [Chapter 5 title]
An Eden for working women [Chapter 2, p. 71]
Our most dangerous competitor [Chapter 4, p. 124]
Nick Carter—King of detectives [Chapter 3, p. 93]
What America teaches us [Chapter 5, p. 223]

∞ The paper used in this publication meets the requirements for permanence established by the American National Standard for Information Sciences "Permanence of Paper for Printed Library Materials," ANSI Z39.48-1984

For sale by the Superintendent of Documents
U.S. Government Printing Office
Washington, D.C. 20402

Contents

Preface

Robert V. Allen, who retired from the Library of Congress on August 1, 1985, knows the Russian collections of the Library better than any other person. This comes from a prodigious memory, an insatiable curiosity, and thirty years of experience in assisting, advising, and listening to scholars who have been attracted from many corners of the world to use the Library's vast Russian holdings. Even so, the richness of the Library's collections impressed Bob Allen all over again when he began exploring them in depth to prepare this book.

The basic idea for the book had been in the back of his mind for years. As he ran across new instances to document his theme, he also became increasingly aware that no one else seemed to be addressing the particular topic. He found areas of Russian-U. S. relations that had been little touched by scholars of either country, in matters of agriculture, technology, education, literature, motion pictures, and even diplomacy. At the time his book went to press, he had accumulated a bibliography of over five thousand items of Russian views on America during the imperial period (the bibliography at the end of this book is barely the tip of the iceberg!). In Bob Allen's words, "there's enough to inspire thirty doctoral dissertations."

Bob Allen is particularly well qualified to write a book on imperial Russia's views of the United States. His doctoral work at Yale University combined a major in Russian history with a minor in American history. His contention during the fifteen years that I have known him and worked with him is that the Russian specialist at the Library of Congress must know American history and culture well in order to interpret the collections and guide the user. He has conducted a lively personal interchange and correspondence over the years with American scholars who interpret Russia and the Soviet Union to the

American public and with Soviet scholars who interpret the United States to the Soviet people.

I hope and trust that the reader of this book will find as much pleasure in it as I had in witnessing its creation and reading the drafts that resulted in this volume.

DAVID H. KRAUS, ACTING CHIEF
European Division, Library of Congress

Acknowledgments

Thanks should be expressed to many people. First of all to those who were my fellow staff members at the Library of Congress during the writing of this manuscript, so many that individual listing is scarcely possible, but including those in the Exchange and Gift Division who acquired microfilms from Soviet libraries of materials essential to this survey, the people in the Microform Reading Room who made it possible to gain early access to these films, those in the Preservation Microfilming Office who accepted my recommendations of titles that deserved priority, all those in the various offices concerned with the management of the collections who bore up under my requests to locate items that had somehow crept out of plain sight, and, most of all, to my colleagues in the European Division who nobly endured both being told more than they cared to know about my discoveries and hearing only somewhat distracted responses to their concerns. Particular thanks are due to David H. Kraus, Acting Chief of the European Division from 1978 to 1982 and from 1984 to the present, and to Clara Lovett, Chief of the Division from 1982 to 1984, for their forbearance in allowing me time to burrow into a vast mass of heterogeneous printed matter, and to take perhaps more than a due share of the time of the division's typists and searcher.

Introduction

As every reader of the daily press or viewer of the television news is aware, the relationship between the Soviet Union and the United States is an important, indeed overwhelming, element in the life of the whole world. In order to avoid the incalculable consequences of a failure to deal with this relationship, it is essential not only that both sides know the daily events in the life of the two countries but that they also understand something of how each views the other and of the factors that have shaped such perceptions. These factors have long roots in history, for it was not a sudden discovery on November 7, 1917, that made the two nations aware of one another. Much of the Soviet attitude toward the United States reflects patterns of thought that developed well before the collapse of the Russian Empire, for there was, if not what may be called a well thought-out and coherent concept of the United States among those people who experienced the transition between tsar and commissar, at least a surprisingly broad body of evidence, opinion, misunderstanding, enthusiasm, and chill disapproval upon which it was possible to base a multitude of interpretations of America.

The pages that follow are but a preliminary survey of the materials from which it is possible to discern something of how Imperial Russia approached the fact, and the myth, of America, a survey that has had to omit much, seizing only on some of the points that show a surprising continuity of interest among those for whom Russian is the principal means of communication with the world. Although one cannot deny that both the Empire and the Soviets encompass a broad spectrum of other peoples, whose own, independent thought about America is of its own value, this study is limited almost totally to materials that appeared in the Russian language and to evidences of use by persons writing in that language of works of American or West European origin. Similarly, while the word *America* has in fact a larger meaning than solely that of the United States of America, a meaning of which pre-1917 users of Russian were well aware, in general practice the expressions *Amerika, amerikantsy,* and *amerikanskii* were then practically without exception applied to the United States.

There are seven chapters in this work, the first of which is a summation of the development of the Russian view of America up to the year 1865. Much has been omitted from this chapter, including such matters as the hopes of Emperor Alexander I that the United States might somehow be persuaded to join the Holy Alliance, a proposal very deftly quenched by Secretary of State John Quincy Adams, or the full details of the construction in the United States for the imperial navy of five, and perhaps six, vessels before 1860. The next five chapters are the heart of the book and are concerned with the years from Appomattox to the February Revolution, taking up the topics of the Russian concept of America as a utopia, assessments of American literature and cinema, the effort Russians made to comprehend the role of American agriculture as an influence on their own position in the international market, Russian investigations of American technology, organizational methods, and education which centered around the World's Columbian Exposition in Chicago in 1893, and, lastly, some phases of Russo-American diplomatic involvement before 1917 that would, with a few editorial adjustments, scarcely be out of place on today's front page. A brief seventh chapter looks at some of Lenin's writings relating to America.

The sources for this study are almost without exception taken from the collections of the Library of Congress, which contain more than 800,000 volumes in the Russian language. A number of the nineteenth-century works cited were originally in the private library of the Siberian merchant Gennadii V. Yudin, acquired some eighty years ago. The long runs of the major Russian journals in Yudin's collection contain an unimaginable variety of articles about American affairs, and surely the Library's many pamphlets and translations into Russian of what can only be called minor fiction, with much about America, are items that he had added to his shelves. Subsequent efforts by the Library of Congress have procured a further rich store of Russian books and of microfilm of newspapers and other journals of relevance, while the presence of many pre-1917 publications in English and other languages make it possible not only to read the Russian reviews but also to examine the French, or German, or other original works. Much of this material had long been held by the Library, but only in recent years has it actually become known to researchers. For example, in answering a reader's request, a Library Staff member found that the official government gazette, *Pravitel'stvennyi viestnik,* was practically complete, rather than the broken set indicated in the reference sources, and a project to collate and microfilm some pre-1917 official Russian serials turned up a very interesting, if partial, run of the *Izviestiia* of the Russian Bureau of Agricultural Mechanization containing much about American agricultural machinery, including the then somewhat experimental gasoline tractor.

The active exchange agreements between the Library and equivalent institutions in the Soviet Union made it possible to obtain a vast quantity of microfilm, including such publications as the annual reports of the Russian civil official who supervised church affairs, a series containing much about the early history of Orthodoxy in America, the official journal of the Ministry of Ways of Communication, with frequent reports on American railroads, etc. From the pages of two filmed magazines devoted to the automobile one can see Russian-language advertisements for such long-forgotten makes as Mitchell, Chalmers, Locomobile, and Detroiter. And the rather ponderous newspaper *Novoe vremia* for 1916 offers advertisements of American films such as "Ne pristavai k moei zhenie" [Don't hang around my wife!].

All the translations, whether from Russian, French, or German, included in this survey are by the author of this book. A number of quotations that appear to be in somewhat awkward English are in the actual English phraseology of Russians themselves, such as the warm appreciation of American attitudes, even in a competitive situation, of a Russian professor who visited America to study its role in the international grain market, or the increasingly forceful English style of Leo Tolstoi as he became more involved in an examination of American writings on nonviolent resistance. In some instances, the author compared recent editions of materials and the scarcer originals in order to understand the possible effect of Soviet editorial practices.

An effort has been made to identify the writers who are quoted and to place them, if only in one or two words, within a framework of personal or intellectual relationships. This was not always possible, because such factors as the transliteration back into the Latin alphabet of European names cited in Russian Cyrillic presented problems defying solution within the available time. Furthermore, transliteration standards varied, so that one finds "Ogaio" and "Okhaio" for one of the American states, and references to an American poet as "Uaitman," "Guitman," "Veitman," "Uitmen," or "Vitman." For less well known places or persons, it is almost impossible to determine the original.

A word should be said about the Russian calendar. Before 1918 (up to and including February 1), Russia used the Julian calendar, so called because it was based on computational methods adopted in Roman times, allegedly in part by Julius Caesar. Errors in these computations had brought about the adoption, by a brief of Pope Gregory XIII in 1582, of the Gregorian calendar, which compensated for accumulated errors. Some of the protestant areas of Europe were slow in accepting these changes; for example, it was not until 1752 that an act of Parliament instituted the new system in Britain and its colonies. Russia, however, retained the old calendar, with the result that differences between the two chronologies in the calculation of leap years brought about an increasing variance between Russian and European dates. The Julian calendar counted the years 1700, 1800, and 1900 as leap years, while the Gregorian did not; as a result, beginning with the Julian date of February 29, 1700, it was necessary to add 11 days to a Julian date to find the Gregorian equivalent, growing to an addition of 12 days in the nineteenth century and 13 days in the twentieth. It is this factor that gives to the revolution in 1917 that overthrew the tsar the name of the February Revolution, though the abdication actually took place in March by Western European reckoning, and creates the seeming anomaly of the celebration in the Soviet Union of an October Revolution with parades taking place on November 7. In this work it should be assumed that all events in Russia are given in the Old Style (denoted O.S.) and those elsewhere in the new (denoted N.S.). There are, however, some ambiguities as, for instance, in the dates given by L. N. Tolstoi in his journal of travels in Western Europe (was he thinking as a Russian, or in terms of local practice?); in other cases, as in references to American motion pictures advertised in the Petrograd newspaper *Novoe Vremia* of 1916, both dates are given in the original source.

The Julian calendar continues to be used by the Russian Church in the calculation of saints' days and church festivals. Because the year 2000 will be a leap year in both systems, the discrepancy—for those who deal in these church matters—will remain at 13 days during the entire next century.

It is, of course, a somewhat biased conclusion to say so, but the work involved in producing this survey appears to be worth it, for it appears that there is no equivalent study, either in Russian or in English. Many of the subjects mentioned in these pages have had no extended treatment in either language, and a diligent examination of guides to American scholarly literature shows but a handful of pertinent publications, and these examine only individual details. Whatever the reader may ultimately have to say about the actual value of what has been produced, it is sincerely hoped that at least a stimulus toward further research has been provided and that someone may take up the job of dealing with this aspect of history as it really deserves.

In addition to the works directly cited in this study, a short bibliography of which is included, the writer has gathered, and is beginning to prepare for possible publication, a bibliography that will include four to five thousand entries citing Russian works published before 1917 that deal with the United States and with materials in other languages that were known to have been used in Russia in that era.

CHAPTER ONE

Russia Discovers America: The Experience to 1865

During the period of the discovery of America Russia was largely isolated from the West, politically and culturally, and references to the new lands across the ocean were slow to appear. While a Greek monk resident in Russia did mention these discoveries as early as 1518, it was only in 1584 that a Russian translation of a Polish chronicle spoke of Columbus and Amerigo Vespucci, and used the word *America*. The seventeenth century did not add greatly to this record. [For a survey of the early contacts between Russia and America see: A. N. Nikoliukin, *Literaturnye sviazi Rossii i SShA; stanovlenie literaturnykh kontaktov* (Literary ties between Russia and the U.S.; establishment of literary contacts). Moscow, Izdatel'stvo "Nauka," 1981. p. 15–26].

It appears, in fact, that the unsigned article "Izviestie o nynieshikh anglinskikh i frantsusskikh seleniiakh v Amerikie" that appeared in the *Sankt Peterburgskie viedomosti* of November 25, 1750 (Old Style) was the first geographical and historical description of North America and its population to appear in Russia, and although this newspaper account is a short one, scarcely 500 words, it provides a thumbnail sketch of the history of discovery, the geographical position of the English and French settlements, and the relations of the two nations with the Indians. There are references to "Iamestovn," (Jamestown), "Viliamsburg," "Mariland," "where there is much timber, tobacco and codfish," to "Novyi Erzei" (New Jersey), and to

"Novaia Angliia" (New England) with its "well-known city Boston." The policies of the French and British in using the Indian tribes as auxiliaries against one another are given pointed attention. "Irokoi (Iroquois) means handsome people, and they are indeed warriors, whom the French fear the most. The Hurons when at war eat human flesh, but in peace live by hunting and fishing" (Nikoliukin, op. cit., p. 386–87). Textual analysis, so Nikoliukin observes, suggests that the author of this short article was the famed Russian historian, poet, grammarian, scientist, and even artist, Mikhail V. Lomonosov (1711–1765), who can be compared in his breadth of activities with Benjamin Franklin.

In fact, Lomonosov, like Franklin, was interested in the nature of lightning, and in 1752, as Franklin's reports were beginning to be assimilated by European scientists, he planned, in cooperation with another prominent St. Petersburg scholar, G. V. Rikhman, a research program to be carried out the next summer. Rikhman was of German background but was born in the Baltic areas of the Russian Empire. As a recent Soviet work has it, "Lomonosov and Rikhman awaited the spring and summer storms of the coming year 1753 with great impatience." They both set up similar sets of apparatus in their houses, which were comparatively close together on Vasil'evskii ostrov, the island across the river from the Hermitage in St. Petersburg. On July 26, Rikhman, after having taken part in a meeting of the Academy, went home to find a storm making up. Approaching too closely to his network of wires, he was hit in the brow by ball lighting and fell dead.

That very day, Lomonosov sent a heartfelt letter to I. I. Shuvalov, a high official, "That I write to your excellency now I consider a miracle, since the dead do not write. I still do not know, or at least I doubt, whether I am alive or dead. I see that Professor Rikhman was killed by lightning under the same circumstances in which I was at that very time. . . .But, in spite of all, Mr. Rikhman died a magnificent death, carrying out the duty of his profession. His memory will never die . . . And that this circumstance not be used against the advance of science, I humbly ask you to have mercy on the sciences."

Clearly, Russia's first acquaintance with Franklin's investigations of natural science was not a happy one, and it was quite a long time before anything similar was repeated by Russians. However, Russian interest in Franklin continued, both in his scientific and philosophic activities. The Soviet scholar Nikoliukin, in pages 77–106 of the work cited above, tells of the broad range of people in Russia who responded to Franklin, from the Empress Catherine, who did not like him at all, to literary figures both of a somewhat conservative and a decidedly liberal outlook. Even in the next century a young military officer who had just been through the harrowing experience of the Crimean War, Leo Tolstoi, made an effort to keep a diary in imitation of Franklin, dealing each day with the evidences of good or of evil that he noted in his own behavior. As early as 1770, while Franklin was still chiefly known as a combination of natural scientist and shrewd exponent of a humane outlook on life, a work of his appeared in the *Trudy* [Transactions] of the Imperial Free Economic Society, the first technical and agricultural society in Russia. And, while the publications listed for sale in 1776 by J. J. Weitbrecht, bookseller to the Academy of Sciences in St. Petersburg, were in French, their availability shows that there must have been reader interest, and it is worth noting that at least one work by Franklin is mentioned, not to speak of others on such American topics as the fauna of the Carolinas and Georgia and the campaigns against the Indians of the Ohio country. The latter two may well have some reflections of Franklin in their pages, for as a scholar he dealt with one, and as a wily politician he had to deal with the other.

Franklin even drew a response from Empress Catherine II (the Great) herself—largely a negative one as she was evidently not amused by the Latin epigram that spoke of Franklin's having snatched the lightning from the heavens and the scepter from tyrants. Though no enthusiast of American liberty, she certainly was well aware of the international political effects, and possible advantages for Russia, of the decrease in British power that would come from American independence, or even from the colonies' unsuccessful, but wearing, diversion of British attention. When, in 1775, George III wrote to his "great and good friend" Catherine, asking to hire Russian soldiers for service in America, she replied noting the political fact that to do so would upset the other powers and create further problems for Russia. She could not refrain from adding expressions that had the effect of saying, "and I did not think that you were in that much trouble." All through the American Revolution the empress took a cool attitude toward the Americans, refusing to give any official reception to Richard Dana, the representative delegated by the Continental Congress to serve in St. Petersburg, and otherwise showing her reserve toward the American cause. However, the Russian attitude toward Great Britain opposed British interpretations of international law and the rights of neutrals, and Russia's participation in what was called the Armed Neutrality, a grouping of various European nations that sought to resist British interference with maritime trade, had in the last analysis an effect on Britain that was favorable to America.

Although there were many foreigners who participated in the Americans' struggle for freedom—not only La Fayette and Von Steuben, Kosciuszko and Pulaski, but also other Frenchmen, Poles, Germans, and others whose names are now less prominent—there seems to have been only one Russian subject who did so. This was the Baltic German nobleman Johann Gustav Wetter von Rosenthal, who served in the American forces under the name of John Rose. He was a member of an expedition against the Indians in the region of what is now Sandusky, Ohio, and he left a detailed, and often rather pointed, critique of some of the flaws of the American commanders in that region. He appears, however, to have won the good will of several leaders of prominence and to have treasured his memories of America until his death in the late 1820s in what is now Estonia.

Throughout the American Revolution and in the years immediately following, the editor of *Moskovskiia viedomosti*, one of the two Russian-language newspapers in the whole empire, was Nikolai I. Novikov, a man of liberal outlook and considerable daring. He had even used some of the satirical journals that he published to cross swords with the empress, who fancied herself a writer, suggesting that some of her ideas really needed rethinking, and his choice of items for his newspaper showed a marked sympathy with the Americans, commenting with evident intent that the moral be applied elsewhere that after the Revolution the American army had been reduced to a mere guard force for the public arsenals. Other Russians also expressed similar admiration. The most important was Aleksandr

I. Radishchev (1749–1802) who had taken advantage of Catherine's relaxation of the ban on private printing presses to publish his own book, *Puteshestvie iz Petersburga v Moskvu* [Voyage from St. Petersburg to Moscow], in 1789. At first appearance this was but another in the rather widespread genre of travel accounts of a lightly liberal and somewhat sentimental nature that had become familiar to the European reading public of the time. In a series of chapters named for the major posting stations along the often toilsome four hundred miles between the two cities, Radishchev tells of the sights seen and thoughts suggested along the way. But the book was actually a scathing account of the situation of the Russian peasants, half of whom were the serfs of an often brutal gentry and the other half, the scarcely less unfortunate wards of the state.

Radishchev went on from his reports of what he had seen to a deeper critique of the Russian system, letting it be evident that he felt that there were underlying flaws in the system of government that needed fundamental correction. One of his most pointed indications of this comes in the pages in which he suggests that the official ban on public discussion needed to be lifted, praising quite specifically those provisions of the constitutions of Pennsylvania, Delaware, Maryland, and Virginia that allowed for the freedom of the press. He also included other remarks on America, noting that, despite protestations of liberty, a large part of the population was then made up of Black slaves, but also praising "Vasgington" (Washington) and including an ode "Vol'nost'" (Liberty) with references to America.

Radishchev's words drew Catherine's wrath and she called him "Even worse than Dr. Franklin." Through somewhat irregular court action he was condemned to death but was later reprieved to exile to Siberia. Zealous efforts to confiscate all copies of his work did not entirely succeed; the first edition became one of Russia's great rarities[1], and only in 1906 was it finally permitted for general circulation.

Although there was some commercial contact between the two countries in the two decades after the American Revolution, this was largely limited to the arrival of American ships to purchase Russian sailcloth, hemp cordage, and bar iron, equiv-

---

[1] A copy is included in the Library of Congress Collections.

alents for which were not produced in America. It was not until the mid-1790s that America was visited by any Russian with the slightest official connections. In 1793, as Britain and Russia were allied against France, sixteen Russian naval officers were chosen for service with the British fleet. One of them, the twenty-year-old Iurii Fedorovich Lisianskii, was assigned to the squadron based in Halifax, Nova Scotia, that watched the American coasts. There were frequent captures both of French and of American cargoes bound for France, and Lisianskii served aboard the British frigate *L'Oiseau* in seizing American vessels convoyed by the French frigate *Concorde*. After two years of this service Lisianskii obtained leave of absence and spent a good part of 1795–96 in the United States. He gave particular attention to the American ports in which at that very time the first frigates—*Constitution, Chesapeake, Congress, Constellation, President, United States*—of the American navy were being built, but there is nothing in his letters to his family to say directly that he had any intelligence mission. However, such a purpose cannot be excluded and perhaps the Public Records Office of Great Britain may contain material on this point.

In more formal relationships, it was not until 1803 that the first American consul in St. Petersburg, Levett Harris, was appointed. A consul's job, at least at that time, was largely the routine one of seeing to it that a ship's papers were made out properly, that equitable treatment was given to the merchants and shippers of the home country, and that sailors in distress were taken care of. He did not deal with the larger questions of international policy, and he had no right of access to the ruler or his minister of foreign affairs. However, since Harris was the one official American representative in Russia, he did upon occasion serve as a channel for more important matters.

One instance of Harris's greater role came in 1804 when America's war against the Barbary States had taken an unfortunate turn. The U.S.S. *Philadelphia* had run aground on an uncharted rock off the harbor of Tripoli, in what is now Libya, and its crew had been captured by the local ruler. Since that ruler owed a rather ill-defined homage to the sultan of Turkey, and since the United States did not have any relations with Turkey, Jefferson hoped that an appeal to the emperor Alexander, who was then at peace with the sultan, might move the Turk to press his not very reliable vassal to refrain from harsh treatment of the American captives. Though this was a subject with which, at least by the formal rules of the time, a mere consul had little to do, Alexander appears to have responded—with what actual effect in Tripoli is not known. In the course of the correspondence on the subject the emperor wrote to Jefferson and, evidently aware of Jefferson's passion for the collection of books, sent him some of the Russian official publications. In one of his letters Alexander told of his pleasure in being in touch with "a man who is as virtuous as he is enlightened," a phrase in harmony with the spirit of the education he had received under his grandmother's control.

It was in 1809 when the first American minister to St. Petersburg was appointed, and he received a good deal of attention from the men in control. Comparatively little of this reception rested on the minister's personal qualities, for he was the "often unamiable," as he himself phrased it, John Quincy Adams. Son of the second, and last, Federalist president, John Adams, he had found it possible to support the Jefferson administration during a short term of service in the Senate and had in other ways distanced himself from the views of the Federalist elite of his native Massachusetts. In St. Petersburg his New England rectitude appeared in distinct contrast to a society that was, at least in the upper levels of the court and diplomatic community, a luxurious and frivolous one in which, as a British diplomat said, Adams sat "like a bulldog among spaniels."

In October 1810, in a meeting with Adams, the Russian foreign minister spoke of his wish to avoid "even every pretext for jealousy or uneasiness. . . . At any rate, I [Adams] might be assured of the continuance of the emperor's amicable dispositions towards the United States. They were as strong and fixed as they ever had been; and, he might say, stronger. 'Our attachment to the United States,' said he, 'is obstinate—more obstinate than you are aware of.'" In January 1811 the foreign minister emphasized that when he had previously been the minister for commerce he had "been extremely desirous of giving every encouragement and facility to the commerce of the United States," and that "he still retained that same ardent desire."

In May 1811 Adams and the emperor met at least twice during their morning walks. On previous occasions of this kind the emperor's principal topic of conversation was the familiar one of the weather, but in this month, after the usual commonplaces, he took care to ask if Adams had any recent dispatches from home and to try to feel out the state of relations between America and Britain, for war was in the air and that would interrupt most of Russia's foreign trade. On June 4, Rumiantsev, the foreign minister, repeated this effort and

asserted his great and long-settled attachment to the United States—the desire which he had so many years entertained of favoring American commerce. It was not only a thing to which he was attached by sentiment, but it had been with him long a maxim of policy. It was the interest of Russia to encourage and strengthen and multiply commercial powers which might be rivals of England, to form a balance for her overbearing power. Russia herself had not the advantage for it. She could not be a great naval power. Nature had in a great measure denied her the means. She ought then to support and favor those who had them.

The most interesting reactions to America among the first Russian diplomats appointed to this country were those of Pavel I. Svin'in (1778–1839). He was a man of literary tastes and aspirations, but these were outstripped by his artistic skill, for he produced a number of watercolor views of American scenes in the years 1809 to 1813 that show an eye for composition and effect that seems somewhat lacking in his prose.

Pictures of such quality from the first couple of decades of the nineteenth century are not common, and Svin'in does seem to have managed both to select people or places that struck him as typical and to present them effectively, if also rather in the sentimental early romantic style of his time. He was, in addition, something of an art critic, for his essay "A Look at the Fine Arts in the United American States," a copy of which is held by a Soviet archival institution, is an informed survey of the status of American art in the era of President Madison, and he had clearly made an effort to see and to study works of Stuart, West, Vanderlyn, Sully, and Rembrandt Peale, as well as examining some of America's major buildings of the time.

Added to Svin'in's interest in art was a very marked one in technology. His essay on American art included some observations on American bridges—not only their design but also their structure—a field in which, indeed, some of the Yankee craftsmen of the time were making new advances. But this topic of bridges paled in comparison with a newer, more exciting innovation, the "stimbot." In *Syn otechestva* (1814, no 36: 135–44; no. 37: 175–82), one of Russia's leading journals, he published a two-part article "Nabliudeniia ruskago v Amerikie. Opisanie Stimbota (parovago sudna)" [Observations of a Russian in America. Description of the 'Stimbot' (steamboat)], which is not only an account of the craft itself but also a series of opinions on America as a whole. It would appear that Svin'in was among the very first Russians to attempt to analyze America's seeming talent for adapting technology to its requirements, an effort to which subsequent Russian generations were to give much attention. He is worth quoting at some length on this:

Craftsmen coming from Europe joined their knowledge and talents with American enterprise, and, encouraged by protective laws and by liberty, surpassed themselves as one might say. Not having English riches for setting up large establishments, and in order to replace somewhat the expense of labor, which is incomparably more costly there than in England, the Americans have turned to the perfecting of various machines, and have made them simpler and lighter in action. In this area they have shown a particularly creative turn of mind, and in everything in which inventiveness was necessary they have attained extraordinary successes. Mechanical inventions have completely replaced human hands in the United States. There everything is done by machine: a machine saws stone, works brick, forges nails, sews shoes, etc. . . .In particular, mills of all sorts are brought to the utmost state of perfection (*Syn otechestva*, 1814, no. 36: 136).

Svin'in is, in point of fact, a bit in advance of the realities of American machinery, for a great deal was still done by hand or by use of only the simplest devices. However, with regard to the topic of mills, he may have reflected something of what he undoubtedly learned in Philadelphia about the millwright and inventor Oliver Evans, who indeed had perfected a grain milling system to the point that one day a visitor to his establishment found no one at home, but the machinery was busy grinding away without a human hand intervening. It might be noted that Evans's name for the device by which grain was raised to the top of the mill so that all other operations could take place sequentially by gravity flow from one machine to the other, the "elevator," was the origin of a term about which we will have more to say later.

The article goes on:

But nothing astonished me as much as the "Stimbot" (steamboat), and the more I inspected it, the more I became convinced of the true value of this extraordinary invention. Thoroughly convinced that its introduction into

Russia might allow me to serve my Fatherland, I used all my time and all
possible methods, not sparing labor or money, to learn the secrets of the construction of the "stimbot." . . .[Svin'in had made the acquaintance of a me-
chanic] with my promise to employ him on the most favorable terms if I
receive from our government permission to introduce "stimboty" in Russia.
To this end, having consulted with our minister in the United States of America and with many notable citizens there, and having acquired plans and models of all parts of the machinery, I have proposed to His Excellency State
Chancellor Count Nikolai Petrovich Rumiantsev a project for this remarkable
invention. Having no motive for any personal gain, I asked the government
only to be employed in the construction of this "stimbot" or to be allowed to
set it up on my own account, but, unfortunately, my letter took an unusually
long time [it appears because of disruption of the already slow normal communications between America and Russia that followed the declaration of
war in 1812], and meanwhile Mr. Adams, the American Minister, asked permission for this from the Lord Emperor for Mr. Fulton, an American engineer, with the right to use this newly invented ship for a period of 15 years.
Even if my labor has been in vain, and if fate deprives me of the happiness
of thus serving my Fatherland, I can at least still be proud of the fact that this
useful and great invention will be introduced among us and that I was the
one who gave the idea to Mr. Fulton (op. cit., 137–39)

The article makes it clear that Svin'in is well aware of efforts before Fulton to build steamboats, for he provides a
couple of paragraphs on both American and European ven-
tures, but he gives Fulton the credit for having made a work-
able combination of known principles to reach success. At the
time Svin'in was writing, he says there were already sixteen
steamboats in the United States, including one each on the Mississippi and Ohio Rivers. Here, he believes, it would be possible
to supplant the boats that floated one-way down these rivers
with the current and to end the need of having to send goods
destined for the area overland from Philadelphia at great cost
(op. cit., 140–44).

I was among the observers in the test made on the Hudson River of the new
steamboat *Paragon*. Of 300 tons burden, going against the swift current and
strong wind, it made five versts (verst = 2/3 mile) an hour. With the current,
and using the auxiliary sails that it has in case of a favoring wind, it went
something more than twice as fast. It has several times gone from Albany to
New York, a distance of 280 versts, in something less than 24 hours (p. 176).

Svin'in was also the author of a four-part article "Vzgliad
na respubliku Soedinennykh Amerikanskikh Oblastei" [View
of the Republic of the United American States] that appeared
in the journal *Syn otechestva* that same year (*Syn otechestva*, 1814,
no. 45: 253–70; no. 46: 3–17; no. 47: 41–57; no. 48: 81–96),

apparently the first substantial work by a Russian observer. He provides a rapid and quite superficial sketch of American history and geography, although he does not lack an eye for the unusual, for he speaks of the colors of the forest in autumn and of the beauties of the tulip tree and dogwood, and he mentions the "nightingale of America, the 'liuken-bart,'" which is clearly a bad rendering of mocking bird.

While he praises the lack of real enmity among the various churches of the country, he says, using a term that other foreign observers were to repeat, that "money is a deity for the American," and he fears that with growing wealth there will be more of the crime and dissolute ways which he then found to be absent (*Syn otechestva*, 1814, no. 45: 269–70). A succeeding installment returns to the subject of technology, and he speaks of factories such as that in "Mattapan," near Boston, that made wool and cotton cards by machinery. Some of this American interest in technology he ascribes to the American system of education in which "the son of the leading banker goes to the same school as the son of a day laborer." In his eyes higher education was somewhat underdeveloped, and he mentions only two universities, those at Cambridge and New Haven, although there is a reference to "academies" in New York, Princeton, and Philadelphia. He was impressed by the role of the American newspaper, saying, "The inhabitants of America of all classes read newspapers, for in addition to the trade reports, which are so closely connected with politics, each citizen, having a voice in the government, wants to know the course of governmental affairs" (*Syn otechestva*, 1814, no. 47: 41–46).

Svin'in praised the range of American philanthropy, noting that this was almost entirely a matter of private initiative, but he also felt that American prisons "are more like factories. Here humanity does not suffer, but is punished. It is not crushed down, but is deprived of liberty, the first of gifts" (*Syn otechestva*, 1814, no. 47: 47–49).

He was not so successful in explaining American politics, as he saw the differences between Federalist and Democrat largely in the light of a supposed attachment each had to Great Britain and France, respectively. Elections were, he wrote, violent and likely to be corrupt. Thumbnail sketches of President Madison, Albert Gallatin, then secretary of the treasury, and other prominent officials appear haphazard and without insight (*Syn otechestva*, 1814, no. 47: 50–55).

Svin'in's last article was taken up with descriptions of the major American cities. Though he had probably never heard of the British visitor who termed Washington a "city of magnificent distances," he did note that, apart from Pennsylvania Avenue and Georgetown, houses were so sparsely distributed that one had to travel a verst to find a neighbor. The Capitol was large and richly decorated, but incomplete, while the White House, "in the eyes of an inhabitant of [St.] Petersburg, does not deserve any attention." Philadelphia made a much better impression, but he had commercial awareness enough to see the potentialities for New York to grow because of its harbor and the Hudson River traffic (*Syn otechestva*, 1814, no. 48: 81–95).

Although Svin'in was not a great reporter of the American scene, apart from his incomparable watercolors, it can be noted that he touched upon themes that were almost universal in foreign writings about America. His sparse words about prisons can be considered in the light of Tocqueville, whose great voyage had as its reason the study of the American penal system, and his references to governmental corruption and electoral practices are a distant foreshadowing of Bryce's *American Commonwealth*. But, even more, these topics, as well as his interest in American technology, the influence of the American press, the spirit of American philanthropy, and the role of education, were to be those of many other Russian commentators throughout the next century. Only two substantial themes, those of agriculture and of the role of American women, need to be added to form the content of most of these later writings.

There were other Russian diplomatic representatives assigned to the United States after Svin'in, but none of them showed either his artistic skill or his broad, if somewhat pedestrian, interest in American life. One of these diplomats, however, did engage in a rather unusual effort to gain information on American moves. On September 25/October 7, 1821, the Russian minister, Petr I. Poletika (1779–1849) informed St. Petersburg that the 90-gun vessel *Franklin* and the brig *Dolphin* were fitting out for the Pacific, ostensibly to protect American commerce along the coasts of what is now Chile, then the scene of clashes between the Spanish and the rebels. It was feared that the Americans might send these vessels to strengthen their claims to the Pacific Northwest by setting up a settlement there, but Poletika writes, "However, nothing in the details of equipment indicates that they have thought about making permanent settlements on the northwest coast. Having recently been aboard the *Franklin* with Mr. Ivanov [Russian consul in Philadelphia] and Baron Maltitz [secretary of the legation], as they were busy finishing loading, I saw none of those articles necessary for setting up forts on a distant and savage coast, such as cannons, munitions, agricultural tools, etc."

So direct an involvement in intelligence gathering was even then somewhat unusual for a senior diplomat, but Poletika's worries were baseless, for the two American ships did, in fact, limit their cruise to Chile and Peru.

Most of Poletika's dispatches from America were taken up with the questions of the Pacific Northwest and alleged American encroachments in what is now Alaska, and his official reports, though of great interest to the diplomatic historian, are principally detailed accounts of what he said to the secretary of state, then John Quincy Adams, and of what the secretary had said to him. Expression of his other views did not come until later when, as many ex-diplomats do, he wrote a book. This was his *Aperçu de la situation intérieure des États-Unis d'Amérique et de leurs rapports politiques avec l'Europe* (Londres, Chez J. Both, Duke Street, Portland Place, 1826, 164 p.). The title page adds only "par un russe," but his identity soon became known. An American translation appeared in Baltimore, also in 1826.

A good deal of Poletika's work seems to have been taken from statistical handbooks and reference manuals, although the preface states that he had had two periods of residence in the United States, the first in 1810–12 and the second 1819–23. Some reflection of his own views does appear in his passages about the difficulty of balancing the interest of the individual states with those of the federal government, and he feels that as more states are added, the central authority will dwindle. This, he writes, impedes the federal government in its relations with foreign countries and hinders the curbing of acts such as the fitting out of privateers to prey on Spanish commerce.

Poletika is somewhat more interesting when he takes up in

his eighth chapter the relations of America to Europe. Although England was the major maritime power, the one most capable of doing harm, and therefore the country for which the United States had least affection, moral ties of common origin, language, and laws existed. America's supposed predilection for France rested largely on a shared antagonism toward Britain.

These same considerations, although in a much less palpable degree, are applicable to the relationships between Russia and the United States of America. One may say that the dispositions of the American government and nation toward Russia are generally amicable. The name of the Emperor Alexander is revered in the United States. This also stems from the moderation with which the imperial government has always treated American interests at a time when they were infringed upon by all the other maritime powers of Europe. Russia, powerful though she may be, inspires no fear in this country. Here one even counts upon support in all the difficulties in which the United States might find themselves engaged with regard to some European powers whose dispositions are less favorable to them (Poletika, op. cit., 81–85).

Further in this book, speaking of the ties that bound the colonies to England, Poletika writes that the principal fact of America is that "the country is new, but the civilization is old," for America drew upon the whole resources of British society and culture in its own formation. Although there were many differences between Americans and the British, it was nonetheless the British influence that was strongest (Poletika, op. cit., 123–36).

In examining this theme of the state of American society, Poletika speaks of a topic that many other Russian observers were to take up until the end of the empire, that of education. The task, he writes, of settling and making useful so vast a country has been so great that, although education was encouraged, the state of the arts and sciences lagged behind that of Europe. Despite this, especially in the north, there was general agreement "on the need for encouraging public instruction as one of the most powerful supports of a republican government. . . . As for primary schools, one finds them scattered over the whole surface of the United States, and in traversing those of the West it is not rare to find huts in which, lacking a better location, the children of the region receive their first instruction" (Poletika, op. cit.: 139–41).

The concluding paragraphs of Poletika's book deserve

rather full quotation. He writes, "What now, in conclusion, is the state of society in which the United States finds itself? A civilized population, but distributed over an immense, still new territory. Everything is in movement there, and proceeds with rapidity toward a better order of things. But this movement, because of the very great disparity between the extent of the territory and the population, is more physical than moral. Human industry seems to be absorbed by the desire for riches, and they do not yet think of enjoying their acquisitions." The country is one in which men can make lucrative use of their physical strength to realize their hopes, given good conduct and sobriety. There will still be some time before the country becomes "the sanctuary of the sciences and the fine arts, of those intellectual pleasures that create the charm of society." In attempting to assess the reasons for many Europeans' lack of fondness for America, Poletika felt that faults lay both in the American excess of egotism and individualism and in the overdemanding attitude of Europeans. His final words are those of a disclaimer of the book being anything more than an essay, for he has lacked the time for the collection of materials "as well as that philosophic comprehensiveness that nature gives to its favorites" (Poletika, op. cit., 161–64).

Basically Poletika's book is rather pedestrian stuff. Although he had lived a total of six years in America, and although his factual material in general is correct, he did not rise to any striking verdicts, perhaps out of an excess of diplomatic caution. This was, it seems, not the case with one of his successors as the Russian envoy to the United States. Later, in 1827, there arrived in Washington Paul Freiherr von Krüdener to take up the post as the tsar's representative. He was, one may note, son of Barbara Juliane Vietinghof, Freifrau von Krüdener, who at one time had been a close associate of Emperor Alexander I, and who is often credited with having inspired the so-called Holy Alliance and given it its name.

In the spring of 1828 he jotted a few fragmentary notes about his views of America, views that suggest, at some distance, the outlook of the well-known Mrs. Frances Trollope:

Society: First evening at President Adams's. Crowd, elbow to elbow. Somewhat coarse aspect of the 'pretty women;' uncultured babble of the men, tobacco chewing. . . .

Description of the Capitol: Its architecture. The senators, feet on the desks! . . .

The history of this country will only be that of parties and always ambitious combinations, and often marred by the vilest egoism. . . .

Constitution of the United States: It is a labyrinth of principles and of interpretations in which a wise people and honest magistrates might perhaps guide themselves. The good sense in the people, the patriotism and honor in those that it is the master of choosing to represent them and to administer affairs, form the guiding thread of Ariadne necessary for proceeding in this labyrinth and for finding the way out.

To escape the Minotaur that awaits his prey, these conditions, this good sense in the populace in the elections, this honesty among those who have known how to be elected, does all this come to pass in recent times? I wonder (Francis Ley, *La Russie, Paul de Krüdener et les soulèvements nationaux, 1814–1858* . . . Paris, Hachette, 1971. 83–84).

Although Krüdener was to stay in America for an extended period, he does not seem to have felt any more at ease there. In March 1835 he was writing to his sister that, "I love Europe with all the profound antipathy that America inspires in me in all its details. . . .You do not imagine how society, marked with the English imprint, makes me suffer, how much this indistinct pronunciation adds to my difficulties of hearing, and therefore to social difficulties . . . to the difficulty of living among a people who are the saddest, the most automatized, and the most unworthy of sympathy that there is on earth" (Ley, op. cit., 109).

A letter to a nephew in August of that year says, "There is no means that a foreign envoy does not use to get out of this execrable sojourn." One lives "in the midst of a bunch of taciturn swindlers, without education, without knowledge, without conversation, without savoir-vivre, who are neither housed, nor fed, nor amused like civilized beings . . ." Even among the "top cream of society," whom Krüdener met at the then fashionable resort of Rockaway, the day passes in "doing nothing:"

One cannot take walks, as it is a plain of sand. One is penned in like sheep in a parlor as big as a riding stable. One walks around, one goes to and fro all the day long under the fire of murderous or languorous glances. It is as in battle, many fewer killed or wounded than one would think from the liveliness of the shooting. . . .When one is tired of the parlor and wants to be alone, one goes to a little cell under the roof where there is a small bed, a table, and a wooden chair. What comfort! Only a death's head is lacking. But the Americans print in their newspapers that Rockaway is a place of delight where one is intoxicated by all the enjoyments that the genius of the Epicureans could conceive. There is in everything the spirit of bold-faced false-hood, dominant in this nation, which shocks and revolts me at all times of the day (Ley, op. cit.: 109–10).

Krüdener, however, "in spite of his personal repugnance toward a people still too young to be civilized," was able to understand that the United States was a great nation, and during his assignment to Washington he had worked sincerely for a Russo-American rapprochement. There were two striking instances in which this attitude took a real form during the seven years or so that he served in America. The first was the arrival in the United States in 1828 of Aleksandr P. Avinov, Imperial Russian Navy, with the mission of observing American naval technology, especially of dockyards, and of acquiring for Russia an American-built armed vessel, the "korvet" *Kniaz' Varshavskii.* Avinov had been in command of a ship of the line at the Battle of Navarino, in which in 1827 cooperating British, French, and Russian squadrons had practically annihilated a Turkish fleet. This action was one of the decisive stages in the liberation of at least a part of the Greek lands and the establishment of an independent state. For this Avinov was promoted to command a 110-gun ship of the Baltic fleet, but the emperor Nicholas I soon gave him the mission to America. His visit to America is not well recorded in the available literature, and inquiries to likely sources of material have not yet yielded positive results.

The second substantive result of Krüdener's mission was his participation in the negotiation of a treaty of commerce between the United States and Russia which was arrived at in 1832. Although the actual formulation of the treaty was carried on in St. Petersburg, Krüdener was in Russia, on "home leave," during the crucial stage of the affair and clearly served as an adviser to the head of the foreign ministry, Count Nesselrode, and to Tsar Nicholas.

The American representative in Russia at the time was the rising and still comparatively young Pennsylvania politician James Buchanan, who enjoyed the confidence of Andrew Jackson, to whom he wrote in copious detail, both officially and privately, about the complications of arriving at an agreement. Buchanan's account of Nicholas having told him of Russia's final acceptance of the treaty in the very public circumstances of a reception at the court, using the British minister as a translator of the emperor's French, makes it quite clear that Russia was making a special effort to win American favor and, at the same time, to score a point against the British. The latter had also attempted to make a commercial pact with Russia, but had failed.

It is not clear, however, whether it was Krüdener or Buchanan who had created Nicholas's own impression of Andrew Jackson, but in 1833, when Buchanan left Russia to return to the United States, the emperor received him in a farewell audience, telling him that it was gratifying to receive an assurance of Jackson's high regard for himself, and saying, as Buchanan conveys it, "He [Jackson] had shown himself to be a man both of integrity and firmness, and he [Nicholas] valued his good opinion very highly. He [Nicholas] felt a great respect for the people of the United States. They were a true and loyal people; and he should always endeavor to promote the most friendly relations with our Country" (James Buchanan, *Works.* v. 2. Philadelphia, J. B. Lippincott and Co., 1908. 378–79).

Nicholas and Jackson were men of somewhat comparable temperament as they tended "to give their orders first and ask questions later," and undoubtedly personal contact would have brought clashes. However, at the distance between Washington and St. Petersburg, expressions of good will could easily be made. There is a tradition that the emperor's good will is still visible at Jackson's home, the Hermitage. Shortly after Buchanan's departure from Russia, the Hermitage burned and Jackson set about rebuilding. Nicholas is said to have sent as a gift toward its decoration the two bronze urns that still stand beside one of the fireplaces there. A recent inquiry to the custodians of the Hermitage did not bring any confirmation, but let us hope that the tradition is true.

Indeed, when Jackson left the presidency, the Russian foreign minister wrote to Krüdener, then still in Washington, conveying Nicholas's approval of "the zeal that you have given to visiting General Jackson to express to him in the name of the imperial cabinet the views and best wishes that accompany him in his honorable retirement. In rendering a fitting homage to the intentions that guided him in his relations with Russia, His Majesty is pleased to receive the assurance that Mr. Jackson has been so good as to give you about the disposition that, on this point, will inspire his worthy successor [Van Buren]" (Ley, op. cit., 108).

There were to be some striking evidences during the Van Buren administration (1837–41) of a continuing Russian interest in American technology. The first was the mission in 1839–40 of the Russian naval officer I. I. fon Shants to supervise the building and delivery of the first steam-powered war vessel ever built in the United States for a foreign navy. The record for this activity is also somewhat scanty, although fon Shants's short article in the professional journal *Morskoi sbornik* offers more detail (1856, no. 3, "Smes'": 149–56. NB: Russian journals of the nineteenth century frequently contained two or more paginations and exact citation of materials is complicated. Since practices varied, readers will need to use care in locating references).

Also in 1839, after there had been much somewhat abstract discussion of the matter in Russia, Nicholas selected two experienced engineer officers to visit America to survey railroad construction. Both countries faced similar problems of transport over a vast area. The United States did have the magnificent network of rivers in the Mississippi Valley leading to the Gulf of Mexico, while Russia's equivalent, the Volga, only fell into the Caspian Sea, which leads nowhere except to Persia, but the two nations needed means of routing people and cargo along other lines to other destinations, past obstacles imposed by shallow streams, mountains, and similar barriers. The railroad was an obvious means of doing this, but in both Russia and the United States a prevailing lack of capital made it impossible to use the high standards of construction of rail lines that the British could afford. American engineers had made some very daring innovations in their railroads, using higher grades, shorter curves, and more flexible equipment, and had thereby greatly reduced costs. These factors were known to the Russians, in whose country there was but one short, experimental rail line between St. Petersburg and one of the suburban palaces, and, though some officials doubted the benefit to Russia of the building of railroads, Nicholas felt it wise to examine the American example.

As one of the two engineering officers selected for the

American mission wrote, "the emperor availed himself of an informed solution to the question . . . for the United States of America have so many points of similarity with European Russia" in factors such as those noted above that . . ."solid data about railroads in America could serve as a possible basis for the investigation of all those points of doubt" that the emperor might have. This officer was Pavel Petrovich Mel'nikov (1804– 1880), who was an honors graduate of the Institute of Engineers of the ministry of roads and communications and who had a solid record in important public works. His companion was Nikolai Osipovich Kraft, whose record was also a creditable one. Selected for their task in June 1839, the two spent almost a year in the United States (P. I. Mel'nikov, "Nachalo zhelezno-dorozhnogo stroitel'stva v Rossii" [Beginning of rail construction in Russia]. In: *Krasnyi arkhiv*, v. 99 (1940): 154).

Mel'nikov appears to have been impressed by the development of American steamboats, for upon his return he published several articles on steam navigation of the Hudson, Mississippi, and St. Lawrence rivers. While a complete run of *Zhurnal Ministerstva putei soobshcheniia* [Journal of the ministry of roads and waterways] was not available in the Library of Congress at the time of writing, microfilm of a substantial portion of this journal has since been received. There are citations in Soviet works to eight publications in that journal by Mel'nikov on steamboats and four on railroads, all clearly of a substantial nature. His companion Kraft was the author of at least one article, on the water supply installations of New York City, that appeared in the same journal in 1842.

Upon their return to Russia the two men were certainly the best informed observers of railroad practices in the country, and their advice helped the emperor make a final decision to commence construction on a line between St. Petersburg and Moscow. There is a legend, one that is very indicative of impressions about Nicholas, that, angered by what he considered too much argument over the route, the emperor seized his pen and a ruler and drew a direct line between the two cities, leaving two bumps where his fingers had protruded, said, "Build it there!" with a result that the final road had two unexplained deviations in its course. The actual process was more rational, for both Mel'nikov and Kraft were members of the commission named to supervise construction and they provided much informed advice.

One of the suggestions was that an experienced American engineer be employed and the two Russian officers named as a suitable candidate Major George Washington Whistler, who had graduated from West Point in 1819 and in 1828 had been assigned by the government to help in the laying out of the Baltimore and Ohio Railroad. Whistler had subsequently taken part in rail construction in Pennsylvania, New Jersey, Rhode Island, and in 1840 to 1842 he had solved a difficult problem in the location of a line in the hills of western Massachusetts, where he had attracted Mel'nikov's attention. The major's son by his first marriage was already a trained engineer and came to Russia with his father, while a son by a second marriage, still a boy at the time, received in Russia some of the training in art that helped him become famous as James Abbott McNeil Whistler. It is reported that the major's wife, the subject of the famous painting, spent some of her time in Russia endeavoring to convert the railroad workmen to a North Carolina-tinged Presbyterianism.

There were other American contributions in this effort. The Baltimore locomotive builder Ross Winans sent two of his sons, Thomas De Kay Winans and William Lewis Winans, to St. Petersburg to collaborate with another American firm, Eastwick and Harrison, in managing for the Russian government the locomotive and car plant at Aleksandrovskii near St. Petersburg, an activity that they continued until 1862. As a result early Russian locomotives and rolling stock showed strong signs of American influence in design. Furthermore, although no American specialist in the field was brought to Russia, the early rail bridges were built according to principles developed by the American, William Howe. These required relatively little iron and a high proportion of timber framing and were thus easily adaptable to Russian conditions, as well as being less expensive. A young engineering graduate, D. I. Zhuravskii, assigned to supervise a major bridge went on to study the principles of Howe's design and to lay some of the foundations of engineering theory in the field. In 1859 Zhuravskii visited America, discovering an interesting device, the "ais-bot" (ice boat) about which he wrote in the *Zhurnal Ministerstva putei soobshcheniia*, but the most important result of his trip was an article in the same journal in 1861 about the interrelationships of American wheat trade and the railroads, a topic about which the Russians were to be much interested in later years (Sergei M. Zhitkov, *Biografii inzhenerov putei soobshcheniia*. vyp. 2. St. Petersburg, Tipolitografiia S. F. Iazdovskogo i. Ko., 1893. 22–46).

During the 1850s one finds an impressive indication of the extent of Russian interest in American technology in the pages of the naval journal *Morskoi sbornik*. In November 1853 the naval officer A. S. Gorkovenko published a report of his visit to Boston and of the way in which the American clipper ships, with their fine lines and high speed, had impressed him. Other articles of his dealt with New York City and American affairs in general, and it is presumably this experience that helped him, after he had been made advisor to the grand duke Konstantin Nikolaevich (1827–1892), who had been appointed head of the Russian navy in 1853, influence a decision to build yet other ships in the United States.

In 1857 the keel was laid in New York for a 70-gun steam ship of war to be named *General-Admiral*, the rank held by the grand duke. A mission headed by Captain I. A. Shestakov, who had designed the vessel, came to supervise its construction and that of two steam transports, one in Boston and the other in New York. In 1858 the launching of *General-Admiral* took place, to the accompaniment of a banquet at Delmonico's that ran to more than ten toasts (one gets the impression that the actual count was lost in the celebration) and many speeches. [On the launch and the banquet, see: *Morskoi sbornik*, 1858, no. 11, unofficial section: 1–17].

Despite his responsibilities, Captain Shestakov had time to write several articles about America that appeared in *Morskoi sbornik* in 1857 and 1858 under the pseudonym "Excelsior," which show him to have been a quite competent observer of the American situation. He was not, however, the only Russian of the time to write about the general topic of the United States, for it was in 1859 that Aleksandr B. Lakier's account of his visit of 1857, *Puteshestvie po Sievero-Amerikanskim Shtatam, Kanadie i ostrovu Kubi* (St. Petersburg, Tip. K. Vul'fa, 1859, 2 v.) was published. This work, which was translated into English in an abridged form as *A Russian Looks at America* (Chicago, University of Chicago Press, 1979, 272 p.) was but the first full-length study and, although of interest, is not of so lasting significance as the similar materials of another traveler, Eduard Romanovich Tsimmerman (1823–1903), whose report first appeared in parts in the journal *Russkii viestnik* in 1859, and in book form that same year. Tsimmerman was to return to the United States in both the 1870s and 1880s, to write a survey of American agriculture in 1897, and, in his last published article in 1903, to contrast the policies by which the Trans-Siberian rail line was built with those of America. He was accompanied on his first trip by the young Prince Mikhail I. Khilkov, who was to make his own repeat visit to the Americas in the 1860s, working in an American-built and British-financed railroad enterprise somewhere in Central America, and to go on to become the minister of roads and communications under whose administration much of the Siberian road was to be built. It was later said that Khilkov while in office was conspicuously friendly to Americans, to whom he spoke with a strongly American-accented English.

Tsimmerman's writings are extensive and full of detail, although he does not appear a strikingly brilliant observer, but the mere fact that they appeared over the course of almost forty-five years would make him a suitable object for a closer analysis, for he provided not only general travel accounts, but dealt with education, the formation of new states, America's world economic role, and other topics. His attitude was largely a friendly one and he seems to have appreciated much about the American outlook. There is, in fact, too much of value in his works to be fairly dealt with in a survey such as this.

Not all Russians revealed so appreciative an attitude toward America as these naval officers and other visitors, as there were many who tended to fear the corrupting influence of American ways of thought on the stability of society. This fear was largely expressed by those who stayed at home and who sought to keep Russian society in its ancient and accepted patterns of control from above. One of the most notable of these was the publisher Mikhail N. Katkov, who was the editor of both the influential newspaper *Moskovskiia viedomosti* and of the solid, but markedly conservative journal *Russkii viestnik*. To the end of his life, in 1887, Katkov was a significant voice for the Russian establishment, often being in such high favor that his publications could deal with subjects that would have drawn the censors' disapproval if presented elsewhere. As the 1850s drew to an end, with increasing tension in the United States over the problem of slavery, and as Russia was simultaneously engaged with the question of how to deal with serfdom, Katkov's organs frequently referred to the American example to show that, while an end of Russian bondage was inevitable, the application of American principles of popular government would erode Russia's foundations.

Nevertheless, the rigidity of Katkov's outlook does not deprive the contents of his two serials of value as a reflection of some aspects of the Russian attitude toward America, an attitude often subtly conveyed as, for example, when use was made of the writings of a quite conservative Swiss immigrant to America to cast a shadow on the idea of popular government. [See the articles by "G. Matil'" (Georges-August Matile) in *Russkii viestnik*, 1860, no. 4, part. 1; no. 4, part. 2; etc.]. There were enough sources of information about America, sources that were neither deeply Russian nor deeply American, for a selection to be made that would, while being quite factual, still convey the view that popular government, as exemplified by America, had failed.

This underlining of American failure was characteristic of the most prominent of all Russians in America, the envoy extraordinary and minister plenipotentiary of His Imperial Majesty Aleksandr II Nikolaevich, Emperor of all the Russias—and a dozen or so additional territorial qualifiers—Eduard Andreevich Stoeckl. This man has been something of a mystery in the history of Russo-American contacts, for even a request to the Academy of Sciences of the USSR has not brought any reply containing full biographical details. However, a discovery at the back of a file cabinet of materials left by a deceased colleague has provided useful, if not entirely proven, information. This was in the form of a typed transcript of Stoeckl's service record, couched in the standard bureaucratic phraseology of the Russian empire and arranged in a satisfactorily sequential manner, testifying to his education and his rise in the bureaucracy. Lists of school graduates, tables of officials in obscure provincial offices, and records of the grants of decorations have offered some confirmation of Stoeckl's path. He had first been named to a post in the United States in 1839, although it does not appear that he actually reached America until 1844. From June 1849 to April/May 1850 he was the chargé d'affaires in Washington, and at that time he collaborated with the Austrian representative in the United States in objecting to American action favoring the Hungarians who were rebelling against the Hapsburgs, a rebellion finally suppressed by Russian intervention. For his assiduous aid to Franz Joseph, the Austrians granted him the Order of the Iron Crown—Third Class. Although appointed consul-general in the Sandwich Islands in 1853, Stoeckl never took up that post, for the Russian minister Bodisco died and he again became chargé d'affaires in Washington, acting as such from March 1854 to January 1857. At last he was named as minister in his own right, and, strangely enough, he took his oath of allegiance to Russia on November 1/13, 1857, dating the document from Washington. By 1860 he had had sixteen years experience in America, having seen Polk, Taylor, Fillmore, and Pierce leave office and having been exposed to a very rough-and-tumble period of American politics. Watching the fumbling of James Buchanan, at least as his dispatches to St. Petersburg indicate, he showed no great depths of understanding, and his immediate reactions reveal a pedestrian mind, attached to conservative/reactionary clichés about the evils of popular government.

After the elections of 1860, he wrote (December 26, O.S./ January 7, 1861 N.S.) to the foreign minister in St. Petersburg,

I have already had the honor to inform Your Excellency in my previous reports about what vicious elements the present Congress includes. As far as demagoguery goes, the two parties have nothing to envy one another, but as far as talent goes, the Republicans are inferior to their antagonists. However extreme the attitude taken by the representatives of the South may be, they have at least the courage of their convictions. . . .The Republicans can only reply by weak, legalistic speeches. They have incited a crisis without having the wisdom to foresee the outcome. . . .They have neither the good sense to accept frankly a plan for compromise nor the courage to propose strong measures which in political turmoil are the only ones to preserve a country." [Copies of these dispatches, which were written in French, are held by the manuscript Division of the Library of Congress.]

In January 1861, as the nation waited for Buchanan to depart and the new administration to be inaugurated, Stoeckl wrote in terms that showed him to view William H. Seward as the strong man of the new administration, criticizing the United States as having "applauded all the convulsions that have broken forth in Europe and in Spanish America. All the agitators of the Old World and the New have been received here with acclaim and, just a few years ago, it was the President and the Senate of the United States that gave an ovation to Kossuth [leader of the Hungarian uprising against the Hapsburgs] who, according to them, was the personification of the liberty of nations."

Stoeckl wrote,

I should add here that the institutions of the United States are not without responsibility for this revolution. The governmental system is completely disorganized. The administration no longer has any power and its action is without effect. . . . Perhaps by some change—that one cannot foresee—the states will still manage to reconcile themselves, or they may reunite later, but the confederation cannot long endure with the Constitution as it now exists. The first problem of any gravity will bring about new dissensions. To consolidate the federal agreement it will be necessary to remodel the constitution, to give the government more extensive powers, to limit universal suffrage, to make less frequent the elections that incessantly repeat themselves and that always give rise to scenes of disorder and anarchy, to create, indeed, laws that can abolish abuses and corruption and put an end, if possible, to the propagation of the revolutionary and socialist spirit, this plague of the present age, that the immigration from Europe of the past ten years has transplanted to this country.

In a long dispatch, dated April 15/27, 1861, after the capture of Fort Sumter, Stoeckl referred to the perilous situation of the city of Washington, and to the qualities shown by Jefferson Davis. Davis had military training and the confidence of his people. "These are the immense advantages that he has over Mr. Lincoln."

For the four years of the conflict Stoeckl remained in Washington, but those years do not seem to have deepened his comprehension. On April 2/14, 1865 he wrote,

The insurrection might have burst out twenty years ago without the talents and the moderation of the men who then governed the country. Unfortunately one no longer finds men of that caliber among the persons whom universal suffrage, as it has been carried out during recent years in the United States, has placed at the head of things. In 1861 the insurrection might have been prevented if there had been in the administration and in Congress such people as Clay, Webster, Calhoun and so many others who were the glory of the American people.

Stoeckl's dispatch of April 2/14 was a long one and undoubtedly required considerable time to prepare in a fair copy for his signature. Certainly at some time while this was being done the White House coachman had been told of his evening's task of driving to Ford's Theater. But one must do justice to the Russian minister, for his dispatch also says, "They [the Americans] have undergone one of the greatest revolutions of this century, so fertile in political convulsions, and they have come out of it with their resources intact, their energy renewed by the thousand difficulties they have overcome, and the prestige of their power greater than ever."

Not all Russian diplomats, however, were of such a cast of mind as Stoeckl. Carl Robert, Freiherr von Osten-Sacken (1828–1906) was one of that group of Baltic Germans who were so frequently found in the upper levels of the Russian administration where they served loyally, if at times somewhat pedantically, the emperors, whose own German backgrounds inclined them toward an acceptance of many Germanic attitudes. Osten-Sacken was appointed secretary of the Russian legation in Washington in 1856, serving until 1862 in that post, then being appointed as the consul general in New York, where he remained until 1871. Resigning his office at that time he made a number of trips back and forth to Europe, finally settling in the United States for the years 1873–77. During all his residence in the United States he seems to have been chiefly interested not in the minutiae of diplomacy but in the description and classification of the diptera, two-winged flies, of North America. He was a frequent contributor to the *Contributions to Knowledge* of the Smithsonian Institution, and he had very close ties with the American entomologists of his time, reporting in an autobiographical and bibliographical account of his works that he had in his files "617 letters received from 99 American correspondents between 1856 and 1872" (Carl Robert, Freiherr von Osten-Sacken, *Record of my life work in entomology.* Reprint: London, E. W. Classey, Ltd. 1978. p. 7). Although he had an additional burden of diplomatic and social duties ("in New York my visiting-list contained over *one hundred* houses where I had been invited to dine"), he undertook several trips such as one in 1857–58 to Cuba, returning via New Orleans, Montgomery, Alabama, Savannah, and the Carolinas, which must have had some diplomatic purpose, although Osten-Sacken speaks only of the season not being a good one for his entomological collecting. Whatever official records of his service may be contained in the Russian archives, fifty separate works from his pen on entomology were published while he was in America, and others reflecting his collecting experiences and knowledge of American species appeared after his return to Europe (Osten-Sacken, op. cit., 6–7, 206–18). His influence on the development of American entomological science was clearly a substantial one, as he himself recognized, calling himself "the grandfather of American Dipterology," and many of the specimens that he gathered and described were given to the Museum of Comparative Zoology in Cambridge, Massachusetts for the use of later students (Osten-Sacken, op. cit. Appreciation and introductory preface by K. G. V. Smith. unpaginated).

However, Osten-Sacken's activities were concentrated largely in fields apart from diplomacy and they were, although of substantial scientific value, of little effect on the Russian view of America, either as expressed by Stoeckl's grumbling about the effects of too much democracy, or by any broad segments of the population. Yet among the last there was, it seems, an interest in American events, largely from those who found that the world view of the United States had elements of possible benefit to Russia. While these dissidents were completely outside the positions of power in the empire, and found it difficult, because of the stringencies of the imperial censorship, even to voice their concepts of the role of America, they still at times had an effect on the Russian view of this country. As the next section of this survey will show, there were some rather surprising evidences of such feelings.

CHAPTER TWO

Simple Gifts: Tolstoi and Others See America as a Surrogate for Utopia

A persistent element in the European view of the United States has been to see it as a surrogate for Utopia. For some, this view has merely reflected a concept of the country's high economic development, but more usually it has included the perception of a land of philosophical liberty, lacking the artificial barriers to development that were felt to impede the utilization of human potential in Europe. Some suggestion of the nature of this mind-set may be found in the character of the reception that the French gave to Benjamin Franklin in the 1770s. This wily politician, philosophical skeptic, and experienced scientist was seen as a type of patriarchal exponent of the simple and honest life of a country that was imbued with doctrines drawn from a sort of natural harmony with the universe itself. America was seen through a mist of preconceptions—based on, or at least in consonance with, the outlook represented by Rousseau—as having freed itself from most of the restraints of the old and imperfect society, and thus attaining a more coherent state of existence, one from which the Old World might well draw useful example.

The Russians were not immune from such an attitude toward America. While late eighteenth- and early nineteenth-century Russia was a country where only a thin minority of the population was even literate—let alone capable of fully participating in a cultural life that might be called completely European—there are many indications of the influence of this current of thought. Striking examples of this are the many strands of evidence of an awareness of American political thought in the current of political dissent that culminated in 1825 in a short and unsuccessful military uprising upon the death of Alexander I. The constitutional plans discussed by the young officers who had hoped for a system of broader liberty often contained almost literal transference of American forms, even to the point that the proposed lower house of the legislative body was called *Palata predstavitelei* [House of representatives] and the oath to be taken by an emperor upon accession was almost identical with that prescribed by the American constitution for the president (G. G. Krichevskii, "Konstitutsionnyi proekt" Nikity Murav'eva i amerikanskie konstitutsii [The "constitutional project" of Nikita Murav'ev and the American constitutions.] In: *Akademiia nauk SSSR. Izvestiia, seriia istorii i filosofii*, 1945, no. 6: 398–405).

Although such plans failed—the uprising was suppressed, several of the dissident officers were hanged, and others exiled to Siberia—there were other, quieter people who remained interested in America as an exponent of a system that allowed popular participation in government. In fact, some seem to have realized that America had thereby gained in stability, since there was a broader distribution of power and of responsibility, thus forming a more coherent system than surface turmoil might indicate. An anonymous article on Ralph Waldo Emerson in the major journal *Biblioteka dlia chteniia* (1847, v. 85, otd. VII: 36–69), the first Russian critical survey of an American writer found thus far, notes that Europe often has a "rather false conception of this remote world. Europeans see it through the prism of the novels of Cooper, and poems of Chateaubriand, and sometimes also through the accounts of the economists." There were, however, places in America where simplicity, religious ways, and family life could be found. This, so one may infer from this anonymous writer, created a potential for order and continuity that had shaped Emerson and out of which he developed a philosophy that would be of lasting influence:

You gentlemen who ask what influence a writer has on his fatherland should take account of the sight that is offered to you by a young people and a nation that has not yet settled down. See how it carries out its training and you will know with certainty the trace that poets and thinkers leave behind them as they change human nature and how, without them, it would be worse than it is. The gradual education of the United States is practically the most remarkable event of our time. It shows in living form before the eyes of the European nations the law of the development of civilization, which these nations thus far have sought out with difficulty in the shadowy traditions of their own history (op. cit., 39).

In the next decade the Russian legal scholar Dmitrii Ivanovich Kachenovskii (1827–1872), in a substantial article on Daniel Webster, showed a surprisingly broad understanding of the underlying stability of America, one that was based on familiarity not only with an edition of Webster's works (a review of which was the ostensible basis of the article) but also with the writings of John Marshall and of John Caldwell Calhoun (*Russkii viestnik*, 1856, no. 3: 385–416; no. 4: 239–78). Kachenovskii refers, as proof of his stability, to Webster's involvement in the "noted political case of Rhode Island," (i.e., Webster's argument before the Supreme Court in 1848 in the case of Martin Luther, Luther M. Borden, and others which arose out of the "Dorr Rebellion," the case citation of which is: 7 How. 1). Webster's speech found European distribution

and everywhere it brought luster to his name. In it are set forth the basic principles of the American system and are expressed the heart-felt convictions of a statesman of the United States. In reading it one may see how mistaken are some of the current concepts of the civil and social life of the trans-Atlantic republic. Here, it is usually said, there prevails an untrammeled democracy; but, actually, from Webster's speech we can see that the case is not at all as simple as it seems to a superficial tourist and that the American system is a quite complicated one of checks and balances, that it has its own history, institutions, traditions, prejudices, unevenness, and that in it is embodied the organic product of the life of the people" (*Russkii Viestnik*, 1856, v. 3: 398).

From these two references, the one to Emerson and the other to Daniel Webster, one can see that there were Russians who looked on America, despite some of the surface manifestations of the turmoil of liberty, as having created a sort of utopia of stability, and that, after all, is what Sir Thomas More's ultimate goal was, to describe a society that was both just and stable, and in the last analysis a conservative one. However, for what seems to have been a larger, or at least more vocal, group of Russians, the utopian aspects of America were seen in its hospitality to experiments and in the flourishing during much of the nineteenth century of efforts to find new and more untrammeled social modes.

The official spokesmen of the Russian establishment were usually hostile to social experiments in Russia and often frowned, even, on the mere discussion of them. However, from time to time there were publications that dealt with these topics, often with marked overtones of favor for radical changes in society. Even the less roseate works at times managed to convey stimulating ideas about American efforts toward building a new and more just system.

Although the Russian press from the 1850s demonstrated a continuing and somewhat scandalized interest in the Latter Day Saints (Mormons)—even a journal edited by Fedor Dostoevskii had an article about this group—most of the comment centered around the interesting question of "plural marriage," and little note was taken of the communal element in the Mormon structure. In the late 1860s, however, largely through the influence of a Russian translation of two works by the lively British writer William Hebworth Dixon, there were signs of interest in the American forms of utopia.

Dixon had visited the United States in 1866, going as far west as Salt Lake City. The Mormons had already had a great deal of attention from other travelers who had produced many solid pages of print based upon two weeks of observations made through a considerable fog of ignorance and prejudice. While Dixon was a facile writer, whose style was not quite so overloaded with the mannerisms of the time as that of others, the British *Dictionary of National Biography* lets it be seen that he was not considered to be always an accurate or fair reporter. Thus one may wonder if the two-volume *New America* (London, Hurst and Blackett, 1867) that was published on his return is correct in all its details, and there is little doubt that *Spiritual Wives* (London, Hurst and Blackett, 1868. 2 v.), a book dealing with "free love" in East Prussia, Great Britain, and the United States, was written so as to heighten the effect of this somewhat risqué topic. Both were translated into Russian, the first in fact appearing in two editions that may possibly present two translations, *Novaia Amerika* (St. Petersburg, "Russkaia knizhnaia torgovlia," 1867. 413 p.) and in 1869 with the same title (St. Petersburg, 1869. 424 p.). The second work was titled in Russian *Dukhovnye zheny* (St. Petersburg, Tipografiia N. Tiblena i Ko., 1869. 380 p.). Examination of the English original of the latter work shows that, despite the emphasis on "free love," a good deal of its American section was but a rewriting of the part of *New America* that had dealt with the quite celibate community of the Shakers. Nevertheless Dixon had left enough other material to draw from the newspaper *Pall Mall Gazette* an accusation of indecency. He sued, and won—being awarded damages of one farthing.

Dixon's *New America* had been the subject of an extended summary and review in the quite liberal *Otechestvennyia zapiski* (1867, v. 172: 82–116; 295–332; 522–64; 702–44; v. 173: 317–59). The next year the same work served as a basis for a four-part article "Sievero-Amerikanskoe sektatorstvo" [North American sectarianism] in the same journal (1868, v. 177: 403–70; v. 178: 273–336; v. 179: 269–318; 324–54) written by the retired colonel turned radical Petr Lavrovich Lavrov, who was in that year undergoing the punishment of exile for some of his previous writings. It was not a harsh exile, for it seems that when he was transferred, a group of the local officials gave him a farewell party complete with champagne.

Lavrov's sources extended beyond Dixon's work to include such people as Tocqueville, the American spiritualist Andrew Jackson Davis, and a Captain W. A. Baker who had prophesied the Second Coming for sunset on September 20, 1878. His message was in essence a radical one, critical of the division of society into a multitude who worked and a minority who consumed the results of that toil, and he emphasized one of the features

of the new sects of America, a feature which has only to a very small degree appeared in the sects of Europe, the consecration of physical toil, as a goal of mankind, as its religious obligation, as important an element of the human ideal, if not the most important, as the element of mental development and religious seeking. Although theoretically recognized, this principle in the Old World has very rarely been applied to practical life; custom and the political structure are against it. Only in America has it found such a firm state of preparation in society that the sects that proclaim it have not only undertaken its serious fulfilment, but have indeed found in it the firmest basis for their development. Labor 'in the sweat of one's brow' is not a curse! It is the best part; it is a service to the high powers; it is an obligation of the loftiest kind!

Physical labor is the way to salvation! (*Otechestvennyia zapiski*, 1868, v. 178: 308).

In addition to the centrality of labor among these American sects, Lavrov also gave attention to their attitude toward the rights of women. He felt this to be a touchstone to evaluate the true progress of society toward rationality and justice, and, drawing on other sources in addition to Dixon, he speaks of the favorable situation of women's education in America, in particular at the women's college in "Paughkcepsie," giving the name in his own version of English, an institution that had the object of offering as broad a level of instruction as that given to men (*Otechestvennyia zapiski*, 1868, v. 178: 318–19). He went on to speak of some of the other movements for women's rights, noting a resolution, for example, of the Women's Rights Convention held in Salem, Ohio, on April 19 and 20, 1850, to the effect that all laws oppressing women should be considered null and void, as well as all those denying them the right to vote, setting any social, literary, financial, or religious distinctions between the two sexes, or establishing any moral double standard between them (*Otechestvennyia zapiski*, 1868, v. 178: 321–36).

Although Dixon's English original had given over fifty pages to the subject of the United Society of Believers in Christ's Second Appearing, commonly called Shakers, Lavrov was rather sparing in using this material and little of the group's simplicity and directness seems to have been conveyed by his articles. However, the first part of Lavrov's article had offered an extended discussion of the views of the American Unitarian clergyman William Ellery Channing, apparently based on Ernest Renan's *Études d'histoire religieuse* (*Otechestvennyia zapiski*, 1868, v. 177: 441–50). These pages constitute a strong statement supporting the rights of men to arrive at their own opinions but denying their right to force those opinions on anyone else. As Lavrov's summary of Renan appears to indicate, Channing felt that all men were part of one another, so long as they strove after the great and good, and that man need not feel himself subject to the Calvinist concept of original sin.

By 1868 Channing was hardly a newcomer to the pages of Russian journals, for there had been a translation of one of his sermons and an analysis of his thought in a major journal in the 1850s, and French translations of some of his writings appear to have been available to Russian readers. When Lavrov's article is added, an article that appeared in a journal that "everyone read"—for *Otechestvennyia zapiski* was a strong voice for a liberal outlook and its influence was stronger than the circulation figures might indicate—one can justifiably assume that many of the leaders of Russian thought might have an awareness of Dixon, of Renan, of Channing, and of some of the utopian elements of American culture.

In the same issue of *Otechestvennyia zapiski* that contained the last installment of Lavrov's article there appeared a short contribution under the title *Iz Ameriki: pis'mo pervoe* [From America: first letter] (v. 179: 180–87) that was unsigned, but that, according to an obituary article in 1912 (Maksim M. Kovalevskii: Ivan Ivanovich Ivaniukov. *Viestnik Evropy,* May 1912: 320–29), was written by the young legal scholar and economist I. I. Ivaniukov. It appears that no other letter was published, although Ivaniukov seems to have intended to contribute others, and its contents are little more than a description of Cambridge, Massachusetts, in the immediate Post-Civil War era with some remarks on life in one of the nearby New England villages. However, the entry for Ivaniukov in the major pre-1917 encyclopedia indicates that one of the motives of his visit was to become acquainted with American communes. While one finds no additional printed reference to this purpose, it is significant that just at this time, as Dixon's works were appearing in Russian translation and Lavrov's articles were providing a synthesis of these and of a range of other materials, a Russian could have been inspired to undertake a visit to America. It was not Ivaniukov, however, who was to be the most remarkable Russian seeker of an American utopia.

That distinction belongs to Vladimir Konstantinovich Geins (1839–1888), who took the name "William Frey," reflecting the German word *frei* (free), and who came to the United States in 1868. Both Frey and some of those whom he later inspired to come to the United States were to be a significant influence on L. N. Tolstoi's attitudes toward America. One of the major sources of information about Geins/Frey's life in America is Nikolai Evstafevich Slavinskii's *Pis'ma ob Amerikie i russkikh pereselentsakh* [Letters about America and the Russian immigrants] (St. Petersburg, Tip. P. P. Merkulev, 1873. 303 p.), which avoids stating the fact that Frey and Slavinskii were brothers-in-law, Frey having married Slavinskii's seventeen-year-old sister shortly before his departure from Russia. [For this relationship, see: A. Faresov, Odin iz 'semidesiatnikov' (One of the men of the 1870s). *Viestnik Evropy*, 1904, no. 9: 238.] There is a certain touch of acidity in Slavinskii's writing that testifies to the adage that no man is a hero to his brother-in-law, but, in spite of this, Slavinskii does say that Frey was

one of those few people of the new generation who value their high and honorable convictions as they would gold and who do not swerve from them even under the most burdensome experiences of life. A serious mind and a full education, acquired in three higher educational institutions, placed G—s on a favorable path, and of course, opened a brilliant career to him. However, the 'subjective' conditions of this person were at variance with the whole condition of his upbringing at home and at school. Continuous and concentrated observation of the 'course of present-day life' soon brought him to a full recognition of the abnormality of the existing order in economic and social relationships.

People with 'this kind' of tendencies do not remain passive; having a character of iron and a remarkable strength of will, they do their own thing ['dielaiut svoe dielo' means, literally, 'do their own thing.'], unrestrainedly, in spite of everything.

Not being imbued with grandiose goals of changing the social conditions in the progress of humanity, etc. and at the same time recognizing reality, G—s began the necessary 'transformation' in himself and, of course not at home or in Europe, where the existing order of things is maintained by strong historical roots, but across the ocean, in a country of the New World, where life has already been established 'otherwise,' where complete freedom in private, social and political life gives to him, who so wishes, wide latitude for carrying out all sorts of experiments" (Slavinskii, op. cit., 232–33).

In a long quotation from an unidentified friend of Geins', his character and the possible reasons for his taking up his utopian socialist views are analyzed, with a number of remarks about the way in which Geins was fated to find quite a different situation in America than he had expected.

"One cannot help but rejoice that V. G—s has seen how people live in America. In many of its relationships this way of life has made a deep impression on him. We consider it a duty to assume that there one finds rivers of milk between banks of pudding," but one has also to admit a tendency toward the greatest possible concentration of capital in the hands of a few. "We are left only with a strong regret for the loss of a magnificent citizen of Russia (a future public figure with a significant sphere of activity), who could have brought positive and not negative good. It seems to me that the youthful life of America, full of the struggle for existence, will take in V. G. sooner or later. Because of his ascetic-political convictions, and of his voluntary infertility (and lack of a wish for contact with real life), he will be left with only his mind, energy, strength of will, firmness, and unshakeable honesty." The forces of his fine nature are better suited to a simple, daily, and active life (Slavinskii, op. cit., 234–38).

Frey and his wife arrived in the United States with about $800 in funds but they showed a frugality that was out of keeping with the stereotypical Russian so that this money stretched over a year and a half. The couple learned how to prepare meals for 80 kopecks a day, about 50 cents at the rate of exchange at the time, and lived quietly in Jersey City (Slavinskii, op. cit., 238–42).

From this vantage point Frey observed American politics, particularly the process whereby in 1868 the Democratic convention, torn by the claims of three leading candidates, finally settled on the rather dark horse Horatio Seymour to head the ticket. The Russian's substantial article on the topic, "Amerikanskaia zhizn'; pis'mo pervoe" [American life: first letter] that was published in *Otechestvennyia zapiski* (1870, no. 1: 215–63) appeared with enough delay to have accounted perhaps for some of the analytical tone of Frey's writing. He was not blind to the flaws of the American political process and he tells of a growing influence of corruption that reduced the honest men to a minority. Yet he did not feel that corruption was a necessary element of the American system, nor was there a connection between wealth and dishonesty.

Everywhere there is a sufficient number of rich and politically honest people, and most especially so in America where the connection between the personal qualities of a man and his wealth serve to the present as a distinguishing trait of society. Most of the present-day capitalists began their careers as ordinary workers, and they owe their success solely to their personal energy and intelligence. Even now, anyone who sets out to gain wealth always reaches his goal if he is sufficiently endowed with the necessary mental and moral qualities. The rich class, until now, has represented the mental force of the people (Frey, Amerikanskaia zhizn' . . . *Otechestvennyia zapiski*, 1870, no. 1: 229–30).

The situation, however, was changing. Economic forces were putting an end to the old system in which there were many small property owners, and creating large enterprises with which these lesser men could not compete. The influx of immigrants was forming a proletariat that had begun to express its discontent at the prospect of endless toil for the benefit of someone else. Workers, in order to counter this, were tending to join in a common effort to face a common foe. "Strikes are beginning, workers' unions and cooperative associations are being formed (these are still quite a few in number, not more than 10 or 15 throughout the Union)" (Frey, Amerikanskaia zhizn' . . . *Otechestvennyia zapiski*, 1870, no. 1: 230–31).

Coupled with these general observations on the trends of American politics, Frey's article provides a sharp description of the Democratic convention in New York in the summer of 1868 and of the situation in St. Louis at election time that year. Frey had decided to move West in the hope of finding employment that would enable him to preserve his small store of cash against further depletion and, choosing St. Louis, arrived there to find the campaign in full swing. The city, which was heavily German in its population, tended to be Republican, while the rest of the state was largely Democratic and Anglophone, and tension ran high. In his telling, at least, there were times in which clashes between the supporters of the two parties came within hairs' breadths of turning into real bloodshed (Frey, Amerikanskaia zhizn' . . . *Otechestvennyia zapiski*, 1870, no. 1: 242–43, 255–57. Slavinskii, op. cit.: 283–46).

Frey had been educated in a Russian institution connected with a governmental agency equivalent to the American coast survey and he was an accomplished draftsman. With this skill he found a job at $40 a month. On that sum, and by cautious use of his reserves, Frey and his wife were able to live sufficiently well. Slavinskii provides figures of the budget for the period September 21-October 21, 1868, as:

Rent	$5.00
Bread	3.25
Sugar	2.40
Tea	1.60
Beef	4.10
Vegetables	1.00
Milk and Cheese	1.70
Butter and lard	1.05
Flour and Potatoes	1.15
Eggs	5.00
Fruit	1.05
Coal	1.20

Supplies	5.30
Books and newspapers	3.09
Horse car fare	1.50
Drinks	.25
Clothing, baths, etc.	7.55
Other expenses and postage	3.00
Total	48.59

(Slavinskii, op. cit., 245–46).

[The family must have been almost addicted to eggs. Also, the very precise total given by Slavinskii comes up sixty cents short, suggesting the likelihood of a misprint in the tea budget figure—$1.60 instead of $1.00.]

However, his wife became ill, requiring him to stay home to care for her, and he lost his job. For three months he took whatever he could get, even the work of a sawyer. In March 1869 he, his wife, and their child returned to New York, but a year later he was again in St. Louis. At that time he and another Russian couple began to consider "the decision to move to the far West, to one of the American communes set up by Longley" (Slavinskii, op. cit., 250–51).

Alcander Longley (1832–1918) was one of the most persistent—and consistently unsuccessful—of those reformers who tried to establish what they considered a rational, cooperative commune in the generally harsh and competitive economic atmosphere of the time. From January 1868 he published, somewhat irregularly, *The Communist,* which was "devoted to the universal adoption of the principles of Communism:—Each for all—all for each. From each according to his ability—to each according to his wants" ["Community of Property and Labor, Unitary Homes, and Integral Education." *The Communist,* v. 1, no. 1 (January 1868): 1]. Each issue contained a text of an "Agreement of the Reunion Community," the set of principles upon which these communes were to be established, and, to judge from the constant changes, Longley's definitions were subject to considerable alteration. Much of the other contents of the journal told of efforts to set up communes elsewhere, as well as providing a quantity of inspirational poetry of rather lame format and in later years a reformed spelling system that appears to have escaped the attention of such writers on the topic as H. L. Mencken.

The issues from January 1868 to January 1870 report

Longley's effort to found a commune on a tract of 160 acres of prairie land located two miles west of Minersville, Jasper County, Missouri. Some of the "weaker vessels" departed, but there was hope for success, despite a feeling of being "whittled down to the little end of nothing." The glowing terms used in describing the location, soil, climate, and water of the chosen site of utopia are very reminiscent of those used by the railroad companies of the period who were boosting settlement along their lines [*The Communist*, v. 1, no. 5 (May 1868): 37–39].

Although the January 1870 issue of *The Communist* tells of an acrimonious departure of a member, the return of whose contribution involved a large share of the community property, it also includes a letter from Frey headed "Williamsburg, New York," in which he spoke of his conviction

that communism, based on liberal principles, is the sole remedy for the present chaotic condition of society. I have an invincible faith that its present struggle with ignorant egotism will be necessarily followed by the great and bright future. But to secure this end it needs now hard work. Only such men must put their hands to the work as are devoted to the principle, and who are ready to sacrifice their means and labor for the development or [sic] this remote aim.

The love to a neighbor—not the egotism—must be the sole and supreme principle among the pioneers of communism. It seems to me that in the deficiency of this sentiment consists the principle [sic] cause of the past failures.

I have recently learned of your Community and of your heroic struggle for existence. I fully concur with your agreement; and now, when you intensely need the help of honest and intelligent men, I would not belong to the mass of indifferentists, who, claiming themselves to be partisans of communism, do nothing to help you, and passively wait the end of your struggle.

I respectfully request you to admit me as a member of your Community. In my native country (Russia), which I left a year and a half ago, I had a brilliant career before me, but I was obliged to leave because of the fierce persecution of the Government against communists, together with the indifferentism of the people to the new ideas, which made impossible either a theoretical propagand [sic] or their practical demonstration. I was an astronomer, and belonged to the Government corps whose duties are similar to the coast survey in this country. My wife and child will be obliged to remain here till next spring, but I can come at any time. Enclosed I send you $2 more as my contribution of $1 per month for the *Communist* [*The Communist*, v. 2, no. 3 (January 1870): 19].

Frey's English, as shown by this letter, is quite good for someone who had only recently learned it; the apparent troubles he has with the use of the definite article are those that are common to most people of Slavic background. As far as his thought goes, he is surprisingly close in his outlook to others among Longley's correspondents, for *The Communist* has many other such contributions from earnest and enthusiastic people who are all in favor of the general ideals of utopian communities, but who seem to have little true analytical or organizing abilities, at least insofar as they were able to express them in ordinary English prose.

In the June issue of *The Communist* it was announced that "On April 12th, Mr. Wm. Frey, with his wife and one small child, arrived with an acceptable amount of money." Others had come in the same period of time, increasing membership to a total of 27, but the same June number also notes, "But within three or four weeks after the arrival of our new-comers, it began to appear that some of them entertained a material difference of opinion or had not yet fully understood the position that we have heretofore taken in regard to marriage [Longley was not a supporter of "free love"], they proposing innovation which we could not agree to either as to principle or policy." These innovators, a majority of the members, withdrew, and the commune was reduced to Mr. Longley and his family, Frey and his, and a Dr. Briggs [*The Communist,* v. 2, no. 5 (June 1870): 36].

At this time, the exact date being uncertain, into the midst of Longley and Frey's high comedy there came the latter's brother-in-law Slavinskii. Without at all identifying Mary Frey as his sister, he says that he found her an energetic woman, in much better health than before and without a shadow of regret for the past, but completely satisfied with her situation amidst her beloved family and two or three good friends, despite modest, even poor, material circumstances. The building of the commune was small and scantily furnished, save that it did contain some bookshelves, a printing press, and an anatomical dummy that belonged to Dr. Briggs (Slavinskii, op. cit., 262–65).

It appears, however, that Slavinskii's visit lasted only a week. *The Communist* appeared in a most irregular manner at this time, so that there is no other report, but it seems that the commune was unable to complete a necessary payment for its land by December 1870 because of the decline in the number of members. Longley returned to St. Louis, to work in the composing room of the *St. Louis Dispatch,* while Frey, who had been joined by another Russian couple, accompanied Dr. Briggs in seeking land for a similar commune farther to the west (Slavinskii, op. cit.: 268–78).

From this time Frey dropped out of Longley's little journal, but the New York Public Library holds a collection of Frey's papers on the basis of which Avrahm Yarmolinsky wrote *A Russian's American Dream: A Memoir on William Frey* (Lawrence, Kansas, University of Kansas Press, 1965. 147 p.). Additional data about Frey is provided by Slavinskii, evidently derived from correspondence with his sister—Frey's wife—and, since other Russians soon appeared to join the commune, there are further references in the biographies and histories of this era of Russian political dissidence.

In the early 1870s some young Russians had sought to foster political opposition to the tsar by a process of "going to the people," venturing out into the villages to live among the peasants and to impart to them the doctrines of brotherhood, equality, and communal life. There were, however, two major impediments. The imperial government was not gentle in dealing with such opponents, and the peasants were often quite suspicious of such newcomers who could not as a rule perform even the simplest of the tasks of rural life. Often, in fact, these intruders were handed over to the authorities by peasants who feared that they were being victimized by such a movement. Given these obstacles to the realization of their hopes, some of these young members of the Russian intelligentsia proposed that they go to the United States to set up at least one communal settlement, if not more, to serve as a sort of training ground and base of support for renewal of the effort in the motherland.

One of the centers from which such proposals came was the university at Kiev. There, in 1871–72, the young Petr Boris Aksel'rod (later to become a leader of the non-Marxist Socialist Revolutionary Party) was approached by a fellow student, Nikolai I. Sudzilovskii, with an invitation to enter a discussion circle that had as its goal migration to America to set up a colony on communist principles. Aksel'rod's own views that it would be better to carry on agitation against the regime within

Russia could only have the effect—so he was told—of fostering the development and the triumph of the bourgeoisie in Russia.

And thus, proceeding from those postulates, since any social activity, even if revolutionary, cannot help but bring about the lordship of the bourgeoisie over the masses of the people, Sudzilovskii attempted to convince me that it was by this very means of organizing communist colonies in America that the Russian revolutionary intelligentsia could most effectively influence Russia toward a socialist outlook and hinder the enthronement there of the bourgeoisie. "By our own example," he declared to me, "we will propagandize for socialism and, insofar as through the influence of our visible example the number of communes set up by Russian socialists in America may grow, socialism will gain strength in Russia."

Since the proponents of such ideas lacked funds, it was suggested that Akesel'rod marry a young lady from a rich Jewish family in Mogilev to whom he had once been a tutor (Petr B. Aksel'rod, *Perezhitoe i peredumannoe* [Experiences and thoughts]. Kn. 1. Berlin, Izdatel'stvo Z. I. Grzhebina, 1923. Reprinted: Cambridge, England, Oriental Research Partners, 1975. p. 80–81).

Although Aksel'rod did not fall in with these plans, he does say that the most active of the young Kievan radicals belonged to the so-called "Americans," and that they soon went abroad, some to America and others to Switzerland where they awaited a time when they could return to Russia. (Despite his arguments in favor of the American scheme, Sudzilovskii did not reach the United States until considerably later, settling in San Francisco in the late 1880s as a medical practitioner, and falling into a feud with the Russian bishop, whom he accused of moral lapses with, it seems, enough evidence to bring the bishop's withdrawal at the urging of the American lawyer who was legal advisor to the Russian consulate. Sudzilovskii, who had adopted the pseudonym of "Russell," and who is generally referred to in Russian sources as Sudzilovskii-Russel', then settled in Hawaii, where he was a member of the legislature of the Hawaiian Republic and presiding officer of the first territorial senate, in a session known as the "Lady Dog Legislature," since its main accomplishment was a change in the dog license fees. During the Russo-Japanese War he carried on socialist agitation among the Russian POWs in Japan, and thereafter settled down for alternate periods of residence in Manila and in

Shanghai. He can be called one of the stormy petrels of the Russian exile community.)

According to Yarmolinsky, by the autumn of 1872 only three young men from this circle had reached the United States, staying but a short time and doing little to carry out the plans drawn up in Kiev (Yarmolinsky, op. cit., 29). Although a mutual aid association for Russian immigrants had been formed in New York in March 1872, the lot of such settlers in America was not an easy one. Slavinskii quotes a letter from his sister, Frey's wife, saying "'Imagine for yourself the horror of those exalted young people who consider themselves almost heroes merely because they have arrived in America,'" for they would need to reshape themselves, a task made more difficult by the conditions in which Frey's commune was living. Mary Frey continued, "'Yet, if our material circumstances were more attractive . . . possibly these young people could reform themselves and might stay with us, but, unfortunately, we live very badly. We eat corn and some sort of bread of wheat flour (which, so these young liberals think, my dog wouldn't swallow). In addition, given that—Oh, horrors!—we do not blush to say that a man who cannot bear up under such a life, 'who loves his stomach more than his conviction,' cannot be one of our comrades.'" Those who did have a capacity for reforming themselves in accordance with the commune's ideals could find a quiet home and brotherly love, but for the others, "'Once again I ask you to tell them, given a chance to do so, about *all this* . . . may they, in the simplicity of their hearts, repeat the well-worn phrases about the joys of rural life, about the pleasures of physical labor, about the grandeur of their familiar ideals . . . and may *they remain* in Russia'" (Slavinskii, op. cit., 296–99).

One of these Russian enthusiasts who did manage to come to Frey's commune was Vladimir Dobroliubov, brother of the well-known radical literary critic, but he proved to be "a halfhearted communist" and "he looked to the settlement as the place where he would undergo a miraculous cure and become a new man." Spending most of his time in bed, he had the habit when he was up of washing his hands twenty times a day. He soon left, borrowing from the impecunious commune in order to do so (Yarmolinsky, op. cit., 35).

In February 1873 another Russian came, the twenty-year-old Grigorii Machtet, who had been discharged as a teacher because of his political views. In company with two others of similar views, Machtet appears to have been a scout for the "Americans" of Kiev. They looked on America as a kind of "rosy Arcady," so Machtet was to phrase it, but the realities of the country brought disillusionment. Although the young Russians were ready to lay down their lives for their fellow men, the Americans "'felt our muscles and eyed us suspiciously, taking us for crooks who had escaped from European prisons'" (Yarmolinsky, op. cit., 37).

Machtet was to become a writer. Although he was not a major figure in Russian literature, his works had a certain popularity among uncritical young readers who were not disturbed by his making his heroes every inch heroic and his villains culprits of the deepest hue. After spending some two years in America he returned to Russia in 1874 and shortly thereafter began contributions on American themes to some of the journals of the time. In 1911–13 a ten-volume edition of his writings appeared, the first volume of which contains a number of short articles on such topics as life aboard an emigrant steamer, spiritualism, the outlook of small prairie towns, and American religious meetings, all of which appear to have been written in the 1870s. One of Machtet's articles, "Pred amerikanskim sudom" [Before an American court], tells of the accidental shooting of one member of his party of Russians by a companion who was put on trial on the charge of murder. Justice appears to have been swift, the court being convened, according to Machtet, in less than an hour, and, in spite of fear that brought the accused to consider suicide, it was surprisingly considerate. The Russians' scanty knowledge of English was pieced out by the German that some of the settlers had in common with them and the proceedings were eased by the fact that the officials, members of the jury, and audience all knew perfectly well that the revolver in the killing was of a make and model that could easily be fired accidentally. Thus, the accused was let off, and, after the public had helped to bury the victim, the men were free to go (Grigorii A. Machtet, *Polnoe sobranie sochinenii.* v. 1. St. Petersburg, Knigoizd. t-va "Prosvieshchenie," 1911. 215–39).

Frey had sought to dissuade Machtet from coming. "No

matter how I might wish to see you here, I consider it my first obligation to advise you to think seriously about it first, instead of rushing here. . . . .We are living very poorly, more poorly even than a Russian peasant, whose hut, even so, is warmer than ours. We have neither tea, sugar, nor coffee; we do not eat beef or pork, and we consider all that very harmful" (Machtet, op. cit., v. 1: 186–87).

Not to be turned aside, Machtet came to the commune. The first word to pass between him and Frey upon meeting was *Rossiia.* "Only in such moments do you know how strongly and passionately you love that which has fed you, consoled you, reared and created you, by which you have lived, and that has taught you to understand. The conversations somehow suddenly ceased to flow . . . something heavy and heartbreaking grasped the soul." Some of these feelings, it is true, may have a certain connection with Machtet's discovery that the commune felt that a wish to eat meat, sprinkle salt over food, to smoke, or to drink coffee or tea was a sign of sinful tendencies and gluttony amounting to "stomach worship." The members of the commune were characterized as having various degrees of eccentricity. One was as "sentimental as a young lady student going home for the holidays," while Frey, though intelligent, was impressionable and inconsistent. Mary Frey was exempted from such criticism, appearing cleverer than the others. All in all, the members were "well-intentioned egoists, for whom people, society, the fatherland, was *nothing*—and personal happiness, peace, their own tastes, habits, and opinions were everything." They were fugitives from real life, but claimed to provide a model for a new system that would bring true happiness and justice (Machtet, op. cit., v. 1: 200–205).

One subject that Machtet does not mention, but that Yarmolinsky does, is that he and the scarcely older Mary Frey became attached. William Frey, despite his support of "freedom," could not avoid feeling jealous and the atmosphere of the little group, already prey to a great deal of petty bickering, was greatly affected (Yarmolinsky, op. cit., 55–57). The younger man soon left the commune, evidently in October of 1873, and broke off all communication with Mary Frey. The latter, however, soon found a new friend in a later arrival, Vladimir Muromtsev, and the situation became even more tragic, for

Mary became pregnant and the two left. It was a scandalous and pitiful happening. Torn between principles and emotion, Frey at last asked Mary to come back—a step that, in fact, was almost the only one open to her, for Muromtsev returned to Russia in June of 1875. Later Frey too was to become the father of a child out of wedlock.

On her return Mary Frey found that, although the commune had grown in size, to include, among others, a Mrs. Robbins who was a medium and clairvoyant, and a young Russian couple who had assumed the name "Right," tension was high. Frey finally declared his willingness to secede and to start a new commune. Those who withdrew received one-third of the communal property and Frey again set about realizing his theories, with a group consisting of himself, his family, the pseudonymous "Rights" and a Charles Small who was also of Russian background (Yarmolinsky, op. cit., 57–67).

By the fall of 1875 this new commune seemed only a step away from dissolution, but on one cold and windy day three men showed up at the bare little farm. They were delegates from Russia, representing a movement that had its origin in a sudden flash of enlightenment experienced by Aleksandr Kapitonovich Malikov which had converted him from a belief in the need for radical political action to the realization that men were indeed partakers of the spirit of the Deity. This transformation appears to have occurred between the end of 1873 and February or March of 1874, as attested to by one of Malikov's friends who, having been absent for just about that length of time, found on his return that Malikov had changed his views:

During your absence I ceased to be a man of the 'old dispensation.' With a strong rush of sympathy toward me, he said, 'Listen, find in yourself the spirit of God. Become a Christian. Turn away from the thought of abolishing force by force, of quenching fire by fire. . . .Let us proceed against force by the means of love. . . .Give me your hand and I will lead you on the way to truth and virtue, to the religious rebirth of humanity. It is not in science nor in political organization that our salvation lies, but in the union of man with man in the name of Christ (A. Faresov, "Odin iz 'semidesiatnikov'" [One of the "men of the 1870s"]. *Viestnik Evropy*, 1904, no. 9 (September): 229–31).

Malikov must have been a man of passion and conviction, with great effect on others, for the same source tells of finding Malikov's apartment filled with people previously known for their extreme ideas to whom he had been expounding his doctrines. "Some of them lay on sofas with compresses on their heads, others complained about a fever, and still others had tearstained eyes, but on all faces there shone the joy and blessing of repentant and forgiven sinners." There grew up around Malikov a band of followers of what he called *bogochelovechestvo* (Godmanhood would be a fair equivalent of this word), and subsequently the authorities, always vigilant over ideological and religious deviation, arrested him. A major of gendarmerie is quoted as having said, "we were all highly interested in the personality of the arrested man. When he was brought to us he spoke of God, of the social organism to which both great and small people were equally essential, as each of us not only needs a brain, but also each finger of the hand." At the end of the questioning, "we stood up from our seats and reached our hands out to Malikov. He was immediately set free." However, Malikov was forbidden to preach his doctrines, and a later, German-language work put forward the suggestion that the commission had considered him to be out of his mind (Faresov, op. cit., 233–35).

The authorities, however, do not seem to have stood in Malikov's way when, as in the case of the students in Kiev, it was proposed that he go to America to create a basis for the conversion of his homeland. It is from the work of Aleksandr S. Prugavin, *Nepriemlushchie mira: ocherki religioznykh iskanii* [Those who do not accept the world: essays on religious strivings] (Moscow, Zadruga, 1918. 45–76) that we have the most detailed account of Malikov's activities, one that, like Slavinskii's, reflects a certain tension between brothers-in-law, for Malikov's second wife was Prugavin's sister.

At the end of 1874 a group of fifteen of Malikov's followers set out for Kansas, at least according to Prugavin (Prugavin, op. cit., 63), but Faresov indicates that it was not until the autumn of 1875 that three delegates knocked at Frey's door. Whatever the chronology may have been, for both records appear to have been reworked several decades later, the tone is remarkably similar. Faresov quotes Malikov as saying,

"Approaching the empty region of Kansas and Frey's settlement, I expected to find a series of cabins, cultivated fields, and the happy faces of new Christians. However, the area was a wild one and the house standing in front of us was so full of cracks that, even at a distance of several paces, we could look right through them at the inhabitants and see what they were doing." They were all protecting themselves from the cold as best they could. Frey himself came to meet us in a soldier's overcoat and with a fever. His wife . . . was in a similar coat, with a sorrowful and resigned expression on her face, as if she had given up on everything earthly. . . . His house was large but clumsily built and was covered by a roof without any ceiling. The grey sky was visible through this roof, testifying even more eloquently to the inability of the settlers to build suitable housing. . . . This pitiful condition of the colony made the most disheartening impression on me and, apparently on my companions as well" (Faresov, op. cit., 238–39).

In spite of these impressions, the newly arrived Russians bought land nearby and invited Frey to join them. He was as insistent in the new organization on his own principles as he had been before. "A negator of artificial civilization, he set up in the commune the most artificial way of life, which tortured us all and in the end sent us off in various directions." Some of the troubles came, however, from a seemingly absolute incompetence in dealing with the ordinary tasks of life. "Our buildings were cold and shabby and had cracks in walls and roofs. No one knew how to finish off milking a cow and we ruined many of them in the beginning." As a further note dealing with animals, the cowsheds were built of such small logs that they fell down when a cow leaned against the walls to scratch herself (Prugavin, op. cit., 67).

"Clothes, which we sewed ourselves, hung like sacks. Food was cooked without any flavor. We did not know how to preserve provisions and we spoiled them. . . .In a word, there was startling impracticality in everything. Any businesslike man would find it repulsive to look at these workers who scratched the ground instead of plowing deeply, who mowed grass with a fear of hitting the legs of those in front with the sickle, who split wood at the risk of hitting their own hand or leg with the ax, etc." The members continued to affirm their spiritual perfection, and, having left Russia to get along without the peasant, still found him necessary. They had drawn pictures based on "ready-made booklets and enthusiastic conversations. Deprivation settled ever deeper into our farm . . ." (Faresov, op. cit., 240–41).

Some of the accounts of this landlocked "ship of fools" are amusing, such as Frey's doctrinaire vegetarianism which denied the use of salt and yeast and even at one time frowned on the milling of grain. Even at this distance in time, however, it is hard to forgive Frey's treatment of his daughter, who was scarcely past six years of age. He set her the problem of multiplying twenty-five billion, two hundred million, one hundred twenty-eight thousand, three hundred fifty-three by one thousand two hundred forty-three billion, three million, forty-nine, and, when the girl began to cry, he poured a bucket of water over her (Faresov, op. cit., 241–54).

Relations among the members were not smoothed by the practice of holding sessions for the public criticism of flaws and errors. These often turned on such matters as the member on kitchen duty having washed a skillet badly. Participants also made public confession of their internal error, and it all became so petty that even Malikov was driven to say that, in place of doing the work of God, people were more like the lamp in front of an icon that was flickering and smoking before going out. Frey's response to this was to urge Malikov, "Remake in one's self the man of decay, in order to be fit for the commune. Reforge the separatist in one's self and make a communist. The commune is the last word of life, but we are not fit for it" (Faresov, op. cit., 245).

Frey's zeal seems, at least for a time, to have reawakened a belief in the calling of the members to remold humanity and to give an example of Christianity. He kept on shouting, "Patience, patience," but also kept on eating his hard, unleavened, unsalted bread, and his affirmation did not alleviate the Russians' growing homesickness. When members fell ill and it was proposed that a doctor be called, Frey would say, "It is your sins and errors that have become illnesses. Free yourselves from the first, and you will be well. Stay in the commune and forget Russia" (Faresov, op. cit., 246–48).

As Faresov's account reports, the Russian believers in "Godmanhood" finally came to the conclusion that they had to return to Russia, quoting Malikov as saying,

"We will never merge ourselves into this country," I was the first to exclaim. "The Americans tolerate us because we, although we deny artificial civilization, still do not go nude into the towns and at home in our private lives we are not *fri-lovery* [a Russian transliteration of "free lovers"]. They are polite and kind to us, but the devil knows what, among themselves, they think about us and what is in the heart of any of them. In Russia I could tell from a man's face and tone of voice whether he was my friend or my enemy; but I will never learn to read an American by face, to see if he is a swindler or if he considers me a swindler. It's murder to live in such an environment" (Faresov, op. cit., 249).

At one time, when feelings such as these prevailed, Malikov's wife, with tears in her eyes, read a poem by Lermontov that included "I love my fatherland, but with a strange love . . . ," and her hearers dissolved in tears, leaving the house to regain their composure. On reassembling, "we were still afraid to remind one another about Russia, as if it were a deep wound in the heart about which everyone knew but no one spoke. We had such a deep longing for home, and thus in the end we hated cosmopolitanism" (Faresov, op. cit., 250).

Finally, in the summer of 1877, the commune split up, after less than two years of existence. Most Russians returned to their homeland, although one, Nikolai V. Chaikovskii, remained two years or so longer, spending some of that time in a Shaker community in upstate New York. From 1879 to 1905 Chaikovskii lived in Europe, going back to Russia to engage in moderately leftist politics. In 1918 he became the head of an anti-Soviet government in the North of Russia, and died in a second exile in Paris in 1925.

After the commune fell apart, Frey remained in Kansas. The years that followed were ones of poverty and grinding work for him, but he continued to seek a realization of his dreams. One of these efforts came in 1882 when he took part in a colony that was set up in an area about 250 miles south of Portland, Oregon, by a group of socialistically inclined Jewish immigrants from Russia. "Even though the land was fruitful, the idealistic colonists insisted on leading a frugal existence. Their diet was confined to beans, peas, and coarse bread. When the food budget rose to eight cents [per person per day], it was considered gross extravagance" (Uri D. Herscher, *Jewish Agricultural Utopias in America, 1880–1910*. Detroit, Wayne State University Press, 1981: 45–46). Frey also continued to try to impose his own specific views on the colonists and at last he again had to withdraw. After a stay in New York, he and his wife went to London where they eked out a bare existence, and in 1885 before his death in 1888 he returned to Russia, visiting

Tolstoi and leaving a certain impression on him of his doctrines, some of which had deep American affinities.

Other Russian members of the Kansas commune also had contact with Tolstoi. Malikov is mentioned a number of times in the index to the *Iubileinoe izdanie,* the most complete edition of Tolstoi's writings, and, following a visit by Malikov in late 1877, Tolstoi drafted a work titled "Sobesedniki" [The Conversation Group] in which both real and imaginary persons appeared as exponents of several different philosophical tendencies, with Malikov included. The work was never completed, but, while the existing draft does not appear particularly coherent, one can see some indication of Tolstoi's awareness of Malikov's views.

In 1877 another commune member, Vasilii Ivanovich Alekseev, became a tutor of Tolstoi's children, from which position, Yarmolinksy holds, he "may have been the first to make him [Tolstoi] feel that it was morally wrong to be a landed proprietor. Tolstoi had intellectual contacts with one or two other God-men at the time when he was turning toward religion, and it is not improbable that their ideas, notably the advocacy of nonresistance to evil, influenced his thinking" (Yarmolinsky, op. cit., 80–81). A note in the *Iubileinoe izdanie* (v. 85: 87) speaks of Alekseev as one of Tolstoi's closest collaborators in a time of spiritual turmoil, and indicates some of his views as having drawn the ill will of Sofia Andreevna, Tolstoi's wife. Perhaps Alekseev's references to the Kansas commune's practice of public criticism and self-criticism affected Tolstoi, who in the summer of 1880 confessed to Alekseev that he was perilously tempted by a "young woman, about 22 or 23, whose husband was away on military service, not exactly pretty but tall, with a strong body, healthy and, all in all, attractive," asking Alekseev to help him resist this temptation (*Iubileinoe izdanie,* v. 85: 88).

It was in 1885 that Frey came to Iasnaia Poliana, Tolstoi's estate, for a visit. In a letter to his sister-in-law Tolstoi wrote that Frey was "interesting and good not only because of his vegetarianism. I'm sorry you weren't here when he was. You would have learned a lot. I was left with the best kind of impression of him. . . . He is interesting because from him there comes a fresh, strong, young breath of the broad world of American life . . . He lived 17 years largely in Russian and American communes, where there is no private property, where everyone works 'not with the head,' but with the hands and where many, both men, and women, are happy . . . very" (*Iubileinoe izdanie*, v. 63. Moscow, 1934. 289).

These contacts with Frey and other participants in the communes in America were not, however, the first that Tolstoi had had with the concept of America. The first apparent mention of anything American to be found in the vast mass of Tolstoi's written record is a journal entry for June 6, 1857 [apparently New Style, since Tolstoi was then in Switzerland], "6 June. Left by carriage at 8:00 from Bern. Flat country with rye and thickets as far as Freiburg. A thirty-year old American, has been in Russia. The Mormons in Utah—Joseph Smith, their founder, killed by Lynch law. In the inns all prices are equal. Hunting Buffalo and deer. I would like to go there. The abolitionists. Beecher Stowe." If one wished to summarize the general store of ideas about the United States that formed a sort of common denominator among literate Russians of the 1850s, this journal entry could scarcely be better, for it included American religious thought, the lack of marked class distinctions, the outlook of the opponents of slavery, and the writings of Harriet Beecher Stowe.

A notation in Tolstoi's notebook, on which his journal appears to have been based, adds the one word "Longfellow." On March 24, 1858 [since he was then in Russia, this is presumably Old Style], he mentions having read articles by Emerson on Shakespeare and Goethe in the *Literarisches Centralblatt*, and two days later he enters a notation about having read "an American tale," which may possibly have been the *Scènes de la vie américaine* by Jean-Baptiste Alfred Assollant that appeared in the *Revue des deux mondes* in that same month (Lev N. Tolstoi, *Journaux et carnets*. t. I: 1847–89. Ed. and annoted by G. Aucouturier. Paris, Gallimard, 1979: 121–128, 490, 492).

In the next year there was a curious juxtaposition of Tolstoi and an American writer that may have been the beginning of an interest that Tolstoi was to show even in his last summer of life. The issue of *Russkii Viestnik* for the first half of April 1859 contained the beginning installment of Tolstoi's two-part "Semeinoe schast'e" [Family happiness], immediately following which was a translation of a sermon on temperance by the American Unitarian clergyman and social commentator William Ellery Channing (1780–1842).

Channing's sermon is in many ways a typical product of nineteenth-century American rhetoric, but it also speaks of the value of a "moral independence, able, if need be, to go counter to public opinion," an independence that is "the sole protection of man. Each time that public opinion is sufficiently enlightened to encourage the development in individuals of this power of the first order, this will be the noblest driving force in the human soul. To thwart this independence would mean destroying the sole base of a thorough and solid reform" (William Ellery Channing, *Russkii viestnik*, April 1859, kn. 1: 506. Passage as translated from the Russian).

There is no available record whether Tolstoi read this sermon or not, nor whether, having done so, he saw a footnote attached to Channing's work that referred to another article on Channing that *Russkii viestnik* had published the preceeding year. This article, titled simply "Uil'iam Channing" (*Russkii viestnik*, 1858. t. 14: 445–512), was written by the earnest, prolific, and not really very talented "Evgeniia Tur," pseudonym of Elizaveta Vasil'evna Salias de Turnemir (1815–1892). It is clear that among Tur's sources was at least one detailed biography of Channing as well as other materials about American social thought. It would require a specialist on Channing to say that she was factually correct about him, but her general references to America have no glaring flaws. [An obituary for Tur in *Mir Bozhii*, no. 5, 1892, p. 41 (3d pagination) calls her article on Channing a "magnificent study" still worth attention.] There is much of what she writes about Channing's honesty and love, about his demands upon himself and about his lack of bigotry, that has a ring of harmony with some of the views that one can find in Tolstoi's correspondence in the months that were to follow. To an elder cousin he wrote, for example, that it had been two years since he had found "that there is immortality, that there is love, and that one must live for others in order to be happy for all eternity. . . .Furthermore, with me it isn't religion that makes life, but life that makes religion. When I lead a good life I am closer to it, and feel quite ready to enter this happy world, but when I lead a bad life I feel there's no need for it. . . .For me nature is religion's guide. Each soul has its own path, and this path is unknown, and is only sensed in the depths of the soul" (Lev N. Tolstoi, *Tolstoy's letters*. v. 1: 1828–79. 125–26).

These factors of the physical juxtaposition of Tolstoi and Channing in *Russkii viestnik*, the availability of Tur's long article about the American, and the tones of a certain harmony between Tolstoi and Channing do not, of course, constitute any really sound basis for assuming that there was a direct transmission of thought from the Unitarian sage to the Russian seeker, but the possibility did exist that, having been interested in Emerson's writings, another Unitarian thinker may have attracted the Russian's attention. One may note additional instances in which, during a period before Frey and the followers of *Bogochelovechestvo* ever came to Tolstoi's attention, there were signs of his interest in America, but it is in the 1880s and 1890s that one finds the most interesting episodes.

The American whose name appears most frequently in the index to the *Iubileinoe izdanie* of Tolstoi's works is the social critic and economic reformer Henry George (1839–1897). Now mostly forgotten, save by specialists in American history, George was a person whose writings and speeches drew much attention in both the United States and Europe in the era from about 1880 to the First World War. Largely a self-taught student of society, George's comments on the inequities of the American system of the late nineteenth century are often just and telling, and his program for a solution to the problems of the time impressed many people as a rational basis for action. The basic flaw, he felt, was that landowners monopolized land and exacted, both from those who used it and from those who acquired its products, an inequitable and unjust rent. The imposition of one single tax to divert this rent toward the use of society as a whole would, in his view, remove these injustices and allow the building of a more harmonious life.

The first major reference in Russian to Henry George appears to have been S. N. Iuzhakov's "K voprosu o biednosti" [On the question of poverty] published in *Otechestvennyia zapiski* (nos. 1,2, 1883) as a survey of George's most famous book *Pro-*

gress and Poverty.[2] Other articles about George appeared in the journals *Dielo* and *Russkaia mysl'* in the same year, with *Russkoe bogatstvo* containing a translation of one of his lectures. Iuzhakov published another article on George in *Otechestvennyia zapiski* in 1884, and one finds additional mention elsewhere (see Nikolai N. Gusev, *Lev Nikolaevich Tolstoi; materialy k biografii s 1881 po 1885 god* [Lev Nikolaevich Tolstoi; materials for a biography from 1881 to 1885]. Moscow, Izdatel'stvo "Nauka," 1970, 385).

In February of 1885 Tolstoi began the reading of George's *Progress and Poverty,* writing on February 24 to one of his disciples that the work had "made on me a very strong and joyful impression . . . I see in him [George] a brother, one of those whom one loves, according to the teachings of the apostles, more than one's own soul." At that time he was also considering making his own translation into Russian of George's *Social Problems* (Gusev, op. cit., 385–86, 389).

Henry George's views clearly made a deep impression on Tolstoi. The American's proposals for what amounted to a nationalization of land seemed to the Russian to give every man an equal access to the resources of the world, an access that would remove from the peasant his heavy burdens of rent, taxes, and unremitting labor. Many times during the rest of his life Tolstoi referred to George and to the benefits that he foresaw from an adoption of his proposals. In the summer of 1894 he was visited by the Russian writer resident in America Varvara N. MacGahan (see chapter 5) who brought with her a number of books given by George himself, and in a thank-you letter to her in September, Tolstoi said that he hoped to be able to get a translation of George's *The Perplexed Philosopher,* a critique of the views of Herbert Spencer, through the toils of censorship (*Iubileinoe izdanie,* v. 67. Moscow, 1955: 103–105, 109, 158–160, 225–227).

There was a direct exchange of letters between the two

---

[2] Iuzhakov's comprehension of George's ideas and of American conditions should be tested in the light of an article in *Sievernyi viestnik,* a journal of which Iuzhakov was an editor, of December 1888 (pages 122–146), signed, however, only with the intitials "S. Iu.," in which (142) there is a reference to [Samuel J.] Tilden's victory in the election of 1877 and to Horace Greeley's presidential campaign in 1881!

men in March of 1896, George announcing a proposed visit to Europe, with a hope of meeting Tolstoi. The latter replied,

The reception of your letter gave me a great joy, for it is a long time, that I know and love you. Though the paths we go by are different, I do not think that we differ in the foundation of our thoughts.

I was very glad to see you mention twice in your letter the life to come.

There is nothing, that widens so much the horizon, that gives such a firm support or such a clear view of things, as the consciousness, that all-though [sic] it is but in this life, that we have the possibility and the duty to act, nevertheless this is not the whole of life, but that bit of it only, which is open to our understanding.

. . . The reading of every one of your books makes clear to me things, which were not so before, and confirms me more and more in the truth of practicability of your system. Still more do I rejoice at the thought, that I may possibly see you" (*Iubileinoe izdanie*, v. 69. Moscow, 1954: 76–77).

The English of this passage, punctuation, "allthough," and other dissonances included, is Tolstoi's own.

The two men never met, for George died in 1897, but the influence lived on. In 1909, when George's son asked if he might come to Iasnaia Poliana, Tolstoi in his reply referred to the elder George as "one of the most remarkable men of the 19th century," and used the visit as the stimulus for a short work in which he again criticized the system of private property in land, supporting the right of every person to live on and be nourished by the land upon which he was born, a right "that was so indivisibly proved by the whole doctrine of Henry George" (*Iubileinoe izdanie*, v. 38. Moscow, 1938: 70–71).

Tolstoi's American contacts of the 1880s were not limited solely to those with the ex-members of the Kansas commune and with Henry George, for he began to receive American visitors and to have correspondence with people of a broad range of attitudes toward social reform. In November 1888 he wrote from Moscow to thank an American woman for having sent him a copy of her book. She was Dr. Alice Bunker Stockham (1833–1912), physician, spiritualist, proponent of women's rights, an educator, and her book was, in its original title, *Tokology, a book for every woman*. First published in 1883, copies issued in 1885 proclaimed on the title page "35th edition." Although there were undoubtedly changes in the text, as Dr. Stockham asked her readers to tell her of their experiences, the 1911 edition is a useful handbook for the pregnant woman, with many commonsense suggestions and a spirit of confidence that must have been helpful, just as the frontispiece portrait of the author shows a person of evident traits of self-command and resolution.

Tolstoi's reply was one of appreciation, but he chose to pick up from Dr. Stockham's book a theme that—at least in the 1911 edition—was rather secondary to her thought. "That sexual relation without the wish and possibility of having children is worse than prostitution and onanism, and in fact is both. I say it is worse, because a person who commits these crimes, not being married, is always conscious of doing wrong, but a husband and a wife, which commit the same sin, think that they are quite righteous" (Tolstoi to Alice Stockham, November 30, 1888. *Iubileinoe izdanie*, v. 64. Moscow, 1953: 202). The subject was one that was important to him at the time, for he was in the process of writing his novel *Kreitserovaia sonata* (Kreutzer sonata) which deals with just such problems of the relations between husband and wife with the implicit view that even in marriage there could be illicit sexuality.

The next year, in October of 1889, Dr. Stockham visited Tolstoi, and he found her a sympathetic person. His diary indicates that they discussed the subject of American religion, although his phraseology is somewhat cryptic, but there is a listing of the Universalists, Unitarians, Quakers "of the new belief only from the year '36," the "majority of the Spiritualists," the Swedenborgians, the Shakers, the Zoarites [a reference to the religious commune at Zoar in Pennsylvania], the Spiritualists who were organized into churches, and to the "Broadchurch" [in English] a representative of which is Hebert Newton, all this is one and the same. All this leads to *practical Christianity* [in English], to universal brotherhood and the sign of this is *non-resistance* [in English] (Diary. October 3, 1889. *Iubileinoe izdanie*, v. 50. Moscow, 1952: 152–53).

But it is also clear from this same day's diary entry that Dr. Stockham was not the only channel through which Tolstoi had received an impression of American religious and philosophical thought along the lines indicated in the preceding paragraph, for he also mentions the title of the journal *World Advance Thought* and the name "Ballou." And, slightly over a month later, he refers on November 12 to having worked on his Kreuzer sonata, with the next day being spent reading "Evans." Although the indexing of the "Iubileinoe izdanie," as has already been noted, is extremely confusing, it only requires a little effort to uncover some quite interesting views of his substantial preoccupation with these three—*World Advance Thought*, Ballou, and Evans—just at the time when he was engaged with a work that has many reflections of their outlook, and of Dr. Stockham's (Tolstoi. Diary. October 3, November 12–13, 21, 24, 28, 1889. *Iubileinoe izdanie*, v. 50. Moscow, 1952: 153, 177–78, 181–83, 185).

The journal *World Advance Thought and Universal Republic* was published in Portland, Oregon, from 1887 until 1918. It was edited and mostly written by Lucy A. Mallory (1846–?), born in Oregon and wife of Rufus Mallory (?–1914), once a member of Congress. There is otherwise little information about Lucy Mallory as she has no works entered in the Library of Congress catalog or in the *National Union Catalog*. Only a single issue of her serial is available in the Library of Congress, one dated 1917, and, if this be representative of the whole, it appears to have been an earnest, and somewhat diffuse, exponent of a Spiritualist outlook. However, in the index to the *Iubileinoe izdanie* there are some ninety-five entries for Lucy A. Mallory and about two dozen for *World Advance Thought*—contrasted with a total of about ninety-five for Henry David Thoreau and all his works. Tolstoi's contacts with Mallory and her journal were to be long ones, for in 1904 he wrote to her, "Though I can not agree with your belief in mediumship and occultism I greatly value your moral teaching and always with great interest read your journal for which I heartily thank you. I find it true and healthy spiritual food and very highly appreciate your activity" (Tolstoi to L. A. Mallory. August 21/September 3, 1904. *Iubileinoe izdanie*, v. 75. Moscow, 1956: 158). In 1906 Mallory wrote to thank Tolstoi for his having sent her a copy of *Für alle Tage*, the German translation of his *Na Kazhdyi den'* [For each day], a book of readings which contained several quotations from her writings (*Iubileinoe izdanie*, v. 76. Moscow, 1956: 287).

And the memoirs of Khristo Dosev, *Vblizi Iasnoi poliany* [Around Yasnaya Polyana], as quoted in the *Iubileinoe izdanie*, report Tolstoi as having said on August 28, 1907, "I think that

Lucy Mallory is one of the most intelligent women (odna iz um-neishikh zhenshchin) both of our time as well as of former times. In her every word is to be seen a concentrated spiritual effort" (*Iubileinoe izdanie*, v. 55. Moscow, 1937: 478). The word *umneishaia* offers a major semantic problem for it can also mean "clever," "wise," "witty," or "sensible," which have quite different shades of meaning.

The "Ballou" mentioned by Tolstoi in the same diary entry of 1889 that tells of Dr. Stockham's visit is the Unitarian pastor and apostle of nonviolence Adin Ballou (1803–1890). In mid-1889 Ballou's work on nonresistance and several of his pamphlets were sent to Tolstoi by the Unitarian pastor and writer Lewis Gilbert Wilson. The Russian replied to Wilson in a long letter, in fluent, sincere, and only infrequently awkward English on July 5:

I have seldom experienced so much gratification as I had in reading Mr. Ballou's treatise and tracts. I cannot agree with your opinion that Mr. Ballou "will not go down to posterity among the immortals . . ." I think that because he has been one of the first true apostles of the "New Time"—he will be in the future acknowledged as one of the chief benefactors of humanity. . . .

Tell him please, that his efforts have not been in vain, they give great strength to people, as I can judge from myself. In those tracts I found all the objections that are generally made against "non-resistance" victoriously answered and also the true basis of the doctrine. I will endeavor to translate and propagate as much as I can, the works of Mr. Ballou, and I not only hope, but am convinced, that the time is come, "when the dead hear the voice of the Son of God; and they that hear shall live" (Tolstoi to L. G. Wilson, July 5, 1889—apparently N.S. *Iubileinoe izdanie*, v. 64. Moscow, 1953: 270. The Biblical quotation is from John V: 25. Tolstoi apparently used the King James version).

Tolstoi did not, however, agree with Ballou's view that force might be used against drunkards and insane people. "A true Christian will always prefer to be killed by a madman rather than to deprive him of his liberty." Nor was there agreement with Ballou's concept of the rights of property. Furthermore, Tolstoi felt that "Government is for a Christian only regulated violence; governments, states, nations, property, churches—all these for a true Christian are only words without meaning; . . ."

"'I am come to send fire on the earth, and what will I, if it be already kindled?' I think that this time is coming, and that the world is on fire, and our business is only to keep ourselves burning; and if we can communicate with other burning points, that is the work which I intend to do for the rest of my life" (*Iubileinoe izdanie*, v. 64. Moscow, 1953: 271–72. The Biblical quotation is from Luke XII:49, also from the King James version).

The letter to Lewis Wilson appears to have been made known to Adin Ballou, for on January 14, 1890, the latter wrote to Tolstoi defending some of his views, drawing an answer dated February 21–24. In this Tolstoi reiterates his views on any use of force, even against a madman "(the great difficulty is to give a strict definition of a madman)", and repeats, "I profess daringly that a Christian cannot have any property—" . . . Tolstoi gave considerable thought to the statement of his position, going so far as to cite a word from the Greek text of Matthew V:22 which he felt was questionably part of the text and wrongly used to support the use of force. The English text of the letter is clear and even forceful (*Iubileinoe izdanie*, v. 65. Moscow, 1953: 34–38. The Greek word translated in the King James version as "without any cause," is omitted in the Revised Standard Version and in other translations).

At the end of June of the same year, Tolstoi again wrote to Ballou, in a letter that, according to the editorial notes, may not have reached the American before he died, expressing his thanks for further books and tracts, and stating, "I quite agree with you that Christianity will never enter its promised land till the divine truth of the non-resistance principle shall be recognized, but not the nominal church will recognize it. I am fully convinced that the churches are and have always been the worst enemies of Christ's work. They have always led humanity not in the way of Christ, but out of it" (*Iubileinoe izdanie*, v. 65. Moscow, 1953: 113–14).

Ballou's views on nonresistance were used by Tolstoi in a substantial section of his *Tsarstvo Bozhie vnutri vas,* . . . [The Kingdom of God is within you, . . .] which he wrote in 1890–93. He had at first thought only of providing a short introduction to a translation of Ballou's *Non-Resistance Catechism,* but the topic took ever greater hold on him and it grew from a short article to a broad survey of many factors of the socio-political life of the time. In doing so, Tolstoi used not only Ballou's writings but also those of the abolitionist leader William Lloyd Garrison, who had also written in his later life of the concept of nonresistance, and about whom Tolstoi had learned as early as 1886. Furthermore, there was a contribution from the writings of the American Mennonite clergyman Daniel Musser, his *Non-Resistance Asserted or the Kingdom of Christ and the Kingdom of the World separated, and No Concord Between Christ and Belial* (Lancaster, Pennsylvania, Elias Barr and Co., Publishers; Pearsol and Geist Printers, 1864, 74 p. Reprinted: Lancaster, 1886). While Tolstoi also made use of the writings of men from other countries, the American influence was strong, and the editorial notes to the *Iubileinoe izdanie* publication of *Tsarstvo Bozhie . . .* show that he was deeply interested in American writings about non-violence (*Iubileinoe izdanie,* v.28. Moscow, 1957: 8–15, 333–42).

The third reference from Tolstoi's diary of October 1889 to be examined is that to "Evans." A close examination of the entries in the index under "Evans, Frederik Vil'iam" shows that the editors, however, have confounded two persons under one heading, for in October 1889 Tolstoi was reading *The Divine Law of Cure* which was by Warren Felt Evans (1817–1889), and he had apparently not yet become aware of the Elder Frederick William Evans (1808–1893) of the Shakers. Both were Americans, and both propounded doctrines that were of interest to Tolstoi and his state of mind at the time. Warren Felt Evans was a Methodist clergyman who had been influenced by the outlook of Phineas Parker Quimby and his doctrines of the mental healing of illnesses, as well as by the teachings of Swedish philosopher Emmanuel Swedenborg. Tolstoi's diaries of November 13, 21, 24, and 28, 1889 indicate that he was interested in W. F. Evans' writings, but not in complete agreement with them: "I am reading Evans. Not bad, but nonsense about curing" (November 13); "I rose very early. I thought and now have begun to read Evans. He doesn't believe himself in what he is saying, . . . but he is a fine compiler and the reading of his book calls up many important thoughts" (November 24); and, on November 28, continuing to read Evans' book, Tolstoi arrives at the thought "but one must firmly base one's whole life on this: to seek, to wish, to do but one thing—good to people—to love and increase love in them, and to lessen non-love in them" (*Iubileinoe izdanie,* v. 50. Moscow, 1952: 177–85).

The other Evans, Frederick William, was a major voice for the Shakers in the years from the Civil War to about 1890. He was a frequent speaker on the platform, even before the "people of the world," and he often found a certain response from them. However, there were also others among the Shakers who spoke to the public, at times in ways that were subtly different from those of Elder Evans, and it was actually from these that there came the first contacts with Tolstoi.

On March 30, 1889 the Shaker woman leader Asenath Stickney sent Tolstoi a letter, together with photographs of some of the group's leaders and with tracts, *The Shaker Answer* and *Plain Talks*, and on September 23 of the same year the Elder Alonzo G. Hollister set forth the Shaker doctrine, emphasizing the tenet of celibacy. Tolstoi replied, October 18, "Last spring I was busy writing a book about marriage and I got quite new views of the matter. At the same time I was reading the books I could get about communiti's [sic] in America. I read Noyes (John Humphrey Noyes, *History of American socialism.* Philadelphia, J. B. Lippincott and Co., 1870, 678 p. Numerous further editions) and a book of a German whose name I forgot [work not identified by the editors of the *Iubileinoe izdanie*, but perhaps Tolstoi was actually thinking of Charles Nordhoff or of Heinrich Semler, both with German names, who wrote on American communes]. In those books I found quite new notions for me about the Shakers." Tolstoi was pleased to receive Hollister's further letter. "I read it all and thank you for it. All this strengthens my views on marriage, which I expose in my book that I am just now finishing. I think that the ideal of a christian always was and must be complete chastity and appreciate very much your books about that matter." He goes on, however, to state some of the points of his disagreement with the Shakers, especially with the revelations of Ann Lee, the founder of the group, but ends, "Please do not deprive me of your love for my boldness; I very much appreciate your good disposition to me and love you" (*Iubileinoe izdanie*, v. 64. Moscow, 1953: 319–21).

The book that Tolstoi mentions was his *Kreutzer Sonata* which examined some of the problems involved in marriage and the fact that, from his point of view, there could be sin in this relationship that was as great as any other form of dissipation. While a direct mention of the Shakers did not occur in the printed version, although it does in one of the drafts, the impress of some elements of their practices can be noted and the general tenor of the work is indeed supportive of the ideal of complete chastity. The novel was considered almost beyond the bounds of what was permitted at the time, and not only was it banned in Russia, but some of the guardians of the public morality elsewhere took action against it. As Robert G. Ingersoll, that bugaboo of all "right-thinking" Americans of the late 19th century, put it in his review of the novel, "a Christian teacher of a Sabbath-school decides, in the capacity of Postmaster-General, that 'The Kreutzer Sonata' is unfit to be carried in the mails." And it seems that Postmaster-General John Wanamaker was assisted in this by the well-known Mr. Anthony Comstock (Robert G. Ingersoll, The Kreutzer Sonata. *North American Review*, September 1890: 289–99). Even one of Tolstoi's American acquaintances, Isabel Hapgood, in her review in *The Nation* (April 17, 1890: 313–15) said "Translation, even with copious excisions, is impossible, in my opinion, and also inadvisable." Nevertheless, the entries in the *National Union Catalog* show that in 1890–91 there were at least four publishing companies in the United States that had issued the novel in three differing translations. Since it was before the copyright laws were changed to provide some protection to foreign authors, there is a question as to whether Tolstoi received any royalties.

Tolstoi's interest in the Shakers did not end with his completion of *Kreutzer Sonata,* for in January and February of 1891 he was writing to the Elder Alonzo Hollister about a continuing response to the community's outlook. He was not convinced by all that the Shakers had to say, but, "I agree completely with your practice of life, but not with your theory, especially about spirits." At the same time Tolstoi also wrote to Elder Evans that he could not criticize the tracts that he had sent, "because I agree with everything that is said in them," adding a statement to show how he had been impressed by Lucy Mallory's journal *World's Advance Thought.* Finally, in March of 1891, in a letter to one I. B. Fainerman, he states,

Now I am going to answer the 82 year old Evans, who recently sent me his autobiography [Evans' *Autobiography of a Shaker*] and other works. If it were not for the spiritualism and the seeing of spirits, this would be the highest embodiment to this time of the teaching of Christ: 1) nonresistance to violence. 2) absence of private property. 3) denial of holy orders, of doctors, of judges. 4) equality of the sexes. 5) striving for purity in sexual re[lationships]. . . . I will unfailingly translate some of their writings. They are mixed with the superstition of spiritualism, but of the highest soulfulness (*Iubileinoe izdanie*, v. 65. Moscow, 1953: 239–42, 272–74).

However, lest it be thought that Tolstoi's views were limited only to the Shakers and to Lucy Mallory, he had written earlier (March 6 to 9 of 1890) that he was receiving other materials that were of interest to him, referring to several American journals which he read with interest (*Iubileinoe izdanie*, v. 65. Moscow, 1953: 42). One of these, *World's Advance Thought* . . . , has already been mentioned. Others were *New Christianity*, published in Germantown, Pennsylvania and devoted to the doctrines of Emmanuel Swedenborg; *Religio-philosophical Journal*, issued in furtherance of the Spiritualist cause; *Dawn* (Boston), the subtitle of which is *A Journal of Christian Socialism*, and which sought to reconcile science and religion; *Ethical Record*, an organ of the American Ethical Union and vehicle for some of the articles of Josiah Royce, Felix Adler, and John Dewey; *Lucifer* (Chicago), which seems to have been almost entirely the work of one Moses Harman and concerned with the then very ticklish question of birth control; and, finally, *Peacemaker* [*and Court of Arbitration*] (Philadelphia). The July 1890 issue of the last-named shows the editorial board to have included Belva A. Lockwood, who was the first woman to have been admitted to practice before the Supreme Court and the first woman to have announced her candidacy for the presidency. On the same page as the list of members of the editorial board are the names of recent subscribers to the journal, including those of Mrs. John Biddulph Martin and Lady Cook, who had been much more widely and scandalously known some fifteen years before as, respectively, Victoria Claflin Woodhull and Tennessee Claflin, sisters, spiritualists, stockbrokers, friends of "Commodore" Cornelius Vanderbilt, outspoken proponents of women's rights, and general disturbers of the settled ways of society. In short, Tolstoi in 1890 had some sort of contact with a very broad range of non-orthodox American thought, and although it seems that only Lucy Mallory's *World's Advance Thought* long retained his attention, no one can doubt that he was markedly affected by their views.

It would again be a subject for prolonged research to examine all facets of the ways in which Tolstoi viewed the United States and individual Americans, but there is an undoubted connection between America and many phases of his interpretation of the world. In 1908, only two years before his death, he was writing to a man in Philadelphia of his hopes that William Jennings Bryan would win the presidency that year. In the summer before his death in 1910 he again referred to Channing, and his last comments on anyone else's published work dealt with Kornei Chukovskii's essay on the baleful influence of the American pulp detective series about Nat Pinkerton. Yet, since Tolstoi was so monumental a personality, with such inner resources of originality, it would not be correct to say that the American factor was an overwhelming one in his thought, for he remained, even in his attempts to become a man of the people and an exponent of the simple life, the quintessential Russian "barin" [landlord and master] who felt that it was both his right and his duty to provide a code of life for his dependents. But, in spite of this, one cannot subtract from his thought the influence of Lucy Mallory, Adin Ballou, William Lloyd Garrison, Emerson, Alice Stockham, or the Elders Hollister and Evans without leaving a very perceptible gap.

The voices from American utopias that Frey, Malikov, and Tolstoi heard were also audible to others, if not in so striking a fashion. Many of the comments that appeared in the Russian press between 1890 and 1917 were not unaffected by such an outlook, and one finds, for example, a flow of interest in the utopian socialist novels of Edward Bellamy. One work about Bellamy, with a title that can be translated as "Socialism with a human face," was even written by a man of conservative outlook who was impressed by the American's non-revolutionary outlook. In another instance, the quite serious economist Ivan I. Ianzhul and his wife, Ekaterina Nikolaevna, were so struck by the data in an American survey of the 1880s of the position of working women, that they titled their article on the topic "Edem truzhenits" [An Eden for working women] (*Sievernyi viestnik*, 1890, no. 5: 76–96). The survey, by the way, found the average wage of all American working women to be not too far from $5.20 per week.

Even in 1905 the obscure Orthodox clergyman Father Grigorii S. Petrov, in his *Lampa Aladina* [Aladin's lamp] (2d ed. St. Petersburg, Tipografiia P. F. Voshchinskoi, 1905. p. 24–46) calls the United States "skazochnaia strana" [a fabulous land], and writes "The newly arrived worker makes do at first with a single room for himself, but the seasoned American cannot think of just a single room. He needs a completely separate, individual house with 4, 5, and even 7 rooms, and inevitably with two floors so that the kitchen is separate. Around the house there has to be a garden," but then goes on to say (p. 34–35), "The internal arrangement of the house of an American is, from our point of view, just an unrealizable dream."

In justice to the Ianzhuls and to Father Petrov, however, one must say that they saw some of the explanation of America's fine state to lie in more mundane causes. Both referred to the influence of education in causing American prosperity, and Mrs. Ianzhul was to become a significant writer on the theme, along with other commentators to be discussed in another section of this survey.

As we have seen, for some Russians America was a utopia, or at least a stimulus to utopian thought. A few of these people had had direct, and highly disillusioning, experience with the subject. Another man, a great and yet flawed man, built a part of his outlook upon interpretations that took some of their rise along rivers of Massachusetts and the Columbia as well as from the "simple gifts" of the Shakers. Others, somewhat better rooted in reality, managed to reflect some impressions of the utopian aspects of what now seem rather unlikely causes for doing so. After all, even in 1890, $5.20 a week was not a lavish wage.

Again, it would be a topic for much further research to uncover all the instances of similar Russian views of America and to interpret their effect.

CHAPTER THREE

Russians Look at American Literature and Film

I f some Russians viewed America as a source for their utopian thoughts, others had a somewhat more sober approach, but at times reached comparably abstract conclusions, for they sought to form a concept of this country based on its literature. Often, of course, that brought them to emphasize more the exotic than the realistic aspects of the United States, for they, like many Western Europeans in the era before the First World War, were attracted by the novels of excitement and adventure that range from the works of James Fenimore Cooper and Bret Harte, which often show considerable literary merit, to the absurd concoctions of specialists in blood and thunder such as the Frenchman Gustave Aimard, who lived for a quarter century on the basis of writings drawn from a few years in the American Southwest, or the questionably literate scribbler responsible for the series of dime novels about the detective Nat Pinkerton. While there were Russians who were aware of Americans such as Hawthorne, Poe, Longfellow, Emerson, Whitman, William Dean Howells, and even Mary E. Wilkins Freeman, there were many more who fed upon works by such people as John Habberton, Josiah G. Holland, Etta W. Pierce, and Maria S. Cummings, or even by European writers about America such as Aimard, the Anglo-Irish "Captain" Mayne Reid, and the German Friedrich Gerstäcker, and it would be difficult indeed to show that these purveyors of excitement and sentiment did not have a greater effect on the

mind of the Russian mass reader than the writers given attention by the professional literary critics.

There is a magisterial bibliography of Russian writings
about American literature during the period from 1776 to
1975, compiled by Valentina Libman, whose diligence is almost
beyond comprehension, *Amerikanskaia literatura v russkikh perevodakh i kritike; bibliografiia, 1776–1975* [American literature in
Russian translation and criticism; a bibliography, 1776–1975]
(Moscow, Izdatel'stvo "Nauka," 1977. 451 p.). It contains 7,551
entries, with a first section citing books and articles dealing with
separate periods or problems of American literature, a second
listing anthologies of translations from various authors, and a
third comprising a guide to materials by and about some 230
individual writers, names which, quite frankly, appear to vary
in their renown from the greater figures of our literature to the
authors of books that have been found to be in harmony with
elements of the Soviet perception of the world. However, one
should by no means overlook Libman's work for, while selective
in its coverage, it is very accurate, diligent in its coverage of the
sources, and highly informative as to how Russians viewed, for
example, William Dean Howells, Bret Harte, Mark Twain, and
others of the nineteenth century. Yet, when one notes that Russians also had a chance to become acquainted at the turn of the
century with such equally American products as Owen Wister's
The Virginian, Frances Hodgson Burnett's *Little Lord Fauntleroy*
(despite her Anglophile touches, Mrs. Burnett can be seen as
being at least as much an American as T. S. Eliot), or Edward
Noyes Westcott's *David Harum,* not to mention novels by such
people as Aimard that were set in America and that purported
to reflect American ways, there is much that is lacking in what
Libman has done. There are many impressions about a country
that are conveyed by the literature that one finds on the book
stands for a season and not in the tomes of the critics, and no
full interpretation can be valid that omits it.

Within the limits of this survey it is not possible to offer a
complete analysis of the way in which the Russian view of
America before 1917 was affected by the various ranges of literature. The record is too extensive, and the relationships too
complex, to do anything more than to select some of the more
revealing facets of the problem, and one can only hope that

some other researcher can at some time pick up the question and give it the attention it deserves.

Among the figures of what one might call America's "high" literature, there are four that seem to have drawn special attention from Russian critics. These are Emerson, Hawthorne, Poe, and Whitman, about each of whom one finds serious Russian reaction.

As was noted in the preceding chapter, Emerson seems to have been the first American writer to be the subject of a serious analysis in Russian. The article in *Biblioteka dlia chteniia* (1847, v. 85, otd. VII: 36–69) is unsigned, but it is a serious and informed one. The author does not merely paraphrase someone else's work about Emerson, but seeks to place the American in a philosophical framework that includes Montaigne, Carlyle, Burke, and the school of Scots philosophers originating in Dugald Stewart, and there is knowledgeable use of a quotation from Margaret Fuller's *Papers on Literature and Art* (New York, London, Wiley and Putnam, 1846. 2 v. in 1), that appears to indicate a continuing effort to follow American thought.

This unknown Russian indicates familiarity with Emerson's essays and with his conviction that men should arrive at their own conclusions by independent thought and not by the adoption of the opinions of others. That there may have been an underlying intention to use references to Emerson in order to convey an outlook that could not easily be expressed openly in the Russian press is indicated by a concluding remark to the effect that, "It would be desirable that Emerson's philosophy, as a protest in favor of the individual, be disseminated in Europe." The article, after all, appeared during the reign of Nicholas I, who did not tolerate open criticism by any means, but whose censors might at times overlook the double-edged quality of analyses of situations in other countries. Readers in Russia were familiar with such techniques and easily understood that, for example, references to flaws in French policy might well be applied to a similar situation in Russia. With America being seen by many Europeans of the more liberal persuasion as a source of inspiration, it was even more the case that praise of her institutions and thought could be taken as a criticism of those in Europe.

It would be difficult to prove, since the author of this first Russian analysis of Emerson is unknown, that it was indeed his intent to apply the American example to Russia, but some of the last words about Emerson's role do show an intent to seek from him guidelines applicable elsewhere. While it is written that man should live in the world, he should not be of the world, taking only those things that are eternal in order to reach an outlook that is "the present task of a wise man. Emerson has reached that goal and points it out to us in his writings. A noble accomplishment of such a nature is enough for an author's glory. Posterity will not forget that he has given to our century that which Montaigne gave to his, a new ideal for wisdom" (*Biblioteka dlia chteniia*, 1847, v. 85, otd. VII: 69).

In 1868 a two-volume selection of Emerson's writings, as translated by E. Ladyzhenskaia, was published as *Nravstvennaia filosofiia* [Moral philosophy] (St. Petersburg, 1868). The entry in Libman's bibliography shows that this edition contains an 80-page introduction, "To Russian Readers," from the publisher. This is, it seems, the longest individual discussion of Emerson in Russian, but the translation is not reported by any American library. However, one can gain some idea of the outlook on Emerson of contemporary Russians from a review in the quite liberal *Otechestvennyia zapiski* (1868, no. 7, Sovremennoe obozrienie: 57–62) which provides a sharp criticism of the alleged tendencies of Emerson to preach self-perfection in place of an engagement in the struggle with outer forces. This leads, the review says, to a withdrawal from life and a reconciliation with even the evils of existence. While the review is unsigned, the attitude toward Emerson's lack of concern with many elements of the world is that of some of the activist Russian thinkers of the time, who felt that men should strive toward changing the world, and one can see that Emerson was felt to preach a passivism that contrasted with the more active programs for change offered by those very American commune members and reformers described in the articles by Lavrov mentioned in the previous chapter, the third of which appeared in the same issue of *Otechestvennyia zapiski* as this review.

It may have been Emerson's doctrine of self-perfection and of, so to speak, rising above some of the troubles of the world

that drew the attention of the legal specialist Konstantin Petrovich Pobedonostsev (1827–1907), tutor to the grand dukes
who were to become Alexander III and Nicholas II, for many
years Ober-Prokuror of the Most Holy Synod, the equivalent
of minister for Orthodox church affairs, rigid anti-Semite, and
a symbol of deepest reaction. Andrew Dickson White, first
president of Cornell University, and, in 1892–94, American
minister to Russia, wrote an article in the *Century Magazine* in
1898 about his interview with Pobedonostsev, writing, "But the
most curious—indeed the most amazing—revelation of the
man I found in his love for American literature. He is a wide
reader, and in the whole breadth of his reading American authors were evidently among those he preferred. Of these, Hawthorne, Lowell, and, above all, Emerson were his favorites. . . .
He also told me that the next book which he translated was a
volume of Emerson's essays; and he added that for years there
had always lain open upon his study table a volume of Emerson's writings" (Andrew Dickson White, "A statesman of Russia." *Century Magazine*, 1898, May: 114). Despite this interest in
Emerson, White reports, Pobedonostsev actually seemed to
view America as a sort of dreamland, and his real interests were
elsewhere (White, op. cit., 116).

Whatever book by Emerson it may have been that Pobedonostsev translated, he does not appear as a translator in any
bibliographic reference thus far available, but it does appear
that the essay "Diela i dni" [Works and days] in his *Moskovskii
sbornik* is a translation from Emerson (Moscow, Sinodal'naia tipografiia, 1896. 304 p. Several later editions. In English as *Reflections of a Russian statesman*, also several editions which do not
include this essay).

Emerson, as an author of essays and works on philosophical subjects did not, of course, have a wide audience, and it is
therefore not surprising that, although some Russians knew of
Emerson, it was the sharper problems of relationships presented by Hawthorne that drew a wider response from them.
During the 1850s, according to Libman, he was the most translated American author. *The House of Seven Gables* appeared in
nos. 9 and 10 of *Sovremennik* in 1852, while *Panteon* (no. 12) of
the same year included the tale "Mr. Higginbotham's Catastro-

phe." In 1853 *Biblioteka dlia chteniia* printed his "The Vision of the Fountain," and *Sovremennik* offered "Rappacini's Daughter," "The Birth-Mark," and "The Snow Image," the two last indicated as having been translated from a French intermediate version. In 1856 *The Scarlet Letter* came out as a 158-page supplement to *Sovremennik*, while *Biblioteka dlia chteniia* contained "How's Masquerade," "Lady Eleanor's Mantle," "Edward Randolph's Portrait," "The Seven Vagabonds," and "The Ambitious Guest," all from his *Twice-Told Tales*. In 1857 the same journal contained "Peter Goldthwaite's Treasure," and in 1858, "Dr. Heidegger's Experiment." In 1859, the children's magazine *Podsnezhnik* printed part of Hawthorne's *A Wonder-Book for Boys and Girls*, a book-length version of which appeared in 1860.

There was little critical reaction to these publications until, in 1860, the radical-liberal N. G. Chernyshevskii used the Russian publication of *A Wonder-Book for Boys and Girls* as the occasion of an extensive essay in which Hawthorne is accused of being too prudish in his retellings of the Greek myths, while his efforts to hide the erotic side of life can only awaken harmful interest in innocent minds. Actually Chernyshevskii is using Hawthorne as a screen from behind which to attack the Russian literary figures of his time.

Our writers treat us as Hawthorne does children. They hide the truth of life from us in order not to tempt or to pervert us. Others occupy us with empty wordiness as if we, like children, found it pleasant to listen to chattering. . . . It would be all right if it were only the writers who treated us thus, if it were only in their tales from the imagination they gave us lies in place of truth and floods of words in place of substance. No, they also treat us exactly in that same manner with regard to subjects upon which our whole lives depend. They consider us children. . . .

. . . Are we so simple that we think that with these remarks we can correct the highly placed personages in literature whose faults we are pointing out? No, it is too late for them to change. They have been too much consumed by the habit of falsification and emptiness (*Sovremennik*, 1860, no. 6, otd. III: 244–45).

In this Chernyshevskii was attacking not so much the American writer as the conformist habit of mind of many of his own countrymen. Mid-19th century Russia had tribes of writers who prettified life, turning out Panglossian works that spoke of society as good and harmonious, though with a few surface flaws. Although it was impossible for him to say so directly in a review of a work by a Russian writer, the not quite "with-it" censors might not notice all the ramifications of what he wrote about a foreign book for children.

If, in this, Hawthorne had only provided a peg on which to hang an excuse for Chernyshevskii to make points against the prevailing deadly conformist atmosphere of Russia, another article, also in *Sovremennik*, is more to the point about Hawthorne as an artist and not as an exponent of views of society. M. L. Mikhailov, in the October issue in 1860, surveys the American's career and provides an over-all survey of his work, reaching one of the highest levels of analysis of an American work to be found in pre-1917 Russia (*Sovremennik*, October 1860, otd. VIII: 217–32). Discussing *The Scarlet Letter* he writes:

In this novel, more deeply than in all previous works by him, Hawthorne delves into those bottomless pits, in Carlyle's expression, of unfathomable darkness that make up human nature. After *The Scarlet Letter* American critics have compared Hawthorne as a psychologist to, and placed him as an equal of, Balzac in the latter's best scenes of Parisian and provincial life.

While actually of equal force in the anatomy and pathology of passion, of sin and transgression, the French and the American novelists are yet essentially different in the character of their analyses. You will not find that merciless, cold—we almost said, dispassionate—analysis that distinguishes the author of *Père Goriot*. In the devices of the latter [Hawthorne] one feels more tenderness, more sympathy with the dark phenomena of life than the bitterness and indignation which give such truth and firmness to Balzac's hand and scalpel. If one might compare these two novelists to experienced anatomists, one cannot avoid saying that Balzac is like a professor who is carrying out a dissection of the body of a stranger in a vast hall and in front of a large audience, while Hawthorne reminds one more of a doctor who, alone, seeks the reasons for the death of his friend, only then cutting into his body" (op. cit., 229).

The December 1860 issue of *Sovremennik* contained the second installment of Mikhailov's survey, largely devoted to Hawthorne's *Marble Faun*, referred to under the title of the British edition, *Transformation*. After a detailed—and, frankly, somewhat boring—account of the events of the novel, Mikhailov asks,

But is it really necessary to tell, step by step, all the actions of these five people in whom the action of the novel is concentrated? . . . The more one turns page after page, the more alive become the traits of the personages, displeasingly at first because of their oddity, and the more one's attention is captured by them in following the drama which unfolds among them. Hawthorne remains faithful in this new novel to a passion for delving into the darkest and most inaccessible corners of the hearts of his heroes and for analyzing those movements of the soul that are most hidden from the eye of the stranger (*Sovremennik*, 1860, no. 12, otd. XIV: 308–09).

The Russian translation of *Marble Faun* appeared as a supplement to nos. 3–5 of *Russkoe slovo* of 1860, which, strangely enough, seems to have been the last instance of any first translation of Hawthorne until 1896, although variant editions of earlier works appeared in the intervening years. In 1900, however, an edition of eleven of Hawthorne's tales was published, and in 1912 two volumes were issued containing *The Scarlet Letter* and *The Blythedale Romance*. After that, apart from two short stories in an anthology of 1946, there was no Russian publication of Hawthorne until a group of his stories appeared in 1965, and *The House of Seven Gables*, with other shorter works, in 1975.

Much more attention was given by Russian critics to Edgar Allan Poe, with just over seventy entries in Libman's bibliography for items about him in the years from 1852 to 1914, while the entries for translations of his works fill eleven pages of her guide. The first appearance of Poe in Russian was a translation of "The Gold Bug," published in 1847, and one finds after that a gradual accumulation of publications both of his well-known and much anthologized works such as "The Tell-Tale Heart," "The Mystery of Marie Roget," "The Cask of Amontillado," and "The Purloined Letter," and also of his lesser writings and, what is a more difficult problem, translations of his poems. The fact that two eminent Russian poets, Konstantin D. Bal'mont and Valerii Ia. Briusov, were among the translators undoubtedly helped the Russian reader arrive at an understanding of Poe's psychological intensities and obscurities. Bal'mont, in fact, was the translator of a five-volume series of Poe's collected works that appeared in three editions between 1901 and 1913.

Interest in Poe, as may be inferred from the rise in the number of references to him, was high in Russia from about 1895 to the outbreak of the First World War. This was a period in which Russian writers attempted to express their view of a strained society in which many of the accustomed certainties of life were being undermined, and they found many of the aspects of Poe's distance from the situation of his own times to be in harmony with their own outlook. One need cite but a single sentence, "Edgar Poe—the underground stream in Russia," that appears in the entry for November 6, 1911 in the journal of a Russian poet even greater than Bal'mont or Briusov, Aleksandr Blok, to see a reflection of this influence. Blok was proposing critical study of Poe the purpose of which was, according to one scholar, to "discover the sources, growth and the ramifications of this phenomenon of literary history: the impressive presence of Edgar Allan Poe in Russia" (Joan Delaney Grossman, *Edgar Allan Poe in Russia: a study in legend and literary influence*. Wurzburg, JAL-Verlag, 1973. p. 7).

Although there was a reference to Walt Whitman in a Russian journal of 1861, it is largely an account of the attempt to suppress his scandalous "novel," and has no indication of awareness of what *Leaves of Grass* actually was. A fourteen-page article by P. Popov (evidently the longtime resident in America and correspondent for several Russian publications Petr I. Popov) that appeared in 1883 is unavailable in the Library of Congress. For 1892, the year of Whitman's death, there are three references to him in Libman, one of them being two pages in V. Zotov's survey of foreign literature in the June issue of *Nabliudatel'* (1892, no. 6, second pagination: 15–16). Zotov had in 1882 edited a four-volume history of world literature, including as pages 349–638 of the fourth volume, his essay on American and British writing, so that he must be presumed to have had a certain amount of knowledge of the topic.

The North American states have lost their best poet, Val't Veitman, dead at the age of 73. European literature is little concerned with trans-Atlantic writers, and they, to tell the truth, do not even deserve attention. Americans, of course, praise them, but who in Europe knows not only the writings, but even the names, "Gol'msa, Vit'era, Merrilia, Griffna, Miss Emmu Latsarus, Adu Isaak, Ellu Ditts, or Tsadel' Gustafson? [Holmes (Oliver Wendell, 1809–1894), Whittier (John Greenleaf, 1807–1892), Merril (sp. ?, unidentified), Griffen (?, unidentified), Miss Emma Lazarus (1849–1887), Ada Isaak (?), Ella Dietz (?), Zandel Gustafson (1841–1917)]. These are all very moral, but also very boring versifiers and not poets. Last year the northern states with special ceremony buried and praised James Russell Lowell, but he was only a clever maker of verses, a witty pamphletist, without, however, any poetic talent. Whitman was, at least, a real poet. The first collection of his works, coming out in 1885, *Leaves of Grass*, is a continuous hymn to nature.

The date 1885 is rather clearly a typographical error, for Zotov goes on to give a short biographical account in which it becomes clear that Whitman first issued his book before our Civil War. In his general evaluation of Whitman, Zotov writes,

He was so poor that more than once a subscription list was set up for him; but he needed so little in life that he never asked anyone for help, but wrote and printed his poems, full of sincere humanism and of unforced poetry. But this poetry, filled with sympathy for mankind and preferring suffering together with the poor to the joys of life, contains such forms, images, and comparisons that an accurate rendering of it in another language is almost unthinkable. He who has soaked up Americanisms, entering into the very skin of a real Yankee, cannot fail to show to this strange poet the same sympathy that he showed to all who were despised and rejected, saying in his poem, "When I meet a tramp with his hands bound and whom they are taking to jail, it seems to me that my own hands are tied and that I also must go to jail with him!" (V. Zotov, Ocherki inostrannoi literatury. *Nabliudatel'*, no. 6, 1892, 2d pagination: 15–16).

Except for Holmes, Whittier, and Emma Lazarus, whose poem is found on the base of the Statue of Liberty, the names Zotov gives are now lost in deep obscurity, and his rather sweeping denial of any great value to American poetry is perhaps an indication that he had not really studied the subject. After all, there had by the time of his writing already been more than 70 publications in Russian of individual poems by Longfellow, and, as we have seen, Poe was not unknown to the Russian reader. But the indication that it would be a difficult matter to translate Whitman into Russian was a perceptive one, and, indeed, somewhat more than a decade was needed before translations at last appeared.

Although there was an 1899 publication headed "From Walt Whitman" ostensibly translated by V. G. Tan-Bogoraz, and one in 1903, translated by K. Chukovskii, it seems that these were written rather in the manner of Whitman. In 1906, however, the young Kornei Chukovskii (1882–1969) and the older Konstantin Bal'mont both published direct translations, including portions of "Drum Beats," "O Star of France," and "To You." Of the two men, it was Chukovskii who was to continue an interest in Whitman to the end of his life, becoming a true specialist on this most American poet.

Because of Chukovskii's attitude toward another facet of literature of American origin that will be mentioned below, his view of Whitman is worth some examination. In 1907 the young Russian published *Poet anarkhist Uot Uitman; perevod v stikhakh i kharakteristika* [The poet-anarchist Walt Whitman; translation in verse and a characterization] (St. Petersburg, Izd. "Kruzhok molodykh," 1907. 83 p.), which contains two essays on Whitman and translations of a number of his poems. Chukovskii's introductory essay indicates that he had made a rather detailed study of Whitman, and that he had looked not only at biographical works but also at the—generally hostile—reviews in American and British journals, and he deals with the question of Whitman's possible homosexuality in a manner that was more direct and open than was possible in most American or British writings of the time (Chukovskii, op. cit.: 9–20).

The poems that are translated are either some of the shorter ones or mere extracts from longer sections. Without making a line-by-line comparison, Chukovskii seems to have conveyed a suitable Russian reflection of Whitman's irregular lines and rhythms, although there is nothing upon which to judge how well he has found an equivalent for Whitman's many Americanisms of phraseology or for his frequent, not quite accurate use of French or other languages (Chukovskii, op. cit.: 21–57).

The second of Chukovskii's essays is more analytical in its treatment of Whitman's poetic method, but it also is an emphatic statement about Whitman's devotion to democracy.

He loved to say that he was born from a new, bold, young democracy. His faults, his attachments, his passions and sufferings, all these he ascribed to that—to that formless and boundless concept. Even the clumsiness of his verses, which were angular and not elegant, because he did not know how to write them otherwise, he based on his democratic outlook. . . . Democracy for Whitman was not a temporary social form, not a political phenomenon, but a sort of element in itself, something of intrinsic value, God-given and all-encompassing. He called it his mother, his child, his loved one, his lady of ladies. It was for him a kind of joy to approach and clasp its knees, and all that before was confused and incomprehensible then became for him quiet, pleasant, and harmonious.

Yet, while Whitman had this attachment for democracy, Chu-kovskii also emphasized his marked individuality, combining in some unfathomable fashion two points of view that, for the Russian at least, were not easily reconcilable. There were, at the time when Chukovskii was writing, two Russian attitudes to-ward Whitman, one, expressed by Bal'mont in 1904, that saw him as an individualist, and the other, in an essay by I. V. Shklovskii (Dioneo) in *Russkoe bogatstvo* in 1898, that dealt with his democracy. "Even Whitman himself does not provide a so-lution," Chukovskii wrote. "If forced to confront his antinomies in earnest, he says:

> Do I contradict myself?
> Very well then I contradict myself,
> (I am large, I contain multitudes.)

[This wording is Whitman's original. Chukovskii's version would be approximately: I, it seems, contradict myself. But what of that? I am sufficiently capacious that I can contain con-tradictions in myself.]

"It is easy to call the merging of these images emotion and not logic. It is easy to speak of the 'flame of the spirit,' which with its fire converts all disparate and all particular things into a new synthesis, into a harmony of a great new awareness of strength.

"But where is this synthesis to come from, this harmony of the new and great, etc.?"

And, referring to the views advanced by Friedrich Nietzsche, to the concept of a "demos," a "proletariat," and to Whitman, Chukovskii concludes that Whitman did not need to justify himself by logic, but that his sincerity, akin to that sincer-ity that Carlyle felt a great man should show, was the reconcil-ing factor. At least, this is the verdict that appears to lie behind the somewhat foggy mixture of Whitman, Nietzsche, and Car-lyle with which this young Russian writer brings his essay to an end.

As a further indication of Chukovskii's reaction to Whit-man one may refer to "Ob Uitmanie, Bal'montie i dr. (pis'mo k redaktsiiu)" [On Whitman, Bal'mont, etc. (Letter to the Editor)] signed by "Elena Ts." that appeared in the journal *Viesy*, a major exponent of the outlook of Russian literature of the so-called

"Silver Age" (ca. 1890–1914), with an extended rejoinder by Chukovskii, defending some of his particular points of view (*Viesy*, 1906, no. 12: 46–51, 52–60). This discussion is in the same general manner as the controversy between Edmund Wilson and Vladimir Nabokov over the latter's English version of Pushkin's *Evgenii Onegin*, and both convey the same impression of being highly erudite, pleasant to the participants, mildly interesting to other specialists, and "caviare to the general." The principal relevance to this survey is that "Elena Ts." and Chukovskii both appear to have cared enough about Whitman to go into print over their differences, and to pose various questions as to whether or not Bal'mont's understanding of the American poet was worth consideration.

It is not part of this survey's purpose to try to explain anything more about Kornei Ivanovich Chukovskii than some of the elements of his interest in two facets of American literature. The second facet (which concerns detective literature) will be discussed later in this chapter. The young man went on to live a long, full life, to become not only the major Russian specialist on Whitman, gradually improving his translations, but also a children's writer of exceptional interest, and, at the end of his life, a grand old man of literature who even dared to point out that the dreadful jargon of the Soviet press was spoiling the Russian language. One account of his funeral speaks of the hovering crowd of police agents that almost seemed to fear that Chukovskii might voice from his bier a thankfulness that he would no longer have to read the grey, cliché-ridden pages of a typical Soviet newspaper.

There were other American writers who may be considered, with Emerson, Hawthorne, Poe, and Whitman, as being among our greatest who were known to pre-1917 Russians, but generally these received much less attention. About a dozen works by William Dean Howells, *A Modern Instance, The Rise of Silas Lapham, A Traveler from Altruria*, and others, appeared in Russian translation. Mark Twain was known both for his now somewhat dated humorous sketches and for his handful of great works. There was a version of part of Thoreau's *Walden; or, Life in the Woods* in 1887, with a complete translation in 1900. But, these men were, as far as Russian critical notice went, rather in the shadows. However, many American writers, and writers about America, were taken up by Russian readers without any particular flow of analysis as to their themes, their styles, or their purposes, and were accepted because of the attractiveness of their humor or the excitement of their plots.

Some of these were certainly as influential and important as Emerson or the others, and they have lasted because of an inner spark that was communicated between the writer and his audience. Others among these authors were merely producers of entertainment, whether of laughter, tears, or excitement, and their works were soon forgotten. There is almost no way of determining how Russian readers before 1917 reacted to most of them, for their works were not reviewed then and subsequent literary history or comment has overlooked them. But, in order to show that America was more widely accepted on other levels of readership, a few of the names on Russian title pages have been chosen to represent the multitude.

The first appearance of any work of literature by an American in the Russian press was a retelling of Royall Tyler's *Algerine Captive*, first published in 1797, with a London edition of 1802, that appeared in *Zhurnal novostei* of 1805. However, it was not until 1825 that any substantial work by an American author appeared in Russian translation. In that year, according to Libman, some of Washington Irving's tales appeared in four different Russian journals: "Rip van Winkle" in *Syn otechestva* (ch. 104, 1825, no. 22, p. 115–45) and a two-part selection from *Tales of a Traveller* in the same journal, as well as others from this book in *Damskii zhurnal*. Russian readers had to wait until the next year to meet Ichabod Crane and share his immortal encounter with the Headless Horseman, which were recounted in *Moskovskii telegraf* (1826, ch. 9, no. 11, otd. II, p. 116–42; no. 12, otd. II, p. 161–87).

James Fenimore Cooper's *The Spy* was also published in 1825 as *Shpion. Novyi roman, soderzhashchii v sebe prodobnosti amerikanskoi voiny s opisaniem nravov i obychaev sei strany* [The Spy. A new novel, containing the details of the American war, with a description of the mores and customs of that country] (Translated by I. Krupenikov from the French. Moscow, Tip. S. Selivanovskogo, 1825, 3 pts.). Libman's bibliography indicates that pages 283–89 of the third part list the Russian subscribers to this novel living in twenty-two cities.

Cooper went on to become quite as popular among the Russians as he was in Western Europe. Aleksandr Pushkin had among his books a fourteen-volume French edition of Cooper's writings, and there are several references to Cooper in the Russian writer's notes and in memoir literature about Pushkin. The most striking is the entry in the diary of a friend that among her circle he was called the "Krasnyi Korsar," a reminiscence of Cooper's *Red Rover* (Nikoliukin [cited above, at head of Chapter 1], p. 237).

Russia, with the rest of Europe, fell prey to Harriet Beecher Stowe's best-seller *Uncle Tom's Cabin,* although it was somewhat later in appearing there because the similarities between American slavery and Russian serfdom were enough to make the authorities hesitate about possible comparisons. In 1857 Stowe's novel appeared as a supplement to the rather conservative *Russkii viestnik,* and the journal's editor, M. N. Katkov, later one of the most influential newspaper publishers in the empire, produced it separately in a 434-page edition. The next year another translation in which five separate people had participated was issued as a supplement to the more liberal *Sovremennik.* From 1871 to 1916 there were frequent editions, some as "retold for children," and the work must have been obtainable practically all through that era. There were even, so it is reported, productions of the stage version of the novel in the 1870s, but the Library of Congress has only a text of the 1890s that unexplainedly omits Little Eva, Topsy, Miss Ophelia, and even Simon Legree and that ends with Tom still alive.

Although both Cooper and Stowe provided excitement, they seem in some ways to have been overshadowed by two writers about America who, though they had lived here, were not Americans at all. The first was Gustave Aimard, the pen name of Olivier Gloux (1818–1883), already mentioned as a purveyor of thrills. He had served as a cabin boy who jumped ship in an American port, making his way to the frontier, evidently into an area in which the American and Mexican cultures were in contact. Returning to France he wrote dozens of adventure tales that were issued in cheap, popular editions. A number of them were, in fact, translated into English and appeared in one or another of the Beadle series of dime novels, while many were also published in Russian. One that was published in all three languages—French, English, and Russian—was titled *Balle-Franche* upon its Paris publication in the 1860s. In 1875 it was issued in English as *The Prairie Flower; or, The Baffled Chief*, and the Library of Congress has a microfilm of a St. Petersburg edition of 1882 as *Mietkaia pulia*, a closer approach to the original French title than the English one.

The story is a mass of absurdities and high-flown language. The Indians of the Upper Missouri enjoy the sport of ostrich hunting, even though the region is haunted by a figure called the She Wolf of the Prairie who proves to be a woman settler who has survived the death of her family and her own scalping at the hands of the Indians, against whom she takes deadly and mysterious vengeance. A French count and his valet, the latter reminding one rather distantly of Phileas Fogg's Passepartout, a grim Indian chief, and a number of American pioneers of curiously theatrical aspect are also among the characters. The style is, in general, one of verbose high-mindedness, and, insofar as the reader is not put off by this, the plot appears to be based on the relentless operation of coincidence. Furthermore, the modern observer finds the repeated and emphatic characterization of the Indians as little more than fiends to be jarring and repulsive.

Gustave Aimard's name was not totally unknown to Russians when his great popularity began in the 1870s, or at least to readers of long memory and wide interests, for there had been a short survey of his works in the journal *Russkoe slovo* in 1861 (no. 8, "Inostrannaia literatura," p. 1–11), which appears to have been intended to tell Russian readers that in 1860–1861, under the reign of Napoleon III, the state of literature had sunk to such a low level that Aimard was practically the only writer who stood out above the crowd. The author of this survey was one V. Popov who noted the rather stereotyped nature of much of Aimard's writing, but who seems to have felt that the Frenchman possessed a certain "Daguerreotype truth" that excelled his artistic truth. Popov repeats many clichés about Americans, some of which are directly quoted from Aimard and others drawn from uncited sources. "No one in the American nations loves money so much as the inhabitant of North America. Gold is everything for him. In order to get money he will sacrifice family and friends without any gnawings of conscience and without pity. In this he has devised the egoistic, vile, and heartless proverb, clearly showing the character of the people, 'Time is money'" (Popov, op. cit., p. 4).

Although, Popov writes, Aimard ranks below Cooper and even Captain Mayne Reid, "in the depiction of nature and the hunt, in which the talented captain is inimitable . . ." he is excellent in the description of the Indians. "Here at every step there is visible a great experience and remarkable powers of observation. It is a pity that M. Aimard did not present his adventures and remarks in the form of memoirs, . . ." (Popov, op. cit., p. 10).

Aimard, so Popov appears to believe, is a star of the first order in the circle of golden mediocrity that comprised French literature of the time, a personification of a country occupied only with the externals of life, and that can only be compared with the landowner who tells his overseer, when the latter reports bad conditions, that he doesn't want to know, for he would be happier that way. But, according to Popov, there will come a new day in which the activity of people will resume with doubled strength (Popov, op. cit., p. 10–11).

Balle-franche was by no means the only work by Aimard to be translated into Russian, and indeed it would be a matter for patient bibliographic research to determine which of his novels, under varying titles, actually did appear in Russia. In the mid-1870s the St. Petersburg publishing house of E. N. Akhmatova issued a number of them, while the 1902 catalog of the major publisher and bookdealer A. S. Suvorin refers to a six-volume edition dated 1895, and, finally, there are reports of other titles that came out in 1908. Present-day Soviet historians of Russian reading patterns have little to say about this element of the public response, but one may note that the *Kratkaia literaturnaia entsiklopediia* (Moscow, "Sovetskaia entsiklopediia") gives Aimard rather favorable notice, and there is a bibliographic mention of a 1958 edition of one of his novels that was apparently supplied with a preface about the work's value for understanding nineteenth century Mexican history.

Something of the role that Aimard had among Russian readers of the 1880's is shown by N. A. Rubakin, the Russian student of the needs and psychology of readers, in his *Etiudy o russkoi chitaiushchei publikie; fakty, tsifry i nabliudeniia* [Studies of the Russian reading public; facts, figures and observations] (St. Petersburg, 1895. [246p.]). He writes,

Some foreign authors are read much more than well-known Russian writers. A Russian who knows literature will be shocked by such surprises. In 1883 in the Nizhnyi Novgorod library Aimard was read almost one-and-a-half times as much as Shchedrin [M. E. Saltykov, who used the pseudonym "Shchedrin," was the author of many satiric examinations of the philistine character of Russian provincial life, and will be extensively quoted in Chapter 4] . . . Let us take, on the one hand, the total requests for Aimard (302), J. Verne (244), Dumas-père (170), Ponçon-du-Terrail (164), Mayne Reid (159), Montepin (145), Marlitt (115), Born (99), Collins (91), Braddon (86), Gaboriau (71)—eleven authors—the sum of requests for them, according to the 1887 report of the Nizhnyi Novgorod library was 1,646. Let us take, on the other hand, Pisemskii (315), Turgenev (350), Goncharov (250), A. Tolstoi (128), Gogol' (127), Grigorovich (123), Pushkin (107), Zhukovskii (43), Nikitin (39), Lermontov (58), Aksakov (56)—also eleven authors—for whom there was a total of 1,494 requests (op. cit., p. 25).

Of the non-Russian authors only three have not by now sunk into deep oblivion—Jules Verne, the elder Dumas, and Wilkie Collins—and none are what present literary critics consider major writers. The Russian authors, however, are among the notable contributors to their country's literature, and some, Turgenev, Goncharov, Gogol', Pushkin, and Lermontov, must certainly be ranked with the great writers of any nation's literature. One might draw inferences from this that are not quite in harmony with claims that the Russian reader has innate good taste, for it really appears that philistinism (the Russians use the word "meshchanstvo"—petty bourgeois outlook) was markedly present among Russian readers, but one may note Rubakin's own verdict on this as a certain mitigation of the situation. Rubakin said that, despite all the flaws of such novels as those of Aimard, they often did attract to the joys of literacy such people as the worker Vasilii Ivanovich Savikhin (1858– ?) who began with works such as *Mustache* of Paul de Kock, Dumas' *Three Musketeers,* Mayne Reid's *Headless Horseman,* and other tales of adventure. "What breadth! What a wide flight over this boiling sea of human activity! What life! How many people! A Struggle! Good . . . I sit on my little bit of plank, for which I paid a ruble and a half, and in candle light I delve into the limitless American prairies, where there are piled up heaps of gold, frightful bands of redskins, and I look at Spain, at France

... Then there fell into my hands a book of another kind, a work of Draper, *History of the Intellectual Development of Europe*. Indeed more than half of this book was incomprehensible to me, or boring. But what I understood did me good service. I gave up reading novels and took up works of a scholarly nature, and read with the same unquenchable internal fire" (op. cit.: 205–06).

Draper is John William Draper (1811–1882), born in England, but active in America, whose criticisms of barriers to freedom of thought were widely read and greatly influential. From the 1860s to about 1905, there were Russian editions of several of his books; critical response in Russia was quite respectful and, as in other European countries, Draper's influence was strong among critics of the existing order. Indeed, Draper's works were considered almost obligatory parts of the reading lists of Russian radicals.

Russian readers did not always proceed from Aimard's preposterous claptrap to Draper's rationalism, for new generations continued to be swept up by Aimard, or by the writings of another creator of spine-tingling adventures in the American West, Mayne Reid. Thomas Mayne Reid (1818–1883), was born in Ireland but came to the United States about 1840. He served in the Mexican War, reaching the rank of captain and acquiring a considerable knowledge of Texas and its people. Upon his return to the British Isles in 1849 he drew upon this background to write novel after novel filled with colorful and bloody adventures. By all accounts he was a flamboyant character, and his style now appears absurdly ornate and overwritten, quite in the same vein as that of Gustave Aimard. However, he was not so much in error as Aimard as to have ostriches haunting the prairies of the Upper Missouri, and his geographic and linguistic references are not outrageously wrong. He did, however, voice doctrines of racial and national superiority, either directly or by his treatment of his characters, that are repulsive. For example,

To talk of their [the Indians] being the aborigines of the country—the real, but dispossessed, owners of the soil—is simple nonsense. This sophism, of the most spurious kind, has too long held dominion over the minds of men. The whole human race has an inherent right to the whole surface of the earth: and if any infinitessimal fraction of the former by chance finds itself idly roaming over an extended portion of the latter, their exclusive claim to it is almost too absurd for argument—even with the narrowest-minded disciple of an aborigines society.

Admit it—give the *hunter* his half-dozen square miles—for he will require that much to maintain him—leave him in undisputed possession to all eternity—and millions of fertile acres must remain untilled, to accommodate this whimsical theory of *national* right. Nay, I will go further, and risk reproach, by asserting: that not only the savage, so called, but civilized people should be unreservedly dispossessed whenever they show themselves incapable of turning to a good account the resources which *Nature* has placed within their limits (Mayne Reid, *The Headless Horseman.* New York, G. W. Dillingham, 1892. p. 292).

When these sentiments are accompanied by a plot in which a man is placed within a noose three times in the course of a single day only to have three different persons show up to interrupt, and when most of the characters speak in a highfalutin language that reflects cheap, bad melodrama it becomes difficult to treat Mayne Reid seriously. Yet, many of the European countries saw a flood of editions of Reid's work in the era from 1860 to the end of the century, with Russia not least among them. There is not enough bibliographic detail to trace all the Russian versions of his novels, but editions of his works were given as premiums for subscription to popular magazines and a 24-volume collection was in progress in 1897. His works continue to be published in the Soviet Union.

There is nothing whatsoever in the written record about whether works by Gustave Aimard or Mayne Reid were included in the stock of books in the Simbirsk household of that truly worthy and intently literate provincial school inspector Il'ia Nikolaevich Ul'ianov [Lenin's father], as the only works by American authors directly mentioned in a study of that family's library are *Uncle Tom's Cabin* and an unnamed book by John W. Draper. However, one can perhaps feel that some possible influence of early reading was reflected in the fact that during an illness late in life Lenin found diversion in listening to his wife read to him from the writings of another teller of adventure tales, Jack London, who was widely read by Russians both before and after 1917. (It might also be noted that some of London's views upon the rights of the strong man can be said to approach those voiced by Mayne Reid in regard to the Indians.)

Although the vogue in Russia for Aimard and Mayne Reid

appears to have lessened somewhat after the turn of the century, the period from approximately 1907 to the end of the Romanov empire was marked by another current of popular literature that dealt with America. This was made up of a vast number of small pamphlets, usually 32 pages in length and retailing for 12 kopecks [about 6 cents at the prevailing rate of exchange] that told of the adventures of "Nik Karter, korol' syshchikov" [Nick Carter, king of detectives] or of "Nat Pinkerton," another detective, and many other bold thwarters of the actions of sinister criminals. Almost all these tales appear to be set in New York City, and there are references to "Garlem," "Sandi Guk," "Kvinz," or, "Zing Zing," and, if memory does not fail, the "Fletairen Bilding." None of the characters, whether on the right or the wrong side of the law, is drawn with any particular differentiation, except that the detectives, while using methods that would draw sharp judicial condemnation these days, voice highminded satisfaction at being able to deal with such threats to the public peace.

These little publications were enormously popular. One estimate, based on extrapolation from a mere two weeks' record in the Russian national bibliography, was that in 1909 there were over five million copies issued of such things. This was apparently a decline from the highest wave of interest, for, as the literary critic Kornei Chukovskii, already noted for his interest in Whitman, wrote earlier, "In St. Petersburg alone during just the month of May of the current year [1908], according to official information, 622,300 copies of detective literature were distributed" (Kornei I. Chukovskii, *Sobranie sochinenii.* v. 6. Moscow, Izdatel'stvo "Khudozhestvennaia literatura," 1969. p. 313).

Chukovskii saw in this phenomenon a sign of the triumph of something that was perhaps worse than mere philistinism. The clustering of people together in anonymous urban masses created a sort of world-engulfing barbarian of the kind that could be interested only in popular singers who were glorified to the heights, a barbarian who replaced the former peasant masses out of whose imagination had come the old gods, knights, and elves, the whole fantasy of which had so enriched the world. Although a state of cultural cannibalism had been foreseen and long awaited in Russian literature, no one, even

those reading the anathemas that Herzen, Leont'ev, Dostoevskii, or Gor'kii had pronounced against such philistinism, no
one could have foreseen such a monstrous situation as was then
facing the country (Chukovskii, op. cit., 129).

It is said that since the time of Herzen and [John Stuart] Mill philistinism has had terrifying successes. Good Lord, is it only successes? Don't you
see that it is as if a dam has broken, and from all sides, over all elements of
culture, over the intelligentsia, the youth, the city, the village, books, journals,
the family, art, these millions of thoroughgoing barbarians have trampled,
and the waterfalls will thunder until everything is submerged. There is no
safe ark in which we might find refuge and float over the waves. We are all
drowned men, each and every one of us. . . .

This multimillion-headed barbarian needs a leader to follow; it needs a
hero before whom to bow. [But this barbarian puts no value on the great
passions that inspired the ancient heroes.] He who laughs when he sees a
saucepan worn in place of a hat, and who cries when he loses a silver ruble,
will indeed not take Brutus, Pericles or the demigod Hector as his hero. . . .

No, it is foreordained by God himself that he [the barbarian] take as his
idol and ideal Peacoat [Gorokhovoe pal'to—identification not established]
and the detective Nat Pinkerton, and that it is this form that embodies all the
ideas of which he is capable about the possible greatness of man's soul.

There was a time when such models as Mikula Selianinov-
ich [one of the Russian folk heroes] or Robin Hood, and, as the
townsfolk rose to prominence, such people as Don Quixote or
Childe-Harold, could serve as the personification of human
ideals. "But it is only recently that we are capable of choosing as a hero such a person as a detective, as Peacoat, or as
the agent of an intelligence service (Chukovskii, op. cit., p.
129–31).

After referring to the six hundred some odd thousand
copies of this detective literature that appeared in St. Petersburg in a single month, Chukovskii notes that during Dostoevskii's lifetime *Crime and Punishment* appeared in but two thousand copies, and that they were on sale from 1876 to 1880
without being sold out. "The best work of an author of genius
in the flower of his fame in a total of 400 copies a year, while
flagrant, unforgiveable trash reaches seven million [Chukov-
skii's estimate of annual sales], and these millions are growing
by unbelievable leaps; now we see ever higher and more impos-
ingly before us the world-famed detective, the all-powerful and
all-knowing Nat Pinkerton" (op. cit., 131–32).

Although Chukovskii avows that the character of Sherlock Holmes served as a distant stimulus for creating Nat Pinkerton, Holmes was an honorable and even knightly man, with qualities of love and poesy in his view of the world and with the ability to subordinate such questions as tangible rewards for his deeds to the deeper values of his own satisfaction with having aided justice. But, somehow, throughout the world, "and first of all in the United States," there appeared book after book about figures who were like Holmes but who had undergone a transformation for the worse. "The millions of American readers, having taken over this character from the English writer Conan Doyle, immediately, invisibly, instinctively, and uncontrollably, began to change him to their own taste, giving him their own spiritual and moral content—and unconsciously killing in him those traits that were foreign to these millions of readers, and, in the end, impressed upon him, on his personality, their own million-headed psyche" (op. cit., 133–36).

Chukovskii asks what is left of Holmes's slender fingers and proud solitude, his taste for Petrarch and for the violin-playing of Sarasate, his work in chemistry, and his honor and self-sacrifice. "All this has disappeared and has been replaced—by the fist" (op. cit., 136).

"'Villain, growled the great detective and with a hard blow sent the criminal to the floor,'—this is the only function of Nat Pinkerton." Chukovskii had read, he says, fifty-three of these little books of the adventures of Nat Pinkerton and was convinced that the sole trait of genius of the American hero was in the distribution of various forms of punches to the ear, hits to the teeth, and frightful blows on the head (op. cit., 137). He was of the opinion that, to judge from Pinkerton's frequent use of the revolver, there ought to be a special cemetery in New York to take care of his victims, whose funeral processions would be endless (op. cit., 138).

Quotations from these tales about the "fitting end in the electric chair" of the villains, and of the "large sums" given to the detective as a reward bolster a final paragraph in Chukovskii's detailed analysis of such works, "It is both pleasant and enjoyable: the criminals are wiped out in the electric chair, the idealized heroes receive fat wallets, and he has the most genius who has the strongest fist. Long live Nat Pinkerton, the ruler, the ideal, the hero of millions of hearts!" (op. cit., 138–39).

It was not, however, merely to call devastating attention to a flood of literary trash that Chukovskii was moved to undertake his analyses, for he felt that there was a tendency on the part of these "millions of urban cannibals" to degrade all phenomena, all ideas, that they might encounter just as Sherlock Holmes had been horribly changed into Nat Pinkerton. It was in vain that philistinism had been so much cursed, and it was in vain that Herzen was saddened by the fear that philistinism was the final form of Western civilization, its maturity. In Nat Pinkerton he saw the "end of our human existence." Although Holmes may have shown traits of bourgeois narrowness, his character nevertheless exhibited a British rejoicing in the human mind and in the limitless force of logic. "For his readers Sherlock is great precisely because of his intellect."

"In Nat Pinkerton, then, as we have seen, the fist takes the place of intellect. The [multiheaded urban] beast, of course, not knowing how to value intellect and blindly hating it, immediately deprived Sherlock of all the folds of his brain" (op. cit., 140–42).

In the last five pages or so of Chukovskii's article, however, something of his real purpose becomes clear. He fears that the transformation of Sherlock Holmes into Nat Pinkerton was an exemplar of the course of evolution of Russia. "And when I see that no kind of an idea, no sort of artistic, moral, or philosophical thought can appear in our society before there is a rush to animalize it, to transform it into the worst kind of kitsch, when I think about the strange fate that has recently touched all movements, all tendencies of our societal life that love the book, and when I think that any high thought can be transformed into something low and bestial, almost quadrupedal, then I understand that this is the action of that mass creativity by which the million-headed beast has changed the intellectual Sherlock Holmes into the head-bashing Nat Pinkerton." Although people such as Shaliapin, Andreev, Serov, and Blok may continue to work, it is the beast who will continue to listen, judge, and evaluate. The beast may even mask itself as a fighter against the philistine spirit, but it will in reality settle into the midst of the intelligentsia, "and suddenly, one fine day, it will turn out that in the spot where for a century we have been accustomed to see the intelligentsia, there will sit a tattooed headhunter, and we will not have noticed this and will, by force of habit, keep on saying, 'our intelligentsia,' 'our cultured society,' 'the course of life of our society'" (op. cit., 143–44).

The worst part of it all seems to be that Russian intellectual life has lost its unity, and has become hospitable to too much variety. There are too many voices at too much variance with one another. "Books are printed, lectures are given, and new writers have appeared—in great numbers—but the intelligentsia has become smaller and smaller. There are many ideas, but not a single unifying one. There are lots of literati, but no literature" (op. cit., 147).

In 1908 Kornei Ivanovich Chukovskii was a very young man, full of the fire of youth, a fire that is fully evident in this essay. He was also given, as young men often are, to the direct and open statement of his views, all passionately and decisively expressive of a clear separation between what he saw as good and what he saw as bad. Furthermore, as we have noted before, he too was using his concept of America as a tool with which to attack the flaws of his own society. Out of the figures of Sherlock Holmes and Nat Pinkerton, and despite his interest in Whitman, apparently possessing no marked understanding of the United States beyond what he found in these little pamphlets on shoddy paper, he has fashioned a spectre of the alleged fate of Russian culture. Such trumpet blasts against the decay of everything and everybody are, of course, commonplaces of much intellectual controversy, and it must be admitted that Nat Pinkerton is fitting and proper thematic material for such music, still Chukovskii has only used the first stick he found to beat the Russian dog. In this regard, at least, he does not seem to have understood Whitman's "I sound my barbaric yawp over the roofs of the world."

Others in Russian life less directly concerned with the actual cultural effects of Nat Pinkerton and similar heroes were not quite so quick to supply such resounding verdicts.

Although the general press of Russia often seemed upset by the flood of tales about Nat Pinkerton and others like him [see, for example, the newspaper *Riech'*, August 24, 1908 and 1909 (no. 198)] and by the sight of students flooding into the market square in Kiev to spend their lunch and school-supply money on second-hand copies of such publications (Hryhorii P. Hryhor'iev, *U staromu Kyievi*. Kiev, Radians'kyi pysmennyk, 1961. p. 60–61), the reaction among educators was not quite so troubled. One N. Verigin, who wrote in the education journal *Pedagogicheskii sbornik* (Literatura syska v otsienkie uchenikov srednikh klassov gimnazii [Detective literature as evaluated by students of the intermediate classes of secondary schools]. 1909, no. 10: 288–302), repeats the general statistical information that Chukovskii used in his essay, but notes that many of the students gave up reading such literature because the issues were becoming repetitive (op. cit., p. 295). He felt that the interest of young people in such literature was an outgrowth of their need to find compensation for the dullness of their day-to-day life and of their search for manifestations of self-sacrifice, bravery, energy, enterprise, and presence of mind (op. cit., 295, 301).

Another of the pedagogical journals even included data from a survey that was undertaken among students, finding that, among 70 students (35 boys and 35 girls) aged 14 and 15, 41 knew about this detective literature, but only 10 of these were girls. The author, one A. Suvorovskii, asked this group three questions: Have you read the tales about detectives, and which ones? Were you interested by this, and by which ones? If you have stopped reading them, then why? Two of those questioned answered in the negative. The others replied that they were very interested by all this, particularly by Nat Pinkerton. "Because of these books, I stopped reading others, in spite of the fact that at home they did not exactly welcome my reading them" (A. Suvorovskii, "Nat Pinkerton v dietskom ponimanii" [Nat Pinkerton as understood by youth]. *Viestnik vospitanii*, 1909, no. 1: 157–59).

The chief reason, Suvorovskii writes, for the interest among young people is that, in their eyes, Nat Pinkerton is an ideal type. They are quite sympathetic to him and are impressed by his intelligence, energy, and selfless devotion to duty (op. cit., 159–60).

Throughout the answers, therefore, there resounds one common note—a liking for Nat Pinkerton as an energetic and strong personality.

Such preoccupation should by no means be viewed as an instance of brutal exploitation: with the idealism of their years young readers in their answers particularly emphasize the ideal—as they see it—essence of the activity of Nat Pinkerton. In his activity they find a 'noble goal, that of abolishing evil,' 'a noble striving . . . the defense of the weak,' and Nat Pinkerton himself is for them 'sympathetic with the innocent and harsh toward the villain, a useful person who roots out all that is evil,' he is 'a fighter for truth' and even 'a great-hearted person, who gives his help to all' (op. cit., 160–61).

Suvorovskii notes that, while Russian literature for young people is filled with works showing pity and sympathy, there is little in the way of writings based on the psychology of daring struggle and activity. There are no active types who might directly affirm the value of a strong will, who could be attractive for their courage, enterprise, and energy. Lacking such works, the young Russians had taken up these accounts of the adventures of Nat Pinkerton and others like him. However, as Suvorovskii goes on to say, many have given up Pinkerton, for his ceaseless activity and unending victories pall after a while, and readers find this whole class of literature unconvincing and even downright false.

Thus, a simple feeling for realism, for the truth of life, as well as the beginnings of artistic taste, bring forth a cooler reaction toward adventure literature and it begins to seem boring and ceases to attract. . . . But it is characteristic that the former worshippers of Nat Pinkerton have only become "artistically" disenchanted with him, while "psychologically" they are still attracted; . . . A practical conclusion among many others is that Russian literature for youth should present more that would be based on the traits of energy, daring, keen observation, and inventiveness. . . . [Thus,] children need characters that show firm will; they seek moral stimuli in books, they wish to experience in their reading a bold struggle and a persistent striving toward a goal. And if we do not give them such reading, then . . . they follow Nat Pinkerton or some other such hero of street-corner literature, and he will lead them into an atmosphere of crime, snooping, and lies . . . (op. cit., 161–63).

Other comments of the time are in general agreement with Suvorovskii's conclusions, but there is no need for extended citation, as they again show that, as we have already noted in relation to other topics, an American theme is being used as the point of departure for analyses that do not really relate to the United States. However, one element that Suvorovskii brings forward, the need for literature for young people that will inspire them to boldness, persistence, self-reliance, and to being able to deal with difficult situations, is markedly reminiscent of the general tenor of the Soviet official outlook toward the role of young people's reading. If one examines the short notations that accompany entries in the section of children's literature of the Soviet pre-publication bibliographic journal *Novye knigi,* one will find many references to the aspects of individual titles that tend to strengthen such tendencies in the reader.

While the attacks, such as those of Chukovskii on the artistic qualities of the Nat Pinkerton literature, or the more analytical conclusions of Suvorovskii about the boredom young people might feel with Pinkerton's unending successes, did have some effect, many of these little books continued to appear. Even during the First World War the Military Censorship on November 18, 1916 [O.S.] passed *Stal'noe zhalo* [The steel sting] (Petrograd, Izdatel'stvo "Razvlechenie," 1916. 32 p. 12 kopecks) in the series "Nat Pinkerton, korol' syshchikov" [Nat Pinkerton, king of the detectives] which told of a mysterious wave of murders in New York. Nor was the taste for such publications lost with the Revolution, for during the early Soviet period some writers attempted to supply a "Soviet Pinkerton," an effort that was heavily criticized by the official guardians of ideology. In spite of such frowns, however, the big box office hit of 1927 in Soviet movies was *Miss Mend* based on a Soviet novel written in clear imitation of the Pinkerton genre. Indeed, although one must beware of the foreshortening that is characteristic of plot summaries, it would seem that many present-day adventure films from Soviet studios have turns that are reminiscent of the King of the Detectives.

Although these references to the literary reception of the theme of America through the works of Gustave Aimard and the many anonymous authors of Nat Pinkerton-type tales show that there was a Russian critical concern with the effects of what might be called quasi-literature, there was very little in the way of reaction to our more traditional forms. As Libman's bibliography shows, there was only one study of any length by a Russian author published in the years 1865–1917 that might be of relevance to American literature. However, since Vladimir R. Zotov's *Istoriia vsemirnoi literatury* [History of world literature] (Moscow, 1874–82) is not reported by any American library, it cannot be determined what the real American content may be of the survey of British and American writing that appears on pages 349–638 of volume 4. Other substantial works that appeared in Russian prove to have been translated from other languages. There was, for example, a Russian version of Johannes Scherr's *Allgemeine Geschichte der Literatur* that appeared in 1880, containing a discussion of literature in English as one of its sections (v. 2, book 3: 3–125). While Pavel Grigor'evich Mizhuev is listed as the author of *Literaturnye faktory amerikanskoi revoliutsii* [Literary factors of the American Revolution] (*Russkoe bogatstvo*, 1900, nos. 5–8. Separately: St. Petersburg, 1901. 252 p.), the work is actually drawn from Moses Coit Tyler's *Literary History of the American Revolution* (New York and London, G. P. Putnam's sons, 1897. 2 v.), and this translation is probably an outgrowth of Mizhuev's broader interest in American affairs, for he wrote several other works on the society and politics of the United States, some of which will be mentioned below.

In 1914 there was a Russian edition of William P. Trent and John Erskine's *Great American Writers* (New York, H. Holt and Company, 1912, 256 p. Russian edition: *Velikie amerikanskie pisateli*. St. Petersburg, P. I. Pevin, 1914. 144 p.), but there seems in fact to have been no general critical work of Russian origin on American literature before 1941, although many short general articles appeared from time to time in Russian journals or as part of larger works. Judging from a very small sampling of these, they leave little impression of real depth. Zinaida Vengerova's contribution on American literature in *Istoriia zapadnoi literatury* [History of Western literature] (Edited by F. D. Batiushkov. Moscow, 1912–14, v. 3: 288–327) is more or less on the level of a survey text for a junior college, and the two articles on the American literary scene in the long, long list of the materials signed "P. A. Tverskoi" (pseudonym of Petr Alekseevich Dement'ev, 1850–1919, who was naturalized in the United States as Peter A. Demens) are only interesting examples of the outlook of a man who was more concerned with the socioeconomic problems of the country (see *Russkii viestnik*, 1895, no. 8: 515–43; and, 1909, no. 8: 671–78). But, since *Russkii viestnik* was a journal that was reported to have been read by both Lev N. Tolstoi and Nicholas II, and since there is a quotation from Demens, albeit at second hand, in the writings of V. I. Lenin, Demens may have been of some influence.

Despite this lack of general studies there was some current of attention to individual American writers. By and large, the critical works that were published as individual books dealt with those authors whose importance lay in their concern with social and economic problems rather than in their more narrowly defined literary artistry. In 1892, for example, Konstantin Golovin published *Sotsializm kak polozhitel'noe uchenie* [Socialism as a positive doctrine] (St. Petersburg, 1892. 246 p.) which analyzed the views expressed in Edward Bellamy's Utopian novel *Looking Backward*. That same year there was E. A. Sysoeva's *Zhizn' Garriet Bicher Stou* [Life of Harriet Beecher Stowe] (St. Petersburg, 1892. 151 p.) which was actually a reworking of Mrs. Stowe's son's biography. Benjamin Franklin was the subject of several works, including M. Rostovskaia's *Ven'iamin Franklin. Razskaz dlia iunoshestva* [Benjamin Franklin. A tale for young people] (St. Petersburg, Vol'f, 1863. 116 p. 2d ed., 1906), A. Liubimov's *Veniamin Franklin, ego zhizn' i ego pravila samousovershenstvovaniia* [Benjamin Franklin, his life and his rules for self-improvement] (Moscow, Universitetskaia tipografiia, 1881. 70 p.), and Z. L. Voronova's *Franklin—tipograf* [Franklin the printer] (St. Petersburg, 1904. 52 p.). For other writers, however, there were only scattered articles, the longest of which, apparently, was V. Sviatlovskii's study "Gaiavata, kak istoricheskaia lichnost' i kak geroi poemy Longfello" [Hiawatha as a historical personality and as hero of Longfellow's poem] in the *Zapiski* of the Neofilologicheskoe obshchestvo pri Imperatorskom sanktpeterburgskom universitatie (1911, vyp. 5: 1–58. Also published separately).

In view of the rather wide knowledge of English among Russian intellectuals there was a certain circulation in the empire of books in that language, as well as in French and German, which were even more commonly known. The import of foreign literature was, in fact, something of a problem for the authorities as it might offer a channel for the introduction of unwished-for materials, and to deal with this there was a monthly bulletin issued to the customs officials at the various border crossing points listing non-Russian publications that fell into the categories of fully permitted, permitted with deletions, and absolutely prohibited. Of course, there is nothing in such a list to indicate that there was any mass importation of materials, but inspection of this bulletin over time does say something about the character of a reading public. The guide, issued by the Glavnoe upravlenie po dielam pechati [Chief administration for press affairs] was titled *Ukazatel' po dielam pechati* [Index to press affairs], and each issue contained a section, "Alfavitnyi spisok sochineniiam rasmotrennym inostrannoiu tsenzuroiu" [Alphabetical list of works reviewed by the foreign censorship]. The guide first appeared in the autumn of 1872, and it was in the third issue that works in English were first noted. A survey of this publication shows that, by and large, materials of British origin tended to predominate, but there were nevertheless numerous listings of American publications. One of the first indicated that the *New York Ledger* had been permitted entry for nos. 1–32, 35–52 for 1871. This publication was famed for its devotion to serial stories, generally of a markedly sentimental or adventurous nature, and, while Robert Bonner, its flamboyant publisher, attempted to display the names of Bryant, Stowe, Longfellow, and Edward Everett as attention getters, the bulk of the contents was provided by such people as the very prolific Mrs. E. D. E. N. Southworth, Sylvanus Cobb, and "Fanny Fern" (Mrs. James Parton) [*Ukazatel' po dielam pechati*, 1872, no. 3: 36–39].

The Russian authorities appear to have been most diligent in trying to exclude material with unwished-for political or religious overtones, but there are at times surprising instances of permission being granted for the import of some rather strange titles. One, which deserves mention if for no other reason than its title, was the Reverend Samuel Watson's *The Clock Struck One, and Christian Spiritualist: Being a Synopsis of the Investigations of Spirit Intercourse by an Episcopal Bishop, Three Ministers, Five Doctors, and Others, at Memphis, Tennessee in 1855; also of Many Eminent Divines, Living and Dead, on the Subject, and Communications Received from a Number of Persons Recently* (New York, 1872, xxxiv, 208 p.) [*Ukazatel'*, 1873, p. 194]. In 1874 one finds an entry admitting: Alger, Horatio. *Ragged Dick; or, Street Life in New York with the Boot-Blacks* (Boston, n.d. 296 p.) [*Ukazatel'*, 1874, p. 87]. And, to show that not all Russian readers had to depend on Gustave Aimard for their excitement, four novels by an American counterpart, Edward S. Ellis, including *Nathan Todd; or, The Fate of the Sioux Captives* were passed, as was Mrs.

Ann S. Stephens' *Malaeska; the Indian Wife of the White Hunter* in a London edition. This last book had been the first title to appear in the famed Beadle series of dime novels in 1860 [*Ukazatel'* . . . 1874, p. 149–50].

Not only did American works enter Russia in their original English, but there were also translations into other languages, as, for example, three German translations of Louisa M. Alcott that were admitted in 1877 [*Ukazatel'* . . . Feb. 1, 1877: 8]. While the inclusion of a work in the *Ukazatel'* . . . does not actually show anything more than that, at one time or another, a single copy had come up for review, examination over a period of time would show something about the breadth of material that people in Russia were apparently willing to make an effort to bring into the country. There is enough to create a feeling that almost any American work had some chance of getting into the Empire. While works of fiction were only rarely forbidden or even ordered to have passages deleted, and while the censors appear to have been distrustful of most social and political comment, still one finds admission of American works on spiritualism, which the Russian churchmen regarded as an abomination, books on utopian communities, and even Thomas Paine's *Rights of Man.* Although circulation of these items may have been limited, they were there, with many latent possibilities for attracting the attention of a reader who might make use of them.

Also, there were numbers of book dealers in Russia who, despite problems with censorship, sold imported books, and some of the more serious journals listed or reviewed them. While these titles were mostly works of non-fiction, readers were often informed of materials about America that might otherwise have escaped their attention. In one volume of the liberal *Otechestvennyia zapiski,* for example, one finds entries for William Dean Howell's *Venetian Life,* a biography of Stonewall Jackson, German works on schools in America, a study of the South in the immediate post-Civil War period, and *Thirty Years of Army Life on the Border* by a Colonel R. B. Macy [*Otechestvennyia zapiski,* v. 168 (1866), "Literaturnaia khronika:" 39–40, 77, 147, 201–02].

However, for the vast majority of Russian readers it was through translation that they became acquainted with America.

The mass of material was a most heterogeneous one, and it was much larger than Libman's quite selective bibliography would indicate. The task of providing a complete view is beyond the scope of this survey but, as a sample, one may refer to some of the works that became available in the ten-year period beginning in 1900. One of the most striking guides is *O dietskikh knigakh* [Concerning children's books] (Moscow. Tipo-lit. T-Va I. N. Kushnereva i Ko., 1908), which was issued by the "Trud" bookstore. Without this volume one might easily overlook a significant factor in the Russian view of America, for the works that it lists are not included in Libman. There were, for example, 21 titles by the Anglo-Canadian-American writer E. Thompson Seton, who often drew on American frontier themes, that were available in Russian [*O dietskikh knigakh.* . . . cols. 469–74]. Twelve editions of *Uncle Tom's Cabin* were listed, some of which were retellings [ibid., cols. 90–94]. Although it is difficult to decide if Frances Hodgson Burnett was an American or an English writer, she lived for a long time in the United States and her most famous work, *Little Lord Fauntleroy,* depends as much on an American background and American characters for its plot as on British ones. Her Russian readers could read about it all in four different translations, including one with the illustrations by Reginald Birch showing little Cedric all done up in curls, lace collar, and velvet suit that stimulated proud mothers to imitation, and small boys to grumbled protest [ibid., cols. 86–87]. And, to show that some sentimental works had a very long life, there is a listing of a 1904 edition of Maria S. Cummings' old tear-jerker *The Lamplighter,* which had first appeared in 1857 as a tale of an old lamplighter's rescue of an orphan who grows up to happiness and a fortunate marriage. The annotation speaks of the book as of interest to girls from twelve to sixteen years of age, and it was apparently something of a standard in Russian book publishing, for several previous editions had been printed, and, in fact, one can be found entered in the national bibliography *Knizhnaia lietopis'* for 1914 [*O dietskikh knigakh,* col. 204].

As for works primarily intended for adults, Hamlin Garland had material in *Mir bozhii,* nos. 4–8, of 1901, the rather forgotten Francis Marion Crawford's *Don Zhuan* was published separately in 1902 (St. Petersburg, Izd. A. Il'ina, 1902. 314 p.), and Paul Leicester Ford's political novel *The Honorable Peter Sterling* made its Russian appearance—also in 1902. That same year *Russkaia mysl'* offered the first part, *The Octopus*, of Frank Norris' projected trilogy on wheat, which *Mir bozhii* continued the next year with the second part of the uncompleted whole, *The Pit*. [We shall return to Norris in Chapter 4, where we will see how his views about the growing and marketing of wheat were noted by a Russian agronomist in his discussion of world markets.] In 1903 the usually quite serious *Viestnik Evropy* presented "Urozhenets Virginii," Owen Wister's famous *The Virginian*. Upton Sinclair's *The Jungle* was available in 1906 in four editions, evidently from as many translators. Two stories by Edith Wharton were published in the October and November 1908 issues of *Russkaia mysl'*, and in 1909 there was a bibliographic reference to what one might call a blending of the Russian and American elements in Aleksandr A. Fedorov-Davydov's *Chernoe serdtse; povest' iz epokha osvoboditel'noi voiny Sievero-Amerikanskikh Shtatov* [Black heart; a tale from the period of the war of liberation of the North American States] (Moscow, Izd. I. D. Sytina, 1909. 151 p.).

Only someone with a good deal of patience and a detailed knowledge of minor American fiction of the years before 1914 could really embark on a full recording of all such publications of works by American authors. However if such a project were undertaken it would certainly become clear that there was much that Libman does not list, and that the Russian view of America was as much dependent upon the ephemeral—or, at a more kindly assessment, the forgotten—works of a season. Furthermore, the whole topic of America in the works of children's literature in Russia is one that, if researched, would also enlarge the picture. After all, some of the impressions of America held by two very opposite men, Adolf Hitler and Albert Einstein, were formed by their youthful reading of the works about the West by Karl May, the German counterpart of Aimard. One need only read Ray A. Billington's *Land of Savagery, Land of Promise: The European Image of the American Frontier in the Nineteenth Century* (New York, Norton, 1981. 364 p.) to see that literature of this sort has an influence that is not lost in adulthood, and one can then perhaps realize that some of Russia's perceptions of America came from just such reading.

An even more effective vehicle for fixing such attitudes as those represented in much of the fiction referred to above is, of course, the motion picture. The cinema was popular in pre-1917 Russia, but it was only just becoming a mass medium; Russian screens had largely been filled with European productions until, in 1914, the coming of the war limited severely the making of movies in the warring countries as well as complicating their international distribution. Thus, while the war brought its problems and American films by no means held any firm position in the Russian market, there is still some interesting information as to their entry into that area.

Evidence for the American film in pre-1917 Russia is rather random in its nature, but one does find, for example, the Library of Congress' one available number of an early Soviet reference work, issued in six numbers, *Amerikanskie kino-aktery* [American film actors] (vyp. # 3: Mak-Avoi - Pringl' [Mac-Avoy-Pringle]. Leningrad, Academia, 1928. 84, (4) p.). This little guide includes such actors as "Kleo Medison" [Cleo Madison] who was first seen in Russia in 1915 "in the renowned movie play 'Troika chervei' [Three of hearts], which had a wild success among us. The lion's share of this success fell to Madison, who created in it an outstandingly brilliant character of a fearless American woman" (*Amerikanskie kino-aktery*, p. 23). In 1915 and 1916 Miss Madison also appeared in films that were given the Russian titles "Chernaia ruka" [Black hand], "Prikliucheniia ledi Rafl's" [Adventures of Lady Raffles], "Mnogozhenstvo" [Polygamy], "Barkhatnye kogti" [Velvet claws], "Orel pustyni" [Eagle of the desert], "V stepiakh Tekhasa" [In the plains of Texas], and "Krovavoe nasledstvo" [Bloody inheritance]. The entry ends on the tragic note that Madison worked only three years, before being killed in an accident while undertaking a movie stunt (*Amerikanskie kino-aktery*, p. 23). (In point of fact, Cleo Madison lived until about 1960, according to a biographic guide to film personages. She is of added interest as having been one of the early women film directors.)

And, for a much more famous actor, it is reported that in 1916 Russian theaters were showing Tom Mix in "D'iavol prerii" [Prairie devil], and "Spasena ot pozora" [Rescued from shame], with other films appearing in 1917. Showing in 1918, despite what must have been enormous difficulties in the supply of films, was "Naezdnik iz Peppl' Sadzh," which is surely the Russian version of *Riders of the Purple Sage* (*Amerikanskie kino-aktery*, p. 35).

While no date is given for any performance of the films of the early comic actor John Bunny, whom the Russians knew as "Pokson," his death in 1914 and references to twenty-three individual titles that had appeared in Russia almost certainly indicate pre-1917 showings (*Amerikanskie kino-aktery*, p. 77). When in addition to the information contained in this single issue of the guide, one notes that the entire six numbers were announced as containing more than five hundred biographies and lists of films by American actors, the names of which include both the stars of the 1920s and names connected with the earlier years of American productions, it is clear that one could find a substantial number of other films that had been viewed by Russians of the last years of the empire.

A somewhat more prosaic view of the American film in pre-1917 Russia is provided by a publication of the Bureau of Manufactures of the U.S. Department of Commerce and Labor, *Daily Consular and Trade Reports*, which offered selections from American consular officials in various parts of the world about local prospects for American trade.

At the beginning of 1911 the American consul general in Moscow reported that there were eighty or so movie theaters in Moscow and about the same number in St. Petersburg, with approximately twelve hundred in the empire as a whole, and in 1910 paid admissions reached 108 million. "On Sundays and holidays the crowds are so great that additional police officers are often required to keep the immense number of people moving and to prevent possible accidents. However, there were few American, English or German films shown, largely because there were no direct agents for these productions, while the French and Italians had branch offices that could supply large stocks. American films could find their way onto Russian screens most easily if there were American distribution offices in the country able to supply a broad range of pictures" (U.S. Department of Commerce. Bureau of Foreign and Domestic Trade. *Daily Consular and Trade Reports*, January 14, 1911: 161–63).

In consular reports in 1912 the situation for American

films seemed to be somewhat better, for the vice consul in Moscow reported, "Various films made in the United States are also used, and those that depict scenes of western or Indian life are held in high favor by the Russians" (*Daily Consular and Trade Reports,* January 13, 1912: 220). However, from Odessa, it was noted that most films shown in that region were from a French house with a local representative, although

many American films are shown and arouse considerable interest. . . . American comics are popular, but all climaxes should be made as plain as possible. There is no doubt that many films made in the United States would meet with good success if properly introduced, but as it is they are all sent though exchange agents in Europe and as a result France and Germany are better known than the United States.

It seems very probable that if scenes from the city and country life of various parts of the United States could be shown they would be popular. For instance, a series of pictures presenting the views that an immigrant would see on his way to the United States and after landing there would probably be well received (*Daily Consular . . . ,* January 13, 1912: 220–21).

Two years later, in the issue of the *Daily Consular and Trade Reports* for July 20, 1914, reflecting the situation as it was about the time that the Archduke Franz Ferdinand set out for Sarajevo, the American consul general in Moscow provided a short but very informative survey of the Russian network of cinema theaters and of distribution practices. He said that most films shown were of non-Russian origin, naming some of the producers, including Pathé, Nordisk, Deutscher Bioscop, Itala, Milano, and others. "A few years ago various American films were shown in Moscow, such as the Biograph, Lubin, Essenay, etc., and proved very popular, and it is thought that they would be much in demand if introduced again in this district." Details as to the duties on imported films, and on censorship regulations were given, and the report was accompanied by lists of theaters, manufacturers, agents, and publications that the Bureau of Foreign and Domestic Commerce held on file for the information of American firms that might be interested in finding Russian markets (*Daily Consular and Trade Reports,* July 20, 1914: 372–73).

In September of that year, the consul in Odessa wrote, "One of the most rapidly growing businesses in South Russia is that of conducting moving-picture shows. There is hardly a town of appreciable size that does not have its place of amusement of this kind, while each city has many in proportion to its population . . . Much interest is always evinced by audiences here in American plays, although they are comparatively seldom seen. American comic pictures are particularly appreciated. The principal makes of films, mostly used in this part of Russia, are the Nordisk, Gaumont, and Pathé." There were suggestions as to the means of supplying American films to Russia, including that of setting up a central distributing agency. Evidently this report was written just as the World War had begun, for it speaks of a time "when conditions in Europe again become normal" (*Daily Consular and Trade Reports*, Sept. 4, 1914: 1257–58).

All these reports indicate that before 1914 American movies were rather infrequently shown in Russia, although there was some audience for our comedies and for adventure films. The war, however, cut Russia off from German films completely and made it difficult to obtain those from France, a country that itself had to curtail productions. Not only was America able to continue the making of films, even increasing it, but one very enterprising French producer, Charles Pathé, whose films had the larger part of the Russian market, shifted much of his effort to American studios and turned out motion pictures in the United States that were distributed in Russia and elsewhere. As a very adroit way of maintaining a presence of his company in Russia, he had, early in the war, given a projector to the young heir to the throne, Aleksiei Nikolaevich, and supplied continuing reels of film for the boy. After Nicholas had assumed the (pro-forma) command of the Russian armies in the late summer of 1915, Aleksiei spent much of his time at Stavka, the imperial headquarters, where the film projector became a rather standard part of the after-dinner recreation. While, except for one picture, to be mentioned below, we have no information as to the actual titles of the films that Pathé's firm offered to this highly placed audience, we do know about those that the French entrepreneur produced in the United States and it can be assumed that the imperial father and son, the attendant generals, and a flock of foreign attachés can have seen a variety of American productions which, to judge by surviving still photographs, were distinguished by florid acting and over-decorated sets [Mitry, Jean. *Filmographie universelle*. Tome

IV: *Primitifs et précurseurs (1895–1915). Deuxième partie: États-Unis.* Paris, Institut des Hautes Études Cinématographiques. 1965. 222. Sadoul, Georges. *Histoire générale du cinéma. 3: Le cinéma devient un art, 1909–1920. Premier volume: l'avant guerre.* Paris, Denoël, 1951. 278; 4. *Le cinéma devient un art, 1909–1920 Deuxieme volume: La première guerre mondiale.* Paris, Denoël, 1951. 37].

While it cannot be said that the movie serial was an entirely American invention—a certain Victorin Jasset in France appears to have produced the first one of the kind, a film version, by the way, of Nick Carter—and while some of "Broncho Billy" Anderson's pictures of 1908 can be considered to be serials, they were not highly popular until 1914 when Charles Pathé, who had had producing interests in the United States since about 1911, collaborated, albeit with some strain, with William Randolph Hearst in making the picture that lives in everyone's mind when serials are mentioned, Pearl White's famous *Perils of Pauline.* The public reaction was so favorable that the Pathé firm quickly began another of the same type, the *Exploits of Elaine,* with Pearl White, Warner Oland, famed for his portrayal of Charley Chan in the 1930s, and Lionel Barrymore (Mitry. *Filmographie . . . ,* v. 4, pt. 2, p. 221–32).

The plot of this serial, as summarized in a Pathé catalog of 1920, was complicated beyond belief. In the first episode, "The Clutching Hand, an unknown person, has committed many murders and the police are baffled. Mr. Dodge, Elaine's father, receives the directions to the Clutching Hand's rendezvous from an old member of the band. That night the Clutching Hand murders Mr. Dodge and steals the envelope which he thinks contains the directions, but is outwitted owing to Mr. Dodge's clever act. Craig Kennedy, the wonderful scientific detective, being called in finds that the Clutching Hand is a past master at crime as is shown by his leaving his own (Kennedy's) finger prints as a clue to the murder." The other episodes are at least equally entangled, and, added to the puzzles of the film itself is the further problem posed by the serial having been titled *Les mystères de New-York* in Europe and often called *The Clutching Hand* in America.

Pathé used the circumstances of the war, and the resulting reduction of French film production, to distribute *The Exploits of Elaine* and other works throughout the parts of the world open to the Western allies, and he did not omit sending a print to the Tsarevich, apparently via Vladivostok. The film had a commercial success in the Russian theaters and it drew an expression of appreciation from Nicholas himself. On December 7, 1916 (probably O.S.) he wrote to Alexandra that, at last, he had found out who the villain was, the heroine's cousin and fiancé, a discovery that had caused a profound sensation among the viewers.

Nicholas was not alone in his excitement at having experienced such a thrill. The major Petrograd newspaper for the war years that is available in the Library of Congress is the conservative and not very lively *Novoe vremia*, which appears to have had ambitions to be a Russian equivalent of *The Times* of London. It did not review films and there were relatively few film advertisements, principally for several theaters along Nevskii prospekt, the city's main street, movie houses that one might compare to the first-run, downtown theaters of the heyday of the American scene. Often the advertisements did not make clear the origin of the pictures shown, and this presents problems of identification. In spite of this one can note that on September 28/October 11, 1916 the Khudozhestvennyi theater at 102 Nevskii prospekt was showing *Chernyi iashchik* [American original: The Black Box, released in March 1915 and including among the actors the famed Lon Chaney]. On October 26/November 8, the same theater included *Chaplin v parkie* [*In the Park,* a Chaplin one-reeler] on its program. Within a few days the Khudozhestvennyi was beginning a "grandiose cine-drama in 11 installments, from the well-known American novel" *Tainstvennaia ruka* [literally "The mysterious hand," which does not, however, appear to be *The Exploits of Elaine* for the number of installments and their titles do not match.]. In succeeding advertisements there were references to further installments such as "In a struggle with the band of the black masks," "The secret of the coffer," "A struggle on water and in the air," and in an announcement in the issue of December 18/31, "The secret is revealed."

The other houses advertising in *Novoe vremia* did not include so much American material although, for example, the *Dzhek Forb – korol' syshchikov* [Jack Forb (sic) – king of the detec-

tives] at the Union, Nevskii prospekt 88, on October 3/16 may
have been American, and three films at Pikadilli, Nevskii prospekt 60, certainly were American ones—*Kupan'e; veselaia amerikanskaia komediia* ["At the beach; a merry American comedy,"
perhaps a Mack Sennett film. October 22/November 4], *Na chto
sposoben vliublennyi; veselaia amerikanskaia kartina* ["What a fellow
in love can do; a merry American film." November 2/15], and
Ne pristavai k moei zhenie; veselyi amerikanskii fars ["Don't hang
around my wife; a merry American farce" November 6/19].

Insofar as these advertisements for the theaters on Nevskii
prospekt indicate, however, most of the films shown in Petrograd at that time were of Italian origin and, given the fact that
several houses announced simultaneous showings of the same
film, it seems that selections were rather limited. As to the programs in the cinemas in other parts of the city, there is no solid
information, but one can assume that, after playing along Nevskii prospekt, the prints were distributed to the houses outside
the center of town and that there too viewers saw some of these
American productions. At any rate, well before the advent of
the Bolsheviks the Russian movie public had been introduced
to the American film and had acquired a taste that was to endure until the time in the late 1920s and early 1930s when Stalin's policies, in culture as well as in economics, cut the country
off from such links with the outside.

As but one instance of the impact of the American film on
the early Soviet period, it was in the summer of 1926 that
"America's sweethearts," Douglas Fairbanks and Mary Pickford,
visited Moscow, to find at least five of their films playing there
that week, including *Znak Zorro* [*The Mark of Zorro*], and to receive a reception that was, according to the *New York Times*,
larger than had been given to any foreigner since the Revolution. And it will be remembered that this was a year after the
appearance of *Bronenosets Potemkin* [*Battleship Potemkin*].

CHAPTER FOUR

Imperial Russia and American Agriculture

The Russia that entered the First World War was overwhelmingly rural. About 80 percent of her population lived in the villages scattered over the countryside, and a large proportion of the city inhabitants were but newcomers to urban areas, often retaining the legal status of peasants as well as close family ties that kept them from being fully urbanized. The size and quality of each harvest was crucial to the national well-being, not only in the internal situation of the country, but also in the empire's international relationships, for agricultural products formed the bulk of exports, with grain shipments consistently accounting for about half of the foreign trade each year, save in times of severe crop failures.

It was because of such exports that during the five decades or so before the First World War Russia usually maintained a favorable balance of trade, thus meeting her international obligations and, what is more important, finding the resources upon which to base her pretensions as a great power. Although Russian industry in the period 1910–1914 had reached such a level that the country was the world's fifth industrial power—the ranking was the United States, Germany, Britain, France, and then Russia—it was the agricultural production of the country, and its sale abroad, that kept Russian bonds attractive to foreign investors and that allowed the maintenance of an army, and increasingly of a fleet, to lend force to Russia's foreign policy. An article that appeared in *The Times [London] Russian Supplement,* December 15, 1911 (p. 32) on the grain trade of Russia begins,

'His Excellency the Harvest' was rightly described by M. Kokovtsov [minister of finance] as the highest authority in Russian finance, for the corn [grain] crop is undoubtedly the determinant factor in the country's balance of trade, in its economic development, and its social and political activities. In a country where only 13 per cent of the people are town dwellers, the good and bad fortunes of agriculture evidently outweigh all other considerations and determine, for the time being, the destinies of the nation.

And this was written in a period when Russia was experiencing a very substantial growth of industry.

However, the returns that came to Russia because of her agricultural exports rested upon the varying situation of the markets to which she sold her goods. And that situation depended upon the way in which those markets might be affected by the presence of other sources of supply. During the five decades from 1865 to 1917 the most constant of those other sources was the United States, a fact of which Russian economists were always aware and about which there is an overwhelming literature. At each harvest season the prognoses of prices and of the likely purchases by Russia's foreign customers were seen to be deeply influenced by what America might also bring to market. The Russian financial press paid a great deal of attention to such factors as good rains in the Dakotas, changes in U.S. rail freight rates, and new American machinery for grain handling, while agronomists spoke of cultivation methods, improved harvesting equipment, and the like, all of which might somehow affect Russia's trade position.

This absolute centrality of agriculture to the Russian Empire, especially of the foreign trade in grain, and the almost constant factor of competition from the United States created a situation in which Russia needed to keep America continually in her sphere of attention (there were, of course, fluctuations over this period and there were during the time other contributors to the market, such as Canada, Australia, the Argentine, and, somewhat surprisingly, India). Although there are many extensive evidences of this in the written record of the time, there appears to have been no substantive discussion of the subject either in Russian or in English since 1917, and, thus, while this chapter can only be a preliminary sketch, this factor is worthy of analysis.

Well before our Civil War, Russians realized that the United States too was an agrarian country with a potential for producing grain on a large scale. However they were not greatly worried that America would be able to dislodge them from the predominance that they then had in the British market, for Britain was in that era the major nation that imported a great amount of grain. Although before 1846 the English Corn Laws set a sliding scale of duties on grain imports, duties that fell as prices rose—a measure to protect the British landlord's profits—merchants in Liverpool and elsewhere usually made substantial foreign purchases, mostly from Russia. America's role in this market was rather limited and Russian expectations were that it would remain limited. In the first year's issue of the significant Russian journal *Biblioteka dlia chteniia* (1834, no. 5, pt.1, "Nauki i khudozhestva:" 35–64) the editors printed a summary of articles from the *Edinburgh Review*, the *Quarterly Review*, and the *Revue Britannique* on the subject of a movement in England to reduce or abolish the duties set by the Corn Laws.

It should be said by way of explanation that it was to the advantage of the British landowner to use the Corn Laws to reduce foreign competition as a means of protecting his profits, but that, with the growth of industry in Britain, it was beneficial to factory owners to keep food prices down in order to avoid having to pay high wages. As the predominant role in politics gradually shifted out of the hands of the landowners, pressure toward free trade in agricultural products became even greater.

The Russian editor noted in his introduction, "There is perhaps no single question of political economy that is more essential and important for Russia, more closely connected with the domestic situation and the well-being of its inhabitants, and less understood by them, than the grain trade. We all feel that it has declined, and that we suffer in pocket and in spirit because of it, but, why did it fall, what are its secrets, what are its mechanisms, and is there a possibility of putting it back on its feet?" (*Biblioteka dlia chteniia*, 1834, no. 5: 35).

If the circumstances in England should change, "our trade in grain would inevitably show a quick and brilliant development, and would draw upon itself all forms of advantages to the state" . . . (ibid., 37).

"There is no doubt that the export of our grain, given the rising commercial activity of Russia, can still maintain superiority over the competition of all other nations. Our northern wheat yields only to that from Danzig in quality. Odessa holds the third place. Hamburg and America, the fourth. Egypt, the fifth and last" (ibid., 40). It is true that there were problems, such as the closure of Russian harbors for a whole six months in winter while Danzig could remain active all winter, and such as the absence of warehouses that could maintain a steady stream of grain to foreign buyers.

Following this introduction the article summarizes British and French surveys of the British import trade in grain. As these sources indicated, America was by no means in a condition to supply British markets more cheaply than Danzig or Odessa. While shipments from Odessa had to face some navigational problems not found in the North Atlantic, they could be delivered, this analysis says, at a lower price than could American grain. As proof of this, it is stated that during the ten years, 1821–31, the average price of American grain had been $1.15 per bushel (four shillings, four pence), with a resulting delivered price in Britain of 50 shillings per quarter (eight bushels, the usual measure in the British grain trade), a price that could easily be met by the Russians (ibid., 57).

Thus, in the early 1830s the Russians seem to have had no fear of American competition, although they were aware that this country was a possible factor in the market, and for some thirty years thereafter, except during such crises as famine in Russia or the Crimean War, Russia remained the major supplier to Britain and, in some degree, to other grain-deficit countries. The repeal of the British Corn Laws in 1846 opened that country to all suppliers, but Russia usually held predominance among them.

Gradually, however, the development of the American rail net, the adoption of such implements as the reaper, and the advance of settlement into the American prairies, which seemed to have been created for grain growing, stimulated production far exceeding the United States' domestic needs, and greater surpluses became available for foreign shipment. Before 1840 U.S. annual exports of wheat were usually less than ½ million bushels or $500,000 in value. In 1854, most likely as a result of interruptions in Russian sales because of the Crimean War, they rose to 8 million bushels, and $12 million. There was an unexpected peak of 15 million bushels, $22 million, in 1857, and a rather surprising level of exports in 1861 to 1864, in the very midst of the Civil War, with volume in those years never falling below 24 million bushels, and $31 million.[3] In both 1866 and 1867 there was a decline, the total in each year being six million bushels and eight million dollars. But, in 1868, sixteen million bushels, valued at thirty million dollars, and in 1869, eighteen million bushels, valued at twenty-four million dollars, left the United States.

The Russians were quick to note this rise. The agricultural specialist Vladimir Ivanovich Veshniakov (1830–1906), who served for many years in the Ministry of State Property, the agency responsible for agricultural administration for much of the nineteenth century, published an article in 1869 entitled "Departament zemledieliia v Soedinennykh Shtatakh" [The Department of Agriculture in the United States] in Katkov's *Russkii viestnik* (1869, no. 1: 252–64). A great part of this article is taken up with a survey of American efforts to foster agricultural science, culminating in the establishment of the Department of Agriculture in 1862. The last two pages, however, deal with changes in the patterns of American grain exports as a factor with which Russians should be concerned. Although he refers to the situation in 1866 and 1867, when the Americans were allegedly so short of flour that it was imported from France and that corn (maize) was bought in Liverpool, Veshniakov says that the future was likely to be different.

In general, according to the remark made by the Commissioner of Agriculture [head of the U.S. Department of Agriculture until 1889, when the position was given cabinet rank] in one of his reports to Congress, American wheat is little in demand in England, its chief customer, when the harvest in Europe is satisfactory and the Black Sea ports are crammed with grain. Only in the case of a significant crop failure in Europe, and given an insufficient supply in the Black Sea ports, does the agricultural administration foresee the possibility of American grain competing with Russian in the European

---

[3] These exports drew Russian attention and expressions of concern. See: Timothy C. Smith, U.S. Consul at Odessa, to Secretary of State Seward, no. 8, October 11, 1862, National Archives.

markets. Upon completion in Russia of a southern network of railroads, which will shift the principal regions of our grain production to our southern ports, the conditions of competition of Russian wheat with American in European markets will become infinitely more favorable for us than at present. Currently the cost of the usual overland transport by our producers of grain to the southern ports greatly exceeds the cost of transport of wheat by its American producers, even from the Far West to American ports on the Atlantic Ocean, because they have already long made use of the beneficial effects of a wide network of railroads, something which only now we are beginning to extend over our fatherland. A final assessment of all the changes of our future competition with the North American Union in the area of grain trade will be possible only when the economic transformation in the economy of the southern states of the Union is completed, to which reference has been made in the report of the Washington Department of Agriculture for 1866, and when our own economy has entered upon a firmer course of development, with the opening of more rapid, more reliable, cheaper, and continuing channels of marketing than at present (*Russkii viestnik*, 1869, no. 1: 264).

There had been references in the Russian press to the subject of the grain trade before that of Veshniakov, but, since only bibliographic citations are available to sources not presently held in American libraries, the exact nature of these items cannot thus far be ascertained. However, some of the titles may be mentioned. In 1868 a Russian trade and industry gazette published a three-part article on the role of the western states of America in the world grain market (*Sodieistvie russkoi torgovlie i promyshlennosti*, 1868, nos. 9, 10, 11). And the powerful conservative newspaper *Moskovskiia viedomosti*, edited by M. N. Katkov, who also published *Russkii viestnik*, included an article titled "America—a Dangerous Competitor in the Grain Trade" in its number 240 of 1869. From that time until 1914 titles of this nature were never totally absent from the Russian press, both general and specialized.

The Belgian-born economist Gustave de Molinari (1819–1912) was a prominent contributor to the French press in the mid-nineteenth century, holding for a number of years in the early 1870s the post of editor of the *Journal des débats*, one of the principal newspapers of Paris, and he had traveled in both the United States and in Russia. Almost doctrinaire in his support for free trade, he contributed a number of articles on economic matters to Katkov's *Russkii viestnik*, and in number 5 of 1870 he included, in his "Ekonomicheskaia korrespondentsiia" (*Russkii viestnik*, 1870, no. 5: 61–103) some references to America's increasing production of grain that he felt would be of interest to his Russian readers, and that would at the same time show the baseless nature of protectionist strivings in agriculture.

The French economist, landowner, and student of the philosophy of Descartes, Comte Louis Alexandre Fouché de Careil (1826–1891) had, so de Molinari writes, spent several months in the United States and had come back both impressed and somewhat alarmed by what he had seen there. If the productive forces of agriculture in what is now for us the old states of Indiana, Michigan, Ohio, and Illinois were great, the potentialities of Minnesota, Nebraska, and Kansas, which the count had also visited, were overwhelming, so much so that he feared the effects on French agriculture. A mere increase in tariffs, which de Molinari says the count felt to be needed, would not recoup the situation, but it would be necessary for cultivators to turn to more progressive means (*Russkii viestnik*, no. 5: 67–69). While de Molinari was not so disturbed, he thought that it should not be forgotten that with America's growing population there would also be an increase in internal consumption that would lessen exports, with a consequent tendency to maintain European prices. Competition might tend to diminish rental payments but would not lead to the ruin of agriculture itself. As with all competition, it would be a stimulus, impelling cultivators to improve their implements and methods.

But, given the extraordinary development of that competition, and the developments still to ensue, should it not be closely monitored by such countries as Russia, for example, which are competing with the United States in supplying the markets of the West? M. Thiers [Adolphe Thiers, politician and historian, first president of the Third Republic] has recently attempted to scare us with 'Crimean wheat.' I do not want to imitate him by brandishing American wheat before you as some sort of scarecrow. But if you study your tables you will see that your export has by no means expanded as rapidly as that of America, and that you have dropped from first to second place, and perhaps even to third. Does that not give you cause to think? Meanwhile your arable lands extend over broad areas, and in quality they by no means rank behind the lands of the Far West, and you *can* have machinery [English word used], capital, and labor such as the Americans have; your position with regard to labor is even more favorable. You can, if you *wish*, recapture for yourself the first place that is slipping away from you" (*Russkii viestnik*, 1870, no. 5: 70).

One of the measures that de Molinari suggests to the Russians is the removal of Russia's barriers against French products, at least to the point of creating more favorable conditions for France's trade with Russia than the Morrill Tariff in the United States had established for the French. There would be, according to de Molinari, an increase in Russia's internal market for domestic manufactures, thereby reducing the strength of Russian protectionist arguments (*Russkii viestnik*, 1870, no. 5: 70–71).

In 1873 when Nikolai Slavinskii published his account of his brother-in-law William Frey's attempts to set up communes in Missouri and Kansas, he included, almost as a passing notice, what is the earliest Russian mention thus far found of an institution to which subsequent writers gave a great deal of attention as being a major contributor to America's advantages in the grain trade. This was the grain elevator, to which Slavinskii refers in telling of his visit to Chicago en route to Frey's Utopia.

The growth of the city began with the grain trade. The first vessel that reached Chicago in 1838 carried seventy-eight bushels of wheat, and in more recent times millions have already been added to that figure. In 1870, up to seventy million bushels of grain reached Chicago; to transfer this grain onto ships or into granaries, twenty lifting machines or elevators have been installed and are in operation at dockside at the large grain warehouses. Elevators consist of a steam engine, of from 100 to 200 horsepower, which drives enormous belts with buckets; there are from four to eight of these at each warehouse. Carloads of grain move along the rails to the grain storehouses and the grain, scooped up in the buckets of the elevator, is conveyed to a height of more than a hundred feet, from which it falls in a broad stream directly into the holds of ships at the dock. The unloading of the ship is carried out in the same manner, i.e., the grain is lifted from the ship by the buckets and is poured into cars which, once filled, move along making room for others. The continuous and rapid loading and unloading of grain into the cars and ships presents an amazing picture. The result of the work of these elevators is as follows: each one is capable, within a ten-hour span, of moving from car to ship or vice-versa more than twenty thousand chetvert' [a measure equal to thirty-six bushels] of grain. To carry out this entire operation, from twenty to forty men are needed at each elevator, depending on its size. The elevator warehouses are so large that they take in grain for storage for a fee of four kopecks per bushel for the first ten days and one kopeck per bushel thereafter. The owners of the grain placed in storage are given receipts which are speculated on in the market on days of good prices for that product (Slavinskii, op. cit., 253–58).

It is rather difficult to sort out the chronology of Slavin-skii's book, but it would appear that his visit to Frey took place in late 1870, so that he undoubtedly learned the word *elevator* at that time, and his use of it is, if not the first, at least one of the earliest ones in the Russian literature.

In May of 1872 the Russian government set up a Commission for the Investigation of the Present Position of Agriculture and of Agricultural Production in Russia, which met in fifty-three sessions to the end of April 1873, submitting a report issued that year. The commission realized that the volume of American production was rapidly growing, having risen from 140 million chetvert' in 1850 to 240 million in 1869. While Russia in that latter year produced more grain than the U.S. (290 million chetvert'), its total volume had increased by only 16 percent in the preceding thirty years. Furthermore, the United States was the leading nation in production per capita—6.2 chetvert' per person, compared with 4.5 for Russia. Although the commission's report did not draw any conclusions about the possible effects that these figures might have on the total amount that would be available for export in the two countries, the relative positions of the United States and of Russia could easily be deduced (Russia. Komissiia dlia izsliedovaniia nynieishniago polozheniia sel'skago khoziaistva i sel'skoi proizvoditel'nosti v Rossii. *Doklad.* . . . St. Petersburg, Tipografiia Tovarishchestva "Obshchestvennaia pol'za," 1873: 9–10).

In 1876 *Russkoe sel'skoe khoziaistvo* [Russian agriculture], the organ of the Imperial Moscow Agricultural Society, published in its issues nos. 9 and 10–11 an article by one N. I. Rimskii-Korsakov (not the composer, who was N. A.) "On the causes of the unsatisfactory state of agriculture in Russia" which is a good example of a voice from within an earnest and scientifically oriented group of landowners, and it can be taken as typical of the serious conclusions of the best of Russian agricultural thought. "There is no need to speak of how harmful is the influence on our economy of the constant dependence on how great or small may be the demand for our raw materials. Recently in our southern ports there have been complaints about the decline in the grain trade. The North American United States are pushing our grain off the English market. This is a further strong

impetus toward manufacturing industry. If there are no purchasers for our grain, then, evidently, we will have to turn our
idle hands and capital to processing our own raw materials ourselves, in place of leaving that profitable business to our neighbors. But there is no doubt that at present the majority of our
factories can exist only in the absence of foreign competition.
Encouragement and strong protection are necessary for them"
(Rimskii-Korsakov, op. cit., no. 9: 92).

In 1878 the Russo-Polish railroad magnate and economist
Jan Gotlib Bloch published a large, five-volume study *Vliianie
zhelieznykh dorog na ekonomicheskoe sostoianie Rossii* [The influence
of railroads on the economic situation of Russia] (St. Petersburg, Tipografiia M. Stasiulevicha, 1878. 5 v.) and in volume
two he provides a survey of the Russian grain trade over the
whole period from 1804 to 1876. Bloch's tables show a rise in
American grain exports to Great Britain from some 1.4 million
chetvert' in 1858 to almost 12 million in 1874, noting that "The
export of grain from Russia to Great Britain in the last two
triennial periods has begun to decline as a result of the successful competition of the United States of North America. One
can appreciate the importance of this competition for the interests of Russian agriculture by surveying the constantly rising
quantity of deliveries of grain from America to Great Britain"
(Bloch, op. cit., v. 2, p. 52). Throughout the period from 1857
to 1872 the proportion of Russian grain imported by Britain
had never dropped below 39.29 percent, and that level was
reached only in the one year of 1861, and had in 1869 reached
the high level of 60.5 percent. In 1873, however, this fell off to
34.6 percent, and only in 1875 did it again reach 39 percent.
In 1872, American and Russian grain provided an almost equal
volume, but thereafter, the supplies from the United States predominated (Bloch, op. cit., v. 2: 45–52).

Of especial importance in this situation was the fact that
the United States was taking the lead in supplying wheat, the
most expensive of the grains, to Great Britain, thereby further
affecting Russia's market position. In the period after 1866 the
volume of wheat imported into Britain was, with some annual
variations, on the increase, while the Russian contribution did
not rise commensurably. Bloch notes, however, that the Russian

export statistics and the English import statistics can not altogether be satisfactorily reconciled (Bloch, op. cit., v. 2: 100–101).

While Bloch's statistics do not provide ruble figures for each grain separately, and while the monetary total for all Russian grain exports reached an annual average, in millions of rubles, of 144.8 in 1869–71, 171.3 in 1872–74, and 193.1 in 1875–76, it is clear that Russia's share of the British market was on the decline, especially in the higher valued wheat.

This situation, one that was clear to most of the Russian interests concerned with foreign trade and the country's whole balance of trade and balance of payments, was in the end responsible for the decision by the Ministry of Finance in 1878 to send to the United States one of Russia's specialists in the grain trade. This was Robert Vasil'evich Orbinskii who spent several months in the U.S. and who produced a very detailed study, published in 1880, *O khliebnoi torgovlie Soedinennykh Shtatov Sievernoi Ameriki* [Concerning the grain trade of the United States of North America] (St. Petersburg, Tip. Trenke i Fusno, 1880. 447 p.). Orbinskii (1834–1892) had taught at the Lycée Richelieu in Odessa, and continued as a professor when that institution was transformed into the Novorossiiskii university. Although his first training was in classical philology, he had become interested in economic subjects and had combined his duties at the university with the office of director of the Odessa Commercial School. It probably did not hinder his progress that he had been a schoolmate of the rising official in the ministry of finance, Ivan A. Vyshnegradskii, or that he had served as secretary of both the Odessa Committee of Trade and Manufactures and of the Exchange Committee.

In the introduction to his work Orbinskii says that, in spite of some gaps in his data, the information is fresh, and that it is "enough to give the reader the possibility of acquiring a sufficiently reliable view both of the grain production of the country, as well as of its export, or, in a word, of that which has brought the United States to the status of being our most dangerous competitor in the field of world trade." He goes on to ask "what do we need in order not to fail in the face of this competitor who is overwhelming us?" However, it is not his mission, Orbinskii writes, to provide an answer to that, for he leaves any resolution of the problem up to the reader (Orbin-skii, op. cit.: iii).

Orbinskii ends his short introduction by quoting from an article on the Russian grain trade that he had contributed to the *Missouri Republican* of St. Louis on August 2, 1879, attaching a footnote with the English text of the paragraph.

We are competitors then, America and Russia, but I never met a competitor so gentlemanlike and noble as your country. Every information I wanted was given to me with a courtesy I could never hope to find. There was nothing of the vile jealousy between rivalizing trade people, which we are accustomed to read in every history of commerce. And, indeed America has nothing to fear from her generous and frank proceedings. We have endless to learn from her; we will make, I hope, some progress in her way; but I think not that we will become her equal. All the advantages and will of man can give are on your side, and all I wish is that my country could follow your example for the benefit of mankind, asking for cheap bread (Orbinskii, op. cit.: v).

The body of the book is a detailed examination of the geographical distribution of American grain production, of its volume, of the land system, of the labor force, and of the major trade centers. Orbinskii has a good deal to say in praise of America, . . . "of all nationals of the world, the American is the one most marked by an ability to stand, so to speak, on his own feet, not needing outside help, and to get along without guidance and special favors. He is in the full sense of the word a 'selfmade' and 'selfmaking' man" (Orbinskii, op. cit.: 38. Words in single quotes in English in the original).

He gives careful attention to the organization of both governmental and private agencies for the fostering of agriculture, and he remarks upon the way in which a well-coordinated distribution system had made it possible for farmers even in remote areas to acquire machinery. He shows awareness of how the Patrons of Husbandry (Grangers) had brought farmers to join together to strive for better methods, both of cultivation and of doing business, as well as for political influence (Orbinskii, op. cit.: 39–73).

Much of the book is given over to a state-by-state review of the agricultural situation, and, in speaking of Kansas, he provides what is probably the first Russian reference to barbed wire, telling of fences made "from galvanized wire with points that make it quite impossible for cattle to get out of the area in which they are enclosed" (State-by-state survey, p. 78–140. Reference to barbed wire, p. 136). Each of the major grain-trading centers that Orbinskii visited is taken up separately, with, for example, thirty pages devoted to Chicago, including the rules of the local elevators, the facilities of the railroads serving the area, and the general type and volume of grain dealt with there. Forty pages cover the major ports handling the foreign grain trade, and an extensive final section deals with the American rail system. Orbinskii is by no means unaware of some of the sharp practices of grain dealers, financiers, and railroad managers, as he speaks of situations in which Indiana growers found it better to send grain to New York via Chicago, a 400-mile detour, because freight rates would be lower, and he knew that at times elevator owners might play games with grading standards, but he seems to have striven for a judicious approach and there are numerous signs of his having been impressed by the size and productivity of America and by the enterprise of the people (Orbinskii, passim).

The book drew a number of reviews in Russia, some of which, in fact, went on to take up the question that Orbinskii had left unanswered, that of what Russia might learn from America. One of the more extensive ones appeared over the signature "Evgenii Markov" in *Russkaia riech'* (1881, no. 3: 216–43). The author was Evgenii L'vovich Markov (1835–1903), a writer and traveler whose outlook shifted gradually toward the right during his lifetime. In the early 1860s he had worked with the liberal to radical *Otechestvennyia zapiski,* then with the liberal *Golos,* and then the moderately conservative *Russkaia riech',* at least according to the leading pre-1917 Russian encyclopedia. As a journal, *Russkaia riech'* did not last long and did not attract any great names, but examination of its content shows that it was not particularly rigid in its approach to topics, and it appears to have covered a wide range of subjects.

Markov's review is somewhat verbose, so that one must cope with a certain nebulosity as he defines his position, but he does make some quite interesting, and straightforward, statements about America. "America is more and more overtaking us as a producer of grain. America is an ever greater threat to us in the grain market of Europe." He notes that Australian wool and American grain had in fact penetrated certain parts of the Russian market, such as the Transcaucasus (Markov, op. cit., 225).

> America is dangerous for us in many ways as a competitor for our grain trade.
>
> Firstly, she definitely produces more grain than Russia does, however implausible this may seem to our frothy village patriots, who think that without Russian grain the whole world would starve.
>
> Secondly, America has a much larger surplus of grain relative to its own needs than Russia; i.e., it can sell more of it without going hungry itself.
>
> Our Russian land often sells to Europe not its surplus, but grain that it needs itself" (Markov, op. cit. 227).

As an explanation of how this had come about, Markov writes, "The Americans are a highly practical nation and not at all doctrinaire and followers of a system. . . . As business-oriented people, and only business, they are completely free of the usual weakness of our educated class that considers itself obliged to believe in one theory or another, whether it be economic, social, or political, and to turn that theory into some sort of unchangeable symbol of faith in liberalism or progress, or, on the other hand, of conservatism and nationalism." The Americans are by no means afraid of the future and they feel that their ingenuity will always allow them to meet the needs of the time. "She [America] believes in herself". . . (Markov, op. cit.: 230–31).

Markov's details about American land laws and rail policies, drawn from Orbinskii's study, do not need repeating, for they are commonplaces of American historical writing, but it is interesting to note his use of expressions such as "wise view," "democracy of property," "America did this in a more practical manner," "rational system," "an American policy as patriotic and moral as it is advantageous for the finances of the state and for national well-being," all in contrast to Russia's having used, "as if it were dead capital," its fertile spaces "under the immobile and ruinous management of the state." It was no wonder that, within just five or six years, America had pushed Russia to the ground and completely thrown her out of the European market (Markov, op. cit.: 232–37).

That Russia was completely out of the European market is, of course, not true. Good quality Russian grain was the equal of any other in the world and could find buyers. Furthermore, the international network of the cable and telegraph system and of the traders in grain, made it possible for buyers in London to shift between purchases in Odessa and purchases in New York, depending on the prices in those markets. Even as small a variation as three cents a bushel would make a difference just one cent shy of $1,000 in a shipment as modest as a thousand tons. And it should be remembered that $1,000 (200 pounds sterling) in those days was quite a decent annual income for many skilled occupations, not to mention being beyond the dreams of most American farmers, even those owning their own land.

Markov, however, feared for Russia's future in the international grain trade, and for the continued well-being of the country. He felt that:

> All our official evaluations, worries, and researches concerning the decline of our economy and the burdens of our peasants' existence should strike any unprejudiced observer as needless hypocrisy or insulting condescension until there has been openly established and firmly implemented the only just and only fruitful principle of our land policy: the land of the state belongs to the people and should be entirely made available to it for settlement and for utilization, for supplying the nation, and for the enrichment of the state.
>
> The parasites clustering around the ministries in St. Petersburg and the lands in Ufa [an area to the East of the Volga then being settled, but with land distribution showing favoritism to officials eager for grants] do not make up the people any more than the drones make up the bee hive.
>
> It is not they who make the nation wealthy, it is not through them that the people secure their industry, trade, and well-being in an incessant struggle with the active and informed forces of other nations of the world (Markov, op. cit., 237).

By contrast, Markov saw the United States as being "a country of bold, boundlessly self-confident freedom of private enterprise. This absolute freedom of private initiative troubles and frightens the unaccustomed observer of American life." Although this freedom may indeed cause difficulties, it carries within itself its own remedy, as there is no barrier against some new force arising to deal with problems. If the railroads ask too much in freight charges, there are canals and rivers, and men can unite either as producers or consumers to win better terms through joint action. The Granger movement of the 1870s was but one example of such a possibility of bringing about lower freight rates or lower prices for farm machinery. The picture that this gives of American life is as frightening to the ordinary Russian as the sight of a steam engine would be to the simple herdsman of the steppes who had become accustomed to the slow pace of his oxen (Markov, op. cit.: 240–42).

America is exactly like this. Our overly cautious turn of mind and too passive wariness have long prophesied for her God knows what sort of catastrophes and dissolution because of an irrational application of the principle of freedom. But during this time she [America] has been flourishing and flourishing, has been growing in wisdom, and becoming richer, and along with that has been pushing us out of the area of general competition and mutual profit.

If American liberty has unleashed across the board the instincts of covetousness and unconscionable exploitation, this same freedom has filled every remote corner of America with agricultural schools, museums, warehouses full of machinery, public lectures, newspapers and magazines, all devoted to the interests of the economy, and with a myriad of active agricultural societies and groups (Markov, op. cit., 242).

It would be the best policy, Markov indicated, if a similar freedom could be attained in Russia.

Without any vice-governors and officials on special assignment the Russian people will comprehend its own agricultural needs, which have long been well known to it, and will be able to explain things to anyone who needs it, and to work accordingly toward their satisfaction. Of course, the Russian, even under new conditions, may be far from able to surpass America. The American is a mighty beast in struggle and in work. It is hard to compete with him not only for our brothers, the out-of-touch Russians, but also for the Western European who was trained much earlier in habits of free initiative and bold thought. . . . We do not know, of course, what role our people ought to play in the international grain trade market under normal conditions of our grain growing. But it is enough for us to realize that the present conditions are not normal, and are too unfavorable and too dangerous for us. The Russian people must, not for the first time and not just in this single field, learn from their competitors.

The Tatars once taught the Russians how to overcome the Tatars, and the Swedes showed Peter how to beat the Swedes. . . .

Why should we limit this characteristic ability of ours only to the single field of war?

In order that our Russia might reach the outstanding levels of American grain production, let us borrow from them in some degree their wise internal policy, which is so simple and so beneficial. Then we can justify the clever statement of the statesman: give me a good policy and I will give you good finances (Markov, op. cit., 244).

Who read this article? What effect did it have? No one can really say, for there were no public opinion polls and no reader surveys. Yet, this was a voice that was part of the give and take of expression in Russia in 1881. Markov was not without a certain standing in the framework of journalism of the time, and the subject was likely to attract attention. Somehow, then, in the Russian press of 1881, the United States had a place not only as a competitor but also as a model to be followed. Markov's article can well be summed up in a phrase that became a cliché in the Soviet Union almost five decades later, during the First Five Year Plan in 1928–32: DOGNAT' I PEREGNAT" AMERIKU! [Overtake and surpass America!].

Another review of Orbinskii's book appeared in the liberal journal *Otechestvennyia zapiski* under the heading "Popytki konkurirovat' s Amerikoi i polozhenie nashei khliebnoi proizvoditel'nosti" [Efforts to compete with America and the position of our production of grain] (no. 6, 1881, "Sovremennoe obozrienie:" 239–66), which contains a forecast that, while it required a century for its eventual fulfillment, is startling, nonetheless:

There is reason to believe that we will not be able to sell [the crops] and that, under present conditions of production, if those are allowed to continue, our role as the granary supplying foreign states is on the decline, if it has not ended altogether. Not only will we not sell, but we ourselves will buy, and for our purchases we will turn to that very America, this not because America overwhelms us with her natural advantages, as it seems to many, but solely because we are not in a condition to compete with her in *production*. However much, in general, our budget relies on income from the export trade, a decrease in the volume of exports, if it were to take place, would not cause us any harm and would not place our national and governmental economy in jeopardy, provided this occurs as a result of changes in the direction of our economic activity . . . Basing our attitude on such a point of view, we definitely see no substance to those conclusions that measure our riches by the size of the grain export and by the sight of digits followed by a long series of zeroes, figures which show our export and glorify our strength in grain. We affirm that this strength does not exist, and, more than that, that it cannot exist, that a digit with a long row of zeroes reveals nothing at all, and if it does prove anything, it—combined with other facts, ones that only a person shrouded in darkness cannot see—merely shows that we are so poor that to meet our daily needs we sell everything with nothing left over. We are forced to do this, disregarding the need to meet the most essential wants of the people (*Otechestvennyia zapiski*, 1881, no. 6, "Sovremennoe obozrienie:" 245).

The author of this review goes on to say, "Our trade is a sign of our poverty, since we sell not the *surplus* of our production, but the *means of our nourishment*. We are slaves to the market, forced to carry to it everything fit for sale, and this is why our export is large. We sell without even taking account of whether this brings profit or loss" (ibid., 246). Drawing on the analyses of the American role in wheat production and export, the reviewer says, "we cannot escape the conclusion that *our wheat is about 2½ times as expensive as that of America*" (ibid., 254).

He continues in a long sentence that, although it has almost Faulknerian complexity, is worth translating in full:

If we then weigh the circumstance that the American economy is moving forward in rapid strides, that it is based on knowledge and on the application of all that knowledge brings, that the American does not glorify routine and does not protect ignorance, that American agricultural societies serve the interests of practicality in the most vigorous fashion, and that they do not rest on laurels that at some time or other were acquired for them by erstwhile active members; if we understand that in America those engaged in agriculture are busy with it and not with completely idle talk, that in America there are no Derunovs or Sladkopevtsevs [characters whose names conjure up the qualities of rapaciousness and of empty words of praise], and that there they do not pay 20 rubles rent for a desiatine [2.7 acres] for a single harvest year and that for people who need land they don't think up any 'easy and accessible credits,' but give them cheap railroad tickets for passage to land that lies fallow; that there isn't any Ufa guberniia there with retired and non-retired civil-servant landowners, that there isn't any red tape and confusion infesting the area of public activity and no slices of the public pie to be eaten by failed landowners—then we must admit that America has not rested on the results she has attained, she had not rested even at that very same stage at which we have yet to begin. 'Well begun is half done,' and although we too boast that we know many truths that are 'old ones' for us, there is still nothing concrete that we can show for that knowledge, and God knows how we will get started. America, however, has achieved half of these things and, working on the other half, she is becoming such a force relative to us that our competition with her looks more like that of a hunting dog with a rabbit. American wheat costs 4 rubles 38 kopecks [unit not indicated, most likely per chetvert'] and ours 10 rubles, and we, knowing an 'old truth,' will prefer to eat new American wheat.

Even so, this might be more advantageous for Russia, as it may truly be the case that American wheat is cheaper than Russian (ibid., 254–55).

The reviewer saw no possibility that Russia might ever win out over America as long as Russia maintained the methods and organization of the time. Devotion to routine and inert expectations of governmental subsidies would certainly not do it.

Emergency aid in time of famine is only a stopgap in a country where agriculture is the basis for national life, and what was really needed was a constant and alert program that would really help the basic producer, the peasant. The peasant did not need the grudging allotment of food and seed grain in time of shortage, but a constant provision of knowledge upon which he could make real progress. But to do this effectively would require a thorough reorganization of the institutions that claimed to be furthering agriculture and spreading knowledge, and reorganization also of the tax system, of the requirement that all peasants have passports in order to leave their native villages, and of the means of providing credit to the peasant (ibid., 261–64).

This article appeared in *Otechestvennyia zapiski* in the June issue of 1881, only three months after the assassination of Alexander II by revolutionaries. The new tsar, Alexander III, disliked the idea that private persons might use the press to criticize, make suggestions, or to complain, and publication of this review required a certain amount of what the French call "courage civique," the boldness to speak up against officialdom, especially since *Otechestvennyia zapiski* had already attracted the disfavor of the authorities. Its editor was Mikhail Evgrafovich Saltykov (1826–89), a journalist of radical tendencies and the author, under the pseudonym "Shchedrin," of many telling satires about the muddle, corruption, and inefficiency of Russian life, especially among the civil servants and petty bourgeoisie. It is, therefore, not surprising to find that a Soviet guide to the anonymous and pseudonymous articles in the journal during the years that Saltykov was associated with it (1868–84) shows him to have been one of the authors of this review. In view of Soviet emphasis on Saltykov-Shchedrin as an exponent of radical criticism not only of Russia but also of the West of his time, it is of interest that he made substantial use of the American example in writing this review, and, given American sales of grain to the Soviet Union in recent years, that even in 1881 he foresaw a possibility that Russia might at some time need to draw upon America's agricultural resources.

Orbinskii's book and the reviews that it occasioned were but a part of a great flow of publication on the topic of Russia's position as a competitor of the United States for the international grain market. Indeed, Orbinskii had apparently been aware of the situation for several years, participating in discussions of the problem even before his visit to America. The United States consul-general in St. Petersburg, in a report dated January 10, 1876, surveying the economic situation of Russia, provides a long survey of the situation of the Russian grain trade, with a quotation from a "memorial from the Chamber of Commerce at Odessa in the fall of 1875," foreseeing that "America will soon absolutely command the English market and reduce the prices to a minimum, with which it will be utterly impossible for Russia to compete" (George Pomutz to Secretary of State, January 10, 1876. In: United States. Bureau of Foreign Commerce. *Report upon the Commercial Relations of the United States with Foreign Countries for the Year 1875.* Washington, Government Printing Office, 1876. p. 1214). And the following year, Leander E. Dyer, consul at Odessa, wrote, "This people regard the United States as a most dangerous competitor in the grain trade," citing in support of this conclusion a report from a committee of the Odessa board of trade that said of America, "'she has now our former position in the English market, and we must be satisfied with quite a secondary position. . . . We cannot therefore hope that a prosperous harvest may turn the scale in our favor and restore us to our former position, but we must believe that the United States will yet take a still higher position among the grain producers of the world. . . . It is impossible to calculate the amount of grain which America will be able to export, and which will render her so completely the controller of the London market that we shall be utterly unable to compete with her. The cheapness and fertility of her virgin soil, her favorable climate, the high class of her agriculture, the substitution of machinery for human labor, the spirit of enterprise and the aptitude of the Americans for organization, are so many proofs that our fears are well founded'" (Leander E. Dyer to Secretary of State, December 2, 1876. In: . . . *Commercial Relations of the United States with Foreign Countries, 1876.* Washington, Government Printing Office, 1877: 799).

Whatever the actual Russian title of the "Chamber of Commerce" or the "Board of Trade" of Odessa referred to in these two reports may have been, it is clear that what was meant was either the Birzhevoi komitet [Exchange committee] or the Odesskii komitet torgovli i manufaktur [Odessa committee of trade and manufactures], in both of which Orbinskii served as secretary. Orbinskii's work was not, therefore, the result of some narrow worry of his own, nor was it the outgrowth of a passing decision by the Ministry of Finance to undertake an investigation into a potential threat to Russia's economic position, but rather it expressed vital interests of a broad sector of the economy that was seeking to deal with a real problem with actual consequences, not only on a nationwide scale, but also for the international financial standing of the empire.

Orbinskii's influence was not limited merely to his book of 1880 and to his probable involvement in the statements of the Odessa commercial organizations. In 1883 he published in Katkov's *Russkii viestnik* "Ekonomicheskoe polozhenie Odessy v nastoiaschem i budushchem" [The economic situation of Odessa in the present and future] (*Russkii viestnik*, 1883, no. 6: 257–276), which, though not a long article, was quite informative in its data on the decline of Odessa's export trade, the basic element in which was grain, especially wheat. His conclusions were not optimistic ones, and he felt that to consider there to be much chance of Odessa's again becoming an equal competitor with the United States was a "false and baseless error." The Odessa grain trade, he writes, had become exploitative and extremely disorganized, and was in no state to face the overwhelming competition of the Americans. He did not think it necessary to go into great detail as to the means whereby Odessa could compensate for this position, feeling in fact that the city's role in the grain trade was perhaps lost, but he did refer to the desirability of efforts to encourage manufacturing. By doing so,

Odessa will follow the example of her younger and more fortunate rival, Chicago. Even there, year after year, factories and manufacturing industry are growing by giant steps and at an even more rapid rate than that of the shipment of grain.

But also for the grain trade of Odessa the present crisis it is undergoing is not the last word. In viewing the growth of our rival America, and falling into a state of horror at the dimensions of this growth, we should not forget the German proverb that God does not let trees grow up to the heavens. With their drive, with their merciless 'go ahead' [English in original], the Americans will soon suffer economic reverses, despite the abundance of resources that they have. It will not be long before the surpluses of their production are absorbed by their own population which is growing by colossal degrees. The system of production itself is an exploitative one, and with it the conditions of their export. Of course, the time for such change will not come quickly, and the present generation will hardly manage to see it come about. But sooner or later it will happen, and then our competition with them will find new opportunities, given, of course, that we ourselves do not yawn away that time, but make use of the American example and American experience, mastering what is good in their methods of agriculture and organizing on this model our own grain trade" (Orbinskii, in *Russkii viestnik*, 1883, no. 6: 276).

One of the pre-1917 Russian biographical sources states that, upon the appointment in 1887 as minister of finance of Orbinskii's former fellow student, the Odessa scholar Ivan Vyshnegradskii, Orbinskii often submitted memoranda on economic matters. Although these documents do not appear to be available in printed form, it is undoubtedly safe to assume, particularly in the light of this article and of his book of 1880, that Orbinskii must have had additional occasions to mention the United States, its role as a competitor of the Russians, and the possible usefulness of some of the features of its system of cultivating, transporting, and selling grain as a model for Russia.

There is much further relevant material to be found in the Russian press of the time. The 1880s saw all kinds of publications, from passing remarks in the newspapers to very substantial volumes of both economic and technical material, that sought to report on Russia's standing in the international grain trade compared with that of the United States and that sought to derive some program that would allow Russia, if not to drive America completely out of the market at least to restrain her from gaining further advantage. It is outside the scope of this survey to mention all of them, but reference to a few items may help show the nature of Russian concern with the topic.

One of the most detailed Russian examinations of the situation of American agriculture in comparison with that of Russia is the work of Ivan Fedorovich Kenig, who was the managing director of the Nikolaevskaia railroad, the empire's major route, running between Moscow and St. Petersburg and serving, as Kenig noted, as the "link connecting Petersburg and Reval [now Tallinn in Estonia] with the network of present and future railroads of the Eastern and Southeastern regions. The success of the operation of these lines now greatly depends, and will continue to do so, on the various facilities which remain to be installed or completed in Petersburg so that our grain trade may be granted conditions that might approach the conditions and advantages held by trade in the United States of America" (Ivan Fedorovich Kenig, *Statisticheskiia dannyia o zemledielii i torgovlie produktami sel'skago khoziaistva v Sievero-Amerikanskikh Soedinennykh Shtatakh i v Rossii* [Statistical data about agriculture and trade in agricultural products in the North American United States and in Russia]. St. Petersburg, Tipografiia V. Kirshbauma, 1880: i–ii). This volume is clearly an official document; not only did Kenig have a major position in the Russian rail net, but also the printing house of the Kirshbaum firm is identified on the title page as being located in the building of the Ministry of Finance on the Dvortsovaia ploshchad' (Palace Square), a building just across the square from the Winter Palace.

Kenig notes that in 1875 Russia exported 22,440,000 chetvert' of grain and the United States, 17,972,000 but in 1879, the figures were 39,729,000 for Russia and about 48,000,000 for the Americans.

The recent increase in the export of wheat from America, capable, it seems, of reaching an even greater extent, has caused varying fears in Europe. English farmers see that, although the harvest per desiatin [2.7 acres] in England is greater than that in America, the cost of tilling, rent payments, and other expenses are so high that competition with America is impossible for them, and they are striving in every way to reduce the sowing of wheat and to increase pasture land and cattle breeding . . .

We have on many sides the worry lest the successes reached in American agriculture be harmful for our export grain trade, which does not have the many conveniences and advantages that exist in the United States of North America (Kenig, op. cit., i).

In his introduction Kenig lists the proposed contents of his work, including a translation of the report for 1879 of the U.S. Department of Agriculture about cultivated land and harvest and about trade in agricultural products, a comparison with the Russian figures, information on the rail and water routes and freight costs in America and Russia, the quantity of grain imported by various European states and the future prospects of this trade, and about "those measures which must of necessity be adopted by us in order that our grain trade is provided the improved grain warehouses and port installations of which it is now deprived. This last defect, wastefully increasing the various charges of loading grain aboard ship, often interferes with the setting of sales prices that might compete with those abroad" (Kenig, op. cit., ii).

One of the elements in the American system of producing grain that the Russians saw as being almost a determinant of our advantages was the grain elevator. As an earlier reference has shown, the word *elevator* was first used to describe the device of an endless chain of buckets used by the American millwright and inventor Oliver Evans to raise grain to the top level of his mill, from which it could flow by gravity through the subsequent stages of processing, requiring so much less handling that it was once reported that a visitor to Evans' mill found the machinery working away without a single person being in the building. In the 1840s, as grain growing in the Middle West began to expand and there was a need to deal with larger and larger quantities of grain, the term was applied to the warehouses that sprang up in major shipping points, such as Buffalo, New York. Efficient transfer of such quantities, however, required that grain no longer be dealt with as the produce of the forty acres of John Jones but as X bushels of a specified quality, and grain was thus transformed into a commodity that could be handled in bulk.

On the basis of such methods of handling there grew up a whole network of financial and trade practices. The grower who sold his grain came to receive in return a receipt showing that he had sold a given quantity of grain of a specified standard, a receipt that could, under varying conditions, be traded in as if it were a kind of commercial paper. The purchaser of that paper, if he presented it for delivery of the grain, would not be given the precise parcel of grain that the original producer had delivered to the elevator, but rather an equal amount of equivalent quality, since the original product might well have already been started on its way to the mills or to the export agents. Furthermore, there came to be a form of trading against the future prospects of the grain market which allowed both those who might need grain and the speculators to anticipate a rise or fall in prices.

There were many opportunities for sharp dealing, and

even injustice, in this system. The standards by which grain was graded were at times manipulated against the producer, who received a lower price than was actually fair, and often the elevator owners or managers, railroad freight agents, millers, village bankers, or Chicago and New York futures traders were not immune to the temptation of business transactions that gave them a profit and left the costs to someone else. The "someone else," at least so many people in America felt, was the individual farmer who had to face a whole complicated chain of people between himself and the consumer. The farmers' resentment of this was a constant element in American political and economic life, and much of the ferment of the period from 1865 to 1914, such as the Granger Movement, the Greenback Party, the Populist Party, the Free Silver Movement, and the Progressive Era, had this as its background.

Yet, despite such flaws, America did have a highly effective method for producing and transferring grain, and to many Russians it seemed that, by close study of this system, ways could be found to make their land an efficient competitor. The literature is large, covering the broad range of the American agricultural scene and dealing with fields such as machinery, crop methods, and freight rates, but there was a marked emphasis on the single element of the grain elevator, an emphasis that may be taken as representative of the whole broader topic.

A bibliography of Russian-language works on grain elevators that appeared in the trade journal *Sovetskoe mukomol'e i khlebopechenie* [Soviet milling and baking] (1929, no. 9: 565–567) includes some 130 references to pre-1917 publications. It is a useful guide, if somewhat flawed in its bibliographic practices, but it is clearly quite incomplete. The highly detailed annual bibliographies that the Russian agricultural authorities began in 1884 and that were continued by A. D. Pedashenko until 1916 confirm this for the period of their coverage, and fortuitous discoveries for the years before 1884 show that this is also true for the earlier time. Though the report of the American consul-general in St. Petersburg for the year 1875 does not directly cite a Russian reference to the grain elevator, he does couple a quotation from a memorial of the Odessa chamber of commerce that speaks of the rising competition of the Americans with his own views that the introduction of the grain elevator into Russia would eliminate excessive physical handling of grain that added to the cost of grain shipped from Russian ports. This cost, "added to the original cost at the place of production, 6.50 rubles [per chetvert', here considered equal to 5 and 19/20 American bushels], swell its price from 10.50 to 11.85 rubles when it leaves Cronstadt for foreign ports. By careful calculation it would seem that the introduction of the American elevator system would insure to the producer a net profit of 2 to 2½ rubles on each chetvert [sic] in the handling and transporting of grain alone, a gain that would act as an incentive to renewed energy in his agricultural pursuit, finally in a great measure to benefit the state" (George Pomutz, General report on the trade, manufactures, and resources of Russia. January 10, 1876. In: U.S. Bureau of Foreign Commerce. *Report upon the Commercial Relations of the United States with Foreign Countries for the Year 1875*. Washington, Government Printing Office, 1876: 1215–16).

The *New York Times* of March 16, 1878, and of May 6 of that same year contains items about a reported contract between the Russian government and a group of Americans for the construction of elevators in the empire, but there is no specific indication of location or capacity of these elevators. Some of the Russian newspapers of the 1870s contain articles about Russo-American competition in the grain trade that also refer to the grain elevator, and Orbinskii's detailed study shows that he gave close attention to the operation of this part of the trade.

Thus, the bibliography in *Sovetskoe mukomol'e i khlebopechenie* is only a fragmentary guide to the subject, for it lists only one reference in 1877 and one in 1878, with nothing thereafter until 1882.

However, at the end of 1883 and beginning of 1884 the question of grain elevators, and of a proposed Russian-American firm to build and manage them, came into some prominence in Russian politics. The project was one that had the backing of Lt.-Gen. P. P. Durnovo and P. P. Demidov— Prince San Donato, both highly placed and influential. Two Frenchmen were also involved, Messrs. de Morny and de la Gante, and, to add the necessary American authenticity, a Mr. Fisher and a Mr. Martin. However, the influential conservative publisher M. N. Katkov opposed it, contending that if the scheme were carried through it would place in American hands a monopoly over the elevator business of Russia. Katkov's newspaper *Moskovskiia viedomosti* during 1883 contained a number of articles that criticized the project and called for its refusal. The subject was taken up several times in the joint meetings of the department of legislation and of the department of state finance of the State Council [Gosudarstvennyi soviet—the highest legislative and judicial body of the Russian Empire before 1905], thrice in October 1883 and once in January of 1884, before being considered in a full assembly of the State Council.

A veritable bureaucratic war broke out over the question of elevators, with the point of view represented by Katkov finally winning out. He had not done this alone, however, for he had gained the support of I. A. Vyshnegradskii, who was to become minister of finance in 1887, following Bunge's retirement; K. P. Pobedonostsev, the Ober-Prokuror of the Holy Synod; the Minister of the Imperial Court Prince I. I. Vorontsov-Dashkov; and, it seems, Alexander III himself. Available bibliographic citations show that there was something of a newspaper war too, but *Moskovskiia viedomosti* is not available at this writing and one is left only some of the short, general statements that appear in Soviet studies.

On Friday, February 10 and Saturday, February 11, 1884 *Moskovskiia viedomosti* published editorial articles devoted to the Russian-American company. The Saturday article was in the nature of a summary. The development of grain elevators was seen in the articles as an unavoidable step against 'American competition,' threatening to 'push out' Russian grain 'from all European markets,' and against crises capable of 'shaking to their foundations' not only the economy but also the state. However the articles spoke out against putting Russian landowners and the Russian grain trade 'as sacrifices to the cupidity' of a foreign company . . .

Moskovskiia viedomosti insisted that the development of the elevator business be concentrated in the hands of Russian private and collective initiative, i.e., that it be assigned to the cities, the zemstvos, and, in particular, to the railroads, but, naturally, with the protection and aid of the government (B. V. Anan'ich and R. Sh. Ganelin, "I. A. Vyshnegradskii i S. Iu. Vitte—korrespondenty 'Moskovskikh viedomostei." In: *Problemy obshchestvennoi mysli i ekonomicheskaia politika Rossii XIX–XX vekov.* Leningrad, Izdatel'stvo Leningradskogo universiteta, 1972. 14–18. See also: Valentina A. Tvardovskaia, *Ideologiia poreformennogo samoderzhaviia (M. N. Katkov i ego izdaniia).* Moscow, Izdatel'stvo "Nauka," 1978. 89–90).

Although the majority of the State Council still favored adoption of the Russian-American project, the emperor himself felt the plan to be dangerous for Russia and he did not confirm the decision (Tvardovskaia, op. cit., 90). This was a fateful step, for the development in Russia of a network of grain elevators was for many years left to ill-coordinated individual effort. Some local governmental bodies, a few of the more enterprising of the separate rail lines, and a number of grain exporters did undertake their construction, with the first being built by the zemstvo authorities at Elets in that same year of 1884. However, it was not until the very last years before 1914 that any concerted national plan was formulated and that the State Bank sought to provide a rational and effective network of elevators. Even so, there were only seventy-five operating elevators in the whole empire in 1910 and forty-seven more were completed in the years 1910–1918.

Although few elevators were thus actually operating in Russia in the thirty years between Alexander III's decision against the Russo-American company and the beginning of the First World War, great interest in elevators was expressed in the Russian press of the time. Some of the material available to the Russian reader was informed and quite technical in its detail and, when taken with the flood of other references to the general economic and agricultural elements of the picture, should have provided much of what was necessary to expand the country's network of elevators to meet its needs.

One of the more extensive Russian studies of the operation of a grain elevator is to be found in the proceedings of a joint session of the Imperial Moscow Agricultural Society and the Russian Technical Society, with additional participation by members of the Statistical Division of the Moscow Juridical Society, the Scientific Department of the Society for Dissemination of Technical Knowledge, the Polytechnical Society, and the Architectural Society. The report of this meeting was published as issue XVII of the *Trudy* of the Imperial Moscow Agricultural Society, and extends over 141 pages of rather close print. The longest single component of this report is a paper entitled "Concerning warehouse-elevators in connection with the reform of the grain trade in Russia," delivered on February 12,

1885, by M. P. Fedorov, who speaks in some detail of American methods as a way of suggesting changes that Russia itself might make. "Indeed, if we turn our attention to the grain trade of America, we see that it is a coordinated system, all elements of which are in complete harmony . . . The cornerstone of this system is the classification of grain into several simple forms."

Grain classification and a fixed set of standards made it possible for America to establish by legislation the relationships between buyer and seller, between creditor and debtor. Grain could, because of this legal structure, be treated as a bulk product and handled in large, standard shipments, without the need to keep each producer's crop as a separate parcel. Thus it was possible, for example, for New York to handle a daily average of 360,000 poods (1 pood = 36 pounds) of grain, while St. Petersburg could handle only 65,000 and even Odessa, the empire's principal shipping point, only 140,000 (M. P. Fedorov, O skladakh-elevatorakh v sviazi s reformoi khliebnoi torgovli v Rossii. In: Moskovskoe obshchestvo sel'skago khoziaistva. *Trudy*, no. XVII, 1885: 31–33).

"The facts in the case are that we are actually suffering failure and are constantly leaving the field to our competitors, America, India, and Australia . . . 1884 was a more unfavorable year for us than even 1880 or 1881, since the decrease then in our export was caused by a crop failure, but now it is impossible to deceive ourselves, since our competitors are winning out over us." One of the reasons for this Fedorov saw in the fact that many European grain traders were losing their confidence in Russian grain. They complained that the Russian product was not of good quality, that it did not correspond with the sample, and that there were even inconsistencies in quality within a single shipment from a single area. Yet, in spite of this, many Russian grain traders were reluctant to take steps to clean and process the grain before shipment, as this would bring extra costs. The prejudice among these merchants, Fedorov writes, was such that they even were inimical to the idea. "This prejudice rests upon the conviction of many grain merchants that the cleaning and sorting of grain would significantly decrease its weight and thus cause them losses" (Fedorov, in *Trudy*, op. cit.: 34–36).

Even though Russian wheat might be better than American in terms of its technical qualities, it suffered in price because of its contamination and lack of uniformity, and Fedorov cites approximate figures indicating the lower prices paid for even some of the best Russian wheat. He proposes the establishment of an official system for the classification of grain being exported, and the chief stimulus for this, he writes, would be elevators in which grain could be cleaned, dried, and sorted. Given this, the situation of Russia's exports of grain would be greatly improved and the country would be able to meet the competition offered by America, Australia, and India. [If the mention of India now seems strange, it should be remembered that in the years from ca. 1880 to 1900 India was a substantial exporter of wheat and a significant factor in the world market.] (Fedorov, in *Trudy*, op. cit.: 36–41).

To provide a graphic description of the arrangement and appearance of an elevator the next speaker, A. R. Kushelevskii, has attached views of three types, a rural elevator at "Meridien" along the "Chikago-Biurlington-Kvintsi" railroad, [most likely this is Meriden, La Salle County, Illinois], a large port terminal elevator in Pavonia, New York, and a floating elevator in Bordeaux, France.

The word *America* appears only once in the short speech of I. E. Adadurov, president of the Moscow section of the Imperial Russian Technical Society, but it is not at all difficult to sense something of his attitude about this country.

Each person interested in the well-being of our fatherland is aware that in the most important function of our export trade, namely that of grain, something untoward is going on. Those close to the business, who themselves feel the burdens of this untowardness, have tried to determine the causes, and they have to admit to the sad and threatening fact that a struggle is now taking place in the European grain market, one in which we Russians have to yield and make room for our strong competitors, America, India, and Australia.

From the information that upcoming speaker Mikhail Pavlovich Fedorov will give you, you will see, among other facts, how in the course of a relatively short time our importance in the grain market is being lost and at the same time a firm position is being taken by other countries. In M. P. Fedorov's report many details are set forth which will show the causes of the decline in our role and of the means with which we can compete. Measures certainly need to be taken.

We have to keep in mind that our competitors are not asleep and that they well understand the whole enormous value of grasping the European market into their hands. They are vigorously developing the growing of grain, its processing and its cheaper transportation. We will not be mistaken if we conclude that, having supplied the market through the development of production, they will be able to close off our access by taking protective measures.

Although quite aware of their strength and of the danger for us, we are still just thinking about doing something, we ponder and we say a lot, we feel sympathies, and, holding to platonic wishes, lose valuable time, which it is dangerous, in this case, to measure in terms of years.

As a remedy, Adadurov repeats in a more succinct form that which Fedorov advances—elevators, better roads and railroads, transport of grain in bulk and not in sacks, and a rational and supple credit system (Adadurov, in *Trudy*, op. cit.: 70–72).

We are close to the main European market, our country is abundantly blessed by nature, and it would seem that in this field everything is on our side. In reality, however, this isn't so. Far away, beyond the ocean, from tens of thousands of versts away, currents of grain flow to fill a market that by every right belongs to us. And that is not all, this grain is valued significantly higher than ours in the European market (Adadurov, in *Trudy*, op. cit., 72).

Discussion of the role of the grain elevator in agricultural trade was not limited to the single session of February 12, 1885, at which Fedorov and Kushelevskii presented their reports. A week later, on February 19, the two societies met again, at which time the floor was opened for discussion. The discussants are, unfortunately, not well identified, so it is not really possible to say that the person named "Vitte" who spoke several times from the floor was indeed Sergei Iul'evich Witte, at that time the manager of a major Russian rail system, who was later successively to become minister of railways, minister of finance, the Russian plenipotentiary who negotiated the Treaty of Portsmouth that ended the Russo-Japanese War, and the person responsible for persuading Nicholas II to grant Russia a quasi-constitutional government. The tone of voice, however, is in harmony with that which one finds in Witte's *Memoirs*, for it is dogmatic to the point of being combative and not especially subtle in its understanding of Russia's position in the grain market. One should, of course, make some allowances for views expressed in a somewhat impromptu fashion in a public meeting, but "Vitte" shows quite clearly that he does not feel that any supposed relative decline in Russia's share of the market is especially harmful, as long as the actual totals are increasing.

"Our problem is wrapped up in the fact that it is all the same to us if we make money, no matter how." He goes on to say, "I touch on that question [of the fall in export figures] because I consider it harmful to spread the view that the export is declining. Dissemination of the opinion that we have entered into a crisis is harmful to Russia." All in all, he felt that there was no crisis and that things were going quite well (Vitte, in *Trudy*, op. cit.: 80–82).

While the other participants attempted as best they could to show that, even if a deep crisis did not exist, Russia stood on the brink of problems that would have to be dealt with, "Vitte" did not feel that the situation was quite so bad, and said only that there were "some signs that will make us get a move on, and if we do not do anything, then our trade could fall off, but I deny that we have at present entered on a decline" (ibid., 85). One of the measures that had been proposed for Russia, that of classifying and standardizing the grades of wheat, mixing the crops of several producers in the process, also did not attract "Vitte's" support, as he felt that Russia had too many varieties of wheat to warrant doing so (ibid., 92–94). In general, "Vitte" felt that Europe would not adopt the transport of wheat in bulk, nor would elevators catch on (ibid., 99–100).

There is no real indication that "Vitte" was in fact Sergei Iul'evich Witte, undoubtedly one of the most influential and effective of Russian statesmen in the last three decades or so of the empire. But the quick and categorical tone of voice encourages such an assumption, one that is furthered by the fact that the meeting was sponsored by organizations in which Witte quite certainly had an interest and dealt with a question that would undoubtedly have had its effect on his work as a railroad manager.

Discussion of the subject was resumed in a meeting of March 13, with I. E. Adadurov in the chair, but without, it seems, the presence of "Vitte." Evidently it was felt that the preceding session had got somewhat out of control, for an agenda of 19 items for consideration was distributed to those present. "The first seven items define our unfavorable position in the international market. In the eighth item measures for improvement are noted, and one must not fail to stress that these measures are presented in close connection lest one measure, unconnected with the other, fail to bring all the expected benefit." The ninth through eleventh of these items touched on means for introducing elevators and the remaining ones related to problems of credit and financial organization. (Moskovskoe obshchestvo sel'skago khoziaistva. *Trudy*, no. XVII, 1885: 103–04).

It does not seem that this meeting was more business-like, although the sharp-minded objections of "Vitte" were absent. One of the participants was Aleksandr Ivanovich Chuprov, one of Russia's most able agricultural economists of the late 19th and early twentieth centuries. He tended to feel that the three major elements of the proposed reforms—classification of grain, transport in bulk, and the setting up of elevators—could be accomplished as separate measures, for there was not any necessary connection among them (*Trudy*, XVII: 107–08). M. P. Fedorov, however, defended the point of view that he had expressed in his original report, the subject of this discussion, and reaffirmed the need for adoption of all three, which he saw as the essence of the American system (*Trudy*, XVII: 111–20).

As a final expression of the joint meetings of the two societies, on March 29, a set of conclusions was presented; one of these spoke of the evidence presented at the meetings to the effect that

... agriculture in Russia is suffering a number of problems, thanks to the lagging nature of our grain trade. From the data presented by the speakers it is evident that our participation in the supplying of the three principal grain markets of Europe—England, France, and Germany—is constantly being eroded and that we are more and more giving ground to our competitors. On this point one of the participants has directed attention to the fact that the nature of our lack of success in these three markets should not arouse special fears, since the figures for total grain export from Russia are not falling.

This last view, however—clearly that of "Vitte"—is based on Russian official statistics, which were termed significantly inflated, and it was said that the situation of Russia's grain export should not be taken lightly. It was necessary to take immediate steps to restore Russia's place in the international grain market (*Trudy*, XVII: 136).

There had been in recent years a growing distrust of Russian grain which had brought about a European tendency to prefer,

. . . especially in the case of wheat, the grain of America, India, and Australia, and thus to a certain discounting in price of Russian wheat in comparison with that of America and Australia.

This difference in price reached rather substantial levels, and the loss to Russia from this single difference comprised for each million chetvert' of Saxon wheat from 200 to 400 thousand rubles, for 'girka' wheat, from 1 million to 1,600,000 rubles, and for winter wheat, from 1,260,000 to 1,830,000 rubles.

This premium in the price of American wheat, previously considered inferior to that of Russia in its natural quality, can only be explained by its incomparably better processing and, most of all, by the uniformity of its shipments (*Trudy*, XVII: 137).

In conclusion, the report restated the view that the three factors of grain classification, transportation in bulk, and elevators were necessary measures to correct the predominance of the United States over Russia in the grain trade. Each one would be beneficial if applied singly, but, if applied together, the results would be even greater (*Trudy*, XVII: 137–41).

On April 29, 1885 the proceedings of these meetings, the reports of Kushelevskii and Fedorov, and the concluding resolution were all forwarded to the Minister of State Properties M. N. Ostrovskii, asking the government to work up proposed laws that would protect the elevator system from falling into the hands of a monopoly, and the producers of grain against excessive charges by elevator owners. "Not deeming itself to have the right of entering into the drafting of proposed laws on this subject, the council considers it a duty only to affirm that which the Russian grain producers have a right to expect from the introduction here of this system of storing and transporting grain which has had such a great beneficial effect on the agricultural production of America . . ." (Moskovskoe obshchestvo sel'skago khoziaistva. *Trudy*, no. XVIII, 1888: 65–66).

It may at first seem excessive to devote such an amount of space to this joint meeting of the two societies, one in agriculture and the other in the field of technology. However, the participants were many of them men of considerable importance in the field of Russian technology and finance. It is not certain that "Vitte" was actually Sergei Iul'evich Witte, but it seems

highly probable that such an identification can be made, for
Witte was later to write on problems of the transportation of
grain, especially with regard to freight charges, and, as minister
of finance, he showed much interest in problems of Russia's
grain export. The Mikhail Pavlovich Fedorov who delivered
one of the reports was later to become director of the Ryazan'-
Ural railroad, which was noted as one of the more "American"
of the Russian lines. Aleksandr Ivanovich Chuprov was an
economist and statistician of significant influence, one who
wrote much about grain harvests and the effect that they had
on Russia's economy. And A. R. Kushelevskii, whose name cannot be found in major Russian reference works, proves to have
been the author of a twenty-page pamphlet, *Ustroistvo magazin-
elevatorov v Amerikie i osushchestvimost' ikh v Rossii* [Construction
of elevator-warehouses in America and their practicality in
Russia] (Moscow, Tipografiia A. A. Kartseva, 1885. 20 p. fold.
plates), one that also appeared in the journal *Viestnik tekhniki*
and that seems from its detail to be based on direct experience,
although this is not stated in the text. In short, a number of
Russians with significant qualifications in the management or
analysis of the Russian economy had engaged in the examination of an American economic institution as a possible source
of ideas for the improvement of Russia's position in a market
in which the United States was a major factor. Whether or not
any of these ideas found quick application in Russia, it is of
importance that they were considered at the time, and these
Russian participants continued to have some measurable influence in the country's affairs. Of course, it would take a full analysis of their writings, and access to their papers, to determine
whether the "American component" of their thought was a lasting and effective one, but, as this survey of the joint meetings
of the agricultural and of the technical societies show, the channel did exist.

During the three decades that remained to the empire
after this conference in 1885, there was a great deal of further
writing about the system by which Russia grew and marketed
its grain and rarely did any of it fail to make some mention of
the practices of the United States. Only a specialist could hope
to deal with this vast and complicated literature, but two authors are worth particular mention. One was Isaac M. Rubinow,

of Russian-Jewish background, who had come to the United States in 1893 at the age of 18 because of the limitations that the imperial government placed on Jews. He became a frequent contributor to the Russian press, especially to serious journals in the fields of economics and social policy, and his many reviews of American books and articles on such topics as municipal administration in the United States conveyed a broad and significant picture of American thought and institutions. He served for a time as an economist for the U.S. Department of Agriculture and his three short works on the Russian grain situation are among the very few substantial English-language studies of the problem, particularly on the competition between the two countries.

Rubinow's analyses, based upon a very close observance of the Russian data, are too fact-laden and intricate in their thought to warrant any great discussion here, other than to say that they have by no means lost their value as an explanation of Russia's place in the world grain market from 1900 to 1910. The one passage from his studies which cannot, however, escape full quotation is taken from his citation of the report of a special commissioner of the Russian ministry of finance charged with investigating new developments in the grain trade:

'On the market place in Nikolaiev (one of the most important southern ports) I had an opportunity to observe a fact which a short time ago would have been altogether incredible. The peasants on arrival at the market with their grain were asking: What is the price in America according to the latest telegram? And what is still more surprising, they know how to convert cents per bushel into kopecks per pood' [Rubinow, Isaac M. *Russia's wheat trade.* Washington, Government Printing Office, 1908. p. 10. (U.S. Department of Agriculture, Bureau of Statistics, Bulletin 65)].

Rubinow's other works are *Russia's wheat surplus; conditions under which it is produced* (Washington, Government Printing Office, 1906. 103 p.) and *Russian wheat and wheat flour in European markets* (Washington, Government Printing Office, 1908. 99 p.).

Nothing else could express so well the feeling, held even among the Russian peasants, that the country's chances for a market, the possibility of receiving a worthwhile price, depended upon developments in America. However one may phrase it, it is almost inescapable to feel that, whatever Russia might hope to do in the international economic—and, therefore, political—field, much depended upon the degree to which its agricultural economy could be profitable in an international situation in which the United States was active, efficient, and powerful.

A somewhat more literary expression is given to this view in a lecture that was read on April 11, 1909 (OS), at the rather out-of-the-way Novo-Aleksandriiskii Institut sel'skago khoziaistva [Novo-Aleksandriiskii Institute of Agriculture] by one Ivan Osipovich Shirokikh, "Ocherki mirovogo proizvodstva pshenitsy" [Outlines of the world production of wheat], in which he begins with a citation of the episode in Longfellow's *Song of Hiawatha* that tells of Hiawatha bringing the gift of grain to man, and continues with a citation from Frank Norris's *The Octopus* about combine harvesters at work in California, ending with a substantial quotation, also from Norris, about the fact that, despite all the ways in which the producers had suffered, their wheat continued to be a force in the market and in the world. It was, Shirokikh said, a matter of national importance that Russia do all that was possible to increase her production of wheat, and the general impression is that the American model of such a system would be of great influence (I. O. Shirokikh, "Ocherki mirovogo proizvodstva pshenitsy," In: Novo-Aleksandriiskii institut sel'skago khoziaistva i liesovodstva. *Trudy*, v. 22, vyp. 2. St. Petersburg, 1909. p. 1–45).

Although Norris did not live to complete it, he had planned a trilogy on wheat. The first two parts, *The Octopus* and *The Pit*, told respectively of the struggles of the producers, the farmers, to earn a living from their efforts, and of the machinations of the speculators in grain that, added to the exactions of the railroads, thwarted their efforts. These were completed, but the third part, a description of the way in which this wheat alleviated the effects of a great famine, was not. However, it seems that Shirokikh in some way understood Norris's purpose and that he saw the great human, as well as economic, importance of this flow of grain through world trade channels.

Although there were fluctuations in the relative positions of Russia and America in their role in the international grain trade, the United States, even during the last two years before the outbreak of war in 1914, continued to be the object of a great deal of Russian attention because of its grain exports. The Italo-Turkish War of 1911–12, and the First and Second Balkan Wars in 1912–13 had either severely hampered or, at times, completely closed the export of grain from Russia's Black Sea ports, her principal outlets for agricultural produce, and created favorable opportunities for the United States. Although, for example, the last half of 1913 was without active hostilities, it was not a good period for the Russians.

Without speaking of the high interest rates which continued during the fall, and which generally are a minor hindrance to our export trade, the most important obstacle to the increase of our export was the low quality of our last harvest and the continuing strong competition on the Western European market from the United States, which had harvested, as in the previous year, a good quality crop and which was able, thanks to that, to retain in its own hands the leading position in the business of supplying the world market (Russia. Ministerstvo finansov. *Narodnoe khoziaistvo v 1913 godu* [The economy in 1913]. Petrograd, Tipografii Redaktsii period. Izdanii Ministerstva finansov, 1914: 25).

In the first part of 1914, before the outbreak of war, the position of the United States as an exporter of grain was a favorable one in general, although Russia, freed from the impediments caused by the Balkan Wars, was again a significant competitor. Hopes of that empire for further growth in trade were, of course, completely destroyed by the war. German blocking of the Baltic routes in August and Turkey's adherence to Russia's enemies in the autumn of 1914 cut Russia's export trade almost entirely, and America took a position as the major factor in world grain movement (*Narodnoe khoziaistvo v 1914*. Petrograd, 1915: 14–15).

There were other aspects of Russian interest in American agriculture besides those of the grain trade and the operation of elevators. During the period from 1893 to 1914, that is from the World's Columbian Exposition in Chicago to the outbreak of the First World War, and most particularly during the last decade before that catastrophe, Russian specialists made frequent visits to the United States to study all kinds of aspects of our agricultural system, and the Russian agricultural press not only provided information derived from them but also direct translations from journals in the United States. The record of all this is by far too extensive to examine in detail in this survey, although some of the more interesting items will be mentioned.

Russian recognition of the position of America as a competitor continued to find frequent expression in the 1880s and 1890s, as did a certain awareness that a close examination of American practices might provide useful suggestions as to ways in which the Empire could improve its agricultural system. There were, for example, scores of articles in the Russian press in 1893 that reflected the observations of visits by Russian agricultural specialists to the World's Columbian Exposition in Chicago in 1893, and there was considerable comment in the general press about the economic effect of American competition on the Russian export of grain. Following the exposition some Russian specialists had visited the United States to study various individual branches of agriculture. Apparently there came to be the feeling that it would be useful to have a continuing Russian presence in the United States, reaching direct expression in a proposal made at the 1902 session of the Sel'-sko-khoiziaistvennyi soviet [Agricultural council] (Russia. Departament zemledieliia. Spravochno-izdatel'skoe biuro. *Agronomicheskaia pomoshch' v Rossii* [Agronomic assistance in Russia]. St. Petersburg, Izdanie Departamenta zemledieliia, 1914: 141–42).

Although no direct steps were taken either then or within the next few years, it seems that one Russian resident of the United States undertook to further the idea that Russia should indeed have what has since come to be called an agricultural attaché in this country. This was F. F. Kryshtofovich who appears to have come to America some time during the 1890s. He had, to judge from some articles of his about Hawaii, visited those islands during the last years before annexation to the United States but had finally settled in Southern California, near Cucamonga, where he had become a neighbor of the earlier Russian immigrant Peter A. Demens. Demens, born Petr Alekseevich Dement'ev, arrived in America in the early 1880s, taking up a role as citrus grower, contractor, sawmill owner, and railroad builder, in Florida. His struggling little road finally made it through the Florida woods to a terminal station that he named St. Petersburg, but the small population of the region, a frost on the citrus crops, and a yellow-fever epidemic caused him to sell out, and he moved to San Bernardino County, California where he also engaged in citrus growing and in the production of wooden builders' articles, as well as in banking, a shaving soap company, and in ownership of a steam laundry. During all this activity Demens also wrote, under the pseudonym "P. A. Tverskoi," many articles about America that appeared in the Russian press, most frequently in the vaguely liberal *Viestnik Evropy,* a journal read at times by Nicholas II himself, as well as by Tolstoi, and—at least on the basis of a quotation at second-hand in Lenin's writings—by the exiled young attorney Vladimir I. Ul'ianov.

Despite Demens' agricultural interests, he had relatively little to say directly about American methods, but his friend and neighbor Kryshtofovich became a quite frequent contributor to the Russian press on agricultural procedures in the United States. The suggestion made at the aforementioned official gathering of agricultural administrators in 1902 that Russia send a permanent agricultural agent to America appears to have attracted his warm interest. [An earlier suggestion that Russia send agricultural attachés abroad, including the United States, appears in "Agronomiia i diplomatiia" (Agronomy and diplomacy), *Novoe Vremia,* March 18/30, 1893, p. 1] While it is not possible, largely in view of the lack of an author index to the entries in many of the annual issues of A. D. Pedashenko's enormously detailed agricultural bibliography, to trace all that Kryshtofovich may have had to say on the subject, the Library of Congress collection of some seven thousand Russian pamphlets ranging in date from circa 1718 to the early 1950s does contain one very significant item. This is A. G. Komsha and L. P. Sokal'skii, *Ob uchrezhdenii russkoi sel'sko-khoziaistvennoi agentury v Soed. Shtatakh Sievernoi Ameriki: doklad Imperatorskomu obshchestvu sel'skago khoziaistva iuzhnoi Rossii* [Concerning the establishment of an agricultural agency in the United States of North America: report to the Imperial Society of Agriculture of Southern Russia] (Odessa, "Slavianskaia" tipografiia, 1906. 41p.), which is a report of the August 1905 meeting of the sponsoring organization. The Library's copy bears, at the top of the first page of the text, Kryshtofovich's signature, while a footnote lists him among the participants and states that he had presented a paper on the matter that had served as a major element in the pamphlet's summary and conclusions.

According to the pamphlet's authors, comparisons between Russia and the United States, especially between the south of Russia and the Plains States, showed many similarities in soil and climate, and these had created in both areas a prevailing reliance on grain as the major crop. America had arrived at its high level of success because of the great successes of American agricultural machine production and because of rational methods of organization. Russia suffered greatly because of the lack of any consistent means for learning about American procedures and machines. Emphasis is given to the great effort that Americans had put into establishing experiment stations and other forms for the study of agricultural production. Drawing upon budget data of the U.S. Department of Agriculture for 1905 it is noted that an aggregate of 5,201,000 rubles (i.e. ca. $2,600,500) were spent on experimental work. "These figures speak for themselves. But they come into even sharper focus if they are compared with the annual budget of Russian agricultural experiment institutions, on which the annual expenditures, in combined state and public organization funds, is about 250,000 rubles" (Komsha and Sokal'skii, op. cit., 15).

The authors write that, taking into account the similarities particularly between the south of Russia and the United States, landowners in Russia ought to pay close attention to the American economy "in order to borrow from America all that is most applicable and useful for our farms." "In all fairness it must be admitted that the rich experience of American [experiment] stations has been about as badly ignored by the practical landlords as by the theoretical agronomists and our professors and experimenters in the field of agriculture." Most of what did turn up in the Russian press, according to the authors, was in the form of translations from German journals, which offered articles on topics of rather remote applicability to Russia (Komsha and Sokal'skii, op. cit., 18).

The lack of knowledge about American agriculture among Russian farmers can largely be explained by the weak development of the knowledge of English, but this language problem did not keep the Americans from making some quite useful borrowings from Russia. When it was seen that the hard "macaroni" wheat of South Russia was highly valued on world markets, the U.S. Department of Agriculture in 1896 sent a Professor "Gansen" to Russia for eight months to study varieties of wheat, and "as a result the United States, adopting the cultivation of several Russian varieties, was already in 1904 putting on the market 10 million poods [360 million pounds—6 million bushels at 60 pounds a bushel] of hard Russian wheat," and it was expected that 1905 would see four to five times as much being grown. Americans were also interested in the alfalfa varieties grown in Central Asia, in cold-resistant apples, and in other Russian crops such as oats, flax, or sunflowers (and it will be noted that the sunflower is actually a native of North America) (Komsha and Sokal'skii, op. cit.: 18–19).

"In the last 5 or 10 years, chiefly under the influence of the articles and letters in the Russian agricultural press by F. F. Kryshtofovich, Russian landlords, particularly in the south of Russia, have begun to show some interest in American farming. Landowners have begun to order American varieties of corn, to be interested in nitrogenous cultures for the inoculation of soil sown to alfalfa, to ask questions about machines for the construction and maintenance of roads, to order sweet potatoes, etc." However, much of the information about American methods has been somewhat irregular, being unplanned and often scattered in time and subject matter. "'During the whole time I have been living in the United States,' writes F. F. Kryshtofovich in his American letters, 'I have received numerous letters from Russian landowners with various questions and commissions. They ask about making inquiries, and about referral to seed traders; they commission the purchase of seeds, and the ordering of machines from factories; they want to know if it is possible to sell Russian grass seeds in America, they want information about where to order road machinery, ditching machines, saws for firewood, presses and forms for glazed (paving) brick, etc., and countless other questions.'" This quotation is, it seems, from Kryshtofovich's article in the major agricultural journal *Sel'skii khoziain* [Landowner], no. 17, 1905 (Komsha and Sokal'skii, op. cit.: 19–21).

Although efforts had been made by Kryshtofovich in 1905 to secure support from the Russian ministry of agriculture for an American agency, the ministry, though expressing sympathy with the idea, had raised some purely formal objections for not going any farther. As a consequence, the authors propose that the matter be taken up by the Imperial Society of Agriculture in the South of Russia, with the cooperation of the zemstva (local governmental bodies) and agricultural societies of the region that included the Bessarabian, Kherson, Tavricheskii, and Ekaterinoslav provinces. The Imperial Society, the authors note, had a long history of furtherance of measures to help agriculture, including such actions as stimulating the building of railroads, the establishment of agricultural education institutions, measures for dealing with harmful insects, etc. By creating an agency in America, the Society "would remain true to its historical responsibility, that of being a representative and an exponent of the interest of the agriculture of the broad steppe region of the south of Russia" (Komsha and Sokal'skii, op. cit.: 21–23).

The pamphlet offers a proposal for the organization of such an agency and says that since the south of Russia is much like the more arid regions of "Vailoming, Kolorado, Nebraska [retransliteration does not change this name], Iuta and, in particular, Kanzas; it is desirable to set up an agricultural agency in Topika [Topeka], the chief city of the state of Kanzas." The responsibilities of this organization would include study of grain cultivation and of food and industrial crops of interest to the south of Russia, methods of grading, experimental work in agriculture in America, livestock breeding and management, machine production, and roadbuilding methods. The agency would not only gather information but also act to procure seeds, animals, and machines, and it could serve as an intermediary in dealing with American purchasers of Russian agricultural products. "Besides this, in the future practical experience will place requirements upon the activity of the agency such as cannot be determined at present." The annual cost is estimated at five thousand rubles (Komsha and Sokal'skii, op. cit.: 24–26).

As a supplement to this pamphlet, illustrating the response of a more local body, there is an account of such a topic being discussed by the Aleksandrovsk uezd (district, subdivision of a province) zemstvo in September of 1905, which was evidently one of the first bodies to respond to the proposals made by the Imperial Society in August (Komsha and Sokal'skii, op. cit.: 29–41). These pages are based on a report made by the zemstvo agronomist A. F. Loginov and published in the newspapers issued by the Ekaterinoslav provincial zemstvo. While it speaks in praise of American technology, it notes that American agricultural machine producers had joined to form a trust, forcing up prices and otherwise restricting the market. However, farmer-consumers had joined to establish their own factories and provide machines at lower prices. "Thus, if Russian zemstvos could join this *organization of farmers* in America, they might thereby avoid the trust and receive agricultural equipment of equally high quality but at lower prices, and at the same time support the union of farmer-consumers in America with material and moral assistance in their struggle with the trust" (Komsha and Sokal'skii, op. cit.: 29–37).

The Aleksandrovsk zemstvo would be willing to contribute 500 rubles annually toward the estimated cost of 5,000 rubles for such an agency, and the zemstvo would support action by the provincial zemstvo as a whole. An American agency would be a response to the deepest needs of the Aleksandrovsk district, and a number of the members expressed their willingness to bear up under some of the preliminary risk that is always connected with any new measure (Komsha and Sokal'skii, op. cit.: 39–40).

These proposals, made in 1905, and the pamphlet, which appeared in 1906, had no immediate response, although in the end they were to bear fruit. However, in 1907, one finds another printed indication of the influence of American agriculture on Russia. This consists of the eight solid volumes that stand on the shelves of the Library of Congress with the polysyllabic title *Ezhegodnik Glavnago upravleniia zemleustroistva i zemledieliia po Departamentu zemledieliia,* dated from 1907 to 1914. After a number of decades' experience with the Russian language, the writer takes this title as it stands, without any particular mental translation, but an inspection of the volumes themselves conveys a very familiar impression. This is a memory of a couple of dark-colored books found among the scant resources of printed matter of a grandfather who was a farmer and a carpenter, issues of the *Yearbook* of the U.S. Department of Agriculture of about the same era, issues filled with similar reports on new crops, methods for dealing with diseases of the horse, and accounts of the life history of various insects, and at last there is a realization that the Russian title, which translates as *Yearbook of the Chief Administration of Land Reclamation and Agriculture of the Department of Agriculture*, is that of a closely parallel publication. There is rather little in these eight volumes that comes directly from American writings or that reports on American practices, but the organization and spirit of the content corresponds with the American series. This is evident in the first few sentences of the introduction to the first volume, that for 1907. "The first venture in the publication of the *Ezhegodnik* is being made in the present year. There has long been felt a need for such a book. In fact, in Russia, where agriculture is the chief occupation of the population, the activity of the [agri] cultural office is of special importance and it is desirable that our landowners have as broad a view as possible of this activity. This [need] is best met, as the experience of the United States shows, by the publication of the *Ezhegodnik,* in which, together with a survey of the activity of the agricultural authority for a given year, the state of the individual branches of agriculture in the country might be characterized" (Russia. Departament zemledieliia. *Ezhegodnik* . . . g. 1, 1907. St. Petersburg, 1908. p. I).

One of the articles in the first volume is "Khlopkovodstvo" [Cotton growing] by A. I. Knize, identified as the secretary of the (Russian) Department of Agriculture's cotton committee, which dealt with the Russian effort to encourage the planting of cotton in Central Asia, thus avoiding the need to import it from America. One of the plates illustrates nine varieties of cotton cultivated at the experiment station in the Golodnaia steppe [Hungry steppe] in 1906, and four of these are named "King's, Russel's, Hawkin's and Peterkin's," and there is a reference in the text to a publication identified only as *Khlopok* [Cotton] by "Berkett," which had appeared in Russian in 1908 and which, upon investigation proved to be Charles William Burkett, *Cotton, Its Cultivation, Marketing, Manufacture, and the Problems of the Cotton World* (New York, Doubleday, Page and Co., 1906. 331 p.), a work that also appeared in Spanish and German translation. There are other references to varieties of cot-

ton named as "Si-ailand, N'iu-Orlean, Tekhas, and Upland."
And the suspenders, sleeve-garters, and hat of a man shown in
another plate supervising the work of four not so easily identifiable figures on riding cultivators almost surely mark him as a
rural Southerner of the period. There will be a further mention of the Russian author A. I. Knize, again in a situation dealing with cotton and with the United States (*Ezhegodnik . . . g. 1,*
1907: 315–61).

Following Komsha and Sokal'skii's 1906 publication, reporting the August 1905 meeting of the Imperial Agricultural
Society of Southern Russia, one finds a number of entries in
Pedashenko's bibliography that take up the question of an official Russian agricultural agency in the United States, unfortunately referring mostly to journals or newspapers not available
in American libraries. However, something of the atmosphere
of literature on the subject can be sensed if one examines the
full, if rather verbose, title of a small work, evidently published
with some official support, that appeared in 1909. This is Vladimir Viktorovich Salov, *Zemledielie—glavnaia osnova blagosostoianiia Rossii. Sravnitel'nyi ocherk sostoianiia zemledieliia v Soedinennykh Shtatakh Sievernoi Ameriki i v Rossii po novieishim dannym.
Miery k podniatiiu v Rossii sel'skokhoziaistvennoi promyshlennosti i
sviazannykh s neiu otraslei narodnago truda* [Agriculture—the
principal basis of the well-being of Russia. Comparative survey
of the status of agriculture in the United States of North America and in Russia, according to the most recent data. Measures
for the increase in Russia of agricultural production and of the
branches of national employment connected with it] (St. Petersburg, Tipografiia Ministerstva putei soobshcheniia, 1909. 143
p.), the publishing house for which was the printing plant of
the Ministry of Ways of Communication, the chief responsibility of which was the railroad system.

Salov's foreword says that his work was inspired by the contrast that he found between the rather unfavorable views of the
role of agriculture in national development expressed by the
eminent chemist and industrialist D. I. Mendeleev in his *K poz-
naniiu Rossii* [On the study of Russia] and those set forth by the
French Vicomte Georges d'Avenel in articles in the *Revue des
deux mondes* of 1907 that emphasized the enormous factor that
agriculture represented in creating the wealth of the United

States. He makes it clear that he has drawn not only on printed works of such people as I. Kh. Ozerov (who is extensively quoted and discussed below in Chapter 5) but also on the advice of a number of high officials of the ministries of finance and agriculture (Salov, op. cit.: xi–xiii).

Abounding in statistics, both for the United States and for Russia, Salov's work is a comparison of the flourishing and well-organized position of agriculture in America with the very ill-coordinated and often irrational state of things in Russia. The underlying tone is one of looking toward the American model not as something to be totally imitated but as one that offers many ideas and approaches that would ultimately benefit Russia. The author clearly supports some of the efforts that Russia, under the leadership of prime minister Petr Arkad'evich Stolypin, had recently made toward fostering the development of individual ownership of land by the peasants in place of the previous system of communal tenure which kept most of the rural population on a low, if ostensibly equal, level.

The work has copious suggestions for steps that might be taken to help Russian agriculture increase its productivity, steps that do not need to be examined in detail except for the ninth item in Salov's proposed series of 27 necessary measures. This repeats a suggestion which was made in 1906 in the Komsha and Sokal'skii pamphlet for the establishment in the United States of a Russian agricultural agency. Russia, Salov writes, had for a number of years had agents of the ministry of finance in various countries, including the United States, and he feels that similar activities in the area of agriculture would be beneficial to Russia as a whole. The road followed by the United States, which had attained such a high development of its economy, could not fail to be highly instructive to Russia at a time when she was gathering all her forces for her agricultural expansion. The Chief Administration of Land Reclamation and Agriculture, as the principal agricultural administrative agency was then known, had in fact made proposals toward such a goal, both in order to establish ties between the experimental bodies of both nations and, given the formation of non-communal private farms by many peasants, to borrow from American practice those measures which would be most applicable in Russia's own situation. The proposed agency's tasks were largely those included in the Komsha and Sokal'skii pamphlet—gather information, acquire plants and seeds, study American agricultural methods, survey machine production and use, and further the sale of Russia's own agricultural products in America (Salov, op. cit.: 88–90).

This time, it appears, something real was done in response to such a suggestion, for the agricultural authorities had requested in their 1909 budget the assignment of 15,000 rubles for such an agency. The appropriation was made and in 1909 F. F. Kryshtofovich was chosen to head the operation in America, but he was sent, not to Topeka, but to the somewhat surprising location of St. Louis.

Kryshtofovich was, however, not the first Russian observer of American agriculture to be assigned to full-time duty in the United States, but merely the first representative of the Russian government itself. There was already an agent of the Ekaterinoslav province zemstvo who had apparently begun operations in 1907 or 1908, for in 1908 the Ekaterinoslav zemstvo printing house issued, as number 1 of its *Izviestiia zemskoi sel'skokhoziaistvennoi agentury v Soedinennykh Shtatakh,* a 137-page work on American agricultural experiment stations, and, as number 2, an 89-page study on dry farming in the United States. Both were signed by I. B. Rozen, whose name appears in quite a number of articles in the Russian agricultural press of the period with references to American topics. Some idea of the general nature of his activities may be gained from a review of his report for the period from December 1909 to April 1910 that was published in the journal *Khoziaistvo* in 1911 (no. 7: 222–33).

The Ekaterinoslav agency was located in Minneapolis and, although it is at times not clear what connection may have existed between it and several other contributors to Russian journals who date their articles from there, one finds, for example, I. V. Emel'ianov writing on the "Fermerskii national'nyi kongress v Sievero-Amerikanskikh Soedinennykh Shtatakh" [Farmers' National Congress in the North American United States] in the *Iuzhno-Russkaia Sel'sko-khoziaistvennaia gazeta* (no. 10, 1911: 10–11), published also in *Khoziaistvo* (February 10, 1911: 180–182), or on the nineteenth irrigation congress in the U.S. (in *Iuzhno-vostochnyi khoziain,* no. 12, 1912. Listed on front cover, but pages missing in Library of Congress copy). Ekaterina Iretskaia took up the subject of the International Congress of Farm Wives, held in Colorado Springs in October of 1911 in conjunction with the International Dry Farming Congress, and she drew upon a work by George Watson Oliver of the U.S. Department of Agriculture to write a survey of new methods of plant selection (*Khoziaistvo,* no. 16, 1912: 525–531). There are several other articles that appear to rest upon the work done by the American agency of the Ekaterinoslav zemstvo, but in early 1912 it was announced that that Russian local government body was giving up its representation in America as a means of protesting against the United States action in late 1911 of abrogating the commercial treaty that Buchanan had negotiated in 1832. That step had been taken as an American response to official Russian limitations on the activities in Russia of naturalized and native Americans of Russian origin and Jewish background, and in Russia there was a considerable reaction among the more conservative and anti-Semitic elements of society. [For references to the motives of the Ekaterinoslav zemstvo, see *Iuzhno-vostochnyi khoziain* 1912, no. 4: 16; no. 6: 5; no. 8: 5–6.]

This cessation of support from Ekaterinoslav, however, did not bring any real interruption in the work of Rozen and his collaborators, for the Khar'kovskoe obshchestvo sel'skago khoziaistva [Khar'kov Agricultural Society] announced that it would take over the agency's operations, and one finds, for example, a rather substantial statement as to the Khar'kov body's operations in America in *Iuzhno-Russkaia sel'skokhoziaistvennaia gazeta* [South Russian agricultural gazette] (August 1913: 13–16). Late in 1914, as the First World War was interrupting the supply from European countries of items needed by Russian farmers, another example appeared in the journal *Turkestanskoe sel'skoe khoziaistvo,* published in Tashkent in Central Asia, which printed an announcement, signed by B. Usovskii as the Khar'kov agent in America, of the agency's offer of services 34 obtaining seeds from American sources (no. 11, 1914: 1038–1039).

However, these local bodies were not so broad in their coverage as the representatives of the central ministry itself, and one finds, even upon a rather rapid survey of the literature, many indications of how Kryshtofovich set out about his job. In *Khoziaistvo* in 1910 he announced availability of his services in ordering seed for quick maturing corn (no. 8: 339–40), and the same journal summarized the results of the first period of the agency's action (no. 23: 1033–35). In 1911 it appears that Kryshtofovich had acquired an assistant, A. Kol', who published articles on such topics as fodder crops and dry farming methods (signed by him as assistant agent) [*Iuzhno-vostochnyi khoziain*, 1911, no. 7: 1–15; no. 11, 1911: 23–25. *Iuzhno-Russkaia sel'skokhoziaistvennaia gazeta*, 1911: no. 23. Article announced on cover but pages missing from Library of Congress copy]. This did not involve any slackening in Kryshtofovich's own work, for he appears several times in the pages of *Turkestanskoe sel'skoe khoziaistvo*, which represented the interests of the commercial farmers in Central Asia—who tended to be of Russian rather than local background—with predominating interests in cotton and fruit growing. However, since that region also had to feed itself, a reprinted report from Kryshtofovich on American quick-maturing corn must have been welcome [no. 4, 1911: 215–16] and, given the aridity of much of Central Asia, another reprint of an article on Luther Burbank's development of thornless cactuses that could be fed to cattle would also have been of interest [no. 5, 1911: 297–98].

However, there was to be a closer relationship between the landowners in Turkestan and Kryshtofovich. The Turkestan journal in its seventh issue of 1911 announced the departure of the Turkestan Agricultural Society's president Rikhard Rikhardovich Shreder (Richard Schroeder, 1867–1944) for the United States to attend the International Dry Farming Congress meeting at Spokane and to view U.S. orchards and cotton growing. The tenth issue of this journal reported Kryshtofovich's views on the way in which the Americans had been quick to adopt Russian varieties of alfalfa which the Russians themselves had not done, on his survey of American silos, and on the fact that he had been a vice-president of the congress at Spokane. The November issue provides both a summary of Shreder's speech at Spokane and a letter by him, dated from Kryshtofovich's farm in California, asking the Turkestan society to suggest that the governor general of Turkestan issue an official invitation to Kryshtofovich to visit Turkestan to demonstrate Californian methods of drying fruit and raisins (*Turkestanskoe sel'skoe khoziaistvo*, no. 10, 1911: 728, 739, 742; no. 11: 831–35, 850–52).

In 1912 the Turkestan journal contained copious material about Shreder's visit in America, not only to California fruit-growing regions but to the Cotton Belt, and in the March issue a summary of the discussion at a society meeting in November of the previous year shows that the proposed visit by Kryshtofovich had been given serious consideration. Previous proposals had been made that A. A. Dylevskii, a local specialist on fruit growing and processing, be sent to America, and hopes were expressed that Kryshtofovich's visit would not replace this plan. The topic was mentioned again in the May number, and in June and July Shreder provided an extensive account of his impressions of orchard management in California. These latter articles were accompanied by supplemental communications, signed by Kryshtofovich's neighbor, fellow orchardist, and correspondent for the Russian press, Peter A. Demens (under his pseudonym "P. A. Tverskoi"). And in November an article by Kryshtofovich summarized a speech on orchard and vineyard operations in California that he had made in August in Tashkent at the Turkestan society's general meeting (*Turkestanskoe sel'skoe khoziaistvo*, 1912, no. 1: 76–77; no. 2: 91–110; no. 3: 162–80; no. 4: 249–81; no. 5: 262–91, 440–41; no. 6: 455–68, 469–78; no. 7: 516–51, 575–85; no. 8: 661–66; no. 10: xi–xii; no. 11: 915–33).

These articles by no means exhaust the American content of *Turkestanskoe sel'skoe khoziaistvo* in 1912, for one may refer to various articles in the journal that, although not always direct translations from American originals, reflect American discoveries and procedures. It would be too much to cite all of them, but some deal with one problem of particular importance in Russian-American economic relations of the era which finds its strongest manifestation in Turkestan. This is the problem of cotton supply to Russia's textile industry. Turkestan was, and is, the region of Russia that offers the most rational prospect in the land for the production of cotton on any large scale, and efforts had been made since the Russian acquisition of the area in the 1860s and 1870s to increase and improve the traditional local cultivation of cotton. Although there had been early efforts to send specialists to the United States to study American methods, these could not really be effective until railroad construction had made it possible to transport bulky and relatively low-value freight such as cotton bales to St. Petersburg or Ivanovo to the East of Moscow where Russian textile plants were concentrated. By 1912, however, Russia had managed to cover almost 40 percent of her needs from production in Turkestan and, to some degree, in parts of the Caucasus, and it is no surprise to find that *Turkestanskoe sel'skoe khoziaistvo* reflects this interest. For example, the August issue of that year has Shreder's long article on American cotton growing, which was continued in September, while October provides a survey of American use of fertilizers in cotton fields, and December printed the resolutions of a congress of cotton growers held in Tashkent from November 25 to December 1. All these issues have on the back cover the advertisement of the firm of P. K. Grosh, successor to Shimunek and Co., based in Moscow and Tashkent, which announced itself as "the sole representatives in Europe and Asia of the well-known American factory of cotton processing machines 'The Brown Cotton Gin Co.,'" which could supply complete equipment for cotton gins "following the most recent American plans," and as a sort of reaffirmation of this, the firm's telegraph address was simply "Tashkent-Dzhin" (i.e. "Gin").

Cotton was much discussed in the Russian press at the time of the American abrogation of the treaty of commerce between the two countries which was announced at the end of 1911 to take effect at the end of 1912. Not only the agricultural but also the general financial press had much to say about improved prospects for Russian growers, comment that was also mixed with the proposal that, in order to make Russian independence complete—Russia also being a substantial importer of American agricultural machinery—Russian landlords and local governments should cease their complaints about the high Russian duties on imports of such equipment. (See, for example: *Promyshlennost' i torgovlia: organ soveta s"ezdov predstavitelei promyshlennosti i torgovli* [Industry and trade: organ of the conference committee of representatives of industry and trade],

no. 1, 1912: 3–6; no. 4, 1912: 209–10; no. 6, 1912: 347. These
articles also refer to letters to the editors of various newspapers
on similar themes.)

However, the cotton growers conference held in Tashkent
at the end of November 1912 makes it fully clear that, no matter how great the desire might be to make Russia independent
of American cotton supplies, any hopes of doing so would have
to rest upon the adoption of the American example. One of the
propositions advanced by R. R. Shreder, who was a leading participant, was that of sending to America an agricultural agent
to deal just with cotton alone, and A. I. Knize, a high official of
the Departament zemledieliia [Department of agriculture] in
St. Petersburg, told the delegates that the authorities indeed
would support such an appointment. Furthermore he said that
in order to acquaint Russian growers with the most up-to-date
American equipment a certain Liubchenko, senior specialist in
the department, had already been assigned to bring from the
United States five complete sets of machines, at least three of
which would go to Turkestan (*Trudy s"iezda khlopkovodov* . . . v. 1.
Tashkent, Tipografiia pri Kantseliarii Turkestanskago general-
gubernatora, 1913: 32–33). This appears to have unleashed a
considerable flow of discussion in which one finds as speakers
not only Kryshtofovich, who by then had served some three
years as the Russian government's agricultural agent in the
United States, but also Stepan Gulishambarov, who was the author of an analysis of the American petroleum industry based
on his visit in connection with the Chicago exposition in 1893
(further discussed below, about midpoint in Chapter 5). The
subject was put to a vote, and it turned out that Kryshtofovich's
feeling that any agent selected should be a person with long-
term experience in the United States was not supported. This
may have been something of a blow to him for he had had at
least 20 years residence in the United States by then (*Trudy* . . .
33–37).

Most of the speeches at the conference, as summarized in
the *Trudy* . . . , dealt with practicalities of irrigation projects,
transport, and labor, but the final meeting, that of December 1,
heard Kryshtofovich state "In almost every report, in every sort
of tone, the words 'America,' 'American success,' etc. have been

used. Russian cotton growers look upon America as an ideal toward which one must strive."

"Long residence in the United States has brought me to the conclusion that the chief cause of American success is the wide application of cooperation. . . ." (*Trudy* . . . 131–32).

The conference report also contains an outline of a talk presented by Kryshtofovich on agricultural cooperative assistance in the American cotton belt, with reference to a "Dr. Nepp," who proves to be Seaman A. Knapp, founder of American agricultural extension efforts, and of the system of county agents. Not only did Kryshtofovich talk about cotton, but he also referred to such means of training young farm boys and girls as "corn clubs," "tomato canning clubs," etc., which gave out prizes. An instance of the use of such clubs in Russia will be noted below (*Trudy* . . . 140–41).

One of the other speakers was the district agronomist of Syr-Dar'inskaia oblast', V. Ia. Anderson, who is listed among the participants as "Vil'iam Iakovlevich Anderson," a form of the name that is an almost certain indication of an Anglophone background, as Russians rather tended to use the Germanic Wilhelm (transliterated "Vil'gel'm"). The region for which Anderson was responsible was a significant producer of cotton and it appears that this experience and his probable ethnic background stood him in good stead, for shortly after the conference had presented its recommendation Anderson was appointed not as a special agent for dealing with cotton but as chief agent in America of the Russian agricultural administration (*Turkestanskoe sel'skoe khoziaistvo*, 1913, no. 8: 806–08). His name can be found attached to many communications from the American agency that appeared in the Russian press and he remained in office until the various representatives of the Russian provisional government dispersed after the October Revolution. Since the National Archives contain some of the papers of these Russian bodies, one can find letters and documents from Anderson in which he signs himself equally skillfully in both English and Russian.

Anderson's English-speaking background is almost wholly confirmed by the fact that he is named as "William Peter Anderson" in the list of participants in an American meeting reported in *Dry-Farming and Rural Homes* (October 1913: 331), a journal devoted to methods of farming in rain-poor regions, which was a subject of considerable interest in Turkestan.

There still remains for both men, Anderson and Kryshtof-ovich, the need for substantial research into the exact scope of their role in informing Russia of American agriculture and into the effect that they may have had on the country. Their writings show them to have been alert and confident men, although perhaps Kryshtofovich tried to cover too much territory with his recommendations on everything from dry farming to fruit growing to quick-maturing varieties of corn, and Anderson seems the better trained, albeit in the single crop of cotton.

At the same time that Kryshtofovich, Shreder, Anderson, and the delegates to the Tashkent meeting were discussing cotton and the applicability of American experience, there was, at the other end of the empire, another effort underway to draw upon our example. For a long time various areas in the south of Russia, including the Caucasus in one corner and the province of Bessarabia in the other, had grown corn (kukuruza in Russian), but poor methods and unreliable seed stock had limited production. There had been several decades of studies, usually not very well coordinated and somewhat remote from the actual peasant farm, about means of improving the situation. There had also been translations of American books, importations of American machines, and other references to our practices, and, at last, in 1910 the Bessarabian province zemstvo decided to bring in an American specialist to provide real "know-how" for the local equivalent of "dirt farmers."

The American chosen for this was the young agricultural chemist Louis Guy Michael, who had studied and worked at the Iowa State College of Agriculture and the Mechanic Arts (now Iowa State University at Ames) developing methods for testing seed corn and for cultivation. The leader in this activity was Professor Perry G. Holden, who traveled over the state of Iowa lecturing farmers on how to improve their harvests, an effort that aroused the interest of the Chicago, Rock Island, and Pacific Railroad, which realized that the more corn grown, the more freight there would be to ship. The railroad provided a special demonstration train to carry lecturers and displays to farmers, and young Michael was among the first of these lecturers. The Bessarabian zemstvo, through the intermediary of agents in Odessa for American farm machines, asked Professor Holden to conduct similar work in their region, but being unwilling to leave the United States Holden recommended Michael. In February 1910 Michael arrived in Russia and in Kishinev, the governmental center for Bessarabia, he met the twenty or so officials with whom he would have to deal (Louis Guy Michael, *More corn for Bessarabia: Russian experience 1910–1917*. Lansing, Michigan State University Press, 1983. 13–15).

"To start my campaign on a high note, I had taken with me a supply of propaganda badges such as those worn in the United States during political or other campaigns. On the button was a replica of an ideal ear of corn in yellow. Around the rim was my campaign slogan in Russian—'More Corn for Bessarabia'" (Michael, op. cit., 15). This very American prop for Michael's enterprise seems to have been puzzling to the Russians, and there also seems to have been some dissension among the zemstvo members that kept bringing hindrances to his efforts. However, he set to work with good will, but was himself puzzled by the great variety of ethnic groups—German settlers, Ukrainians, Moldavians, and others—to whom he was expected to give his information. Some of the major landowners were more absentee landlords than active managers, while the peasants on the other hand were so wrapped in tradition that, when it was suggested that they could improve their crops by some very simple procedures of seed selection, they said, "We are all children of God. If He wants us to have a good harvest, He will give us one. It is sacrilegious to do anything in opposition to His will. All is as God wills" (Michael, op. cit., 27).

As one means of coping with such reluctance, both of large landowners and of the peasants, Michael adopted the approach of asking teachers to organize some of their pupils into corn clubs for both boys and girls. "Each club member was to be instructed how to select good sound ears of corn from his own father's crib. These ears were to be brought to the school, where a few kernels from each ear would be tested for germination strength and the best ear would be selected for seed. Each club member would plant the kernels of this best ear in a single row on a plot of the school land. He would then cultivate his own row of corn during the growing season and at the end of the season the three pupils making the best records would receive cash prizes" (Michael, op. cit., 35–36).

Through these and other methods, Michael endeavored to spread improved methods of growing corn not only to the students in school but also to their elders. And it appears that he had some success, for some of the younger peasants asked him to stop wasting his time on children and show them how to do it (Michael, op. cit., 50). Not only did he teach by example, but he appeared in print, adapting to Bessarabian conditions Professor Holden's *ABC of Corn Culture* (Springfield, Ohio, Simmons Publishing Co., 1906). [Russian edition reviewed in *Iuzhno-Russkaia sel'sko-khoziaistvennaia gazeta*, no. 25, 1912: 25.]

Further information about Louis Michael's experiences in Bessarabia can be found in three reports from John H. Grout, U.S. consul in Odessa, that were published in the Department of Commerce and Labor's *Daily Consular and Trade Reports* in 1911 through 1913. Quotations from Michael's own letters that were conveyed by Grout show his optimism for the outcome of his efforts and his recognition that, if the dispersal of the large landed estates were to continue, the future of agriculture would rest in the hands of exactly those peasants and small farmers whom Stolypin had wished to benefit. In 1911 Grout ended his report by writing, "It is predicted by advanced Bessarabians that, as a result of Mr. Michael's efforts, the time is very near when the Province will lead all other Provinces in Russia in corn cultivation, and, after supplying home demands, will do a large export business" (*Daily Consular and Trade Reports*, January 18, 1911: 216–17). A year later Grout told of further work by Michael that promised well, although the growing season had been wet and cold. While American varieties of corn had not been particularly successful, American methods of seed selection and cultivation could be profitably applied to the local cultivars and the local authorities had recognized these benefits by increasing funds from a previous 20,000 rubles to 60,000 (*Daily Consular and Trade Reports*, January 25, 1912: 409).

And the next year, although the weather was again uncooperative, American methods had once more proven themselves. The appropriation had been increased from an equivalent of $18,540 for 1912 to $64,325 for 1913, and individual landowners were acquiring an increasing number of tractor plow outfits, as well as all kinds of American corn tools (*Daily Consular and Trade Reports,* April 5, 1913: 109).

All in all, it appears that the six years, 1910–16, during which Michael was employed by the Bessarabian zemstvo were productive ones for him. There was at least some measurable progress toward increased quantity and quality of corn production and, though many landowners still remained unconvinced that the reforms begun by Stolypin would be helpful, the agriculture of the area did benefit. Michael was not, of course, the only corn specialist at work in Russia, although no other American's name has thus far come to light, and there were many more items in the Russian agricultural press besides his edition of Holden's book. One can find many pages in the Russian agricultural journals of the period telling of experiments elsewhere with varieties of corn named "Broun-kounti," "Liming," "Minnezota," and "konskii zub" (Brown County, Leaming, Minnesota, and horse tooth), and the advertising pages of these journals included notices of both American imports and Russian models of machinery for cultivating or processing corn.

When one adds this element of corn and its production to the other factors of cotton and its machinery, and of Russian analyses of the wheat production system of the United States, there is no doubt that there was an appreciable transfer of technology from America to Russia. Yet, as has been stated at several other places in this survey, it would require much detailed research, using many varieties of evidence, to determine what the actual weight of this influence was. Russia, after all, with the adoption of the measures proposed by Stolypin, had entered upon her own independent course of development and, while the American example could be helpful, the determinant elements were those arising from her own situation. Information from the period, whether statistical or based on educated inference, does seem to show that, had the processes of the period from 1907 to 1914 been allowed to continue, the peoples of the Russian Empire would soon have reached a stage of development that, as things turned out, did not come to pass until several decades later—if, indeed, such a stage has yet been reached.

As a somewhat unexpected result of examining the materials relating to the establishment and operations of these agencies of both the imperial agricultural authorities and of the two more local bodies, there proved to be a quite serious Russian interest in an agricultural tool then only in its developmental stage. This was the tractor. Efforts had been made, from the 1860s or so, to adapt steam engines to the tasks of plowing, but these machines were large, heavy devices, which generally required a trained operator and often complicated procedures for use.

In the very late 1880s, as gasoline engines became practical, various American inventors built quite a number of odd looking devices that, they claimed, could plow, run threshing machines, and provide power for other tools. Apparently the first one of these things to be sold to a customer in the United States—and stay sold—was one produced by the Charter Gas Engine Company of Sterling, Illinois in 1889 (Charles H. Wendel, *Encyclopedia of American farm tractors*. Sarasota, Florida, Crestline Publishing, 1979. p. 5). The one, slightly blurred, photograph of this contraption that is available shows it to have two enormous flywheels and what appears to be gearing designed by Rube Goldberg, but it seems to have worked (Wendel, op. cit.). In 1900 two engineering students at the University of Wisconsin, Charles W. Hart and Charles H. Parr, began efforts to design gasoline traction engines and by 1903 they had progressed far enough to have built fifteen of them. It took a great deal of developmental work before these could truly be suitable for pulling plows, rather than merely being stationary sources of power for threshing or silage cutting, but by the end of the first decade of the century the Hart-Parr machine was far enough along to be considered an efficient replacement not only for the horse but also for the steam plowing engines that were also being produced. There is a claim by the man who was the sales manager for the Hart-Parr Company that he had invented the word *tractor*, a word that he used in the company's advertising in 1907 (Wendel, op. cit., 133).

Whether this claim of primacy in the use of the word *tractor* is valid or not, for the word may have originated elsewhere, the Russians quite soon were using it. Pedashenko's agricultural bibliography for 1908 has three entries dealing with "traktory" in the journals *Khoziaistvo* and *Khutorianin*, which unfortunately are not available in the Library of Congress for that year. However, there are other indications in the years that followed that some Russian agriculturalists were interested in the idea of the tractor. The rather short-lived but very interesting journal *Amerikanskoe sel'skoe khoziaistvo* [American agriculture] published in St. Petersburg by one George Grigorieff, in its first issue, that of September 1909, had an article on the use of kerosene tractors for plowing and other uses in the United States. The same journal for 1910 and 1911 had a two-part article for which only the title needs to be cited to show its general approach, "The development of plowing with the aid of mechanical power sources in the United States: Economy and practicality resulting from mechanical engines for heavy agricultural work." [*Amerikanskoe sel'skoe khoziaistvo*, no. 9 (September 1910): 4–5; no. 1, 1911: 5–8.] In the December 1910 issue of *Iuzhno-Vostochnyi Khoziain*, an organ of the Imperial Don-Kuban-Terek Agricultural Society, there is a reference to a tractor of the International Harvesting Machine Company having been displayed at work, though not tested, at the society's testing station (*Iugo-Vostochnyi Khoziain* 1910, no. 12: 44).

Even more significant evidence of the Russian interest in tractors is provided by the official *Izviestiia* [News] of the Biuro po sel'sko-khoziaistvennoi mekhanikie [Bureau of agricultural mechanization] of the Uchenyi komitet [Scientific committee] of the Glavno upravlenie zemleustroistva i zemledieliia [Main administration of land reclamation and agriculture], issued from 1909 until 1916. Many articles in this journal deal with tractors, some being translations from American sources, others reprints from the Russian agricultural press, and yet others reports of the Bureau's own studies. In 1910 there is, for example, a report of the Third Winnipeg Tractor Competition, which was an annual event between 1908 and 1914 at which both Canadian and American producers of gasoline and steam tractors presented their products for testing. This article rests upon materials taken from the American journals *Farm Implement News* and *American Thresherman* and is filled with data on fuel consumption, tractive effort, weight upon driving wheels, etc., of the various models shown, most of which were American (*Izvestiia . . .* 1910, no. 2, otd. 2: 261–72).

The next year there is a reference to an article that appeared in *Sel'skii khoziain* (1912, no. 1: 18. Not available in the

Library of Congress) that told of the first Hart-Parr tractor having reached Russia in 1910—purchase arranged by F. F. Kryshtofovich (*Izviestiia* ... 1911: 718. NB: The contradiction in dates of the two sources appears to have rested on the delay in appearance of the last issue of *Izviestiia* ... for 1911).

In 1911 the journal *Khoziaistvo*, issued weekly by the South Russian Society for Encouragement of Agriculture and Agricultural Industry, included in the issue dated February 24 an article "Traktory v Sievernoi Amerikie" [Tractors in North America] by an author whose name at first gave rise to some speculation, for it is signed "V. Benzin," and "benzin" is the common Russian word for gasoline. But reference to other Russian agricultural literature and to the National Union Catalog of the Library of Congress showed that the name was not at all pseudonymous and that Mr. Benzin had been a student at the University of Minnesota, a contributor to other Russian journals on both American and Russian topics, and, after the Russian Revolution, apparently an emigré who wrote on Alaskan agriculture. His article on tractors is concise, illustrated by several photographs or sketches, and includes a map that marks the distribution of tractors in the United States. It appears that the particular areas of concentration were the Dakotas, Eastern Colorado, and the Texas Panhandle, regions in which wheat was the chief crop. However, Benzin's text, based on data from the Department of Agriculture, states that there were only something over 500 tractors in use. Benzin's interest in tractors was apparently of some standing, as he had, three years before writing, heard a lecture on the advantages of tractors from one of the members of the Hart-Parr firm, and he offers some preliminary cost analyses showing that while horse-plowing was still a cheaper way of doing the job ($1.20 to $1.30 per acre by horse as contrasted with $1.40 for the tractor), the speed and convenience of the tractor work was an advantage.

His last sentence was "One must think that the introduction of tractors at home in Russia would be, in suitable areas, of the same character in the steppe region of the South and, possibly, in Siberia." This is signed from "N. America. Minnesota experiment station" (Vasilii Benzin, "Traktory v Sievernoi Amerikie." *Khoziaistvo*, no. 8, 1911: 237–42).

That this interest was not entirely a mere expression of surprise at the development of new and clever machines seems to be proved by the fact that later that same year this same journal, *Khoziaistvo,* contained a three-part article "Some data about American steam and gasoline tractors and about one threshing machine (From an answer to inquiries from Novorossiia)" which was written by A. Kol', who is identified as the assistant agricultural agent in the North American United States. Kol', as did Benzin, provides some cost figures for the machines, but is somewhat more descriptive of the types of soil and operations for which tractors are best suited. He did not feel that the steam tractor was the total answer to the farmer's need, but that, since it was easier in Russia to find a steam engine operator than a man familiar with gasoline engines, they might still be useful there. Even if gasoline motors were used, single-cylinder forms would be more easily dealt with, since "in place of four riddles they presented the operator with only one."

Yet, some factors favored the gasoline machines, and Kol' proceeds to examine them in detail. He differentiates three major types—one or two cylinders, four or multicylinder, and crawler tractors. The first were necessarily heavy, especially in the fly-wheels which had to supply enough momentum for continuous power, but vibrated greatly, nonetheless. The four-cylinder tractors, smoother in their operation, tended to have very large driving wheels which often became mired. The crawler tractor avoided some of the problems of the other two types, but had its own difficulties because of its more complicated transmissions.

Kol' clearly had made a thorough investigation of the major types of American tractors and had also inquired as to the terms upon which the makers could supply them for export.

The Holt factory [predecessor of the Caterpillar firm] offered the following conditions to me for export to Russia: they will send the machine no later than 10 days after receipt of the order. The price is $4150, which includes packing for export and delivery to dockside in New York. Payment of $1,500 is due with the order and the balance after 30 days. Because of the distance to Russia, one should, at the time of purchase, order the major spare parts, as recommended by the factory, in case of breakage or the need for repair. The plant estimates the cost of such material at from $200 to $300.

Kol' also gives similar figures for the Hart-Parr, Rumely "Oil Pull," Gas Traction Company, and Flour City tractors. It would be difficult, he writes, to recommend any particular make or model, but advises would-be purchasers to take into account the experience and reliability of the various makers, and, while some of his remarks indicate that he was not yet completely certain that tractors could be easily introduced into Russia, which lacked some of the skilled mechanics needed for their maintenance and repair, he gives the names and addresses of six American firms to which inquiries might be sent [A. Kol', "Niekotoryia dannyia ob amerikanskikh parovykh i gazolino-vykh traktorakh i ob odnoi molotilkie (Iz otvieta na zaprosy iz Novorossii)" *Khoziaistvo*, no. 10, 1911: 305–11; no. 11: 336–41; no. 12: 370–75].

Later that year, in *Khoziaistvo*, no. 39, there is a short note signed by I. B. Rozen, "Eshche nieskol'ko slov ob amerikanskikh kerosinovykh traktorakh" [A few more words about the American kerosene tractor]. Rozen, as the representative in the United States of the Ekaterinoslav province zemstvo, was charged with acquiring information on American agriculture and assisting in the ordering of machines, purchasing of seed, etc. He offers some figures on the cost per acre of plowing which differ markedly from those given by Benzin, as they run to 37 cents an acre for kerosene-powered tractors, 51 cents for gasoline, and 89 cents for steam. There is a clear preference shown for the product of the Gas Traction Company for, although a Hart-Parr machine with equivalent plows would be six to seven hundred rubles cheaper, the economies of operation were not in its favor.

"Either tractor, as well as the Rumely and Kinnard-Hains, may be ordered directly from the manufacturer through the Ekaterinoslav agency, by writing to the agronomy section of the Ekaterinoslav province zemstvo board" (I. B. Rozen, *Khoziaistvo*, no. 39, 1911: 1247–48).

And, to prove that this was not entirely an abstract enchantment with new gadgets, the quite business-like "Mezhdunarodnaia kompaniia zhatvennykh mashin v Amerikie" [International Harvesting Machine Company in America] in its advertisement on the inside front cover of the June 1911 issue of *Iugo-Vostochnyi khoziain* included among its offerings "Traktory, t. e. gruntovye lokomotivy s plugami" [Tractors, i.e. land locomotives with plows] and some of the journals of 1912 contain advertisements for the Rumely or Hart-Parr firms with illustrations of massive and complicated-looking machines traveling down endless vistas of furrows with a number of plows in tow.

In 1913 there was an extensive article, the title of which may be translated as "Report of field observations on the work of tractors on private estates in the south of Russia in 1912," that told of the experience of nine estates with fifteen different machines. These machines included those produced by the Hart-Parr Company, the International Harvester Company, and the Rumely firm (the "Oil-Pull"). Only one tractor, the Stockmotorpflug, was not of American make. There are many pictures and much comparative data, and, although the problems of spare parts and of finding skilled repair men were mentioned, the general conclusion seems to have been that the applicability of tractors to Russian agriculture deserved full and careful attention (A. B. Treivas, ed. by A. A. Baranovskii. Otchet ob ekskursionnykh nabliudeniiakh nad rabotoi sel'sko-khoziaistvennykh traktorov v chastnykh imieniiakh iuga Rossii v 1912 g. In: Biuro po sel'sko-khoziaistvennoi mekhanikie. *Izviestiia*, 1913, vyp. 1: 203–64).

For one last look at the Russian interest in tractors in the era before the First World War, there is the article on the All-Russian Exhibition in Kiev in 1913 that appeared in the *Ezhegodnik* . . . of the Russian agricultural administration for 1914 (p. 84–97). This covers almost 14 pages and includes a number of photographs, both from the makers' catalogs and from field trials held at the fair. One needs to look carefully back and forth between two of these photographs, comparing the catalog illustration of placement of exhaust pipes and gear handles, to determine that one of the cuts does indeed show a Holt Caterpillar tractor, largely obscured by the accompanying groups of prosperous looking gentlemen whose nationality is established by the presence of two typical Russian bureaucrats in the uniforms that were obligatory even for civil officials at the time. The text tells the results of the field tests, which showed the Holt firm to have been the winner, although the others represented—Hart-Parr, Pioneer, Case, Rumely, and the German firm Stock—were satisfactory, save for the German make Stock.

There is no doubt that tractors and various self-propelled machines attracted the greatest interest in this [machinery] section among the landowners, since the cost of labor and of work stock for some time now has placed in the forefront the question of the effectiveness of motorized agriculture in Russia. Although this problem had already been solved, theoretically, its practical realization among us presents many difficulties, the chief one being that all machines for motorized agriculture, beginning with the tractors themselves and with other motors and ending with the tools that operate under their power, will have to be ordered by us from the North American States, which costs a great deal, and moreover, they are produced in a country that presents a great variety of climatic, soil, and economic conditions, a fact that explains the great variety of types of American machines and tools for motorized cultivation (*Ezhegodnik* . . . 1914: 84).

This variety of equipment is confusing to Russian landowners, who would have to cope with the flood of catalogs and descriptions, "filled with artful advertising," and thus it would be desirable to set up exhibits and competitions of tractors and the machines they operate and to publicize the results, especially in grain or sugar beet growing areas, where the problems of labor and work stock were particularly severe. The article then examines in some detail the tractors displayed and it becomes clear that each of the American firms already had representatives in Russia, and therefore must have had some reasonable expectations of sales.

In one of the concluding paragraphs the article speaks well of the tractors of the International Harvester Company, which were displayed but which did not compete at the Kiev exhibition, saying that the 20 to 25 HP models "bring the tractor close to the means and needs of the smaller farms; and if only there would appear 10 to 15 HP tractors, they would be suitable in price even for the small farmers, who constantly are asking the editors of agricultural journals where they can get tractors or self-propelled machines with multi-share plows in a price range that would not exceed 3 to 4 thousand. Such machines might be acquired by groups of small farmers on a cooperative basis." Here, in a somewhat generalized form, is a thought that the Soviet regime was to use as the basis for its ultimately quite different system of organizing agriculture, which was to collectivize the use of the tractor as a means of control from above, and not as an outgrowth of mutual agreement among the peasants. It may also be pointed out that the Soviet statistical handbook for many years held to the practice of reporting the national stock of tractors in terms of 15-horsepower units (*Ezh-egodnik* . . . 1914: 84–97).

However, the most telling figure of all, not about tractors, but about the overall role of American agricultural machinery in the Russian Empire, is found in a survey on the problem of agricultural machines in wartime that appeared in the *Izviestiia* of the Main Administration of Land Reclamation and Agriculture on October 12/25, 1914. Of all the harvesting and mowing machines in Russia, 44.5 percent were of American make, and 47.8 percent were from Russian factories, and thus, since grain was an absolutely central element in the Russian economy, American machines were equally essential to its production. Loss of this American machinery would have meant a catastrophic decline in Russia's ability to keep herself supplied with grain and at the same time to maintain an army from among those laborers whom the harvesting machines set free from their toil in the fields (Russia. Glavnoe upravlenie zemleustroistva i zemledieliia. *Izviestiia*, 1914, no. 41: 994).

It was not, however, always the complicated agricultural devices that drew Russian attention, for in *Zemlediel'cheskaia gazeta* (no. 4, 1914: 116), one finds, in the form of a translation from the American journal *Country Gentleman*, an article "Prostoi ovoskop" [A simple egg-candler] that describes one of the typically American improvisations that helped a farmer do his work. An egg-candler, for the benefit of the urban reader, allows the inspection of an egg to determine if it is fresh, which is done by holding it against a concentrated light source so that the position of the yolk and the internal air space, determinants of the age of the egg, can be seen.

Russian fiscal and tax policies were such that they tended to favor the marketing, at whatever cost to the producer, of the year's crop as soon after harvest as possible, an outlook expressed by the statement of Ivan Vyshnegradskii, minister of finance in the era 1887–1892, to the effect that Russia might starve but that she would continue to export. That this was indeed the case is shown by the very great delay in placing an embargo on the export of grain during the great famine of 1891–1892, a period in which one may observe a sharp peak in the statistics of American grain exports. Even in years of better harvests there was a constant awareness of the "konkurrentsiia amerikantsev" [competition of the Americans], with items appearing in such publications as the ministry of finance's official *Viestnik finansov* about such topics as rains in the Dakotas or new freight rate structures among the Trans-Mississippi railroads.

It was, however, a more intricate problem for the Russians to proceed from such an awareness of the American factor to any practical measures for improving their own position. As has been shown, there was much discussion of the American marketing system, as typified in Russian eyes by the grain elevator, but there were few results, for scarcely 100 elevators were in operation as the war began in 1914, and the Soviets inherited only a couple of dozen or so more that were completed or under construction by the end of 1917.

One of the major impediments, of course, to any great application of the American model was the prevailing organization of Russian agriculture under two differing modes of large estates, generally property of the landed gentry, and of the communal lands of the peasants. The latter were, until the adoption of some drastic but belated reforms, held within the bounds of a form of management that almost totally prevented any broad individual enterprise, keeping agricultural methods to a narrow and unproductive traditional pattern. The administration of Stolypin, the bold prime minister of the period 1906–1911, did undertake to allow individual peasants to receive their land in full property, so that, as Stolypin indicated, the strong and efficient peasant would not be held back by his less enterprising fellow villagers. Some Russian critics of Stolypin's policies, including V. I. Lenin, recognized that, in effect, the end result would be the creation of individual farms of a type that might be compared with those of America.

In the vast flow of literature on this subject, however, there is relatively little directly said about the United States, but the increased attention to American methods, as shown by the establishment of the official Russian agricultural agency in this country, does seem to imply a wish to draw upon the American experience in a more direct and persistent fashion than had been the case with the grain elevator. While the financial statistics for official support of agricultural activities in the last years before the First World War do not show the expenditure of any really great sums of money in comparison with the United States, the total had in fact grown from some 3.9 million rubles in 1904 to 34 million in 1914 (i.e., from about 1.9 to 17 million dollars), and one finds a number of direct comparisons of Russian and American policy in the field of governmental agricultural activities. That the interest in the American model was not confined solely to the central government and its agencies is shown by the work undertaken first by the Ekaterinoslav zemstvo and then by the successor body of the Kiev agricultural society, as well as the broad American content of the Turkestan society's journal, and by the Bessarabian zemstvo's employment of the corn specialist Louis Michael. Further instances could be cited from the available literature, but these examples suffice to show the general thread of Russian reaction.

It was, however, impossible to avoid the inclusion of a rather detailed survey of the pre-1914 Russian interest in the tractor, an implement that, although produced in other countries, was largely an American innovation in those years. When, at the end of the 1920s, the Soviets reached the decision to base their agricultural system on a combination of the collective farm and the tractor, they were not at all acting in a vacuum. There had been a long history of experience with the management of agriculture through the medium of the large estate, and much of the way in which the landed gentry had exercised control over their peasants was not all that different from the measures applied by Stalin; at the same time, the years 1908–1914 had seen an effort to study the usefulness of the tractor, with at least some preliminary introduction of tractors on the part of some landowners. Indeed, as indicated by the citation to the report of tractor tests at Kiev contained in the 1914 issue of the *Ezhegodnik*, some of the smaller landowners—including ones, apparently, of peasant status—were beginning to consider the subject. And the very publication in Russia of advertisements for Hart-Parr, Rumely, IHC, and Holt Caterpillar machines is an indication that a market was felt to exist.

Much more evidence could have been cited in respect to each of the three major topics of this chapter—the grain trade, the presence in America of official representatives of Russian agricultural bodies, and the interest in the tractor—but the foregoing seems sufficient to support the conclusion that among all the factors in Russo-American relations before 1917, that of agriculture had the greatest ultimate effect. Furthermore, the Soviets in no way appear to have expressed any attitude toward American agriculture that cannot find its parallel in the observation of Russians from the days of the empire.

Saltykov-Shchedrin foresaw a possibility that Russia would one day import grain from America, a prophecy realized under L. I. Brezhnev. The Bessarabian zemstvo hired the Iowa corn specialist Louis G. Michael, while Nikita Khrushchev, rather deprecatingly known among some of the bolder Soviets as "Nikita-kukuruznik" (Nikita the corn grower, from "kukuruza," corn), visited Roswell Garst's farm in Iowa. Stalin's thundering platitudes about the role of the tractor in transforming Russian agriculture merely echoed, in a much diminished form, statements of people such as Kol', Rozen, and the very appropriately named Benzin.

There is much that needs to be done to study this aspect of Russo-American relations. While this chapter is apparently the first broad survey in print of the topic, it is only intended as a preliminary guide to what has been found to be an enormous literature, often of a most informed and serious nature, that shows pre-1917 Russians to have been unshakably aware that much of the economic situation of their nation could be understood only against the background of the United States, both as a competitor and as a role model. Further detailed examination of these records would clearly repay the effort in any attempt to understand relations between the two major powers of the present world.

CHAPTER FIVE

Forty Commissars in Chicago: Russian Perceptions of American Technology, Methods, and Education

Russian interest in the American example was not limited solely to agriculture. It has already been noted that the early development of the Russian railroad system was based quite firmly on a direct transfer of technology through the advice of Major George Washington Whistler, the bridge designs of William Howe, and the locomotive and car design of the firm backed by the Baltimorean Winans brothers and by Harrison and Eastwick. In the period before 1865 there were other instances in which the Russians showed a close interest in the ways in which Americans did things, and it would indeed require a long and detailed study to cover the topic as it deserves.

For example—by way of a rapid summary—at least five vessels were built in America for the Russian navy before 1860. In that same year a Russian officer, present at ordnance tests at Fort Monroe, Virginia, was able to acquire knowledge of a new, more evenly burning cannon powder developed by Major T. J. Rodman which was to serve as a basic feature of Russian artillery practice for the next twenty years. Early in the Civil War a Russian officer visited the United States to study its telegraph system, and the Grand Duke Konstantin Nikolaevich, the General-Admiral of the Russian fleet, within weeks of hearing in March of 1862 of *Monitor* and *Merrimack,* sent a delegation of four officers to examine America's ironclads. As a result, the Russian naval appropriations of 1863 included funds for ten single-turret monitors, almost rivet for rivet copies of Ericsson's original design. The Russians, however, also did not fail to note Confederate practices, for they ultimately built two and acquired another of what an 1890s Russian newspaper called "merrimaky." And their policy on the building of coastal fortifications took into account the conclusions expressed by Major General Quincy Adams Gillmore, whose operations had succeeded in an attack against Fort Pulaski at the mouth of the Savannah River, but that had failed against Fort Sumter. And for quite a number of years the prevailing infantry arm in the Russian army was a rifle converted to breechloading action that had been developed by Colonel Hiram Berdan of a Civil War unit known as Berdan's Sharpshooters, a weapon known to the tsar's soldiers as a "berdanka."

It was not merely the military face of American technology that was of interest to the Russians. Several missions were sent after the Civil War to study American railroads, and, at the time of the Philadelphia Centennial Exposition in 1876 a number of Russian experts came not only to enjoy an excursion, but also to examine broader aspects of American technology. While no American library appears to have reported holding Ivan Sytenko's report on the pneumatic and hydraulic brakes used by American railroads, one does find his *Gorodskoe khoziaistvo v Soedinennykh Shtatakh Sievernoi Ameriki* [Municipal services in the United States of North America] (Moscow, Tip. I. Chuksina, 1877. 124 p.), the title page of which explains his variety of interests by identifying him as "Engineer of the lines of communication, heading the Moscow city water system."

The mining engineer Konstantin A. Skal'kovskii, whose list of publications shows that he evidently prided himself on a broad outlook, for he wrote not only on professional topics but also on ballet, women, and trade in the Pacific Ocean area, published *Gornoe zakonodatel'stvo v Soedinennykh Shtatakh Sievernoi Ameriki* [Mining law in the United States of North America] (St. Petersburg, Tip. A. Transhelia, 1876. 63 p.) and also collected travel articles he had written for the conservative *Novoe vremia* of St. Petersburg into a somewhat sour *V stranie iga i svobody; putevyia vpechatleniia* [In the country of the yoke and of freedom; travel impressions] (St. Petersburg, Tip. T-va "Obshchestvennaia pol'za," 1878. 415 p.).

A much more important visitor to the United States in 1876 was the great chemist Dmitrii Ivanovich Mendeleev, whose brilliant arrangement of the chemical elements resulted in the chart that hangs in every chemistry laboratory and classroom. He came in order to study the American petroleum industry and his observations resulted in *Neftianaia promyshlennost' v Sievero-Amerikanskom shtatie Pensil'vanii i na Kavkazie* [The petroleum industry in the North American state of Pennsylvania and in the Caucasus] (St. Petersburg, Tip. T-va "Obshchestvennaia pol'za," 1877. 304 p. Reprinted in *Sochineniia*, v. 10. Moscow-Leningrad, Izdatel'stvo Akademii nauk SSSR, 1949), the title of which shows his intent of contrasting Russian and American practices and, if possible, of drawing on technological solutions that could be adopted in Russia. It should be noted that Russian methods of the time tended to be somewhat primitive and that, as a result, there were substantial imports of American kerosene into the empire. Mendeleev's impressions of America, both technological and social, were less than favorable. Here is a sample: "It was clear to everyone that in the North American states it was not the best but the mediocre and worst aspects of European civilization that had been expressed and developed. . . .The new dawn is not visible on that side of the ocean" (op. cit., 151).

It appears that not only did Russians visit America in search of technological information but they also read some of America's technical literature. The extent of this is not wholly clear, for it would require a close survey of the Russian publications of the time to find evidence of this. However, there are such indications as the advertisement of the subscription agency "Buchhandlung von Carl Ricker in St. Petersburg" which by chance is bound in with the Library of Congress copy of the December 1878 issue of *Viestnik Evropy.* Among the journals listed are *American Law Register, Official Gazette of the United States Patent Office, American Chemist, American Medical Journal,*

New York Medical Review, Popular Science Monthly (then a most serious publication), *Scientific American, American Brewers Gazette, Bulletin of the American Iron and Steel Association,* or the *American Educational Monthly,* to mention only those titles that are immediately identifiable as of American origin. A short session with a publishers' guide of the period would probably add others to this list.

Russians were not only concerned with the nuts and bolts of American technology but they sought to learn of the structural and conceptual framework that made this technology possible. One early expression of this was a short article that appeared in the professional journal of the Russian navy, *Morskoi sbornik* (no. 5, 1860: 55–72) under the signature of Mikhail Khristoforovich Reitern, a rising young civilian administrator who had been sent abroad, including a visit to the United States, to study accounting methods and the organization of pension funds. His article, "Vliianie ekonomicheskago kharaktera naroda na obrazovanii kapitalov" [The influence of the economic character of a people on capital formation], was in essence an argument in favor of economic freedom, on the American model, in place of the controlled pattern of the Russian system. The enterprise and adaptability of the Americans is compared with similar qualities of flexibility and presence of mind among the Russians, but the difference in the attainments of the two systems is explained by the fact that in Russia everything is controlled from the center, hedged in by prescriptive rules, and subject to all kinds of governmental action, or nonaction. Reitern refers to the impeding effects of slavery in the American South as an example of the way in which compulsion in economics is in the end counterproductive. His remarks about the American situation demonstrate rather considerable knowledge and a good deal of thought, and they are basically intended to be used as a means of analyzing the harm that the Russian system of serfdom and centralized control brought to the nation. The poor development of trade and industry in Russia is explicable,

Not only because there exists a class of serfs, but because the economic initiative of all the others . . . is held in a tight framework which determines from birth for each his sphere of activity, out of which he can transfer only with great effort. It is also because, in order to keep everyone in his place, a general police surveillance is necessary that stifles the initiative of the working classes and burdens the administration with enormous, fruitless work. We are convinced that any step toward the easing of these bonds, which restrain the economic activity of the people, will be a step toward the development of national well-being, as well as toward the improvement of our administration" . . . (Reitern, op. cit.: 71–72).

There seems to be nothing else that directly reflects Reitern's experience in or thoughts about the United States, but it is significant that within two years of the publication of this article, in 1862, he was appointed minister of finance, a post that he held until 1878. During that term of service Reitern had to face three major problems, stabilization of the Russian currency, which was based on silver and which fluctuated against both gold and paper money; the furtherance of railroad construction; and the extension of the Russian industrial system. These problems were in their general outlines the same as those that the United States had to deal with in the period following the Civil War. Close study of the details of Russian fiscal policy in the time of Reitern's ministry would undoubtedly permit one to reach some verdict as to how far the attitude toward the United States expressed in his article of 1860 affected his official decisions and policies.

Another frequent commentator on the American economic system was Nikolai Khristianovich Bunge (1823–1895). His first major work, *Teoriia kredita* [The theory of credit] (Kiev, V universitetskoi tipografii, 1852) included references to the writings of the American economist Henry Charles Carey (1793–1879), considered by many Europeans to be America's most prominent thinker in the field. Bunge's later works include further comments on Carey's thought, and in addition draw on many American examples, in order to support an argument that, for instance, a banking system should be relatively free of artificial restraints, for it would be "(a) safer and more solid; (b) cheaper; (c) more responsive [to the needs of the situation]; and (d) more natural" (Bunge, *Otechestvennyia zapiski.*, v. 125, 1859: 463).

An article by Bunge in 1867 in the rather conservative *Russkii viestnik*, "Bumazhnyia den'gi i bankovaia sistema Sievero-Amerikanskikh Soedinennykh Shtatov" [Paper money and the banking system of the North American United States] (1867, no. 8: 311–77) dealt with the American approach to the problem of re-establishing the currency in the post-Civil War period, a problem that very closely paralleled the Russian situation in the aftermath of the Crimean War of the 1850s, but that, even after more than a dozen years, had not been solved. Another article in *Russkii viestnik* in 1867 (no. 10: 431–62; no. 11: 5–47) examined the foreign trade positions of Russia, Great Britain, France, Austria, the German Zollverein, and the United States, and, although somewhat indirectly, expresses a certain concern with the way in which America's railroads would allow that country to be an active marketer of agricultural products.

Although there is relatively little discoverable in the printed record of Bunge's views in the 1870s and 1880s, it is significant that in 1882, after four years of interim holders of the office, Bunge was appointed minister of finance, a post that he held until 1887. Again, the sources are somewhat obscure and the tasks of uncovering them are complex, but it would certainly be worth the effort to determine the way in which Bunge may have included the American situation in his decision-making process. He had, for example, to continue to deal with the problem of restoring Russia's currency, for, just as Reitern felt that he was close to a solution of the problem, the empire found itself at war with Turkey, a war that it won militarily, albeit after some difficulties, and the monetary system of the nation was again unsettled. This happened just at the time when, at the beginning of 1879, the United States returned to a freely convertible monetary system in which one did not have to examine the daily papers to find out how much a paper dollar was worth in terms of coins.

Some of the Russian observers of the time looked even deeper into the American situation than the mere factors of technology or of fiscal policy, and saw a more basic explanation. America's strength, in their view, rested not on machinery, and not on the currency system or similar factors, but on the existence in the United States of a broadly educated, alert and—to use a rather horrible expression of German origin—goal-conscious people. The central cause of this was, so many wrote, the American educational system. Only a trained and efficient work force would explain so productive and well-organized an economy. There were, as a result, numerous Russian publications examining the structure of American schools, the outlook that they inculcated, and the enlivening effect upon the country as a whole. Some of these publications were translations from the writings of Western European observers, but a few were by Russians themselves. Again, any full analysis of this literature would call for both broad and detailed references to the unexpectedly rich sources that exist and would also go far beyond the limits of the present study.

However, as a way of demonstrating something of the nature of this three-pronged Russian interest in America's technology, industrial organization, and educational system, one particular event may be singled out for examination. That event, which stretched from May 1 to October 31, 1893, was the World's Columbian Exposition in Chicago, held to mark the 400th anniversary of Columbus's voyage. It displayed so many facets of the culture, technology, and economy of the world that, even now, more than ninety years later, it is difficult to comprehend its impact. For the many Americans and foreign visitors who came it was a revelation of how broad the human experience could be, and, if one were to select one single sentence to express the feeling, it would be Hamlin Garland's message to his parents that said, approximately, "Come, even if you have to sell the kitchen stove."

The whole world came, not only as visitors, but also as official exhibitors or delegates. The British formed, it is said, the largest contingent. The next was that of Russia. "And I remind the Russian reader that we have in Chicago *forty* commissars for a survey of the exposition" (M. I. Veniukov, "Illinois i Chikago." *Nabliudatel'*, May 1893: 273). The official report on Russian participation in the exposition, however, lists 59 people who were sent to Chicago by various ministries and public agencies, as well as some people in high places who came as "private" visitors, such as the Ober-shtal'meister [Master of the Horse] Count Orlov-Davydov and the Governor-General of the Amur Province, General-Lieutenant Dukhovskoi. This report is a quite substantial volume, filled with a good many high quality photoengravings and copious details not only about the exhibits but also about the way in which some of the visitors extended their survey to include inspection of broader operations of the American economy.

In this respect it must be said that factories and all sorts of technical establishments of America were widely open for visits, and all, especially engineers and professors, had free access to study them as they wished, with all possible cooperation on the part of the owners, managers, or engineers. Nowhere in Europe is there such free access as in America for a detailed survey of technical equipment and plants, not excluding the most specialized, and this was particularly so during the period of the Columbian Exposition. Here there was no policy of jealously guarding special installations from the eyes of those who were interested in them, as there was in general little in the way of trade secrets. In particular our Russian delegates could make free use in this respect of the openness of Americans since between the two distant countries there can be no question of mutual competition through jealousy (Russia. *Otchet General'nago kommisara russkago otdiela Vsemirnoi Kolumbovoi Vystavki v Chikago Kamergera Vysochaishago Dvora Glukhovskago* [Report of the general commissar of the Russian section of the World's Columbian Exposition in Chicago Gentleman of the Imperial Court Glukhovskoi]. St. Petersburg, Tipografiia V. Kirshbauma, 1895. 150 p.).

There was some quite serious preparation on Russian's part for the exposition, including at least three substantial official publications, one of which, *Fabrichno-zavodskaia promyshlennost' i torgovlia Rossii* [The Factory-Mill Industry and Trade of Russia] (St. Petersburg, 1893. 320, 352 p.) was noted as having been edited by D. I. Mendeleev himself, while another, a catalog of the Russian exhibits, appeared in both English and Russian and ran to 577 pages. [See review in: *Sievernyi viestnik*, August 1893: 64–67.] One finds other indications, such as an advertisement in the major St. Petersburg newspaper *Novoe vremia* of January 17/29, 1893 (p. 6) by an English engineer offering his services as a representative of firms wishing to participate in the Chicago fair, followed by a similar advertisement a week later from a Russian, already an agent for a number of companies (*Novoe vremia*, January 24/February 5, 1893: 6). In February a classified advertisement read: Une anglaise de Londres cherche des leçons avec des personnes qui vont à Chicago. S'addresser par écrit à. . . . (*Novoe vremia*, 16/28 February 1893: 5).

On April 1/13 (p. 3) a correspondent of *Novoe vremia* writing from Paris offered advice on how to reach Chicago, and on

April 22/May 4 (p. 1) the Norddeutscher Lloyd advertised its ships and other services for those going to America. The April 26/May 8 issue (p. 1) contained an announcement of the Torgovyi Dom L. i E. Metsl' i Ko. which could place advertisements in all Chicago newspapers. More detailed advice on American travel, including side excursions to Niagara Falls and discussion of the advantages of, say, the Pennsylvania Railroad over the Baltimore and Ohio route, appeared on April 30/May 12 (p. 2) dated from New York over the signature of one N. P. Mel'nikov. Similar advertisements of travel companies and of people offering themselves as guides continued to appear throughout the summer, although one might ask how many Russians could actually afford such a voyage, for the International Sleeping Car Company (Compagnie Internationale des Wagons-Lits) on August 5/17 (p. 4) stated that its excursions ranged in price upwards from 1,900 francs (about $400), an enormous sum of money in comparison with the average Russian income.

Although most Russians had to stay home, some very substantial information was available to them in the general press. Among the most productive writers on this theme was Varvara N. MakGakhan (as she transcribed her name into Russian), the Russian-born widow of the American newspaper correspondent Januarius Aloysius MacGahan (whose reports on the repression of the Bulgarians in the era of the Russo-Turkish War of 1877–1878 had done a great deal to create sympathy for their cause; J. A. MacGahan, in fact, is still regarded as a hero in Bulgarian eyes). Mrs. MacGahan had settled in the United States and from the 1880s was a frequent contributor to the Russian press on American themes, largely to the journal *Sievernyi viestnik*. Although this publication had a rather small circulation (an inventory of the 1880s showing only some 3,500 copies printed), her collaboration was a lengthy one, and her accounts were detailed, usually thoughtful and correct, as well as being imbued with a great deal of the spirit of the socially conscious elements of the Russian intelligentsia. Even before the exposition opened, she was discussing its plans, and some of her articles during the spring and summer of 1893 were almost stupefying in their detail (V. MakGakhan [MacGahan], Pis'ma iz Ameriki. XX. Vodovorot amerikanskoi dieiatel'nosti i ego zhertv [Letters from America. XX. The watershed of

American activity and its victims]. *Sievernyi viestnik,* January 1892: 103–14). In spite of the rather gloomy sound of the title of this article, it is principally concerned with the Chicago exposition and with the growth of New York City. [For the exposition itself, see her "Pis'ma iz Ameriki. XXXVII. Vsemirnyie kongressy na kolumbiiskoi vystavkie" (Letters from America. XXXVII. World congresses at the Columbian Exposition). *Sievernyi viestnik,* June 1893: 68–74.]

Other reports, which reached a larger public than did *Sievernyi viestnik,* appeared from the pen of V. V. Sviatlovskii in the newspaper *Novoe vremia.* At least 39 articles by Sviatlovskii were published, usually under the running head "V strane dollarov" [In the land of the dollar] between April 12/24 and September 13/25, dealing not only with the exposition itself but also with topics such as the treatment of the American Indian, the petroleum industry, Niagara Falls, and the allegedly good situation of the car builders at the Pullman Company under the beneficent policies of George Pullman, workers whose resentment was to burst forth in the famous strike of 1894. The writer appears to have been a competent reporter, if not particularly profound or colorful in his style, and the general effect is that of an informative series, undoubtedly touching on numbers of topics of interest to the Russian reader.

It appears, however, that there were enough Russian visitors to Chicago, in addition to those sent officially, to make it worthwhile to publish a few guidebooks in Russian. One of the most interesting of these was N. Pliskii's *Podrobnyi putevoditel' na Vsemirnuiu kolumbovu vystavku v Chikago 1893 goda* [Detailed guide to the World's Columbian Exposition in Chicago in 1893] (St. Petersburg, 1893. 125, vi., 32 p.). It is full of all kinds of information, from the procedures for obtaining a Russian passport for foreign travel, to the methods for checking baggage on the North German Lloyd ships, to the costs of hotels in New York. These, it is said, range from 25 cents to 3 dollars a day, but one can live more cheaply in a "berding-khouz" [boarding house]. The reader is told how to buy a railroad ticket and it is explained that, "In the front of the locomotive there is attached an apparatus called the catcher of the cows (cow cather) [sic—in English] which throws wandering cattle, stones, timber off the road." American railroads are praised, although the present-day reader may find it hard to believe that Pullman cars "are outstandingly ventilated, so that passengers in 103° (32° Reaumur) in the shade, and wearing light flannel clothing, feel quite comfortable" (Pliskii, op. cit.: 7–52 passim).

The traveler at last reaches "Chikago. Tsaritsa Zapada" [Chicago. Empress of the West] where one can find even a number of twenty-story buildings that are justly called "skai-skrepers" [sky scrapers], in a city populated by at least 30 separate national groups, ranging from 292,463 Americans, including Blacks, to 2 Sioux Indians. It is a growing city, for in 1891 alone building permits had been granted for 11,805 new structures. Turning to Chicago's role in food processing, Pliskii then provides a good deal of information that can perhaps best be summarized in the words of Carl Sandburg, "Hog-butcher of the world" (Pliskii, op. cit.: 62–65).

After his general survey of the city, Pliskii gets down to the topics of hotels, hack fares, and other matters of daily life. A page and a half is devoted to "pivnyia zaly," which he gives in English as "salloons."

Many of these saloons are decorated with great elegance, expensive mirrors enhance the walls, the floor is often in mosaic or in other fine material. All is well cleaned and bright. Such places often yield nothing to the hotels in their exteriors. There is nothing in them that might shock the most demanding visitor.. . . .Very good beer is sold there, and in particular there is an endless series of strong drinks from whiskey or schnapps (vodka) to the most fantastic mixed drinks, . . .

Some of these saloons might well be recommended to the visitor to the Exposition, since they outstrip all others in the grandeur of their decoration, comfort, high quality of beverages, speed and courtesy of the staff. As a result of these features they enjoy the very high patronage of the most outstanding people in Chicago.

Was it not said of Chicago saloons of the time that, when [a new one] opened, the owner walked over to Lake Michigan, threw the door key into the water, walked back to his place of business, and never closed his doors again? And were not some of these men very influential politicians? (Pliskii, op. cit.: 75–76).

Of course, the truest voice of all saloonkeepers in Chicago had not yet appeared in early 1893, for it was not until October that the public heard from Martin Dooley, of "Archey Road" in Chicago, whose most telling phrase was, in mentioning Theodore Roosevelt's account of his experience in the Spanish-

American War, to say that if it had been his book he would have titled it "Alone in Cubia." Yet, somehow, Pliskii in his further listing of bars, wine stores, beer gardens, and the like does not seem to have totally missed the target of conveying something of the spirit of Chicago, for his detail is never quite out of harmony with the clumsy, often boring, but yet telling method by which Theodore Dreiser was soon to create his lumpy masterpieces.

Finally, after this generous imparting of information about Chicago, which occasionally affords a more personal glimpse of Pliskii's approach to comprehending a colorful and varied city, he deals with the World's Columbian Exposition itself. One's discovery that pages 105–112 in the Library of Congress copy of his guide had never been opened in the intervening 92 years says something of how far out of sight the topic of foreign participation in the exposition has sunk, but these pages, even if Pliskii has been superficial and maybe not always well-informed, deal with the description of the agricultural, horticultural, forestry, fisheries, mining, and industrial buildings, which, as later reference will show, were central to the Russian view of the Chicago exposition.

Included as a supplement are a number of pages containing useful English phrases for the visitor, printed in both languages, and in a Russian phonetic transcription. Rendering some of these back into the Roman alphabet, we have: uan, tu, zsri, for, faiv, seks; Kebman, tu Broduei; Dzet iz tu dir; Gav mi e glas of uoter; Ai em et e boll' enekspektedli tu-dei; and the understandable, if quite unorthodox, Khou mech du iu wil' dzet uosh e shert? But it is unkind to make fun of all this, as one can remember the harmless merriment caused in Rio de Janeiro by a similar use of a phrase-book to find some corn plasters.

Furthermore Pliskii was no greenhorn when it came to American matters, for he appears in the Library of Congress catalog as the author of two other works dealing to some degree with this country. In 1893 there appeared his *Prichiny bystrago obogashcheniia amerikantsev i prevoskhodstva amerikanskikh millionerov nad evropeiskimi* [Causes of the rapid enrichment of the Americans and of the superiority of the American millionaires over those of Europe] (St. Petersburg, Nevskaia artis. Tipo-lit.

Stefana i Kachka, 1893. 27 p.) and in 1894 there was his *Rek-lama* [Advertising] (1894. 175 p.) which speaks of America as the home of the advertising man. As his guide to Chicago shows, he had some comprehension of the points that were important to his audience and of ways of telling its members in simple language the things that were most essential to his purpose. And that is the core of the advertising man's effort.

All in all, the Russian traveler who reached Chicago with Pliskii's guide in his hand could not have gone too far wrong, and its information had the potential for being of interest to some users who might at first impression seem unlikely customers of the bright, cheerful, and comfortable saloons of the city. The Institutions of the Empress Mariia, which supported institutions for the training of the blind and deaf and other charities, chose as its delegates to Chicago O. K. Aderkas and a Mrs. Siemechkina. In an article in the education journal *Obrazovanie* for September 1893, Mr. Aderkas tells of the installing of the Russian exhibits, including those of his own institution, and of the ceremony of formal dedication that took place on June 9/21. All Russians in Chicago were invited, as well as a number of others, and a total of 60 persons gathered for the ceremony in which Nikolai, Bishop of the Aleutians and Alaska, blessed the premises. Following this, "all those present went into the neighboring room, where a table had been prepared, decorated with palms and flowers, and laden with hors d'oeuvres, cooling drinks, tea, fruit, etc." Aderkas spoke, thanking the bishop, and saying that, after the fair, most of the exhibits would be given to American charitable and educational institutions.

He ended his speech with a toast to the health of the Lord Emperor and the Lady Empress, answered by all those present with a loud hurrah.

After this there were toasts to Bishop Nikolai, to Count N. A. Pratasov-Bakhmetev and Gentleman of the Chamber D. V. Kniazev (chairman of the St. Petersburg committee that prepared the exhibit), to the general commissioner of the exhibit, to the delegates of the Institutes of the Empress Mariia, to the success of the Institutes of the Empress Mariia, to the guests that were present, etc. (O. K. Aderkas. Na vystavkie v Chikago [At the exposition in Chicago] *Obrazovanie*, September 1893: 115).

There followed, Aderkas writes, a detailed inspection of the displays.

Despite these festivities, the educational specialists who visited the exposition actually accomplished some quite serious work. The most striking proof of this is Evgraf Petrovich Ko-valevskii's *Narodnoe obrazovanie v Soedinennykh Shtatakh Sievernoi Ameriki (vysshee, srednee, nizshee)* [Public education in the United States of North America (higher, intermediate, lower)] (St. Petersburg, Tipografiia V. S. Balasheva i Ko., 1895. 592 p.), which is a telling witness to the Russian view of the role of education in American life.

Through great good fortune the bound copy of this work in the Library of Congress includes the original paper cover. It shows, on the left, the Statue of Liberty, with rays emanating from the torch, between which are the figures and abbreviation for $200,000,000, and on the right a portrait of Horace Mann, the founder of American pedagogical methods. Below the title is a box reading "23% of the population in Educ(ational) Inst(itutions)." On handling the book it almost automatically falls open at the one folded plate it contains. This shows "a city primary school in the city of Indianapolis (state of Indiana, North American United States)," with students seated at rigidly aligned desks in a room that with its blackboards, portraits of national leaders, and architectural proportions recalls the atmosphere of an old-fashioned public school in a depression-ridden town in Illinois in the early 1930s, but that also conveys something of the same message, to the effect that the pursuit of knowledge might be a path to future benefits.

The impressions conveyed by these two single artifacts of the paper cover and the folded plate are such as to make it almost excessive to survey much of the text, but it is worth noting some of the more specific indications of Russian attitudes toward the American experience in education.

In issuing, with the assistance of the Ministry of Public Education, this modest work, the compiler hopes that the information imparted in it will present a certain degree of interest for our thin pedagogical literature and that it will direct the attention of persons involved in education toward the energy and liberality, which is worthy of attention, that has been evidenced in the field of education of the people of our Transatlantic competitor.

Fervently striving toward the attainment of universal education, Americans do not forget that the development of industry, agriculture, commerce, and the trades is directly proportional to the amount of knowledge possessed by the people and that this knowledge is one of the signs of the strength and power of the country.

But the republic does not only aim at mere material well-being, spending ¼ of its budget on the education of the people and having in its schools 23 percent of its population. It seeks, and attains, a spiritual development of the people, and this development, while it cannot be valued in money, is immeasurably higher than any material benefit; it is a result of the system of public educational institutions of the country, and it comprises an object of justifiable pride and moral satisfaction of every American [Evgraf P. Kovalevskii, *Narodnoe obrazovanie v Soedinennkykh Shtatakh Sievernoi Ameriiki (vysshee, srednee i nizshee)*. St. Petersburg, Tipografiia V. S. Balasheva i Ko., 1895. viii. Hereafter: Kovalevskii, *Narodnoe obrazovanie* . . .].

There is much in the pages that follow these introductory remarks to reinforce memories of the remarks of older relatives who, with varying degrees of interest or success, were touched by the education system of late nineteenth century America, as pupils, as teachers, or as poorly educated parents who still appreciated the possible value of an often seemingly hopeless striving for improvement. There is something of the memory of the one-room country schools, now frequently decayed into casual shelters for the neighboring farmer's corn, that lay strewn along the muddy roads which followed the unmitigatedly rigid lines of the land-survey system. The compilers of this Russian work had some awareness of the many variations among the states as to just how the task of funding and controlling these schools was carried out, and they recognized that there were many other difficulties, but it would be an imperceptive reader indeed who could fail to note their admiration of the general results. Nor can one avoid some impression of the presence of other social factors in the Russian analysis, as, for example, "Women may be elected to positions on the school board in Massachusetts, Pennsylvania, Rhode Island, Kansas, Colorado, California, Idaho, and elsewhere" (Kovalevskii, *Narodnoe obrazovanie* . . . p. 25, fn. 3).

A telling indication of one facet of the Russian view of American education is the illustration on page 65 that shows the teacher and pupils of an ungraded school somewhere in Kansas, posed in front of a building that is nothing more than the traditional "sod shanty on the plains," built of blocks of turf cut from the prairie soil.

The work covers problems of organization, financing, teaching methods, the compulsory education laws, secondary schools, university and college training, teacher education, physical education, school buildings and furnishings, and the training of the deaf and blind. Footnotes show the use of a most varied number of sources, from the school legislation of Indiana, to Lester F. Ward's *Dynamic Sociology,* James Bryce's *American Commonwealth,* and the Harvard catalog. The general attitude is one of respect and even of admiration for the way in which Americans have spent so much effort on education, although flaws in the system do not go unnoticed.

Almost two hundred pages of Kovalevskii's work deal with the subject of education as presented at the Chicago Exposition both by America and by other countries. There are reports on such special features as exhibits dealing with kindergartens, reform schools, societies for the prevention of cruelty to children, and the congresses of educators held in connection with the Exposition. There is no summation to the whole work that draws a set of conclusions as to how all this could be applied to Russia, but there is a very interesting report of a conversation with an unidentified American professor who had lived for some time in Moscow and St. Petersburg, and who had traveled through Russia, which conveys some of the responses that a person trained in the field might have as to the applicability of the American example to Russia. There is a temptation to put a name to this anonymous American professor and to say that Kovalevskii had been talking with Andrew Dickson White (1832–1918), who had been the first president of Cornell University and had served as the American representative in Russia and Germany. From 1892 to 1894 he was our minister in St. Petersburg, meeting such representative, if incompatible people as Konstantin Petrovich Pobedonostsev, Ober-Prokuror of the Most Holy Governing Synod, an equivalent of minister for church affairs, and L. N. Tolstoi, by then a thorough opponent of Orthodox doctrinal rigidity. White is the only American whose name rises immediately to mind as having had the Russian experience, and American educational qualifications, to say what is conveyed in these remarks.

At any rate, use of such remarks attributed to an anonymous American professor offers an excellent way of advancing proposals for Russia that, if uttered in Kovalevskii's own voice, might have posed problems for him. If for no other reason, the "American professor's" suggestion that, before anything be undertaken, local leaders be consulted, "who, without doubt, are more competent in questions touching their local interests than you officials sitting in the bureaux in St. Petersburg," could be seen as an expression of support for the *zemstva*, the Russian local government authorities chosen on an electoral basis, even if the representation of the various social groups was an unbalanced one. The *zemstva* were looked on with marked disfavor by the more conservative elements of the government, and the new emperor, Nicholas II, had upon his accession referred to the "senseless dreams" that the zemstvo principle could lead to some form of public participation in the national government. Furthermore the American noted that, since Russia lacked any fixed tax for educational purposes, schools depended on the varying allocations of funds made by the *zemstva* out of resources that were already quite limited. Thus, there were variations from province to province in the support of education (Kovalevskii, *Narodnoe obrazovanie* . . . 536–37).

Kovalevskii also reports the American's remarks about the censorship. "In order that a certain woman landowner, Ivanova, in, for example, Vologda province might read in winter to a group of peasants a few little books specially intended for public reading and having passed, as I found, three censorships—general, religious, and educational—she must obtain the consent of two ministries and the Ober-Prokuror of the Synod" (Kovalevskii, *Narodnoe obrazovanie* . . . 542). The Ober-Prokuror of the Synod from 1881 to 1905 was that dessicated scholar of law, tutor to both Alexander III and Nicholas II, arch-Antisemite, passionate enemy of freedom of expression, and, quite oddly, a dedicated reader of the works of Ralph Waldo Emerson, Konstantin Petrovich Pobedonostsev. While Andrew D. White's article about the man that appeared in the *Century Magazine* in 1898 suggests that he was not quite so rigid a personality as myth would have it, Pobedonostsev was feared and hated by many of the Russian intellectual class. It was he who in 1901 was to further the excommunication of Tolstoi, an act that had a certain justification, for Tolstoi had certainly gone beyond the bounds of Orthodoxy, but one that was carried through with unnecessary strictness and that served to generate a great deal of reactionary polemic.

The American had favorable opinions as to the quality of

Russian education of girls and of technical instruction, but felt that teacher training needed greater attention. Furthermore, Russian schools tended to emphasize Latin and Greek to the disadvantage of the natural sciences. Even those schools that emphasized science and commercial studies, modeled after the German Realschule, lacked laboratory facilities, while language instruction tended to slight the teaching of English. Worst of all, the fact that graduates of such institutions could not easily enter the universities was viewed as a defect in the system, and it was suggested that these graduates might be admitted on the basis of examination and some supplementary training.

The impression that the "American professor" may indeed have been Andrew D. White is strengthened by statements of support of the "elective system" at the university level, for Cornell University under White's administration was one of the American pioneers in allowing students to chose some of their courses. There was also a proposal for activities that might be compared to university extension classes and to similar reading circles (Kovalevskii, *Narodnoe obrazovanie* . . . 543–44).

In the last two pages of this "conversation with an American professor," Kovalevskii reports the American's views on the great role that a national system of education would have as a unifying institution.

The role of the public school in Russia is truly enormous. Only by making use of it is it possible to set the people on the path of moral improvement and to improve its material well-being. But, in addition to that, a school in the hands of the government is a powerful tool for the unification of the various tribes and peoples, scattered over the broad face of the Russian land. Only by means of the school, open equally to all children of school age, independently of their class, sex, and faith, a school with instruction in the national language, is it possible, *as the experience of other countries shows* [Italics added], to unite students differing from one another in language, faith, and customs (Kovalevskii, *Narodnoe obrazovanie* . . . 544–45).

In its spirit and in its fundamentals the public school should be marked by a national character. To bring from a foreign country any sort of ready-made school is impossible, for the school is indissolubly bound up with the conditions of life of the country in which it functions and is under the direct influence of the social views and convictions that prevail in a given epoch. . . .On the other hand, a complete separation of the school from the general movement of culture and a derisive denial of the value of what is being done in other countries certainly cannot at all be justified. In order not to fall behind the others, and especially if one wishes to progress, one must know what is being done by them and be able to make use of all that is good among the neighbors, accepting and applying only the spirit of improvement, but not its letter, and certainly not in any servile manner and on faith, but with rationality, and in conformity with one's own national traits (Kovalevskii, *Narodnoe obrazovanie* . . . 546).

These views, whether they were actually those of Andrew D. White or were Kovalevskii's manner of advancing opinions that might draw fire if he were to present them as his own, were not at all totally new in the Russian literature. By 1893 there had already been an extensive number of publications about the American school system, some of which were translations of authors such as the French writers Celestin Hippeau and Émile Jonveaux, or the German Rudolf Dulon, and others were produced by such Russians as Eduard R. Tsimmerman or, in sections of his works, by the theologian Aleksandr Lopukhin. However, the participation of Russian specialists in education in the activities of the Chicago exposition appear to have had some lasting effects. Kovalevskii contributed an article to the *Report* of the U.S. Office of Education for 1902 (Washington, Government Printing Office, 1903. 1139–46) on Russian education, containing no direct views on the American situation, but testifying to a continuing interest in maintaining relations with educators in the United States.

Almost twenty years after the Chicago exposition, a two-volume work appeared in St. Petersburg that brought together Kovalevskii's speeches, reports, and articles in the years 1907–1912 in connection with the problem of education in the work of the Third Gosudarstvennaia Duma, Russia's quasi-parliament, *Narodnoe obrazovanie i tserkovnoe dostoianie v III-i Gosudarstvennoi Dumie* [Public education and church resources in the Third Gosudarstvennaia Duma] (St. Petersburg, 1912. 2 v. in 1), containing, it is true, only two or three direct references to the United States, but presenting a view of Kovalevskii's activities as one of those who felt that the Duma, despite its limitations, was an institution in which there could be a gradual, step-by-step construction of a real edifice, "although the circumstances of Russian political life make this slow and modest effort especially difficult and unrewarding. It is not enough merely to lay 'brick upon brick,' to go 'step by step,' but one must also struggle, be vigilant, and defend each new brick and

each step forward" (Kovalevskii, *Narodnoe obrazovanie i tserkovnoe dostoianie . . .* Introduction by A. Ol'ginskii. p. I-II).

In reading this volume one gains a clear view of a trait of
persistence and devotion in Kovalevskii's attitude toward the
problems of education that at first seem greatly out of harmony
with the fact that on page 131 (footnote 3) he is identified as a
member of the Octobrist Party, often presented, especially in
Soviet works, as a group of hidebound reactionaries, dead set
against any efforts to widen access to education. However,
going on to consider the views Kovalevskii expresses on pages
298–303 on the widening of possibilities for graduates of the
"real'nye uchilishcha" to enter the universities, it is clear he had
remained true in the years 1907–1912 to ideas contained in his
1895 report of the conversation with the "American professor."
And, toward the very end of the volume on education, Kovalevskii is quoted as having said on June 5, 1912 (O. S.), "It is
impossible to stop the development of universal education, for
the whole country firmly demands it!" (Kovalevskii, *Narodnoe
obrazovanie i tserkovnoe dostoianie. . .* 353).

Of those who took part in the publication of the 1895 volume on education at the Chicago exposition, Kovalevskii was
not the only one to continue an interest in the American school
system. In fact, much of the subsequent activity of Pavel Grigor'evich Mizhuev, who had supplied the chapter on American
secondary education in Kovalevskii's study, was connected with
America. Not only did he write about schools, he also produced
volumes on American history, and he continued his writing
about the American educational system into the early years of
the Soviet regime. One of his works, published in 1925, dealt
with the same theme of secondary education in the United
States that he had written about in 1895. It is again a problem
for a specialist to determine the full extent of Mizhuev's knowledge of the United States and the depth of his understanding
of our educational system. However, from an examination of
but one of his volumes, it is clear that he had a very good knowledge of the literature in the field, ranging over some forty years
of the printed record, for in his *Sovremennaia shkola v Evropie i
Amerikie* [The contemporary school in Europe and America]
(Moscow, Knigoizdatel'stvo "Pol'za," 1912. 247 p.) he draws on
sources ranging from an 1870s translation of the work of a

British visitor to this country, Bryce's *American Commonwealth*, a book on the evolution of the Massachusetts public school system by a certain Martin, and the 1907 report of the United States Commissioner of Education, to mention only those items that have an American aspect.

Even a somewhat superficial comparison of the chapter on the American high school that Mizhuev had contributed to Kovalevskii's Chicago exposition volume (Kovalevskii, *Narodnoe obrazovanie* . . . 187–230) with his more extended discussion of the subject in 1912 shows that he maintained a consistency of outlook and that he continued to feel that the broad scope in America for individual, nongovernmental effort in education had been a major element in the advancement of the country. Although, by 1912, there had been criticism of the fact that American high-school students were too involved in what we now would call extra-curricular activities, he wrote, "However the ability acquired in youth to work together in one or another activity and through such joint effort to reach this or that set of goals turns out later to be useful in the highest degree, for it is quite beneficially reflected in the most varied aspects of American life. This goes a long way toward explaining the fact that in America the organized initiative of private individuals often attains kinds of success which, apparently, the social forces of European peoples cannot reach" (Mizhuev, *Sovremennaia shkola* . . . 220).

A more statistically based effort to examine the role of education as a contributor to the American economy, with resultant lessons for Russia—an effort that was also based on experiences arising from the Chicago Exposition—is to be found in Ivan I. Ianzhul, *Ekonomicheskaia otsienka narodnago obrazovaniia* [Economic evaluation of public education] (Moscow, Tipografiia I. N. Skorokhodova, 1896. 87 p.), which included contributions not only by Ianzhul himself, but also by his wife Ekaterina Nikolaevna, by A. I. Chuprov, who has already been mentioned with regard to his views on American grain elevators, and by other educational specialists. The immediate background of this small volume is the Second Conference of Russian Workers in Professional and Technical Education, held in Moscow in 1895–96, but the deeper origins lie in the American experiences of the Ianzhuls themselves.

Ivan Ivanovich Ianzhul (1845–1914) was left an orphan at an early age. Living in the provincial town of Ryazan' to the north of Moscow, he diligently sought an education, and through his having attended a theatrical performance of the Black American actor Ira Aldridge—whose success in Russia was a deep one—the young Ianzhul was inspired to learn English, setting himself a goal of fifty words a day. This enabled him to study in Britain in the 1860s and to write his dissertation on England's tax system. In 1876 he became a professor at the University of Moscow, and in 1881 he was appointed to membership in the first group of factory inspectors under a new system established as part of an effort to mitigate some of the worst abuses. Ianzhul's reports on his work are earnest and honest accounts of the situation of the Russian factory worker of the time. But in 1887 he resigned when minister of finance Nikolai Khristianovich Bunge (already noted as a commentator on the American economist Henry Charles Carey) was replaced by Ivan Vyshnegradskii, the harsh proponent of maintaining Russia's trade balance at whatever cost ("Russia may starve, but she will export [grain]"). Ianzhul continued to write about Russia's economic situation and was a frequent contributor to *Russkiia viedomosti*, considered an organ of the liberal intelligentsia. His wife, Ekaterina Nikolaevna Veliasheva, who was an able collaborator and supporter of his views, was particularly interested in problems of education, and the two formed a most effective team. The crowning event of Ianzhul's career was his election to membership in the Academy of Sciences of the Russian Empire, a body that at times chose persons not totally in harmony with the views of officialdom.

In 1893 the couple visited Chicago, from where they contributed numerous articles on American affairs to *Russkiia viedomosti*, the husband specializing in items about the American economy and the wife, in education. These articles, along with a sustained interest in America, were to result in works by both of them, which will be mentioned below, as well as in the above-mentioned cooperative volume on the economic assessment of education. This last publication seems to have met with favor, for in 1899 there was a revised and enlarged edition, almost double in size. (This is not at present available in the Library of Congress.)

As the foreword to the first edition states, the volume was published not only to draw interest to the schools of the Imperial Russian Technical Society but to promote, as well, "the furthering of the idea of the economic value of education. 'If Russia is educated, she will also be rich,'" I. I. Ianzhul says in the conclusion of his article, and then goes on to say:

Riches will be brought by the industrial development of the country, but this development requires fundamental support for the expansion of education. This is why the proponents of primary technical education strive above all to increase literacy among the workers and the most elementary form of general education. The arguments brought together in the present book clearly show that literacy and a concomitant mental development of the workers, in themselves, increase the productivity of labor; as a result, expenditures on education are not inherently an act of philanthropy but contribute directly to satisfying the needs of the country in the sphere of the productive results of its efforts (Ianzhul, *Ekonomicheskaia otsienka* . . . III–IV).

Professor Ianzhul's article, "Znachenie obrazovaniia dlia uspiekhov promyshlennosti i torgovli" [The significance of education for the success of industry and trade] is the lead article in the volume (pp. 1–26). Much of his argument is based upon citations of such sources as the *Circulars of Information* of the U.S. Bureau of Education, the writings of the American statistician Carroll D. Wright, the eighth annual report of the U. S. Commissioner of Labor, and reports of American consuls in various European cities. His major premise is that only an educated working force can allow a country to develop its industrial system, and in support of this he emphasizes the American experience.

What are the results of those enormous expenditures for public education in all its aspects in America? The Americans have adopted the rule, as we see, in their budgetary policy that each extra kopeck spent for education inevitably brings whole rubles back to the nation in the future. Indeed, they have not been mistaken in their calculations: thanks to the broad availability of education the American nation has transformed its working classes into exemplars of the most intensive labor force in the world and thereby created its extensive industrial and economic preeminence. Universal education and the development of the nation, these are the true sources of those colossal riches, which cause everyone to stand in awe . . ." (Ianzhul, *Ekonomicheskaia otsienka* . . . 12).

In a striking instance of prescience, Ianzhul goes on to say that America is not the only country to show the importance of education, for another land can serve as a prime example. This is Japan, which is beginning to win victories in a field that may be dangerous to Europe, that of industry. Through expansion of its education and its trade and manufacturing, Japanese competition is being felt in old Europe and causing public concern, and Ianzhul quotes a businessman in Hamburg as having told him "Japan ist das höchste Unglück für Europa!" [Japan is Europe's greatest misfortune!]. Indeed, Ianzhul gives so much attention to the topic of Japan that one feels that even eight years before the Russo-Japanese War some in Russia were already deeply concerned by possible dangers of a clash (Ianzhul, *Ekonomicheskaia otsienka* . . . 13–14).

In summation Ianzhul repeats his view that only through an expansion of education could Russia advance.

. . . I sincerely believe that the statement so often made recently by us, about the need for increasing education, of making it *really* universal and accessible, will not be an idle one but that it will quickly mature and bear fruit, and the most obscure worker in the field of public education may rest assured that his work too will serve as one of those many, many millions of bricks from which, in the more or less near future, will be built the magnificent structure of Russia,—a *Russia* that will already be a country of education, a Russia in which every person will enter into life through the school doors. . . . And, if Russia is *educated*, she will be *rich* (Ianzhul, *Ekonomicheskaia otsienka*: 26. Italics in original text).

Yet, as has already been pointed out, sixteen years later E. P. Kovalevskii was still speaking of the need to defend every "brick" in the structure of education, and every step forward that had been made, and was still pointing to the American example as an inspiration to Russian action in the field. Why so little progress seems to have been made in all that time is an inviting subject for a great deal of demanding and detailed research, to look into the political and financial sides of Russian life as well as into the socio-economic situation. That is not the purpose of the present survey, the intent of which is rather to point out the persistence of America in Russian discussions of the topic.

In some ways an even more striking use of America is to be found in the second article in *Ekonomicheskaia otsienka* . . . , A. I. Chuprov's "Znanie i narodnoe bogatstvo" [Knowledge and national wealth] (p. 27–51). Chuprov perhaps tries to deal with too many theoretical and historical questions, as he provides a sort of capsule history of educational thought, but he proceeds to a summary examination of the workings of universal education in Britain and in France, with data on the accompanying rise in national well-being that, in his eyes, is a result. He then writes, "All that has been done in the area of education in Europe pales before the North American United States." He cites figures to show that the proportion of students to the total population there is not to be matched in any other country of the world, and mentions in particular that in America the average monthly pay of a male teacher in 1889 was $42 and of a woman $34. He refers to institutions based on private philanthropy, such as the Drexel Institute in Philadelphia and Cooper Institute in New York City, as well as to the land grant colleges, and to the educational work of agricultural societies and other organizations. This effort in agriculture, according to Chuprov, had had a major effect on the role that the United States had played as a producer and, although here he does not directly refer to Russo-American competition, the undertone is there, but there is a much more direct statement about the prospect of American gains in the field of industry. Production of iron and steel, of cotton cloth, and of industry as a whole had increased at an unheard-of rate in the United States, with total manufacturing output growing by about 65 percent in the period 1880–90.

In view of these major successes, which in terms of their size and rapidity cannot be matched in all of history, pessimistic forebodings are already beginning to appear within the European industrial world. In the course of over two thousand years European culture set the tone for the whole world; but now they fearfully await the moment when America will leave old Europe behind in the main branches of industry. One of the contemporary German publicists notes with despair, "culture, like the sun, moves from east to west. From Babylon, Athens, Rome, it passed to London and Paris, and now is moving across the Atlantic Ocean to New York and Chicago." The exposition in Chicago can offer, perhaps, still greater grounds for such gloomy conclusions.

Chuprov provides a footnote that appears to indicate that the German "publicist" probably was Hermann Julius Losch (1863–1935), but does not identify the work quoted.

"What can account for this colossal growth of industry and wealth?" It was not, Chuprov says, the treasures of soil and cli-

mate, nor the ethnic make-up of the population, nor the reserves of capital nor the size of the labor force. . . . "no, these
ordinary explanations are not the ones that one can put forward as solutions to the riddle of the unparalleled economic
progress of America. In the opinion of the experts in the field,
the only, or at least the underlying, factor must be seen as the
broad-scale harnessing of the forces of nature to serve man's
ends. The American, wherever it is possible, puts the forces of
nature to work, and does it with a rare courage and knowledge"
(Ianzhul, *Ekonomicheskaia otsienka:* 45–46).

All this contrasts, Chuprov writes, with the situation in
Russia. Only about one-sixth of the population between seven
and fourteen was in school, and in the fifty major provinces this
meant that only some 2.5 percent of the whole population was
being educated. The male-female ratio was unbalanced, with
one fifth of the boys and only one-fifteenth of the girls in class.
On the average, Russia spent but seventeen kopecks per capita
of the population on schooling, while the United States figure
was equivalent to four rubles sixty-five kopecks. Statistics for
literacy showed, for example, that in 1882 in Moscow city 43
percent of the men and 61 percent of the women were illiterate. While in Prussia and Switzerland only 2 percent of army
recruits were illiterate, the data for 1874–1884 in Russia rose
to 77 percent (Ianzhul, *Ekonomicheskaia otsienka . . .* 46–48).

Chuprov's statistics on Russian industry, in comparison
with other countries, are also not glowing ones. Even major industry, protected by high tariff barriers, frequently showed adherence to outmoded methods, and in agriculture truly primitive ways prevailed.

There are, of course, more than a few causes that retard the development of
the Russian economy, but among them we must place in the most visible spot
that almost universal illiteracy which so sharply sets our fatherland apart
from any other cultured country. How can the idea for any kind of improvement reach our farmer and agricultural manager when he is not open to the
basic tool for the transmission of ideas, literacy? Mired in centuries-old routine, the farmer slavishly bows to the conditions that surround him and, un-
moved, watches while, from year to year, the harvests from his land fall . . .
It never even comes into his head that sometimes but a step away from him
there is some new, better form of application of labor, and that a minor improvement in the construction of a plow or in the tilling of fallow land might
increase his crop by half, etc.. . . .

. . . " One must not forget that the single means for coping with poverty is found in an increase of the productivity of labor, for which the best means is knowledge and education" (Ianzhul, *Ekonomicheskaia otsienka* . . . 48–51).

A third contribution to Ianzhul's survey is his wife's "Vili-ianie gramotnosti na proizvoditel'nost' truda" [The influence of literacy on the productivity of labor] which is almost entirely based upon the results of an inquiry begun in 1870 by the United States Commissioner of Education to elicit the views of employers on the value of educated workers in comparison with others. The findings were reported in the Bureau of Education's *Circulars of Information,* no. 3, 1879, showing that education was indeed a factor in indicating the level of skill and application in employment. Ekaterina Ianzhul's article is a short one, but, in addition to the above-mentioned source she has consulted other materials and there are some reflections of her own experiences during her visit to Chicago. There is a telling contrast between her reference to an opinion voiced in one of the Russian provincial zemstva that a carpenter needs an axe and not a school and her quotation from the secretary of a labor union in Massachusetts that no one should enter into the field of life without a fitting primary education, "for the class of uneducated workers is an eternal danger and hindrance to the interests of labor in any human society and any state" (Ianzhul, *Ekonomicheskaia otsienka* . . . 52–60).

Ekaterina Ianzhul continued to write about American schools, and in 1901 published the first edition of *Amerikanskaia shkola* [The American school], which was issued in at least four editions. The Library of Congress holds the second one of these, the full title of which is *Amerikanskaia shkola: ocherki metodov amerikanskoi pedagogii* [The American school: survey of the methods of American pedagogy] (2d. rev. and enl. ed. St. Petersburg, Tip. M. M. Stasiulevicha, 1904. 374 p.). One need not go into any lengthy discussion of this work, as the Ianzhuls' previous writings provide a sufficient definition of their views. However, it may be noted that Ekaterina Ianzhul appears as the author of works on education published even after the Bolshevik Revolution.

Professor Ianzhul's principal publication based on his visit to the World's Columbian Exposition was *Promyslovye sindikaty, ili predprinimatel'skie soiuzy dlia regulirovaniia proizvodstva, pre-*

imushchestvenno v Soedinennykh Shtatakh Sievernoi Ameriki [Industrial syndicates, or unions of entrepreneurs for the regulation of production, principally in the United States of North America] (St. Petersburg, Tip. M. M. Stasiulevicha, 1895. 459 p. At head of title: Ministerstvo finansov. Departament torgovli i manufaktur [Ministry of finance. Department of Trade and Manufactures]). The tone of the work may perhaps best be conveyed by the quotation on the title page from a French dictionary of political science, "In summation, there are acceptable and useful monopolies, as there are detestable and harmful ones. One should not let oneself be frightened by a word which furthermore is sometimes badly applied."

Ianzhul's investigation of American organizations to regulate production was undertaken as a mission for the Ministry of Finance of Russia, which was particularly concerned with the role of producers' syndicates in the petroleum and sugar industries, in which Russian production and trade were substantial. In his introduction Ianzhul writes, "Since similar syndicates, under various names such as, 'Trusts,' 'Pools,' and the like, in the United States comprise a majority of the chief branches of industry, and the legislatures of the various states have already made a series of enactments in regard to them, it is quite desirable for the Ministry of Finance *to become more closely acquainted both with American laws on this topic as well as with their results.*" [Italics in original] (Ianzhul, *Promyslovye sindikaty:* III–IV).

Two introductory chapters take up the general question of producers' combinations both on the theoretical level and throughout the world, and chapters three through six (p. 146–328) provide what is in essence a history of American organizations of this kind. Ianzhul describes such specific groups as the "Whiskey Trust," "Kentucky Distillers' Agreement," "Oil Cloth Trust," and the "Michigan Salt Association," as well as the Standard Oil Company and the agreements among the sugar refiners, in both of which Russia was most interested. The footnotes show that he had a broad knowledge of the technical economic literature on the question, and was aware of some of the works of controversy that had appeared in the general press. He often arrives at conclusions that were not in accord with much of the public opinion of the time, or of later scholarship, when, for example, he states that the Interstate Commerce Act of 1887, the first major federal enactment to regulate the railroads, was perhaps not all that beneficial. There was, he states, a fall in the financial standing of the railroads that led to a loss of some $500 million in stock values, and he cites an evaluation of the act in the *Political Science Quarterly,* calling it the poorly thought-out result of the ignorance of demagogues (Ianzhul, *Promyslovye sindikaty* . . . 187–94).

Ianzhul's sources also cover legal publications, and he provides a clear statement of the role of "judge-made law" in the American system, as well as of the interrelationships between state and federal law, case law, and common law. As with the works of many other Russian authors already mentioned, it would require detailed research to determine the depth of his understanding and the precise validity of his sources, but, on the whole, his book impresses the reader as being a serious scholarly effort to understand the role of agreements among American producers to control the market in relation to the larger economic picture. Given the rise in Russia of similar organization over the next two decades, it might indeed be useful to investigate whether Ianzhul and his views of America were influential in that movement.

In his general conclusion the Russian economist states that it would be impossible and undesirable to attempt to halt the development of industrial syndicates through legislation. The syndicates themselves however should assume responsibility for bettering the lot of the workers, going beyond mere philanthropy, if for no other reason than their own self-interest for, as one may summarize, higher wages mean more consumption and therefore more production (Ianzhul, *Promyslovye sindikaty* . . . 374–429).

Another author whose work is based on his visit to the Chicago exposition is Stepan Iosifovich Gulishambarov, whose special interest was in the petroleum industry and who wrote *Neftianaia promyshlennost' Soedinennykh Shtatov Sievernoi Ameriki v sviazi s obshchim promyshlennym razvitiem strany* [The petroleum industry of the United States of North America in relation to the general industrial development of the country] (St. Petersburg, Tip. V. Kirshbauma, 1894. 184 p.), which was sponsored by the Department of Trade and Manufactures of Russia. Gulishambarov not only went to Chicago, but also visited American oil regions, refineries, commodity exchanges, transport companies, etc., and he sought to place the whole industry into the framework of the national economy. He too provides much material about the Standard Oil Company and it is clear that he is concerned with that company's role in an international market for which Russia was also a producer.

Again one must refer to a need for detailed study before any substantive evaluation of Gulishambarov's views can be made, but also the broad nature of his sources must be mentioned. One detail, however, that may surprise the present-day reader appears in a table of the annual production of petroleum in the United States from 1859 to 1892 that lists only 54 barrels as having been produced in Texas in 1891, with none being reported for 1892! (Gulishambarov, *Neftianaia promyshlennost'* . . . 17).

Sergiei Dem'ianovich Kareisha's *Sievero-amerikanskiia zhelieznyia dorogi* [North American railroads] (St. Petersburg, 1896. 774 p.) is stupefying in its detail. The reader almost feels that, apart from the lack of machinist's blueprints for locomotives and rolling stock, the man who mastered this book could be fairly successful in building and managing a road, for Kareisha was most diligent in gathering information. Not only did he go to Chicago, but he also traveled over the Pennsylvania, Chicago Northwestern, Union Pacific, Southern Pacific, Santa Fe, Wabash, New York Central, and other lines to a total of 7,103 miles, and he visited such firms as Baldwin Locomotive, Carnegie Steel, and the Pullman Company, and also viewed grain elevators in Pittsburgh, Chicago, and St. Louis. His search for data was, he writes, facilitated by the fact that he was a Russian, to whom the majority of Americans were favorably inclined. He expresses thanks to the more than 40 governmental agencies and rail firms that helped him (Kareisha, *Sievero-amerikanskiia* . . . 2–4).

As has been said, Kareisha's detail is copious almost beyond belief, and there is no need for more than a superficial look at most of it. There are, for example, notes to the effect that American horse-drawn earth-moving machinery is of such a size as to require 12 horses with two drivers, but that, after his having seen one of these machines in operation in Russia, one would need to use 16 of the smaller Russian horse, with four drivers, in order to do the same work (Kareisha, *Sievero-amerikanskiia . . .* 96).

However, the discussion on pages 322–329 and 597–624 of the relationships between railroads and grain elevators is yet another indication of the Russian interest in the latter institution as one of the explanations for America's having outstripped Russia in the international market. While he provides a full translation of the rules for grain classification of the railroad and warehouse commission of the state of Illinois (p. 605–606), and of the various forms used as receipts, certificates of inspection, etc., it seems that, as with previous Russian examinations of the subject, this generated little in the way of actual, operational results.

The Russian literature that stemmed from the World's Columbian Exposition in Chicago does not end with the publications that have already been mentioned, for one can go on to cite A. D. Gattsuk on American machine tools, D. P. Konovalov on the chemical industry, D. N. Golovnin on irrigation, V. D. Tishchenko on naval stores production, and the military officer G. A. Zabudskii, who dealt with explosives manufacture. There were other writings on technical subjects, and works on social phenomena as seen by Russian visitors to Chicago in 1893 range from serious, book-length studies to passing articles in the general press.

The total effect of Russian publication about America that grew out of the World's Columbian Exposition must have been a substantial one, although, again, it would require much research to determine just what its actual extent may have been. It is, however, sufficient to note that in 1894, a year later, there was a dinner given in St. Petersburg for those who had been exhibitors or otherwise participated in the exposition, with those attending including S. Iu. Witte, minister of finance, I. D. Delianov, minister of education, A. S. Ermolov, minister of state property and agriculture, A. D. White, United States minister to Russia, and Savva T. Morozov, a major Russian industrialist. There were many speeches, congratulatory telegrams, music, and an abundance of toasts, and it is a bit difficult to note any particular connecting thread in all this, except that Ermolov, in speaking about the relationships between the two nations, noted that the Chicago fair had shown Americans

something about Russian industry as well as about agriculture
of which they already had some awareness. "In the future there
may arise in this area [industry] competition and even a clash,
but an honorable and useful one, not destructive but capable,
rather, of strengthening the organisms of the state" (*Novoe vremia*, June 10/22, 1894: 2).

From the end of the 1870s a rising flow of publications had
emanated from Germany concerned with the problem of
American competition in industry as well as in agriculture, and
it appears from citations in the Russian economic press that
many of these publications were read in Russia. However, there
was among the Russians little of the German emphasis on "die
amerikanische Gefahr" (the American peril) in the spirit of
combatting an insidious threat to economic stability. Most Russian response spoke of "honorable and useful" competition
aimed at "strenghthening the organisms of the state," to use
Ermolov's phrase.

While it does not seem that Ivan Khristoforovich Ozerov
(1869–1941) had himself visited or commented about the Chicago exposition, his writings are indeed a striking expression
of a wish to strengthen Russia through drawing upon American experience. Ozerov was one of the very, very few Russians
who had managed to make the long and difficult ascent from
peasant to a position as professor in Moscow and St. Petersburg
universities, and, ultimately, after the introduction of Russia's
quasi-constitution in 1905, to membership in the partially
elected Gosudarstvennyi soviet (Council of State), the upper
chamber of the legislative body. Although any tie with Chicago
is a remote one, it is still worth discussing Ozerov as showing
a certain ideological continuity between people such as the
Ianzhuls, Mizhuev, or Kovalevskii.

As an example, in 1903 the April and May issues of *Russkoe
ekonomicheskoe obozrienie* contained his "Amerika idet na Evropu" [America is gaining on Europe], with footnotes that show
that he had been reading some of the French, British, and Germans who were busy, as he phrased it, "ringing the alarm bells
in foretelling the storm [of American competition] that was approaching Europe ..." But the Russian author is somewhat
quicker in stating his interest in discovering the causes for
America's strength than were the German authors, for Ozerov

in his third paragraph asks, "Why is America developing so much? Indeed, in America there is protectionism, just as there is here, but America is marching with giant steps, while we have a lot of people and no work. In America famine is unknown, life is rapidly moving forward.... There aren't enough people" (Ozerov, "Amerika idet ..." *Russkoe ekonomicheskoe obozrienie*, April, 1903: 1). There follow some eight pages of data about America's economic growth up to 1900, a flow of details that add up to a view of startling economic progress, and it is only on page 10 that, finally, Ozerov observes America's poor position in commercial shipping. But then the account of American expansion resumes, and the first installment is something of a song of praise for a powerful country. "In America they attempt to develop the moral forces of the people, initiative, energy, the spirit of unity, to enlighten its mind, to enrich it by knowledge. To make use of man only as a beast of burden is viewed there as irrational, uneconomical, equal to using gold as paving for the streets, or wheat as fuel for the furnaces ..." Ozerov clearly did not know of those evil years in which Nebraska farmers burned their crops because prices were so low that they could not afford fuel (Ozerov, op. cit., 15).

It is true that there is also exploitation of child labor in America, but those enormous resources that are spent there on public education show that America values more highly than all crops, more highly than the cultivating of wheat or the hoisting of coal, the culture of the mind, the cultivating of man, which is what gives her predominance in the world....in America much attention is given to this cultivating of the mind; 25 percent of the world production of wheat is grown there, 20 percent of the gold, but to the training of the mind are allotted 40 percent of all funds used for this purpose by humanity (Ozerov, op. cit., 17).

Ozerov points out that this training of the mind was predominantly directed toward the practical tasks of life, and notes with interest such phenomena as the development of a poultry industry making wide use of incubators, heated chicken coops, etc., and the efforts in the school of agriculture of the University of Minnesota to cross-breed wheat that would be more productive and resistant to weather (Ozerov, op. cit.: 20–22).

It was true, however, that America did strive to conquer markets, and he quotes some of the complaints of, for example, British publicists who lamented the fact that America was taking over in Britain in such fields as typewriters, ladies' blouses, photographic equipment, many electrical parts, shoes, and even "pills of various kinds." From a German source he takes a reference to the fact that America is attacking Europe not with armies or with new religious or political ideas, as had been the case with previous conquests, but with bales of goods that tear old pricelists to shreds and that may act as destructively as the most modern explosive shell, "and by competition and reduction of prices they are destroying and overturning long-established ways, closely bound up with political and social relationships" (Ozerov, op. cit.: 25–27).

Although Ozerov saw some reason to expect the financial crisis in America that many Europeans were predicting, he felt that the country's balance of payments would continue to be favorable, and thus a crisis would be a passing one. More possible, however, was a sharp conflict between capital and labor, and Ozerov's evidence for this is telling and generally correct in its outlines, as there are references to the difficult position of most labor unions of the period and to the way in which the authorities tended to side with capital (Ozerov, op. cit.: 27–36). And yet,

At the present time it is hardly possible to deny that, as far as the heaping up of riches and the development of industry and of all forms of material progress may go, the United States will unquestionably take first place within a very short time. . . .Its population enjoys an education lagging only behind Germany and Switzerland and standing higher than any other European country. Their natural resources can match the resources of all of Europe. The energy of the Americans exceeds the energy of England, and their intelligence is hardly surpassed by that of the Germans or the French.

Their social and political system is more favorable to material development than any other organization ever devised by man. It is flexible and allows much scope for action. This unusual combination of national and social qualities coupled with boundless physical resources cannot fail but to give America an unquestionable edge in all material progress (Ozerov, op. cit., 36).

Thus, as one of the major reasons for America's progress Ozerov turns to the field of education, and cites data similar to those of Kovalevskii, Mizhuev, and the Ianzhuls about the proportion of the population in schools, the rates of literacy, and the total expenditures on education. To this he adds a survey of the influence of the press, "another important factor in this colossal development of the United States."

A free press is light for public life, and only in the light can one struggle with nature, creating new forms of life. In the darkness you would not risk dealing with this material. Here they make use not of clay or marble, but of the living hearts of men and their brains. We have already said that one needs above all the cultivating of the mind of man.

The subtle work of man's culture does not call for hired hands, but calls for spirit, for the free human heart, and for eyes wide open to God's world.

Europe, pay attention . . . (Ozerov, op. cit.: 42–44).

In the second installment of this article Ozerov goes on to speak very favorably of America's readiness to introduce new machinery and, what is more, to discard old but useful tools when new ones would provide greater economic benefits. These factors, in Ozerov's view, help to explain the industrial expansion of America, but, an even greater element perhaps, is the governmental structure of the United States. He quotes an unnamed American ambassador in London as having said that the civil equality of all citizens, improved education, and the fact that each citizen is not only an elector but eligible to be elected had created the industrial prosperity of America, and adds in his own words, "Here a wide field of activity is open before each person, and this stimulates him to work. Nine out of ten leaders of industry began with nothing, but the road was open before them, and the wide expanses beckoned them forward" (Ozerov, "Amerika idet . . ." *Russkoe ekonomicheskoe obozrienie*, May 1903: 1–2). Perhaps these words reflect something of the outlook Ozerov had formed from his own experience of having been one of the very few and very fortunate persons to have risen from the ranks of the peasantry into the intelligentsia in a career that culminated with his becoming a university professor and a member of the upper body of Russia's quasi-parliament.

However, in his next statement as to the elements fostering America's economic development Ozerov somewhat negates that viewpoint, for he says,

In addition to these general conditions of American life, quite favorably affecting the development of industry, a major role was played by the organization of American industry into trusts and syndicates. This created the possibility of working with enormous capital funds, sparing no expenses, introducing new improvements (as, for example, in the petroleum industry, etc.), hiring the best technicians, acquiring patents at the proper time, and not worrying about losses during the first period of the conquest of markets. Depriving American industry of the right to form syndicates would be, to a significant degree, a cutting of its wings. These giants were formed for the very purpose of struggling with European industry and America cannot make any deals with Europe in the question of a struggle with the syndicates. This would be the equivalent of disarming oneself industrially (Ozerov, op. cit., 2).

This very same process of the formation of large industrial units did not seem to be recognized by Ozerov as a limitation on the ability of other men to start with nothing in their own advance along an open road of progress. Yet, it was true, as Ozerov cites much evidence to show, that the large units of industrial management and production in America were economically more efficient, more "elastic" as he phrases it, than those of Europe. Although he does not provide the same kind of detailed information about the methods and organization of American industrial corporations that Ianzhul did in his book of some eight years previously, Ozerov repeats his general conclusions about the favorable effects of large-scale enterprise, especially in competition with foreign countries (Ozerov, op. cit.: 2–3).

It was only on the basis of these general conditions of American life and industry that a policy of protectionism could really bear fruit. This statement may perhaps be the core of Ozerov's article, for Russia too had a policy of high tariffs as a means of protecting her industries, but her development lagged greatly behind that of the United States or of the other industrial countries. If Russia were to benefit from such a system she too, so Ozerov appears to have felt, needed such elements as an educated working class, freedom of the press, a good transportation system, a policy of favoring innovation, and a more coherent and efficient form of industrial organization (Ozerov, op. cit.: 4–5).

Ozerov's survey of American methods goes on to praise the energy and knowledge of American workers which, he writes, makes them more productive than those of Europe, and he tells, in what now seems a somewhat exaggerated manner, of the generally good relationship between employer and employee. Yet, as other sources prove in abundance, America's development in the years between the Civil War and 1914 was indeed a major element in the world economy and some of that development did rest upon American energy and the generally tranquil nature of our economy. For almost twenty pages Ozerov repeats his high praise of the American system, its enterprise and flexibility, and its productivity, but finally comes to the question as to how, once America has supplied its own market, surplus production will be disposed of. The answer, he says, is that of increased export to Europe (Ozerov, op. cit., 5–23).

> The vast domestic market of the United States has so far protected Europe from being flooded with American goods, but as soon as that market is satisfied, America will begin to send to Europe an immeasurably greater amount of goods than it does now. The syndicates, trusts, and the high tariff make it possible for them to send wares to Europe at extremely low prices. Yes, the American danger is not something vague that may or may not come to pass, it is a real fact of the highest degree, which must come to pass, and if it still is not so much felt for the present, this can be explained by the enormous domestic demand which swallows up the production of the United States, so that little remains for exports (Ozerov, op. cit.: 26–27).

Much of America's ability to compete with Europe, Ozerov writes, was provided by Europe itself. ". . . European immigrants cultivated the virgin soil of America, European capital helped grow the wings of American enterprise. . . . Europe itself is arming its opponent across the ocean; such is the irony of fate." Some people had proposed, according to Ozerov, stringent measures to prevent European capital from being used to finance overseas endeavors, in order to retard the growth of such competition. However

> the stuffy, confined atmosphere of Europe forces out capital, and the spirit of freedom attracts it across the seas and oceans. . . .In Europe the established interests, the interests of the land owners, leave no room for capital to move its arms and legs. In Europe capital is hobbled, and the future brings a decrease in the purchasing power of the population. The new countries have knocked out from under Europe the foundation of agriculture, and capital is very sensitive, it foresees that the edifice might crumble . . ." (Ozerov, op. cit.: 28–29).

It cannot be said that Ozerov's phraseology is particularly clear and direct in this, for the preceding quotations have too many of the flowers of rhetorical embellishment, but his general thought is quite comprehensible. Somehow, he even brings up the instances of European grandees coming to America in search of rich wives, which were so much a topic of interest in his time, and points to them as a sort of proof of American predominance. Such measures would not, however, retard for long the the disappearance of the old feudal structure, as the American heiresses' fathers and brothers will continue their production of goods that will explode the old system and the struggle will go on. "But for the present Europe is not prepared for a struggle with the United States" (Ozerov, op. cit.: 30–31).

Much of the explanation can be found in the fact that in Europe the younger generation is trained in habits of obedience and of submission of one's will to that of higher authority. It is quite different in America, where the effort is to inculcate habits of enterprise and responsibility for one's own acts. Old feudal ways are dead there and the possibilities for the young to apply their talents are not thwarted as they are in Europe.

In his last pages Ozerov takes up the consideration of the varying effects that American competition would have on the individual countries of Europe, saying that this competition was giving rise to a spirit of protectionism there. England was being beaten both in its foreign and its domestic markets. However, "Russia is protected from the American danger by a high tariff, but this weapon is extremely double-edged, and while it may avoid the danger at a given moment, it makes us weak industrially over the long run." Europe is being flooded with a wave of competition that, at first, brings savings and improvements, but that is later seen as having a double role with consequent decline in Europe's economic ability to cope with the situation. "We have come to one of the most frightening and darkest turning points of our history; the time has come to utter a cry of alarm." This alarm, Ozerov states, has reached the point that some in Europe are even considering the need for a war with America, but there was also a fear that such a war might be lost, playing into the hands of the proletariat. This prediction, at least as it applied to Russia, was not such a bad one, but such general statements were not unparalleled at the time (Ozerov, op. cit.: 34–38).

The other solution, that of a European economic federation, might, Ozerov says, enable Europe to resist America. He cites in support of this an article in the newspaper *Torgovo-promyshlennaia gazeta,* an organ of the Ministry of Finance, reporting Andrew Carnegie's speech to students at St. Andrew's University in Scotland that proposed such a European union, failing which Europe's fate would be lamentable, leaving the nations to revolve like lilliputians around the great American Gulliver. Ozerov goes on to cite an article on the advantages of such European unity by Professor Freiherr August Sartorius von Waltershausen, published in the *Zeitschrift für Socialwissenschaft* in 1902, which urged such unity as a means of combatting American competition, a unity the feasibility of which Ozerov doubted (Ozerov, op. cit.: 38–40).

In his—admittedly somewhat over-decorated—summation, Ozerov speaks of the need for dealing with America by using America's own weapons, those of knowledge, efficiency, and persistence. Europe can only free itself from America if it learns the lessons America has to teach.

> But while we, the near-sighted ones, find it advantageous for our own petty, selfish reasons to keep large groups of the population in the situation of blind moles, delving in the earth and never raising their heads to the skies, it would be insanity to believe in a victory over America.
> We will win one fine day, when everyone, boldly and proudly—from the small to the great, from those living on the mountain tops to those living beneath—looks with wide open eyes at the world, at the sun, at the shining sun itself (Ozerov, op. cit.: 45–46).

Even with this detailed look at Ozerov's article it is difficult to define what his view of America really was. Much of what he writes is based on a surprisingly close attention to American materials, for he draws on such widely varied sources as a description of the labor and mangement system of the Baldwin Locomotive Company, the *New York Journal of Commerce,* the proceedings of the annual meeting of the American Economics Association, and writings of both Henry Adams and his brother Brooks Adams. Yet, somehow, he draws a greater amount of inspiration from the American model than, perhaps, reality actually offered, for there is a certain touch of what might be called abstractionism in his view of the country. There is too much of the bright colors of American success and not enough recognition of the flawed reality of our frequent failures. Nevertheless, Ozerov did arrive at one major conclusion—that

American advantages in the economic struggle of the nations rested on an element of economic rationalization that of necessity would have to be recognized and, with some local variations, followed by others who hoped either merely to preserve themselves from our competition or possibly to rise above us.

Also, as has been pointed out previously in this survey, Ozerov used the American example as a means of making editorial comments about the Russian situation that might have been forbidden by the authorities of the time if he had spoken in his own voice. It is again a matter of a need for further research into Ozerov's writings and his sources of information about America to come closer to determining if he was dealing with a real America or with a concept of America that he had constructed as a form of counter-balance to Russian realities. Whatever it all may have been, though, we have here a serious Russian economist, with a basis of detailed information about us, using the American model in order to construct his view of the world and to suggest paths by which Russia could cope with its own problems.

Ozerov's article was published separately that same year as a pamphlet, issued by the publishing house of V. Kirshbaum, known to be a publisher for the Russian ministry of finance. And, that same year, in the journal *Russkaia mysl'*—a serial of a clear, but somewhat restrained, liberal orientation—he published an article of similar nature, "Otchego Amerika idet tak bystro vpered?" [Why is America advancing so rapidly?], that repeated, in different order and with somewhat different emphasis on specific topics, the major points of his "Amerika idet na Evropu." Whatever the differences in detail between Ozerov's two articles may be, however, both are surprisingly strong statements to the effect that, while some of America's progress rested on its natural conditions, "on the other hand they are making progress; their social institutions, their way of life, allow them to make a magnificent use of human energy" (Ozerov. "Otchego Amerika . . ." As published in his *Iz zhizni truda* [From the life of labor]. Moscow, Izdanie D. S. Gorshkova, 1904: 273). Again there is reference to America's advantages of education, of self-reliance and initiative, and of a capacity for organization. And there is the same emphasis on Russia's intellectual retardation, which can only be overcome by a conscious effort to take up new ways. The first step, Ozerov writes, would be to build school after school. Without this, the contest with the New World would be impossible (Ozerov, op. cit.: 274–93).

In 1908 Ozerov published a second edition of his *Amerika idet na Evropu* but under the title *Chemu uchit nas Amerika?* [What does America teach us?], with over 200 pages of text. Still other writings of his touched upon the American example, as, for instance, an article "Chiem pobiezhdaiut" [With what they are conquering] in his collection *Na temy dnia* [On themes of the day] (Moscow, "Khudozhestvennaia pechat'," 1912: 86–141), which was a further statement in support of a strong policy of fostering Russian industrial development, including many references to American topics. Even in 1916, in the midst of the difficult situation in which Russia found herself during the First World War, he again took up the topic of America as a source of ideas about industrial organization, etc.

As with so many other persons who have been mentioned in this survey, it would require a long and patient research effort to discover the full range of Ozerov's views on the United States and to determine exactly what effect his expressions of them may have had on Russian thought as a whole. However, the positions that he held as a university professor and as a member of the Gosudarstvennyi soviet, as well as the nature of the organs for which he wrote—including newspapers such as the organ of the Constitutional Democratic Party *Riech'* and journals of the type of the *Russkoe ekonomicheskoe obozrienie*—show that he could be presumed to have an audience. There were other people of the time who published similar indications of interest in the possible lessons of the American economic system that might be applied to Russia, but these too can only be studied at the cost of much research.

However, one can cite, as a quite superficial indicator, some of the articles or book reviews on American themes that appeared in the *Russkoe ekonomicheskoe obozrienie* in 1903, the year of the first work by Ozerov mentioned above. The January issue of that journal included a questionnaire as to reasons for the decline of the export of Russian wheat to England and as to possible measures for its restoration, which grew out of an inquiry conducted by I. M. Gol'dshtein, who immigrated to the United States after 1917 and can be found in the Library of

Congress catalog as Joseph M. Goldstein, author of various economic studies. There were, in addition, a report on the U.S.-Cuba trade agreement, a review of an article on the Trans-Siberian railroad written by E. R. Tsimmerman, whose visits to the United States have previously been mentioned and who in this last article compares the Russian and American railroad systems, and a review of an article on American trusts written by "I. Rubinov," who is the Isaac Rubinow discussed and cited in Chapter 4. There is a long summary of an article in the French *Revue d'économie politique* on grain cultivation and export in the United States. Finally, "I. Rubinov" contributes a long review of a work on savings institutions by Professor "Games" [James] Henry Hamilton of Syracuse University. In the May issue, in which the second part of Ozerov's "Amerika idet . . ." appeared, Rubinow published a substantial review of the work of Edwin R. A. Seligman, a professor at Columbia University, on the economic interpretation of history. In August Rubinow's article on labor legislation in the U.S. Congress appeared, as well as his review of an American work on reciprocal trade agreements. In the September issue a reviewer signing himself "I. O—v," probably Ozerov himself, dealt with *Le péril améri-cain*, by the French engineer Paul Sée, which "does not present anything original but which is characteristic of our time, when everywhere people begin to shout about the American danger." The November issue summarizes an article in a major Russian journal on stock speculation in the United States, and provides a review of *The Principles of Money* by J. Laurence Laughlin of the University of Chicago. There were numbers of additional, lesser notes about American topics, but there is no need to add to the list, as there is enough to show that the American economic system was quite closely observed by Russians and that from this one journal a reader could obtain a fairly detailed and often quite informed view of our developments.

When one considers that there were many other sources of information about American economic matters, ranging from the general interest press to specialized organs such as *Birzhevyia novosti* [Stock exchange news] or the official publication of the Ministry of Finance, *Viestnik finansov*, all of which contained much America-related material, the picture becomes even more impressive and one can find many observers contributing to the discussion.

There were others beside Ozerov among the Russian economists who wrote on the contrast between the productivity of American industry and the alleged retardation of Russia in that field. Again, much research would be required to understand that subject in its fullest extent, and one can refer to only a few indications that have been found about the Russian concept, at least in some areas, that there was much in America's industrial system that might be beneficial if adopted in Russia. One single example will have to suffice here. The journal *Promyshlennost' i torgovlia* [Industry and trade], organ of the Komitet s"ezdov predstavitelei promyshlennosti i torgovli [Committee of the congresses of representatives of industry and trade], which can be compared in some ways to the National Association of Manufacturers in America, published in its issues for the years immediately preceding the First World War many articles that discussed American topics. In no. 10 for 1912, dated May 15, it included (p. 520–21) a short article, by one I. P. Glivits, "Dorogo stoiashchaia deshevizna" [An expensive cheapness], the conclusions of which are actually contained in the sub-head, "A metallurgical worker in a major plant in the south of Russia receives an average of 434 rubles [i.e. $217.00] per year, and in America, 820 dollars. However, for every ruble in wages in an iron mill, there are in Russia 34 kopecks of profit, and in America, 88 kopecks."

Other articles, and other journals, sounded a similar note, speaking of America's economic progress and prosperity. At times, of course, there were remarks about the clear evidences of capitalist exploitation of the American worker, with forecasts of growing social tension as labor began to realize the need for struggle. However, there was a prevailing recognition of the generally high level both of American efficiency and of the well-being of the average worker, particularly as the latter was compared with the laborer in Russian industry, and there were many attempts to explain the causes of all this.

Even in October 1915, Nikolai Andreevich Borodin (1866–1937), a Russian engineer specializing in cold storage enterprises and the preservation of fish, who had been one of

the Russian specialists visiting Chicago at the time of the Co-
lombian Exposition and who had returned in 1913 to study
American methods, wrote in *Viestnik Evropy:*

The American seeks good fortune along various paths and only after great
effort does he find his calling. The *Pioneers* of Fenimore Cooper, the adventurous types of Mayne Reid remain essentially what they were, and it is only
that the field of their activities and adventures has been shifted from the
mines and wild places of the country to the wave of broad industrial life in
which an American customarily seeks challenges in order to overcome them,
taking risks, in hope and faith, in order to attain success, and astonishes the
world by the boldness of his undertakings and the genius with which these
are carried out, as well as by their breadth of scale, one that is unknown in
Europe, but more comprehensible and close only to us Russians.

"Thus energy and independence are the basic traits of the
American." . . . While these might, Borodin writes, cause dangers for the organized course of society, his experiences convinced him that there is a basic unity in America that is an essential element of the country's culture. And, again as with
Ianzhul, Kovalevskii, or Mizhuev, Borodin returns to the subject of the American school as an explanation of this unity. "As
of January 1, 1910, the number of schools in the United States,
with its population of 90 million, was 270,008 and the number
of students 20,812,686, while in Russia, with 160 million, there
were but 117,941 schools and 7,687,843 students. The percen-
tile of students in the total population in the United States was
22.6, and in Russia 3.7 (Nikolai A. Borodin, "Amerika i amerikanskaia kul'tura." *Viestnik Evropy,* no. 10, 1915: 263–89).
   Even though Borodin recognizes some of the flaws in
American life, quoting, among other writers, Woodrow Wilson's *New Freedom,* in confirmation of this, he also emphasizes
Wilson's expression of belief in the possibility of correcting
these flaws. "Thus, one of the characteristic traits of the American citizen at the present time is the recognition of the defects
of the contemporary economic and social system, combined
with the striving toward broad reforms in this sphere" (Borodin, op. cit.: 299–300).
   In this article, which also appeared as a separate publication that same year, an informed Russian with substantial experience in America views the United States as a country still
marked by the attitudes that he felt to be present in the writings

of Cooper, and even in those of the often absurd Mayne Reid, a land that, largely because of its system of education, is able to undertake major economic enterprises, and at the same time to retain its national unity as well as its faith in the possibility of rising above its errors. Although he says nothing explicitly about any Russian adoption of the American model, there is an almost inescapable conclusion to be drawn from Borodin's presentation that the American experience did indeed offer useful lessons.

Thus, as the Russian Empire was less than eighteen months away from its collapse, there was one final expression of the spirit that had taken such a concentrated form in the writings of those Russians who had drawn upon their experiences in the World's Columbian Exposition. N. A. Borodin was himself a participant in the Russian representation at Chicago, so that his article of 1915 is perhaps not an unexpected echo from twenty-two years before, but it should be emphasized that there were other Russians, even earlier, who had shown a similar interest in the way in which American education, organization, and technology had combined to make the United States so effective an economic unit. Many of their writings could be cited, but to do so with all the necessary detail would inflate this chapter to something approaching the fabled ten-volume German work titled "An introduction to the study of the elephant," and thus consideration here had to be limited to a sampling of a much richer literature, concentrating chiefly on the materials that grew out of that event in Chicago in 1893 that, as the years pass, is seen as a landmark in American social and cultural history, and that, as these pages have attempted to show, was not without its influence in Russia. Omissions had to be made, many of them painful ones. Unfortunately, nothing could be said at length about the direct presence in Russian life before 1917 of certain rather startling aspects of American technology, so one can only mention the Volga steamboat entrepreneur A. A. Zeveke whose riverboats were exact copies of American sternwheelers, with old photographs of craft named "Alabama," "Niagara," etc. anchored off some Volga town, traditional Russian onion domes in the background, looking like an impossible collaboration between Mark Twain and Leo Tolstoi. Nor is there space available to say more than that *Novoe vremia* in 1907 had advertisements for "bezshumnyi amerikanskii av-tomobil'—Kadillak" [The noiseless American automobile—Cadillac]. And in a more serious vein, one had to omit discussion of the frequent, informed, and very earnest articles on American topics in the official publication of the Ministry of Finance, *Viestnik finansov*, not to mention the rather large number of Russian translations of, and articles in professional journals about, the writings of William James on education.

And yet, it is hoped that the materials which have been cited at some length will suffice to show that in pre-1917 Russian eyes America served not only as a technological model, but also as an organizational, and in the field of education even as something of an ideological one. In none of these aspects was America, of course, a determining factor, but increasingly her experience was an influential one. It may perhaps seem somewhat exaggerated to say it in exactly the following words, but the inclusion of the Statue of Liberty on the original publisher's cover of Kovalevskii's study of American education was indeed intended to represent "Liberty enlightening the world." Even now, after years of tension and many changes in both nations, Americans can well be proud of their image in Russia before 1917 as a land of progress, efficiency, learning, and freedom.

CHAPTER SIX

Russian Diplomacy and America, 1866–1917

At the end of the Civil War the United States had two major diplomatic problems facing it. One was to secure from Great Britain some form of recompense for that country's unneutral acts in allowing Confederate cruisers to fit out in British ports for action against the North. The other was to pressure France to withdraw its troops from Mexico, where they had intervened to install and support as emperor the Austrian Archduke Maximilian, a man of good intentions and even more magnificent whiskers. With almost all other countries our relations were placid, often to the point of somnolence, and American representatives in most capitals had to face only routine correspondence and the dangers of surfeit in partaking of the elaborate menus of official dinners. Although this was basically the situation in our relations with Russia, there does seem to have been on both sides a certain expectation of warmth in spite of a recognition that the two systems of government were so widely different, and the tone of the newspapers and of official attitudes expressed this.

Some of the nature of this feeling was evident when, on April 4/16, 1866, an attempt was made on the life of Emperor Alexander II. The United States Congress adopted on May 10, and President Johnson signed on May 16, a resolution congratulating the emperor on his escape. In order to lend emphasis to this resolution it was decided to send a special delegate to Russia with the message, and Gustavus Vasa Fox (1821–1883), who had just left the post of assistant secretary of the navy, was chosen for the position. At his own request a monitor was assigned to take him to St. Petersburg, and the vessel chosen was the U.S.S. *Miantonomoh*, one of America's most powerful craft. She was 259 feet in length, 14 feet 9¾ inches in draft, of 1,225 tons measurement and was armed with four 15-inch Dahlgren smooth bore guns. The most remarkable item in her description was that her deck was only thirty-one inches above the water, and one may suppose that even the slightest of waves would wash over her deck (Joseph F. Loubat, *Narrative of the mission to Russia, in 1866, of the Hon. Gustavus Vasa Fox, Assistant Secretary of the Navy.* New York, D. Appleton and Co., 1873: 16–17, 29).

The mission set out in June. Although that is likely to be a favorable month for a North Atlantic passage and although *Miantonomoh* was towed some eleven hundred miles of the way by one of the two vessels accompanying her, Mr. Fox was certainly not engaged in any pleasure cruise. That there was something more to his trip than a mere message to the tsar was shown by the fact that the ships paid rather demonstrative visits to both French and British ports. On July 17 *The Times* (London), in commenting on *Miantonomoh's* presence at the British naval base at Sheerness on the Thames, ostensibly so that Victoria's sailor son, Prince Alfred, Duke of Edinburgh, could see her, described the ship as "something between a ship and a diving-bell . . . almost invisible, but what there was to it was ugly, at once invulnerable and irresistible . . ." around which were moored "a considerable portion of the navy of this great maritime power [Britain]," ships among which there was not one of them that the foreigner could not have sent to the bottom in five minutes, had his errand not been peaceful." The British, however, were massively kind, giving Fox tours of their dockyards and providing him large quantities of naval information and official publications, as well as inviting him to a ball at Buckingham Palace. The French were similarly hospitable, with Napoleon III himself receiving Fox in audience, and with the minister of the navy, the director of naval construction, and the director of naval artillery, as well as other specialists, being shown the monitor.

With scarcely more than this somewhat indirect indication

of American power, both European governments were made to sense something of the force that America had at her command, and were thus undoubtedly warned to pay serious attention to her discontent with their policies. Once this had been done, *Miantonomoh* was able to proceed placidly on toward St. Petersburg to carry out the announced purpose of her voyage. She met with no obstacles on the way, save perhaps for the effects on both officers and crew of the broad hospitality she was shown in Copenhagen, Helsingfors, and Kronshtadt. On the passage from Helsingfors to Kronshtadt the Americans were met by a Russian squadron that included four of the single-turret monitors that had been built for the imperial navy in 1863, and among the Russian officers assigned to welcome them were Rear-Admiral Lesovskii, who had commanded the squadron that visited the United States in 1863–64, Rear-Admiral Gorkovenko, who had toured America in 1853, and Colonel Pestich of the naval artillery who had been part of the study mission of 1862 (Loubat, op. cit.: 36–79).

Loubat's account is of such lavish banqueting and such quantities of toasts to Russian-American friendship that one wonders that the guests were able to endure it all. The municipality of Kronshtadt provided four different soups, four types of meat pies, and something entered in the menu as "yellow tea," and the evening was crowned by the making of punch in the Russian style. "It is made of rum, sugar, fruit, etc., set on fire, and after burning for some time, is quenched with champagne" (Loubat, op. cit.: 119, 125). A banquet at Moscow included two menus, one of which was meatless because of an Orthodox fast day, but this does not seem to have affected the number of toasts or the volubility of those who made them, and Loubat runs to twenty pages in his description (Loubat, op. cit.: 242–62).

There is a natural question as to how much all this toasting and banqueting really meant. However it does appear that the men in power in Russia had a serious purpose in trying to win American favor. The account of the visit that appeared in the August 1866 issue of the professional naval journal *Morskoi sbornik* offers some indication of this in its emphasis on the British fears in 1863–64 that America and Russia were drawing together, because of a shared concern with Britain's overweening power, and the naval journal's other articles about the technical side of armored ships and naval tactics showed close attention to the role that America could play in maritime affairs. There were also articles in the public press in Russia, as well as pamphlets with titles such as *Amerikantsy v Peterburgie. Druzhestvennyi soiuz Rossii i Ameriki. Podrobnoe opisanie Miantonomo* [The Americans in Petersburg. Friendly alliance of Russia and America. Exact description of Miantonomoh] (St. Peterburg, V tip. i lit. S. Stepanov, 1866. 16 p.). Even *Pravoslavnoe obozrienie* [Orthodox review], a voice of the Russian church, is reported to have had a fourteen-page article on the topic.

The most telling evidence of the Russian attitude came with the grandest of all the banquets in this series, one held at the very aristocratic English Club. There were but ten courses and three toasts, but at the serving of punch afterwards there were further speeches. One was delivered by Prince Aleksandr M. Gorchakov, foreign minister and vice chancellor of the empire. Gorchakov was a highly skilled diplomat, able to express the policy of his government without leaving too many verbal hostages to the future, and he spoke of Russian friendliness toward the United States. "I have no need to emphasize the manifestations of sympathy between the two countries. They are bursting into the light of day." No documents existed that affirmed any entente, but Gorchakov spoke of it as being "instinctive" and "providential." He went on, speaking with an elegance of phrase that, to judge from other reports, was habitual with him, and that was also quite clear of any definite commitments, to welcome an entente between the two countries, one that was "neither a menace nor a peril for anyone" (Loubat, op. cit.: 437–39. Gorchakov's speech is cited from the French text on those pages and not from the English version on p. 341–46).

At the time Gorchakov's speech attracted a great deal of attention and Loubat reports, "On the same evening of the banquet, Mr. Oscar G. Sawyer, correspondent of the *New York Herald*, telegraphed to that journal the entire speech of Prince Gortshakoff [sic.], at a cost of seven thousand dollars." The Atlantic cable had been successfully completed scarcely a month before, and the charges were approximately five dollars a word, but the two James Gordon Bennetts, father and son, publishers of the *New York Herald,* were fond of splashy gestures, and this may have been one of them.

There was no American action to follow some of the possibilities that the Russian attitude seemed to leave open, although the very elaborate welcome given *Miantonomoh* and Mr. Fox seems to have had some such end in view. America's long-standing policy of aloofness from Europe, and the many domestic problems left by the Civil War, kept America remote from Gorchakov's fine-spun diplomatic maneuvers. However, within slightly over six months, the United States and Russia had negotiated a treaty that ceded Alaska to the United States, in return for $7,200,000, a move that allowed Russia to give up a remote, not too profitable colony, which might otherwise have fallen prey to the British. During the quarter-century or so that followed, while the two countries had no formalized agreements, the language of diplomatic contacts was always cordial and there were several instances in which America proved a useful element in Russian policy.

Quite soon after the acquisition of Alaska it became clear that the strong, and even threatening, fleet that the United States had had at the end of the Civil War was being allowed to dwindle into a sort of genteel decay. By 1873 when trouble arose with Spain over the treatment of Americans involved in the Cuban Insurrection, the American navy was spoken of as "too weak to fight and too slow to run away," and through much of the era the older naval "brass" was admonishing the commanders of our ships to keep the consumption of coal to a minimum and to rely on sail during most sea passages.

Russia, however, still had her eye on the strategic advantage of American ports as a point from which, at least on the outbreak of a war, their navy might be able to move against Britain, avoiding being bottled up in the Baltic by the Royal Navy, and there were events such as the visit to New York in November of 1871 of three vessels, the frigate *Svetlana,* corvette *Bogatyr',* and clipper *Abrek.* The welcome in America was an enthusiastic one. Even Alexander II telegraphed to his wife Mariia Aleksandrovna on November 10/22 that on the previous day there had been a welcoming crowd of thousands on the New York streets, and Vice-Admiral Pos'et, commanding the Russian squadron, noted in his diary the constant American expression of sympathy for Russia (Gennadii P. Kuropiatnik, *Rossia i SShA; ekonomicheskie, kul'turnye i diplomaticheskie sviazi, 1867–1881*. Moscow, Izdatel'stvo "Nauka," 1981: 210, 212).

One of the reasons for such enthusiasm can be assumed to arise from the fact that one of the Russian lieutenants was the Grand Duke Aleksiei Aleksandrovich (1850–1908), the emperor's fourth son. The young man had, it appears, managed to "entangle" himself with a woman from whose influence his father wished to remove him, and this mission to America offered a perfect chance to do so. Although members of other royal families had visited the United States before, there had been no one of quite so exalted a family as the House of Romanov, and, when in addition the visiting prince was young, strong, and handsome (if somewhat "muffin-faced"), with an eye for the ladies, the welcome was a very lively one.

An excursion to Washington aboard a three-car special train was organized, with the grand duke being received by President Grant, Secretary of State Fish, Secretary of the Navy Robeson, Postmaster General Creswell, and other dignitaries. The warmth of this reception was marred, however, by the fact that the grand duke was accompanied by the Russian minister to the United States, Konstantin Gavrilovich Katakazi, whose meddling habits and outright untruths had aroused the anger of Secretary of State Hamilton Fish and of Grant himself. There are many details of Katakazi's very checkered career to be found in Allan Nevins's biography of Fish, including the fact that as a young man Katakazi had caused a scandal in Rio de Janeiro by running away with the young wife of the Neapolitan minister to Brazil, and that, in America, he had bought a site in New York for a Russian church with paper currency but had billed the Russian foreign office in gold, thus making a substantial profit. He then managed to make such sharp criticisms of the American administration over a matter of the claim against Russia of an enterpreneur from Massachusetts that Fish was on the point of asking his recall (Allan Nevins, *Hamilton Fish; the inner history of the Grant administration*. Revised edition. v. 2. New York, Frederick Ungar Publishing Co., 1957: 503–510).

As a result, the atmosphere of the presidential reception was a bit strained. "Grant and Fish made it plain that while Catacazy [sic] was still nominally Minister, he was tolerated only for the purpose of attending the Grand Duke, and was not to receive diplomatic honors. . . . The Russian Government grasped the situation, and Catacazy was overtaken in St. Louis by peremptory orders to return home" (Nevins, op. cit.: 510–11).

Katakazi had quite clearly forgotten the words addressed to him by the emperor himself upon being appointed to the post in Washington: "You must always remember that our best friend is the American people" (Alexander II to Katakazi, as stated in the St. Petersburg newspaper *Golos,* December 23, 1871/January 4, 1872. Quoted in Kuropiatnik, op. cit., 51). However, those accompanying the grand duke had apparently taken the emperor's views to heart, and the young man was taken to many places in the United States: Annapolis, West Point, Boston, Lowell (Mass.), New York, Buffalo, Cleveland, Chicago, Bridgeport (Conn., to visit the Union Metallic Cartridge Company), Springfield (Mass., to visit the Smith and Wesson factory), Philadelphia (to see the Baldwin Locomotive Company, which had business ties with Russia), and other places. The most exciting part was probably the hunting trip into the Western plains, where Aleksiei hunted buffalo and observed the Indians and their riding skill, which the Russians said could only be compared with that of the Don Cossacks (Kuropiatnik, op. cit.: 215–16, 220–21). There is, in another source, a further record of this hunting trip in the form of a photograph of Lt. Col. (brevet Maj. Gen.) George A. Custer, the Grand Duke Aleksiei, and William F. (Buffalo Bill) Cody.

From the Plains, the grand duke visited Topeka, Memphis, New Orleans (a reference to his visit formed part of one of the popular songs at Mardi Gras that year), Mobile, and Pensacola, where he rejoined the Russian fleet to sail around the Cape of Good Hope to the Russian Pacific coast. He himself left no particular record of his impressions, but Vice-Admiral Pos'et's report indicated that he "was surprised and impressed by the sincere good wishes of the broad masses of the people, thus far never seen by him in any other country. . . . exchanging views with the officers he came to the conclusion that the United States and Russia had much more in common than was usually assumed." He noted the obvious similarities in extent, in climate, and in many products, saying that these created a likeness of character in both Russians and Americans (Kuropiatnik, op. cit.: 222–23).

The Winter Palace appears to have been quite pleased with the general outcome of this visit, which the Soviet scholar Kuropiatnik views as having had major diplomatic significance. One of Kuropiatnik's footnotes reads, "'We read with great interest the journal of K. N. Pos'et about your travels in America!' Grand Duke Aleksandr Aleksandrovich [later Alexander III] informed his brother, March 18/30, 1872" (Kuropiatnik, op. cit., 223, fn. 132).

Although Kuropiatnik does not supply any supporting details, he is of the opinion that, on the American side, the State Department used the fact of the visit of the Russian squadron to influence the successful completion of a settlement of America's claims against Great Britain, the so-called Alabama Claims, for her allowing Confederate cruisers to be fitted out in her ports. And, in reporting on March 27, 1872, his reception by the emperor on arrival to take up the post of American minister, James L. Orr informed Secretary Fish that Alexander viewed the reception given the Russians in America as a sign of friendship and respect for the empire, "an old and faithful friend of the American people in Russia."

One does not, however, find—at least in Kuropiatnik's work—any indication that America's settlement of her claims against Great Britain formed a precedent by which Britain in turn could object to American actions that might favor Russia, should hostilities break out between those two European powers. Although the British had had to admit their error, and pay the sum of $15,500,000, it was a small price to pay for such extensive ultimate benefits. Nor, in fact, despite a number of articles in the general Russian press on the subject of the Alabama Claims, does there seem to have been any unofficial reference to such a limitation.

Russia continued to express a direct interest in having American good will. When, on April 23, 1872 [O.S.?], there turned up in Sevastopol, aboard—of all possible conveyances— the steam yacht of the Sultan of Turkey, General William Tecumseh Sherman, he was met by expressions of friendship from broad sections of the population, and was able to visit the Caucasus, Moscow, and St. Petersburg, with facilities to see everything that he might wish to see. In St. Petersburg he was received by the tsar and had an official conversation with Gorchakov, who repeated that the Russian government wished the friendliest of relations with the United States (Kuropiatnik, op. cit.: 226–27).

Upon the death in St. Petersburg of the American minister, James L. Orr, the leather manufacturer and former governor of Connecticut, Marshall Jewell, was named to the post, with the hopes of negotiating agreements with Russia to protect trademarks, to provide for mutual extradition of criminal fugitives, and for Russian acceptance of the principle that immigrants to the United States, if naturalized, would be treated as American citizens if they should return for visits. The first task was accomplished, but the remaining two were more difficult. Russia was not willing to admit that its subjects could become citizens of another country. "Voluntary emigration was viewed as treason to the motherland. The laws most strictly forbade emigration into any other country. In case of a return to the territory of the Russian Empire of her 'loyal subject,' who had left the motherland without permission from the highest level and without the required 'written certificates,' there awaited him by law a lengthy incarceration in prison or forced labor in Siberia. If, in addition, he were subject to military service, he was also considered guilty of avoidance of service in the armed forces" (Kuropiatnik, op. cit.: 229–30).

It appears that much of the activity of the American legation in Russia consisted of correspondence on exactly such problems, as our diplomats attempted to protect naturalized citizens. Despite our wishes to provide some means for lessening the problem, any Russian agreement appears to have rested on a corresponding concession by the United States for the extradition of criminals charged with Russian crimes, and, in general, American opinion felt that these procedures might be used against political exiles. Both matters remained in abeyance, until, in the late 1880s, an extradition treaty was arrived at, a covenant that was not ratified by the Senate until several years had passed, during which some Americans protested strongly against possible Russian efforts to apply the treaty to its emigrant dissidents (Kuropiatnik, op. cit.: 231–37).

Kuropiatnik speaks of other instances in which, in his view, the Russian government was interested in establishing good relations with America, such as an effort to gain American participation in a conference held in Brussels in 1872 to discuss the international laws of war, or the furtherance of Russian participation in the Centennial Exposition in Philadelphia in 1876. In general, he indicates, relations between the two countries were those of good will and harmony, despite some differences in detail (Kuropiatnik, op. cit., 246).

It was well for Russia that this was the case, for the years 1875–78 were to bring complications for the empire and to create circumstances in which there was a quite definite reliance on America's good will.

Although there never appears to have been any real expectation that America would take open action on Russia's side, America's geographical position and its general attitude of favor for Russia was of advantage to her. The problems arose in 1875 as members of the Christian population of the European part of the Turkish Empire began armed action against the sultan's forces. Since a large proportion of these rebellious Christians were both fellow Slavs and fellow members of the Orthodox communion, Russian sentiment was on their side. Austria-Hungary, however, which had its own ambitions in the Balkans, tended not to favor these insurrectionists, while Great Britain felt that if the Turkish Empire were to be seriously weakened the Russians might be able to break through into the Eastern Mediterranean, upsetting the balance of power. The chronicle of the situation is a long one and, as far as the Christian peoples of the region goes, a bloody one, and there is no need to go into the whole topic here. It is sufficient to say that with the passage of time the continuing backing that Great Britain gave to the sultan—whoever he may have been, as there were three men who held that post in 1876, changes being brought about by palace intrigue—strengthened Turkish resistance, as well as Russo-British animosity.

The treaty that ended the Crimean War had forbidden Russia to maintain naval forces in the Black Sea and, although this prohibition had been annulled in the aftermath of the Franco-Prussian War of 1870–71, there had not been time for Russia to do more than provide a weak coastal defense fleet as a replacement. The major element in Russia's naval forces was

the Baltic Fleet, some elements of which were "fast steam corvettes and clippers," and in March of 1876 the small Russian
squadron in Greek waters, commanded by Rear-Admiral I. I.
Butakov, was reinforced by the corvettes *Bogatyr* and *Askol'd*
and the clipper *Kreiser* (Kuropiatnik, op. cit.: 250, 256). With
these additions it was expected that "From thence in case of a
conflict with Turkey Russian ships could cut Turkish lines of
communiction and seize ships laden mostly with English weapons" (Kuropiatnik, op. cit., 257). With the increasing tension
between Russia and Turkey, and given the openly pro-Turkish
attitude of the British, it became strategically questionable to
leave the Russian ships, even if reinforced in number, in the
Eastern Mediterranean. On September 30/October 12, 1876,
Butakov, then in port in the somewhat ticklish city of Smyrna,
received orders to leave Turkish waters immediately, "without
arousing suspicions," and go to Trieste. This difficult task was
accomplished with the aid (most likely unwitting) of a British
naval officer, for "to Smyrna on a return voyage from the Crimea there came, aboard the imperial yacht *Livadiia*, the Duch-
ess of Edinburgh, Mariia Aleksandrovna, daughter of Alexander II who had married the British duke, who had been visiting
there." This Duke of Edinburgh was Queen Victoria's second
son, the Prince Alfred for whom *Miantonomoh* had put into a
British harbor in 1866 so that he might visit her. He had made
a career in the Royal Navy and was, it seems, a competent commander, even if what the French call "la petite histoire," and the
Germans, "Hoftratsch," said that he was an unpleasant man,
given to drink and to boorishness toward his wife, as well as
being an excruciatingly bad performer on the violin (Kuropiatnik, op. cit.: 258–59; Kenneth Rose, *King George V.* New York,
Knopf, 1984: 40–41).

Early on the morning of October 1/13, *Livadiia* and the
English frigate "Relli" [Raleigh ?] left Smyrna. "'Following the
lead of the imperial yacht, the ships of the squadron,' it is noted
in Butakov's report, 'began one after the other to raise anchor
and, forming a line ahead, set out to sea. The fine speed of the
imperial yacht did not allow the squadron to keep up with her,
and *Livadiia*, accompanied by the frigate *Relli*, the best sailer in
the British fleet, quickly began to draw ahead.' As soon as the
yacht, the British frigate, and the Turkish coast disappeared

over the horizon, the admiral made a signal to the frigate *Svet-lana* to detach herself and follow *Livadiia* to its destination, Malta, while he himself, in command of *Petropavlovsk, Bogatyr'* and *Askol'd* headed to the roadstead at Cape Corfu to take coal. There a new order awaited him, to go with his squadron to winter in Italian ports. Butakov was still en route to Naples when from Livadiia [the emperor's Crimean palace and not the yacht] there came a change of orders—to send the squadron to U.S. ports in place of those of Italy" (Kuropiatnik, op. cit., 259).

On October 7/19 the emperor, still in the Crimea, informed his brother, Konstantin Nikolaevich, General-Admiral of the Russian navy, that he foresaw a break with England and that within three weeks it would be desirable to have Butakov leave the Mediterranean. "'Do you think that he will succeed, and what ports to recommend to him. Answer immediately.'" That same evening a reply was made to the tsar. "It was utterly clear and laconic and foresaw the taking of concrete action. 'I feel that three weeks are entirely enough to move out of the Mediterranean Sea into the ocean. The best place for the squadron is the ports of North America, to which orders can be transmitted by telegraph, . . . '" (Kuropiatnik, op. cit., 260).

Some of the complicated problems of dispatching, supplying, and controlling such a naval move into distant waters were dealt with by the resurrection of the orders that in 1863 had been given to Admiral Lesovskii when, in comparable circumstances, a Russian squadron had visited the United States. Further support was provided by the assignment as the Russian agent in America of the naval officer Kroun [it is uncertain which of the two brothers of that name, A. E. or F. E. Kroun, is meant; they were the sons of a man of British origin named Crown who had served in the Russian navy], who had had that post under Lesovskii. The emperor told his brother, "'Issue orders immediately to Butakov and the whole squadron to proceed to one of the ports of North America, as you determine, and give him the same instructions as in 1863. . . . Order Aleksiei [Grand Duke, and previous visitor to the U.S.] from me to join Butakov in Naples'" (Kuropiatnik, op. cit., 261).

In a week new telegrams to Butakov read, "The situation is close to a break. Make all effort for the quick completion of all work and fitting out with provisions." Among the officers and crew of the ships any talk about the forthcoming voyage was forbidden, as a security measure. Despite the efforts of the Russians, it took not three but five weeks to get ready for the voyage, but in mid-November the Russian ships left Genoa, Naples and Spezia under the cover of night and, passing Gibraltar also at night, set out for America (Kuropiatnik, op. cit.: 261–62).

Similar measures were taken with the small Russian squadron in the Pacific, which was sent to San Francisco. And, once the fleet movements were under way, the Ministry of Foreign Affairs was informed of the matter, and that ministry finally let the American minister, G. R. Boker, know that the Russians were coming (Kuropiatnik, op. cit.: 263–64).

This sequence of events, the dispatch into neutral waters of the naval forces of a country feeling itself in imminent danger of war, without any preliminary consultation with the host country, is a rather bold one. It is, mildly speaking, a step of rather shocking condescension, as well as a sign of a marked confidence that Russian and American interests were close enough for it even to be contemplated. Kuropiatnik's extremely well documented study of the subject has quite literally nothing to say about any previous contacts with the United States, nor does there appear to be any reference to possible American reluctance to face complications that might arise if her ports, even with strict observance of the formal obligations of neutrality, were to become a factor in Russian action against British maritime trade. America's experiences with the British attitude toward the Confederate cruisers, and the negotiations for the settlement of the Alabama Claims, certainly must have alerted American statesmen to the dangers of the situation, for the British would have been in an excellent position to raise complaints.

The Russians, however, went boldly ahead in laying their plans. Admiral Lesovskii, who had commanded the squadron sent to America in 1863 and who was then in command in the Baltic, asked the foreign ministry to inquire of the Russian minister in Washington whether any trace could be found of the plans of that earlier time for Russian ships to cruise against British commerce. Although nothing could be found, it did develop that there was then present in the United States one of the Russian officers who had drawn up such plans in 1863. This was L. P. Semechkin, who held the post of adjutant to the commander of the Russian naval forces and who was in America as representative of the Russian navy at the Philadelphia Centennial Exposition.

He had an outstanding memory. Without any particular difficulty he reconstituted the general outlines of the plan for cruiser operations in 1863, supplementing it by his notes on the most recent practice of American compliance with the rules of neutrality . . .

Semechkin developed the argumentation of his paper taking into account the 'assistance that our fatherland might find in the United States.' This included the statement that, from a strictly technical point of view, 'the construction in a short time of twelve naval ships does not present any particular difficulties . . . ' But from the point of view of international law, 'a certain degree of caution is required in order that the national laws of the United States not be violated. As long as Russia has not declared war on any other state whatsoever with which the United States is in a state of friendship, she has until then a full right to enlarge her fleet with the help of American industry. But as soon as the break has taken place, she loses that right and if construction has been begun it must be halted till the end of the war.'

As a way out of this possible interruption in the acquisition of ships, Semechkin proposed the purchase of commercial vessels and fitting them out as auxiliary cruisers (Kuropiatnik, op. cit.: 265–66).

The passage of the Russian squadron across the Atlantic was a stormy one, and this appears to have forced some dispersal of the ships, for only *Svetlana* showed up in Hampton Roads on the Chesapeake on the morning of December 31, 1876/January 12, 1877, while others arrived in Charleston and Port Royal, South Carolina. Whatever the doubts may have been among the American international lawyers, the reception, both of the public and of the officers of America's decidedly obsolescent navy, was a warm one. Kuropiatnik gives many references to the way in which the Russians were met, at all levels, and were given facilities for repairing ships, buying supplies, and securing treatment of Russian seamen in naval hospitals (Kuropiatnik, op. cit.: 266–69).

There is an index to *The Times* of London, but its organization is not always immediately clear. Examination of the quarterly issues of this period under a variety of headings referring to America, Russia, the "War in the East," and naval and military "intelligence" (i.e., news), does not indicate any major press reaction to this Russian visit to America. However, it is probably the case that when the ships appeared in American ports there was a flurry of activity in the British legation in Washington seeking to pull together a variety of reports as to the Russian purchases of coal or stores, their requests for charts of foreign waters, or the gossip that passed at evening receptions attended by Russian officers. Most likely a few days spent in the Public Records Office in London would turn up thick dossiers of documents in the case, but no entry in either the index to *The Times* or in that to the *New York Times* conveys any great sense of concern about the possible complications of the presence of these Russian ships in American waters.

One of the developments of the situation was that, although the Grand Duke Aleksiei was in the United States for the second time, it did not seem a favorable moment for his paying a second visit to the White House, at least not until the new administration had taken office. After the elections of 1876, there was still a question as to which set of electors in some of the states would be recognized and, thereby, whether it would be Rutherford Birchard Hayes or Samuel Tilden who would become president. The chances of the grand duke's having another interview with the outgoing U.S. Grant vanished when Fish informed the Russian minister, Shishkin (a name based on the word *shishka*—pine cone—and reminiscent of the expression *bol'shaia shishka,* more or less equivalent of the colloquial *big cheese*) that the president would not pay a return visit to the young Romanov. There was, it appears from Kuropiatnik's account, a great deal of correspondence on the matter of whether Ulysses S. Grant should call upon an unmarried young man who was, after the Grand Duke Aleksandr Aleksandrovich, his eight-year old son Nikolai Aleksandrovich, and his other son Georgii Aleksandrovich, very far down the line for the throne (Kuropiatnik, op.cit.: 269–70).

Most of the difficulties were solved after March 4, 1877, when Hayes took office and, five days before the outbreak of war between Russia and Turkey, gave a large formal dinner for the Russians. There were similar demonstrations of good will toward the Americans in St. Petersburg, formally undertaken by the Russians who had been members of the commission managing the Russian exhibits at Philadelphia in 1876. The quotations from the newspapers that Kuropiatnik cites, as well as from the American diplomatic correspondence, show that the imperial government was making a concerted effort to win the good will of the United States (Kuropiatnik, op. cit.: 270–73).

On 12/24 April 1877 the imperial manifesto declaring war with Turkey was issued. Butakov and his squadron were in New York, and were informed of the state of war by a telegram from St. Petersburg that further instructed them to stay there until they received further orders. The admiral asked St. Petersburg, "Should we begin the capture of contraband of war exported from American ports under English, American and other neutral flags?" It is easy to imagine the complications that would have ensued for American relations with Russia, Great Britain, or any other maritime country from action of this kind, and it is good to find that the authorities in St. Petersburg realized the situation, for General-Admiral Konstantin Nikolaevich in a marginal note on Butakov's telegram referred to such measures as not being allowed by the international law of the time. However, it would appear from Kuropiatnik's account that the Russian still expected some favors from the American government in the way of providing barriers to the export of contraband of war to Turkey, an expectation that was cooled by an explanation from the Russian minister in Washington to the effect that the Americans would have to act even-handedly and thereby prohibit export of materials to Russia as well as requesting withdrawal of the Russian ships (Kuropiatnik, op. cit.: 281–83).

Despite the formal neutrality of the United States, as shown by the foregoing, the diplomatic corps in St. Petersburg saw matters somewhat differently. To them it appeared that in reality the Americans had shown a clear support of the Russians through acts such as the friendly reception given to the squadrons in New York and San Francisco, "the sudden appearance of an American squadron in the Bosphorus a few days before the declaration of war,"[4] the delivery of American

---

[4]With no apparent realization that the American navy of the time was of very uncertain quality, and that quite clearly the new Hayes administration had no real intention of improving it. Richard W. Thompson, 1809–1900, was Hayes's secretary of

weapons, the emphasis at the official level of close and friendly ties, and the mutually favorable tone of the press of Russia and America in relation to one another (Kuropiatnik, op. cit., 284). The American representative in St. Petersburg, Atkinson, was even seriously asked by another foreign diplomat there whether our sending ships to the Black Sea region was not the result of an agreement with the Russians to give them support (Atkinson to Secretary of State Evarts, April 25, 1877, as quoted by Kuropiatnik, op. cit., 285).

In May of 1877 the Russian ships left both American shores and were for the moment no longer a direct factor in Russo-American relations. The Russian war with Turkey proved to be a more difficult matter than had at first been supposed, for the "sick man of Europe," with a certain amount of British backing that hovered just on the outer edge of being downright aid, put up a fight holding Russia all through a good part of 1877–78 along the line of the Balkans. The principal center of Turkish resistance was at Plevna and the Shipka Pass, and for days the Russian communique contained the disheartening phrase "Na Shipkie vse spokoino," which has come to be the equivalent in Russian of "All quiet along the Potomac" or "Im Westen, nichts neues." But, finally, the Russians, a good part of whose infantry, by the way, was armed with what they called the "Berdanka," a single-shot rifle reprocessed to allow breech loading by a method developed by Col. Hiram Berdan of the U.S. Army, acting against the Turks, some of whom had Remington repeating rifles, managed to break through and to advance to the outskirts of Constantinople. There was a great amount of international concern with this situation. Neither Austria, which had its own ambitions in Southeast Europe, nor Britain, which feared that somehow a Russian occupation of Constantinople would threaten England's valuable new route to India via the Suez Canal, wanted the Russians to retain all their gains. At the suggestion of Bismarck, who claimed to be only "an honest broker," a major international conference was called in Berlin to deal with the problem, and as a result some of Rus-

---

the navy, an appointee from Indiana, known as the "Ancient Mariner of the Wabash," and, according to anecdote, so surprised at his first visit to a warship that he said, "Why, the durn thing's hollow!"—H. J. Eckenrode, *Rutherford B. Hayes; statesman of reunion.* Port Washington, New York, 1963. 242.

sia's first claims were given up and not quite so much was lost by Turkey. Britain occupied the island of Cyprus and Austria occupied Bosnia and Herzegovina; Bulgaria north of the Balkans became an autonomous principality, Serbia and Montenegro received more territory, and Romania declared its independence. None of this quite removed all possible problems, and the region remained one of confusing national antagonisms and a fertile object for international intrigue. Was it not Mark Twain who said of one country there, "It produces more history than it can consume locally"? But, for a time at least the Conference of Berlin did alleviate the immediate situation.

In the interval, however, between the Russo-Turkish armistice signed at Adrianople on January 19/31, 1878, and the final act of the Berlin meeting, tensions still remained high. There was a great storm of reaction in Great Britain, one that, because of a popular song of the time that ran, approximately,

> We don't want to fight,
> But, by jingo, if we do,
> We've got the ships, we've got the men,
> We've got the money too.

gave rise to the expression *jingoism*. The demonstratively bereaved "Widow of Windsor," Victoria, was abetted in her pro-Turkish outlook by Lord Beaconsfield [Disraeli], and there were mysterious comings and goings of British ships in the Eastern Mediterranean, resulting in all kinds of worries about the possibility of war between Russia and the English.

The Russian admirality felt that, should war come, their most profitable target would be British commerce. The old-style method of using private armed vessels had been forbidden by the Declaration of Paris of 1856, but there was nothing to prevent the use of auxiliary cruisers that formed a part of the national naval forces. Lacking sufficient swift ships that could be refitted for such a purpose, the Russians looked toward America as a source of these craft. On March 27/April 8, 1878, the Emperor Alexander ordered the immediate dispatch of a group of naval personnel to the United States with the purpose of acquiring at least three or four ships—in place of the originally proposed twelve, a number that available financial resources would not cover. On that same day the naval ministry selected four officers of the rank of "kapitan-leitenant" (equivalent of commander), and L. P. Semechkin—previously mentioned as a participant in the Russian delegation to the Philadelphia Exposition—was also sent to America as Russia's chief agent in the organization of cruiser action.

In what followed, a present-day reader may possibly be reminded of an adventure film of sorts.

Within two days [evidently March 29/April 10, 1878] a detachment of 660 sailors crossed over from Kronshtadt [the naval port near St. Petersburg] on the April ice to the shore at Oranienbaum and a special train, making a circle in order not to go through St. Petersburg, arrived at Baltiiskii Port [a naval base on the Baltic]. Here the sailors changed their naval jackets and caps for civilian clothes. The day after the detachment went aboard the German steamer *Cimbria*, chartered from the Hamburg-America Company by the naval attaché in Germany, Kapitan II ranga [captain, bottom half of list] N. A. Nevakhovich for an 'unknown destination' for six months. According to the contract the steamer was for this period entirely at the disposal of the charterer. When the sailors embarked on *Cimbria* each had a passport for foreign travel. In these was entered one of the completely civil occupations—cabinet maker, carpenter, baker, gardener, waiter, etc. The embarkation of the detachment was wrapped up in such secrecy that no one, including the commander of the detachment, even knew the point of destination (Kuropiatnik, op. cit., 304).

Out at sea on April 1/13 Kapitan-leitenant [Cdr] Grippenberg, who had been put in charge of the detachment, opened the sealed orders instructing him to pass to the North of the British Isles and to proceed to a small port in the State of Maine to await further orders. One of the participants in this expedition, I. Butkovskii, reported some of the experiences of the voyage and the general attitudes of the officers in an article that appeared only five years later in *Istoricheskii viestnik* (I. Butkovskii, "Tainstvennaia ekspeditsiia v Ameriku v 1878g." [The secret expedition to America in 1878]. *Istoricheskii viestnik*, 1883, no. 6).

In spite of all the efforts to assure that the English would not learn of this move, it appears that British agents worked quickly and accurately, and the British ambassador knew the purpose of the trip and had a list of names of the officers. What is worse, however, it seems to have been as much as a week after *Cimbria*'s departure that the American chargé d'affaires in St. Petersburg, Wickham Hoffman, was able to report to Washington that the Russians were coming, adding later a confidential report about their purpose. Hoffman did not see anything that would prevent the Russians acquiring ships in America, "But, having in view the fact that the present relations between Russia and Great Britain threaten to break out in war, I thought that you [Secretary of State Evarts] possibly would like to know of this situation and therefore I have telegraphed to you." This confidential report, Kuropiatnik says, did not reach the Department of State until a week after *Cimbria* had entered the little known port of South West Harbor on Mount Desert Island in Maine (Kuropiatnik, op. cit., 305).

In other words, without any preliminary consultation with the United States or any of its representatives, the Russians had quite high-handedly again taken action that could have brought rather grave consequences for the United States. The days were gone when *Miantonomoh*, as *The Times* (London) had phrased it, could have sunk the whole British fleet, and that was only twelve years previously. There were, it is true, 142 vessels on America's naval list, but most of those were either rusty monitors of no seagoing capacity or aging, weak wooden vessels. None of them could have done the Royal Navy, despite its own flaws, any essential damage. Yet, the dangers to the United States of this quite unexpected intrusion of the Russians ought to have been obvious.

It appears, however, that the Russian's very theatrical efforts at clandestinity did not particularly serve to mask the mission of *Cimbria* and its passenger list of "cabinet makers, waiters, and bakers," for quite soon after the ship's arrival there was a cluster of reporters, surprised American naval officers, and some undoubtedly quite gentlemanly but persistent inquirers with scarcely concealed ties to the British legation. Most likely the tale told by the Russian officers, that these people were emigrants from Russia seeking refuge in America, did not prove quite convincing, since it must have been impossible to conceal the attitudes of the naval officers among them, and it was also probably hard to reconcile this story with the fact that from South West Harbor Kapitan-leitenant Grippenberg had sent to St. Petersburg "an extremely long telegram made up only of figures." When, after a day or so, an American revenue cutter arrived, there was a visit to *Cimbria* and an inspection of documents. The "commander of the group introduced himself as an agent assigned by the Russian government to see to it that the 'emigrants' properly settled in and adapted to the U.S. The customs officials courteously viewed the sea chests, filled with naval uniforms" (Kuropiatnik, op. cit., 306).

In the traditional Punch and Judy puppet show there is often the scene in which Punch "confidentially" announces to the audience his "g-r-r-reat secret," for which there is a French phrase, apparently not paralleled in English, "secret de Polichinelle." The Russians had, with all their efforts to be clandestine, created something of that kind, sending 660 sailors under false passports giving what were undoubtedly blatantly inaccurate entries as to occupation—it is very difficult to disguise a boatswain's mate as a pastry cook—aboard a German ship to a supposedly out-of-the-way little port in Maine, one that was in full telegraphic communication with the rest of the world. Very shortly reporters began to turn up and the newspapers were supplied all kinds of details. This brought in other visitors, including British naval personnel attached to the legation in Washington, and unluckiest of all, Her Majesty's Vice-Consul in Portland. *The Times* of May 18, 1878 (p. 7, col. c.) reports, "The steamer is steadily watched by the British Vice-Consul at Portland, who passes his time chiefly on the wharf." May on the Maine coast has weather that can only be described as "brisk," and there are frequent fogs. One hopes that the British officers shared their high-proof rum with the poor diplomat. All in all, *The Times* contained at least twenty dispatches on the subject during May, including several of the traditional letters to the editor, one from a retired colonel who was nevertheless willing to offer naval suggestions. On May 24, it was reported that the British gunboat *Sirius* had *Cimbria* under observation and that the Royal Navy forces in Halifax were following the situation closely.

Kuropiatnik tells of a very complicated amount of diplomatic maneuvering, as the Russians made arrangements to buy three fast merchant vessels, and to have a fourth one built, all of which could be rearmed as auxiliary cruisers, and the British undertook to raise objections to any threatened violation of international law. The Russians entered into an agreement with the Philadelphia banker Wharton Barker that would allow Barker to have a rather fictitious ownership of the four ships, under pretext of establishing a line to ply between San Francisco and Alaska, but in actuality to take the ships to sea, there to transfer them to the Russian navy. It appears that coordination between the naval ministry and the ministry of foreign affairs was not always smooth. Although the Russian minister Shishkin had letters from the navy urging him to give all possible aid to this project, the diplomatic authorities in St. Petersburg were counseling avoidance of any clash or even of any unpleasant need for making diplomatic explanations to Washington. Secretary of State William M. Evarts found himself the recipient of communications from Sir Edward Thornton, the British minister, and from N. P. Shishkin, his Russian counterpart, each decrying the activities or interpretations of the other, and seeking to win a favorable view by the American government. The Russians, it seems, had enough of a realization of the nature of American politics to take at least two rather adroit steps. Through Wharton Barker ties were formed with the Industrial League, a group of industrialists and bankers, which promised cooperation with the Russian fleet; and the support of two eminent Republican leaders, Benjamin F. Butler and James G. Blaine, both men of flexible outlook, was obtained. Leading American authorities on international law were consulted for opinions that there was no barrier to foreign acquisition of ships and arms during time of peace—and, despite all the tension, Britain and Russia were at peace in the spring and early summer of 1878 (Kuropiatnik, op. cit.: 309–19).

Fortunately the tension between the two European powers was, if not totally removed, at least reduced below the danger level by the Congress of Berlin which, as noted above, took away some of Russia's first gains but brought about enough involvement of the other nations to ensure a sort of equilibrium. A mere inspection of the entries in the index to *The Times* shows that, even in June 1878 the British were no longer quite so worried about *Cimbria* and its project, although to the end of the year and into 1879 there were references to the Russian acquisition of four auxiliary cruisers in the United States.

The Russian representatives in the United States, whether those of the Imperial Navy or of the Ministry of Foreign Affairs, do not, however, appear to have slackened their efforts to complete the purchase, equipping, and arming of the four ships. Three of them were already afloat and had been engaged in various commercial voyages, and all that the Russians had done was to buy them from their owners to be refitted in the shipyards of William Cramp and Son in Philadelphia. The fourth, however, was built by Cramp, to Russian designs and under the strict control of that country's construction officers. The process was greatly smoothed by Russian efforts to win the support of the influential Industrial League and by the care that was taken to conform to most American interpretations of the laws on the subject (Kuropiatnik, op. cit.: 321–22).

The creation, in difficult diplomatic circumstances and despite the pressure of Britain, of a small but powerful and modern squadron of cruisers was a visible confirmation of the reality of cooperation of the two countries. "The successful completion of the cruisers in the United States, under rather difficult political conditions existing in Europe, gives Russia grounds even in the future," noted the ship constructors who had had many months of experience in joint work with the Americans, "to rely upon America in case of new difficulties with the maritime powers."

In the period of work on the construction and fitting out of the ships the Russians and Americans became better acquainted with one another. The Americans were imbued with respect for Russian specialists, who applied the most recent innovations of their country's engineering thought and who made many constructional changes in the completion and rigging of the ships. The ships were built in American yards, with American materials and basically by American works. "Although they were neither built nor armed in Russia, they should in all justice be called Russian," stated a report written from New York, "because, beginning with the general concept and ending with the most minor detail, these cruisers were created by Russian thought and Russian naval experience, which proved to be at its height . . . The Americans were only executants, in large part unsuccessful ones because of their lack of practice in naval ship construction" (Kuropiatnik, op. cit., 323. Citation is made to documentation in the Central State Archive of the Naval Fleet of the USSR).

In the final report on their mission in the United States the naval specialists wrote of the "advantage that Russia had gained from the expedition, namely, the moral impression left in America. In case of a naval war our fatherland will have only one well-wisher, the United States, for operations in the open sea" (Kuropiatnik, op. cit.: 323–24).

During the 1880s and 1890s there was no such dramatic evidence of the Russian hope that the United States could perhaps provide support to her, even that of mere benevolent neutrality, if troubles should develop in Europe. Americans gradually changed their attitude of good will toward Russia, under the influence of such works as George F. Kennan's *Siberia and the Exile System,* first published in 1891, and other accounts of the severities of the imperial regime. This change was strengthed by the fact that from the 1880s there had been a growing immigration into America of Jews of Russian origin, fleeing the restrictive laws that limited their areas of residence, barred them from education, and otherwise hampered them. An expulsion of the Jewish residents of Moscow in 1891 that had been reported to *The Times* (London) by its American-born correspondent Harold Frederick (author of the significant novel *The Damnation of Theron Ware*) had attracted wide attention, with serious impact on the state of opinion.

By the turn of the century, at the time of what is called the Boxer Rebellion in China, America had begun to worry that Russia was perhaps seeking to assume supremacy in the northern regions of China. She had acquired the right to build a railroad across Manchuria as a shorter route to Vladivostok and had been granted the naval base at Port Arthur in the south of that province—an action that would close Secretary of State Hay's "Open Door in China."

As a result of such factors, the American reaction toward Russia when that country's difficulties with Japan resulted in war in 1904 was not exactly a friendly one. The war had begun in February 1904 by a surprise Japanese attack on the Russian fleet that was very similar to that at Pearl Harbor. By the end of 1904 Russia had to surrender Port Arthur, which was its major naval base in Asian waters. Its armies were being pressed back into the Asian hinterland, with all the land combat taking place within the bounds of the Chinese Empire, contested predominance in which had been the major cause of the Russo-Japanese conflict. In May 1905 elements of the Russian fleet, sent all the way from the Baltic at vast cost and with many signs of inefficient command, were resoundingly defeated by Japan at Tsushima. Some of Russia's problems arose from those "slow ships" that the buffalo-hunting General-Admiral Grand Duke Aleksiei had favored along with the "fast women" mentioned by one of his relatives. None of these military acts had really damaged any vital centers of Russian power, but it was impossible for her to carry on a war so far from her real bases of strength, especially since everything had to be transported over a rail line that was not yet actually completed, and Russia was almost at the end of her ability to do more than relapse into a stalemate.

Japan, although it had enjoyed many victories, was also coming close to exhausting its financial resources and to perceiving the impossibility of doing vital harm to Russia. Both nations had arrived at a point at which some determined force could, perhaps, suggest a way out of their common dilemma. In this case the determined force was Theodore Roosevelt. It was perhaps with some relief that Roosevelt found both nations in a position of relative equilibrium and, acting on this situation, in the summer of 1905 he undertook a complicated diplomatic action to bring the two countries to the negotiating table. Neither wanted to be the first to agree, and Roosevelt at times found cause for irritation with both, expressing himself with some vigor about the vacillations of Nicholas II.

At last, both Russia and Japan agreed to send a delegation to the United States, and both selected serious and able men to serve as members. The Japanese were in the fortunate position of being able to choose a Harvard classmate of Roosevelt's as one of their delegates, a diplomat of considerable experience and ability. The Russians on their side named as their chief delegate Sergei Iul'evich Witte (1849–1915), a man of definite and forceful opinions, with no hesitancy about expressing them, qualities that the vague and malleable little emperor did not enjoy (cf. the views of "Vitte," probably S. Iu. Witte, on the grain situation, Chapter 4).

Witte served from 1892 to 1903 as the minister of finance, years in which he was able to establish a solid currency system, based on gold, and in which the empire began a period of impressive industrial development. Russia's prosperity, however, did not yet have deep roots and Witte, like his predecessors in office, did not favor adventurous policies that might lead to war. His opinions were in a large part the cause of his being removed from the finance post to be appointed to the resounding but not very influential position of Chairman of the Committee of Ministers, one which was nothing more than the presiding officer of a group of officials who had their own independent access to the emperor. However, the emperor, who tended to cringe away from forceful men and to find sly ways of dealing with them, must have found it a relief not to have to hear from the blunt Mr. Witte the even blunter tale of Russia's financial problems.

Yet, Witte was a loyal Russian, and was certainly not in favor of weak acquiescence to Japan's proposals for peace. Between his firmness and Nicholas' tendency to vacillate, Roosevelt had a considerable problem in securing Russian agreement to meet with Japanese emissaries. In a confidential letter to his long-time friend Henry Cabot Lodge, the president expressed his exasperation about the Russians, "they are hopeless creatures with whom to deal. They are utterly insincere and treacherous; they have no conception of truth, no willingness to look facts in the face, no regard for others of any sort or kind, no knowledge of their own strength or weakness; and they are helplessly unable to meet emergencies" (Roosevelt to H. C. Lodge, June 5, 1905. *Letters of Theodore Roosevelt*, v. 4. 1204–05). He was not quite so harsh about the Japanese, but this same letter contained forebodings about possible future clashes between the United States and Japan, particularly if some elements in America continued to provoke the Japanese by policies of exclusion and racial superiority while failing to maintain naval strength (op. cit., 1205–06). The sequence of acts by which Roosevelt finally managed to bring both sides together is a complicated one, and the details do not belong in this survey, but it is worth noting that all three participants, the warring Russians and Japanese and the go-between Theodore Roosevelt, were not in a good mood about one another, so that it is no surprise that the chief Russian delegate had some sharp things to say about America.

As Witte expressed it, on his departure for America, he was not entirely in good standing with Nicholas, and he had to undertake a job that would be distasteful to any loyal Russian, but he also tended to do all this in a spirit of "I told you so," which never exactly placates one's superiors after their policies have proven to be disastrous. His mood, therefore, was not particularly good, but he apparently retained full awareness that he was the only leading Russian who could carry out such a task. One point upon which he laid particular emphasis was that upon arrival in America he would need the good will of the American people, as a form of counterweight against any tendency to favor the Japanese—although the Russians had begun to exhaust their reserves of American public favor—so he was most careful to cultivate the press and to give signs of being affable, approachable, and benevolent.

Witte's memoirs appear to have been compiled in the form of individual segments, sometimes of several paragraphs each, that rather lack coherence and that, perhaps, reflect various dates of composition and some shifts of his points of view. It is, therefore, difficult to be quite sure whether his writings are indeed the thoughts that he had at the time of the events he describes or are, to vary the definition somewhat, "emotions recollected in rancor," a rancor that with him increased with age.

However, he sets forth a five-point program for his activities, one that he drew up during the six days of his Trans-Atlantic voyage.

(1) By no means show that we want peace, and act so as to give the impression that if the Emperor agrees to negotiations, it is only because of the general wish of almost all countries that the war come to an end; (2) Act as the representative of Russia should act, that is, as the spokeman of a great empire which has had a mild setback; (3) In view of the great influence of the press in America, behave especially cautiously and adopt an open demeanor to all its representatives; (4) In order to win over the people of America, who are extremely democratic, be completely open with them, without any condescension and in a democratic manner; (5) Given the particular influence of the Jews, especially in New York, and of the American press in general, do not adopt a hostile attitude toward them, which, indeed, corresponds to my views on the Jewish question in general" (Sergei Iul'evich Witte, *Vospominaniia*. v. 1. Moscow, Gosudarstvennoe izdatel'stvo, 1923. 340–41).

Upon his arrival, Witte writes that he showed himself willing to do such things as pose for tourists' cameras, to answer correspondents' questions, and to go up to the locomotives of trains upon which he had ridden to shake the engineer's hand. "I do not doubt that such behavior on my part—which placed a great burden on me, especially because of my inexperience, since in essence I had constantly to be an actor—greatly helped, in that gradually American public opinion, and consequently the press, more and more inclined their sympathy to the chief representative of the Russian tsar and his aides" (Witte, *Vospominaniia,* op. cit., 342).

Roosevelt's sympathies, Witte writes, were on the side of the Japanese, although as we see from Roosevelt's letters the president was actually rather cool toward them too, perhaps less critical than toward the less coherent Russians but still not without a certain tone of irony.

Upon landing in New York Witte was housed in "the best hotel on the best street. In this hotel a large suite was prepared for me, consisting of a bedroom, a room for my servant, a bathroom, two offices, a large living room, and a dining room. For this suite I had to pay 380 rubles a day . . ." [$190 at the prevailing exchange].

On my arrival in New York they warned me not to go into the Jewish areas. At that time there were up to 500 thousand Jews, most of whom had left Russia chiefly because of the difficulties of earning a living and in part because of the Jewish pogroms. Probably they expected attacks from this area.

On arrival I hired an automobile and rode in it with one of the officials of the embassy into all the Jewish parts of town. The Jews soon recognized me. At first they looked askance at me, then with equanimity, but when I spoke with some of them a few words in Russian and greeted them, they generally responded to me hospitably and favorably (Witte, op. cit.: 343–44).

It is difficult within the bounds of a single paragraph to explain the connotations of the preceding paragraphs. Suffice it to say that Jews in Russia were, by law, confined to only a few regions of the empire, that they were limited in their civil and economic rights, and that even those who had been naturalized in America had to observe all the galling rules of the Russian bureaucracy should they return for a visit. Many Russian officials had almost openly encouraged pogroms against Jews, in which quite innocent people were attacked, and even killed, merely because they were Jewish. As a result, Jewish immigrants of Russian background in America were on the whole bitterly hostile to "Nikolasha" (their nickname for the emperor), his Cossacks, and their whips.

The day following his arrival Witte went by train to visit Roosevelt at his house at Oyster Bay on Long Island. "The president's villa, which belongs to him personally, is extremely simple—the ordinary villa of a not very wealthy citizen." T. R.'s manner of living and the food served were not particularly to Witte's taste, and he did not like the idea that ice water was the only beverage served. He did not feel that Roosevelt was particularly pleased with the conversation that followed the luncheon, a feeling in which Witte was probably quite correct as, even as late as November 1 of that year, T. R. was writing, "Witte impressed me much while he was here, but by no means altogether pleasantly" (Roosevelt to Cecil Spring Rice, November 1, 1905. *Letters of Theodore Roosevelt*. v. 5. Cambridge, Harvard University Press, 1952. p. 61).

Following that meeting, Witte and the Russian delegation proceeded in a somewhat leisurely fashion toward the appointed meeting place at Portsmouth, New Hampshire. For part of the route Witte and the Russian delegation were aboard the presidential yacht *Mayflower*, which put into Newport, Rhode Island, so that Witte could meet with some of the vacationing grandees there. Witte then went by train to Boston, stopping to visit Harvard, and then on to Portsmouth. The other delegates, still aboard *Mayflower*, arrived in Portsmouth on August 8, where they and Witte were welcomed with considerable ceremony.

The reception did not, however, smooth Witte's state of mind particularly. He was further irritated by the quarters that he was given in a "largish wooden hotel, built for the summer visit of not very well-off people. In that hotel were quartered the delegates, their advisers, a herd of correspondents, and a mass of witnesses eternally coming and going and wanting to be in the very cauldron of the great diplomatic drama that was taking place. Undoubtedly this year was surprisingly fortunate for the owners of this hotel!" (Witte, op. cit., 348).

The hotel, adjudged by Witte as being intended for the more unprosperous summer visitors, was in fact the Hotel Wentworth, which is described in some detail in a 1969 study of the treaty negotiations.

Still in business at the present time, and well worth a trip to Portsmouth, it was, at the turn of the century, one of the finest resort hotels in the United States, easily as impressive as other spas American-style, such as the Broadmoor in Colorado Springs or French Lick in Southern Indiana. The Went-

258   Russia Looks at America

worth had opened in 1867. Guest lists read like a *Who's Who* of eastern society. On a hill overlooking the bay stood the huge white frame structure of four stories divided into three sections joined by roofed-in passsages.

Nor did Witte find the food especially to his taste. "American food at this time was quite different from European and Oriental, and the chefs were undecided what they should prepare. At the beginning of the conference they prepared many dishes, hoping the delegates would find something to their tastes." One menu, admittedly from a banquet for the reporters, included "Chicken Pot Pie, with Dumplings," which may have been an obscure and unconscious answer to some of the things served Gustavus V. Fox on his visit to Russia (Eugene P. Trani, *The Treaty of Portsmouth; an adventure in American diplomacy.* Lexington, University of Kentucky Press, 1969: 69, 125–26).

One of Witte's most extensive comments about America itself, rather than about the difficulties of the conference and of relations with the press, deserves extensive citation, as it represents the view of a significant, and still familiar, facet of American society. The translation is made for this present survey, rather than being taken from the published English edition of Witte's memoirs.

Some of the specific features of American life surprised me greatly. For instance the majority of the waiters in the hotels and restaurants, i.e., the people serving food and clearing the tables, were none other than students of higher educational institutions and universities, who by this earned their way, since in summer the personnel in restaurants are paid a comparatively large sum, reaching 100 dollars, i.e., about 200 rubles, total.

And these students are by no means shocked by such duty. They don the requisite garb of a restaurant waiter, serve during dinner in the most exact fashion and clear the table (they do not do the dirtiest work [Witte must be referring to dishwashing]). Then, after dinner or after lunch they change clothes, like all the others, sometimes put on their club badges, pay court to the ladies and young girls living in the hotel, go with them into the parks, play games, and, when the time for dinner comes, they go away, again put on their waiters' uniforms and serve table just like the best of waiters.

This feature of American life surprised me very much since, not to speak of the fact that according to our way of doing things nothing of the sort could happen in Russia, and in spite of the fact that our poor students go hungry, sometimes living on 10 to 20 rubles a month, they would, nevertheless, be shocked if it was suggested to them that they serve table as a lackey, even in the best restaurants. Besides, it is not only in Russia but, most likely, in the other areas of Europe that they would look at it in that way.

It also surprised me that young girls of quite good families, living in the hotel, did not consider it shameful of an evening, in the dark, to walk out with the young people. A young girl, tête-à-tête with a young man, goes into the woods, or into the park, they both walk together there for hours on end, go out in boats, and no one takes it into his head to consider this in the slightest degree demeaning. Quite on the contrary, any base thoughts that might come to the mind of outside observers in relation to these young people would be considered prejudiced (Witte, op. cit.: 351–52).

The story of the negotiations that ended in a peace treaty that Russia could accept without too deep a blow to her prestige, and that Japan could feel presented some reward for her series of victories, does not belong here, and most of what Witte writes about the effort is not at all part of his view of America. However, once the agreement had been made there was a period in which he undertook several visits to American institutions, one of which in fact was a quite serious element in his whole visit. In one of his encounters, at Columbia University, he talked with a professor of political economy, asking him if he informed his auditors about Henry George's book on the nationalization of land. The professor answered that of course, he did so; "firstly, George is one of our most talented writers, and, besides this, I consider it useful to acquaint my listeners with his view on the land question in order to explain his lack of foundation!"

"For many of our home-grown Russian economists it would be useful to hear these lectures, even for such a great writer, but naive thinker, as Count Lev Tolstoi." Although Henry George had died in 1897, this episode from 1905 shows that his outlook was still present in the mind of a person such as Witte, who continued to fear the effects of George's teachings (Witte, op. cit., 362).

But the most important of his post-treaty activities was Witte's meetings with the very powerful financier J. P. Morgan the elder. The war with Japan had, as was customary with Russia, severely unsettled the country's finances and it was felt necessary to turn to the foreign money market to borrow enough upon which to keep the situation within manageable bounds. Although Russia had, since the early 1890s, relied on French loans for most of her foreign credits, there was a hope that Morgan and the interests that he represented could provide additional sums, or at least serve as a lever with which to bring better terms from other lenders.

The two men, Morgan and Witte, traveled up the Hudson

River together, aboard Morgan's yacht, to visit the military academy at West Point, and there was one feature that the Russian greatly appreciated. Going up river he had lunch and coming back down he dined,

and this was the only time when I, during my stay in America, really had lunch and really dined, since, when I stayed in the hotel, in spite of the completely fantastic prices that they charged me, such as 380 rubles for the room, and for dinner from 30 to 40 rubles per person, and that for the most modest of dinners, the food was still completely vile.

Aboard the yacht I had talks with Morgan and asked him if he would take part in a loan that Russia would have to make in order to liquidate the consequences of the war. He not only agreed but also expressed himself on the topic and insisted that I would not carry on negotiations with another group, a Jewish one, at the head of which was Schiff. I did not do so (Witte, op. cit.: 362–63).

While there were other reasons for Morgan's not having, after all, participated in such a loan, there may have been some influence arising from Witte's tactlessness about something from which a really good briefing would have spared him. J. P. Morgan the elder suffered from a very conspicuous skin disease that affected his nose, enlarging it and damaging the skin. No one with any knowledge of the man whatsoever dared to mention it to him, for he was sensitive on the subject and he was, when aroused, a person of truly formidable coldness. Witte did so however, telling the American banker of a famous professor in Berlin who could perform a wondrous operation. As far as Witte's memoirs show, Morgan concealed his famous truculence and answered in a rather restrained negative manner (Witte, op. cit.: 363–64).

There followed a quick visit to Washington and to Roosevelt's home at Oyster Bay for a farewell interview. Here Roosevelt brought up a question which was to play a major role in Russo-American relations in the years before the end of the empire, the problem of unfavorable Russian treatment of American Jews who visited Russia. The American interpretation of relevant clauses of the Treaty of 1832 was that no such differentiation would be made, but, on Russia's side, the officials maintained that American Jewish visitors could be treated only in accordance with prevailing Russian practices. During Witte's service in the cabinet a commission had been set up to consider the problem, but this body did not report until several years later, and finally, by the end of 1911, the Americans had been driven to abrogate the treaty because of the Russian actions in this field.

The treaty came to an end after the expiration of a year's grace late in 1912, and until 1914 there was no American ambassador in St. Petersburg, matters being handled by subordinate diplomats. Many Russians of a strongly nationalist outlook criticized America for advancing claims for the equal treatment of all our citizens, including those of Jewish background. Some of this was of an undisguised anti-Semitic nature and it was said that the American effort to secure equal treatment in all parts of the Russian Empire for all Americans, of whatever background, was the result of insidious machinations by inveterate enemies of Russia, and that, in excluding Jews or in limiting their rights, the country was only defending itself against "a refractory and non-assimilable tribe, refusing to take upon themselves an equal and just share of the common burdens in the life of the country" (V. P. Egert, *The conflict between the United States and Russia.* St. Petersburg, 1912. p. 8). Although in his introduction the author disavows any official connection with the imperial government, and although no publisher of this squalid pamphlet is indicated, there is on the reverse title page a little series of Russian letters reading in transliteration, "Tip. Gl. upr. ud.," and these can, upon comparison with another of his writings, be expanded into "Tipografiia Glavnago upravleniia udielov" [Printing House of the Main Administration of Lands of the Imperial Family]. Egert was also the author of *Iz amerikanskikh vpechatlienii* [From American impressions] one issue of which was published in 1911 by the same printing house (no further entry appearing in the Russian national bibliography 1911–14), this time shown in its full Russian title. There is no need to repeat Egert's language, save to say that Streicher and Goebbels could scarcely have added to it, and to cite his allegations that the United States in its protest against Russian official mistreatment of American citizens was "carrying out not their own, but a Jewish policy" (Egert, *Conflict* . . . 26).

As war came in 1914 there is no Russian evidence that that empire took great notice of America's position or of its potential power. In contrast to the events of 1876–78, there was no direct effort to "play the American card" in any direct diplomatic sense of the word, although quite soon Russian purchasing missions were to appear in the United States seeking supplies of all kinds, from harness for horses to motor trucks, from shoes to horseshoes. These operations were hampered by problems of finance, and by the fact that the war had cut off access to Russia's ports on the Baltic and on the Black Sea, leaving access only by various round-about routes, including the Trans-Siberian rail line from Vladivostok and the hastily built line to Murmansk on the empire's north coast. There is an important body of records of the chief Russian purchasing mission in the National Archives in Washington and, although there appear to be gaps, these materials would be well worth serious investigation.

Despite these economic matters, one finds, at least thus far, very little from the higher levels of the failing imperial regime as to its view of the United States. There were, it seems, too many other problems, those of military defeat as well as those of political ineptitude, to allow for any large attention to a country whose reserves of good will, so much spoken of four decades before, had largely been exhausted.

The three episodes discussed in this chapter were chosen with a certain amount of malice aforethought for, although the most recent of them—Witte's visit—took place over eight decades ago, they reflect attitudes that may still be felt in relations between the Soviet Union and the United States. Even to this day official visitors to the USSR are accorded receptions which can easily be compared to that given to Gustavus V. Fox and the crew of *Miantonomoh* in 1866, with speeches of just such impressive generalizations as those of Prince Gorchakov. This writer can, on a rather lower level, testify to two similar instances in his own experience, one when, as an aide to the then Librarian of Congress, he took part in a very well orchestrated series of lunches, theater evenings, and official viewings of Soviet library treasures—with a grateful memory of being left with praise, given in English and in the hearing of the Librarian, of his ability to cope with the translation of Russian speeches—and the other as he made an independent official two-week visit, with one of the guides being a woman who had previously accompanied Indira Gandhi, Jacqueline Kennedy Onassis, and . . . Imelda Marcos.

In the case of the *Cimbria* affair in the 1870s, one must refer to the marvelous flexibility of the Russian language in which, by the careful use of prefixes, terribly precise, and sometimes equally cutting, turns can be given to almost any verb. The word "khitrit'sia" means, approximately, "to act cleverly, to approach things slyly," and so on, but with the use of the prefix "pere," it becomes "perekhitrit'sia," which can be best rendered by the colloquial "to outsmart one's self," or even "to shoot one's self in the foot." This, certainly, is what the dispatch of *Cimbria*, with 660 unconvincingly documented pastry cooks, gardeners, and coachmen did for Russian efforts to be clandestine. G. K. Chesterton's detective Father Brown is reported to have said that the best place to hide a pebble is on the beach, and some other British writer of the same era referred to an acquaintance as "a bull who carries his own china shop with him." Russian unawareness of these two truths brought about the appearance in the allegedly out-of-the-way South West Harbor, Maine of a large (or at least largish) steamer, crammed with male passengers, whose officers immediately sent off long telegrams in cipher addressed to St. Petersburg, all about as easy to conceal as a kettle drum in a string quartet. Any alert newspaper reader will remember instances of a comparable nature in the Soviets' management of their foreign relations.

As for Witte's visit to he United States in 1905, the quotations from his memoirs testify to a conscious effort to exhibit understanding and affability toward Americans—as shown by his various forms of "stroking" the press and public—that actually overlaid a combination of incomprehension and of bad briefing. Witness, for the last two factors, Witte's lack of understanding of the way in which American college students could "lower themselves" to take up summer jobs as waiters in hotels, and his failure to be informed that one did not *ever* mention J. P. Morgan's nose to J. P. Morgan. It is easy, and would be superfluous, to refer to Soviet visitors who have shown similar lack of perception.

Indeed, this record, from a span of almost four decades, from 1866 to 1905, can be interpreted as showing that, despite the many evidences of Russian understanding of the United States which can be found in other fields discussed in this book, imperial officialdom knew rather little about the United States and was not intent upon adopting any particularly subtle approach. Even today analytical reading of official Soviet pronouncements often demonstrates that similar attitudes prevail. Unfortunately, a similar attention to much of the equivalent phraseology at high levels on the American side often reveals an equal lack of knowledge and a comparable avoidance of anything except unthoughtful preconceptions.

At any rate, the Soviets in many ways appear to be the inheritors of methods of diplomacy that were habitual among the servants of the tsar, and it could in fact be said that very little has changed in the psychologies of those in charge of the country's foreign affairs. Certainly there is other proof of an essential continuity between the American policies of the Empire of Russia and of the Union of Soviet Socialist Republics that could be found by closer study of the materials for which this chapter had no room.

CHAPTER SEVEN

After 1917—A Brief Look

In late December 1916, as Russia was reeling under defeat after defeat at the front and the effects of economic disorganization and political turmoil at home, a group of inept conspirators—including a grand duke, the son-in-law of another grand duke, an extreme right-wing deputy to the Duma, and an army doctor—undertook a step that, they thought, would save Russia. If, they reasoned, the influence of the enigmatic Grigorii Efimovich Rasputin could be ended, the emperor would be able to free himself from that man's wiles, as exercized through the distraught and hysterically inclined empress, and to set things right both with the war and with the country. Luring Rasputin to the palatial residence of the grand duke's son-in-law, the plotters sought to eliminate him. They poisoned his wine and pastry, and he lived; they shot him, and he continued to walk; they pushed him under the ice, and the autopsy, so it was said, indicated that he had died by drowning. As all this was taking place, so one of the conspirators recorded, the stage effects for this macabre event included a phonograph playing *Yankee Doodle!*

The murder did not, however, have the desired effects. In the eight weeks that remained to the regime previous policies continued, with rapid-fire changes of political appointments and further evidences of military and economic mismanagement. The honorable, charming, and inept emperor continued to hold to his view that God had selected him to govern Russia, and his wife repeated her admonitions to him to show himself as the master of all these lesser folk, without any concessions to the calls from every part of the political spectrum for a government more open to public participation. The British ambassador, Sir George Buchanan, an almost perfect example of The Edwardian Gentleman with finely honed aversion to abrupt and intrusive actions, at last took his career in his hands and, in a final interview, urged the emperor to regain the confidence of his people. The emperor replied by asking if Sir George did not really mean that the people should try to restore the emperor's confidence in them.

Within a few weeks the increasingly difficult problems of food supply to Petrograd brought riots in the capital which, when joined by the disaffected garrison, ultimately brought Nicholas to abdicate, giving way to a Provisional Government. The long series of Russian monarchs came to an end, as T. S. Eliot wrote of the end of the world, "not with a bang, but a whimper." The old regime had left Russia not only many problems but also a great, at times even a magnificent, legacy. One of the elements in this legacy, as this study has attempted to show, was a large range of information about and attitudes toward the United States, ranging from solid scholarly studies to the transient kitsch of American film comedies and the tales of Nat Pinkerton, and all this remained part of what has been called the "furniture of the mind" of those who attempted to restore some sort of order and then to remake a vast, disorganized, but essentially powerful land into something conceived to be a juster and more rational one.

A major agent in this reshaping of Russia was a man who had spent the previous ten years in exile in Western Europe and who, in fact, had experienced either exile to Siberia or to Europe for most of the time between his twenty-fifth and forty-seventh birthdays. His brilliant mind and his cutting prose style had largely been engaged with abstractions about the need for revolution according to the formulae he derived from the works of another great exile, Karl Marx, as mingled with some of the more elemental tendencies of Russian radicals toward violence as a political tool. His major experience with the administration of any organization whatsoever was that of attempting, through any necessary deviousness, to remain in control of a small group of radicals, most of whom were also political exiles, in anticipation of the coming of a day of revolution and destruction of the old order.

This exile, Vladimir Il'ich Ul'ianov, who used the party name "Lenin," included among his stock of abstractions some that dealt with the United States, which he chiefly used as debating points in his efforts to squelch his adversaries. While some of these debating points show perspicacity, and often provide unexpected opinions, there was little evidence that he had sought understanding in depth. Though the index volume to the fifty-five volumes of the so-called *Polnoe sobranie sochinenii* [Complete collected works, Hereafter PSS]—the completeness of which has been disputed by some scholars—contain numerous entries under headings relating to America, most are either passing references or demonstrate the tendency already noted with regard to others mentioned in this study of employing an American theme to advance an argument in an essentially Russian context.

Nevertheless, some of his writings from the years before 1917 are of interest. One of the most striking was the article "Kapitalizm i nalogi" [Capitalism and taxes] that he contributed to *Pravda* in 1913. That newspaper, one must note, appeared quite legally in St. Petersburg from 1912 to the outbreak of the war in 1914, although at times the title had to undergo cosmetic changes (from *Pravda* [Truth] to *Rabochaia pravda* [Labor truth] or *Put' pravdy* [Path of truth]) to avoid the censorship, and the imperial authorities were well aware, especially since at least one of Lenin's associates was an informer, that some of the articles the paper published were contributions from the exiled attorney and member of the hereditary gentry Vladimir Il'ich Ul'ianov.

In his article Lenin examined the subject of the American income tax, then just going into effect as a result of the ratification of an amendment to the Constitution. The rates of tax, as Lenin gives them, seem impossibly mild to present-day observers, for incomes of less than $4,000 would be exempt, and only 1 percent would be levied on those up to $20,000, while the man who earned a million dollars would pay only 3 percent. There would still remain, Lenin writes, a need to levy various indirect taxes, which would weigh hard upon the mass of the population, which, according to his calculations, would pay an equivalent of seven cents per dollar of income while the capitalists (those with $11,000 or more) paid but little more than one third of a cent per dollar. One of his conclusions was,

We see that the demand of the social-democrats for a complete abolition of all indirect taxes and their replacement by a real not feigned progressive income tax is completely attainable. Such a measure, not infringing on the bases of capitalism, would immediately give great relief to nine-tenths of the population, and, secondly, would serve as a giant stimulus to the expansion of the productive forces of society as the consequences of the growth of the internal market and as a result of the freeing of the state from the clumsy hindrances to economic life brought about by the levying of indirect taxes (Lenin, *PSS*. 5th edition. v. 23. Moscow, 1961: 242–45).

In essence, Lenin is saying that the income tax would be beneficial to capitalism for it would increase purchasing power among the masses, and it would also be helpful to the state, reducing the problems caused by a system of indirect taxes. However, "the only difficulty is the class greed of the capitalists and the existence of undemocratic institutions in the political structure of bourgeois states," and he evidently did not feel that the capitalists would actually comprehend the situation (Lenin, op. cit., 245).

A second major American institution about which Lenin wrote was the New York Public Library. Although his years of exile had taught him a great deal about the scholarly libraries of Western Europe, from which he had drawn masses of social and economic data to bolster his political views, it was not the New York Public Library as a resource for scholars that drew his attention, but rather the library as an agency for making knowledge available to the masses about which he wrote. On July 18, 1913 (O. S.) in *Rabochaia Pravda*—one of the changes of title that kept the newspaper in being—there was published his "Chto mozhno sdelat' dlia narodnogo obrazovaniia" [What can be done for public education]. It is quickly evident that Lenin in this case was using the quite familiar technique, already mentioned a number of times, of using an American example as a club with which to beat a Russian reality. The West, he said, had many prejudices from which "sviataia matushka Rus" [Holy Mother Russia] was free. There they think that libraries are for people and not for some guild of professors, specialists, and technicians. "Our careful authorities guard us with concern and minute attention against the influence of these prejudices and preserve our rich public libraries from people off the streets and out of the crowd" (Lenin, *PSS*. 5th ed. v. 23. Moscow, 1961: 348–49).

The West, the unregulated West, does things differently and to show this Lenin refers to the 1911 annual report of the New York Public Library. This institution has forty-two branches—no matter where one travels in the city, a branch is no more than ¾ verst (ca ½ mile) away—and there is an effort to make books available to all classes of the population. He cites circulation statistics and gives particular attention to the library's work with children, contrasting it with the way in which such activities are slighted in Russia. "That's the kind of thing that exists in New York. But, what about us?" (op. cit.: 349–59).

Somewhat more significant insofar as any effect on the Russian economy may be concerned was Lenin's rather detailed survey of the writings of the American industrial engineer Frederick Winslow Taylor (1859–1921), who had studied the performance of workers, seeking to arrive at methods for the elimination of lost motion and for the increase of the efficiency and speed of production. To many people Taylor seemed to open a way to a new era of improved operations and lower cost, but others, particularly among the workers, felt that he had merely offered means for employers to raise their profits without a corresponding rise in wages. As early as 1908 there had been references to Taylor in the Russian press, and between 1909 and 1914 the engineers A. V. Pankin and L. A. Levenstern had translated four of his books into Russian. There were also writings by Henry Laurence Gantt, Frank B. Gilbreth, and Frederick Augustus Parkhurst, all of whom were Americans applying similar time-and-motion-study procedures. Furthermore, there were at least ten other books or articles, some by Russian authors, that appeared in the pre-1917 era with titles that included Taylor's name, and about fifteen other titles of those years that deal with industrial efficiency and that most probably refer to the American investigator. [For pre-1917 Russian publications on F. W. Taylor and his system, see: Osip. A. Ermanskii, *Nauchnaia organizatsiia truda i sistema Teilora* (The scientific organization of labor and the Taylor system). Moscow,

Gosudarstvennoe izdatel'stvo, 1922. 367 p. Pages 355–60 provide a bibliography of Russian-language works from which information about publications with Taylor's name in the title and about other possibly relevant items was obtained. Information as to the role of A. V. Pankin and L. A. Levenstern was derived from entries for Taylor, Gantt, Gilbreth, and Parkhurst works in the national bibliography *Knizhnaia lietopis'* for 1909 to 1916.]

Thus, by the time of the appearance of Lenin's first reference to Taylor, in his "Nauchnaia' sistema vyzhimaniia pota" [Scientific method for squeezing out perspiration], which first appeared in *Pravda* of March 13, 1913 (presumably Old Style), he was not a pioneer in the field. The article, which is a short one, is relatively unfavorable, but it appears that Lenin had read one of Taylor's books (Lenin, *PSS.* v. 23: 18–19). The next reference, just a year later, in the March 15, 1914 issue of *Put' Pravdy,* was "Sistema Teilora—poraboshchenie cheloveka mashinoi" [The Taylor system—the enslavement of man by the machine]. In this the undesirable features of Taylor's methods are noted, such as their use to enable employers to exploit the workers without any commensurate increase in pay and the effects of this increased effort on health among the laborers, but in his last paragraphs Lenin writes,

> The Taylor system, without the knowledge and against the will of its authors, is preparing for the time when the proletariat will take into its hands all social production and will appoint its own workers commissions for a just distribution of the sum of social labor. Large-scale production, machines, railroads, telephones, all this will give thousands of possibilities for decreasing the work time of organized workers by a factor of four, assuring them a greater well-being, by a factor of four, than at present.
>
> And the workers commissions, with the help of the labor unions, will be able to apply these principles of rational distribution of work when this work is freed from its subjection by capital (Lenin, *PSS.* v. 24: 369–71).

A footnote to this article in Lenin's collected works says that the original manuscript had remained unknown until 1959 when it was discovered in the Central State Historical Archives in Moscow in a collection "Items in evidence" that had been compiled by the imperial Department politsii as proof of *Pravda's* antigovernmental activities (Lenin, *PSS.* v. 24: 467).

There is no surprise, then, when one finds that within a

few months after the October Revolution, Lenin was speaking of the need for the Soviets to adopt the Taylor system, applying it to the benefit of the workers (Lenin, *PSS.* v. 36: 189–90, 212–13, 260, 279. Materials dated: between March 23 and 28, 1918; April 1, 1918; April 29, 1918; May 9, 1918). His last mention of Taylor came in an unfinished review of the book by Ermanskii cited above, written sometime after September 10, 1922, during the last few months in which his health still allowed him to be an active participant in affairs, in which he says that, were it not for Ermanskii's prolixity, the work would well deserve to be a text for trade and secondary school use (Lenin, *PSS.* v. 45: 206–07).

Given the fact that all three of the editions of the *Bol'shaia sovetskaia entsiklopediia* speak of "Teilorizm" as having, despite some of its harmful effects when used by capitalism, contributed significantly to the formation of Soviet work methods, it may indeed be the case that one of the most significant items in the Soviet inheritance of the pre-1917 view of America was in this field of industrial management. Although the slogan of the era of the First Five Year Plan (1928–32) *Dognat' i peregnat' Ameriku!!!* [Overtake and surpass America!!!] was not used by Lenin in just that form, his drawing of lessons from F. W. Taylor, and from other aspects of American industrial methods, was entirely within its spirit. And, as we have seen from some of the materials in preceding sections that deal with the grain elevator and with agricultural methods, there were others in pre-1917 Russia who would have found such a motto to echo their own thoughts.

However, Lenin's most extensive commentary on the United States appears to be that which he made in the course of criticizing the imperial government's reforms in the system of peasant landholding. The courageous and efficient Petr Arkad'evich Stolypin (1862–1911), who followed Witte as chairman of the council of ministers, had undertaken measures to allow peasants to opt out of the traditional Russian institution of communal landholding and to consolidate their land into individual tracts on which there was no longer a need to conform to the cultivation times and crops of their neighbors. There would be, Stolypin was well aware, many peasants who would fail in this effort, but he said, in effect, that Russia should not attempt any longer to maintain a system that holds almost everyone down to a low, common level, but that she should "bet on the strong and able" who would show enough strength and enterprise to rise toward new productivity. For the radical segment of Russian public opinion, this was a horrifying introduction of the capitalist principle into agriculture, one that destroyed the communal aspects of peasant life and that would, so these radicals felt, hinder the transition of the whole country to socialism.

Lenin wrote in 1908 in opposition to Stolypin's changes in the agricultural system in Russia, stating that "after the 'solution' of the agrarian problem in the spirit of Stolypin, *no other revolution capable of seriously changing the economic conditions of life of the masses of the peasants can ever exist*" (Lenin, *PSS.* 5th ed. v. 17. Moscow, 1961: 32). Despite this awareness of the possible effect of Stolypin's measures in eliminating any chance of a revolution in the countryside, Lenin had little to say about any relationship that might have existed between these measures and the American model until in 1915 he presented an analysis of the situation in the United States in his *Novyia dannyia o zakonakh razvitiia kapitalizma v zemledielii. vyp. 1: Kapitalizm i zemledielie v Soedinennykh Shtatakh Ameriki* [New data on the laws of development of capitalism in agriculture. v. 1: Capitalism and agriculture in the United States] (Lenin, *PSS.* 5th ed. v. 27. Moscow, 1962: 129–227). This was largely based on the volumes of data resulting from the U.S. census of 1910 and it sought on that evidence to show that the "inevitable" laws of capitalism tended to squeeze the small farmer more and more out of competition with larger landowners. Lenin's conclusion was to the general effect that, as in the United States, so it would be with the small farms created by Stolypin's reforms and that, therefore, Russia should not take this path which would only end in the concentration of property in the hands of a few. His footnotes and other remarks indicate that one of his purposes was to counter arguments made by some of his socialist opponents—in the broad sense of the term socialism—who were somewhat more favorable to some of the Stolypin changes, particularly the views of Nikolai Gimmer-Sukhanov as expressed in a 1913 article in the journal *Zaviety* [not available in the Library of Congress].

It may be argued that Lenin's tendencies toward viewing the world as an abstract pattern of forces, without any great evidence of awareness of the often chaotic and contradictory interaction of real life, have shaped all subsequent Soviet thought. Certainly a strong case may be made with regard to the Soviet attitude toward the United States, at least as this is reflected outwardly. Insofar as one may draw one's perceptions from the publicly expressed record, the years since 1917 have seen a narrowing of both the volume and the outlook of material about the United States and, if one were to express it in musical form, the range of tones has been sharply diminished. Yet, as in so many other areas, the experience of the years before 1917 has not ceased to affect present-day Soviet perceptions, and, despite the influence of almost seventy years, older attitudes have not been erased.

While Imperial Russia was, even during the decade of quasi-constitutional government, a state that relied largely on central control of both governmental acts and, as far as possible, of information and opinion, there was a breadth and richness of thought and interpretation that formed a great intellectual heritage. And, the theme of America is one of the strands in this legacy. Even now, the Soviet concept of America continues to draw upon much more than the history of the times since November 7, 1917.

Conclusion

A ll the preceding has been but an introduction to a topic about which much more can, and should, be written. The Russian Empire that vanished in 1917 had available to it a vast body of information and opinion about the United States, greater in scope and in detail than any single piece of analysis can ever encompass, and the new regime that took power, proclaiming a break with all the patterns of the past, did not in reality interrupt a continuity of knowledge of and interest in American affairs that is still influential almost seventy years later. Indeed while the Russian journals of, let us say, the 1880s were filled with painfully long analyses of Gladstone's policies toward Ireland or Egypt, the passage of time has robbed these articles of their immediacy but the materials on the United States often show attitudes that still appear in present-day relationships between the two countries. Even if the remarks of Mikhail Evgrafovich Saltykov-Shchedrin in *Otechestvennyia zapiski* of June 1881 (see Chapter 4 above) to the effect that, perhaps, Russia would some day become a consumer of American wheat reflected only a lucky guess, influenced by a sharply negative attitude toward the system that held the peasantry in subjection, there were many other indications that the American experience was present in many Russian minds as a stimulus toward guiding Russia's own development. At the same time, however, one must enter the observation that Russia's own background and needs, as well as the strength of her own culture, provided the real basis for national development. No nation, even the seemingly weakest one, can fail to draw more upon its own cultural resources in shaping its future. As many analytical treatises since 1917 have made clear, the Soviet Union includes quite as much, if not more, that comes from the centuries-old patterns of the mingling of steppe and forest, Or-

274

thodox Christianity and autocratic rule, than from the teachings of Karl Marx and his followers. With all these influences, the relatively few decades of interest in America can, of course, play only a limited role, but, as the foregoing chapters have shown, the American presence cannot be denied. Nor can one fail to see that the Russian Revolution did not, in fact, interrupt many elements in the relationships between the two countries. Although some journalists, and even those of more scholarly intent, seem to assume that it was only with Lenin's advent to power that the people of Russia took any great interest in America, the evidence presented here shows that for at least a century Russians had had an interest in American affairs, an interest that was reflected both in many translations from English or other West European languages and in a very substantial body of writings by Russians themselves.

Of course, not every Russian mention of the United States deserves belief. Often one finds absolute misstatements in quite serious journals, such as that in *Sievernyi viestnik* of December 1888 to the effect that Samuel Tilden had won the presidential election of 1877 and Horace Greeley had run in that of 1881! This article is signed only with the initials "S. Iu.," most likely those of S. Iuzhakov, one of the editors of the journal, and while one need not demand great knowledge of American politics from the editor of a middle-level Russian publication, there is still a question as to how well Iuzhakov, if this author indeed were he, managed to present the thought of Henry George whose works Iuzhakov was among the first Russians to examine at any length (see *Otechestvennyia zapiski*, 1883, nos. 2 and 3). Other Russian writings about America seem intended chiefly to amaze the reader with the doings of these wild men in the West, an outlook reinforced by several decades of repeated editions of the adventure tales—thrice-repeated efforts at a hanging or ostriches along the Upper Missouri—of Mayne Reid and Gustave Aimard. Then, too, many of the translations from American writers served only to divert the reader with material of the "soul butter and flapdoodle" school of literature exemplified by the long publishing history in Russian of Maria S. Cummings's sentimental novel *The Lamplighter* (from the late 1850s to 1914), not to mention similar writings.

However, as other citations in the previous pages have

shown, there was a serious core within all this, and one may derive from it conclusions as to a definable Russian attitude toward America in the years before 1917. Imperial Russia had no single, obligatory, or imposed interpretation of the United States, and there were many differing opinions. Some writers saw the United States predominantly as an exemplar of progress and justice, while others felt that it was, so to speak, a suspect and unsuccessful experiment. It is perhaps unsound to engage in retrospective assessments of the relative weight of these two points of view, but it does seem that it was the former that set the tone of most of the Russian discussions of America. There was comparatively little in the published material of the time that approached in its venom the language that has been employed at times in the Soviet press, and one finds no consistent image of the United States as a source of most of the ills of the world. Indeed, even though Robert Orbinskii realized that his visit to the United States to study the grain trade related to an absolutely vital element of Russia's economy and that U.S. competition did indeed present serious difficulties to his native land, his letter, in somewhat awkward English, in the *Missouri Republican* of August 2, 1879, did not breathe a spirit of harsh antagonism. "We are competitors then, America and Russia, but I never met a competitor as gentlemanlike and noble as your country. Every information I wanted was given to me with a courtesy I could never hope to find. There was nothing of the vile jealousy between rivalizing-trade people, which we are accustomed to read in every history of commerce" (see Chapter 4 above). Nor is any reflection of antagonism to be found in the book on American education by E. P. Kovalevskii, published under the auspices of the Imperial Ministry of Education that, as its original paper cover shows, was from the very beginning a statement in praise of the beneficial influence of education on America and, by inference, a demonstration of the need for Russia to adopt similar policies (see Chapter 5 above). Even as the possibility of an industrial competition between Russia and America began to be discussed, A. S. Ermolov—admittedly somewhat less directly concerned with this problem, since he was Minister of State Property and Agriculture—spoke of such future "competition and even a clash" as "an honorable and

useful one, not destroying but rather strengthening the organisms of the state" (see Chapter 5).

It is true that there were instances of harsh words directed
at the United States. Encroachments by American sealing vessels in Russian waters of the North Pacific, rumored plans by
the American railroad magnate E. H. Harriman to set up enterprises in Siberia, or American press agitation against the imperial policies toward Russian Jews, all drew criticism, and one
may see evidences that as the Russo-Japanese War began in
1904 prevailing American sentiment felt it desirable that Russian advances into China be thwarted. Yet, on many levels—
education, agriculture, literature, certain aspects of social and
governmental policy, or the organization of industry—Russians
continued to express favorable views of the United States.

It was an often repeated opinion that the two countries
have many traits in common: broad expanse of territory, inhab-
ited by a mobile and enterprising people who breathe a com-
patible spirit of enterprise—enterprise, however, that the Russian structure tended to inhibit but that would, given the
opportunity, so many said, reach as high a level as among the
Americans. The two countries had in many ways developed
outside the often closed and codified patterns of the other
lands of Europe, and both tended to be seen by Europeans as
somehow not quite civilized participants in world affairs.

Yet, if one were to make an estimate based solely on un-
quantified impressions, it appears that the extent of pre-1917
Russian knowledge of America by far outweighed the corresponding American resources. As but one strand of quasi-
evidence in support of this, mention can be made of the types
of references to Russia that were found in the entries in the
Index to the *New York Times* for 1913. That newspaper's reports
on Russia seem to have centered around somewhat stereotyped
concepts of tsar and revolutionary, of Cossack and whip, and of
a nation of boiling discontent. Little of an analytical nature was
visible. And this outlook may be reinforced by inspection of the
themes of articles listed in the *Reader's Guide to Periodical Literature* for the whole era from that work's beginning in 1900 to the
outbreak of the First World War.

While, as the preceding pages have noted, there was much

Russian reliance on what has been called the "gee-whiz factor" in dealing with America, there is more to testify to a wider, more differentiated outlook on the part of many Russians. In America then, as in America now, knowledge of Russian and any close experience with the country was rare, while in Russia, at least among the educated elements of the population, habits of intellectual interest and the much commoner knowledge of foreign languages had enlarged the body of evidence and opinion that might be drawn upon in assessing the United States.

From a perspective acquired during several decades of almost daily rummaging through the largest collection of Russian writings outside of Russia, which afforded a unique opportunity to indulge a special interest in Russian writings about America (of which a mere representative slice is specifically noted and discussed in these pages) and a natural and concomitant awareness of American attitudes and writings about Russia (which are outside the scope of this survey), it seems to this writer fair to say that before 1917 Russia knew America better than America knew Russia, that this knowledge continues to have its effect on the present-day Soviet Union, and that, despite all kinds of variances in styles and content of information, the Soviet awareness of America continues to be a good deal broader than the reciprocal United States awareness of the Soviets. If we Americans are to understand the way in which the Soviets may respond to us, we need, therefore, to take into account not a mere seventy years of controversy, often couched in terms that would disgrace a barroom brawl, but the longer and much more varied record of the Russian attitude toward the United States. Failure to comprehend this involves the possibility of unimaginable calamity.

Bibliography

This bibliography includes only the major works that have been discussed in this study. Some titles that have been cited only by way of example—and that have been given in sufficient detail to be found in library catalogs—are omitted from this section. It should not be thought that the present list is by any means complete or that it even provides all books and articles that exist on any of the subjects examined in the foregoing pages, for there are quite literally thousands of references that have been found to the United States in pre-1917 Russian publications, and the preparation of an exhaustive guide to them is a task that may in fact be impossible. There is, however, in the materials brought together by this writer, a file of perhaps 5,000 cards dealing with items of relevance. They range from some woman's article on New York that appeared in *Modnyi zhurnal* (a serial title that needs no translation) to the publication of short stories by the entirely forgotten American writer John Habberton, and to dozens of long and often agonized analyses of the unfavorable position of Russian grain in the face of American competition for the European market. All in all, it may be said that there is enough in the pre-1917 Russian literature to provide useful support for research by a very broad range of American scholars. The task appears one that would repay the effort, for, in this writer's opinion, there is little hope for a real American understanding of the Soviet Union until the Russian view of America is understood—and that view is, as this study has attempted to show, one that has roots older than the year 1917.

Adams, John Quincy
    Memoirs of John Quincy Adams. Philadelphia, J. B. Lippincott and Co., 1874–1877. 12 v.   E377.A19
    This edition includes Adams's diary which for the years 1809–14 deals with his service as America's first minister to Russia. There is much to show

the Russian interest in maintaining America as a counterbalancing force to Britain, especially in the maritime carrying trade, in a period when the United States, pinched between France and Great Britain, was only precariously safe from the European turmoil of the era.

Aderkas, O. K.

Na vystavkie v Chikago [At the Exposition in Chicago]. Obrazovanie, 1893, September: 113–21.   L51.O3

Otto Karlovich Aderkas attended the Exposition as a delegate of the Institutes of the Empress Maria, foundation for charitable works established by the imperial family. Upon return to Russia he prepared a report on the education of the deaf and blind in America, *Obuchenie glukhoniemykh i sliepykh v Sievero-Amerikanskikh Soedinennykh Shtatakh* (St. Petersburg, Tip. V. S. Balasheva, 1895. 52 p.—   HV2545.A4)

Aimard, Gustave

Balle-Franche. Paris, Amyot, 1867. 144 p.   PQ2152.A2B2 1867

Mietkaia pulia [The sharpshooter]. St. Petersburg, 1876. 357 p.

PQ2152.A5M6

The prairie flower; or, the baffled chief. London, New York, Ward, Lock and Co., 187–. 360 p.   PZ3.A294pr

This is one work by Aimard that is available in the Library of Congress in its original French as well as in English and Russian translation, and it is a fitting example of the absolute absurdities of plot and setting that are characteristic of Aimard. The Indians of the Upper Missouri River enjoy riding over the prairies hunting—and catching—ostriches. The style is melodramatic and the characters unbelievable. However, Aimard was widely translated into several European languages, and the Library of Congress has about a dozen titles in Russian. Russian book dealers were advertising Aimard's books well past 1900, and Soviet editions of some of his novels have appeared in the years since 1945. Even the *Kratkaia literaturnaia entsiklopediia* [Short literary encyclopedia] (Moscow, Izdatel'stvo "Sovetskaia entsiklopediia," 1962–1978. 9 v. PN41.K7) refers to Aimard with a certain respect.

The Altruist

January 1868–1900. irreg. Title varies: 1868-Feb. 1885. The Communist. Edited by Alcander Longley.   HX1.A2

Alcander Longley (1832–1918) was a persistent, and unsuccessful, proponent of utopian communal life. It was to his settlement in Missouri that the Russian William Frey (name taken by Vladimir K. Geins) went in 1869 and from which Frey was to go on to further, and equally vain, attempts of the same kind. In addition to Longley's own earnest strivings, his little paper has much about similar settlements elsewhere, as well as an effort to foster a specially devised alphabet for a more rational English spelling—one that appears not to have been known to H. L. Mencken in his writing of *The American Language*—and also a proposed new system for the notation of music.

Amerikanskie poety i romanisty

[American poets and novelists]. Sovremennik, 1860, no. 10, otd. III: 217–32; no. 12, otd. III: 305–24.   AP50.S695

Unsigned but known to have been written by M. L. Mikhailov, this is an article concerned principally with Hawthorne and Longfellow. The most interesting sections are those dealing with Hawthorne, about whose *Scarlet Letter* it is written, "In this novel, more deeply than in all previous works by him, Hawthorne delves into those bottomless pits, in Carlyle's expression, of unfathomable darkness that make up human nature." There is in Hawthorne, Mikhailov writes, more of tenderness and more sympathy with the dark phenomena of life than of the bitterness and indignation characteristic of Balzac. In the years that followed Mikhailov's review, however, interest in Hawthorne—who had been the most widely translated American writer in Russia in the 1850s—appears to have diminished and there were few references to him until the 1960s.

Amerikanskoe sel'skoe khoziaistvo mashiny i orudiia
[American agricultural machines and equipment]. St. Petersburg, 1909—1911.

This journal was not a lasting publication, but it shows the way in which Russians looked at the American agricultural system as a source of possible examples for Russian landowners. It was among the first Russian publications to deal with tractors and their applicability to Russian conditions. Other material deals with such topics as road building, cattle feeding, and fruit growing. Microfilm has been received in the Library of Congress. Microfilm in processing backlog.

Benzin, Vasilii M.
Traktory v Sievernoi Amerikie [Tractors in North America]. Khoziaistvo, 1911, no. 8: 237–242.   S13.K36

Upon first discovery of this article it was thought that the author's name was fictitious, for "benzin" is the Russian word for "gasoline." However, Vasilii M. Benzin was a frequent contributor to the Russian agricultural press on American agricultural topics, having been a student at the University of Minnesota. This article is one of the earlier indications of Russian interest in mechanization of plowing and cultivation.

Biblioteka dlia chteniia
[Library for reading] 1834–   AP50.B5

The first of the so-called "thick journals" that provided 19th century Russia a broad selection of literature, criticism, articles on world affairs, and the merely interesting facets of things. Even today the major Soviet journals reflect some of its organization and content. From the beginning its American content was substantial, and its 1834 article on the British Corn Laws was among the first in Russian to speak of the role of American grain in world trade, a theme to be a large one in the Russian press later in the century.

Bolkhovitinov, Nikolai N.
Russko-amerikanskie otnosheniia 1815–1832 gg. [Russo-American relations: 1815—1832]. Moscow, Izdatel'stvo "Nauka," 1975. 623 p.

E183.8.R9B58

Dr. Bolkhovitinov is the leading Soviet specialist on early Russo-American relations. This volume deals with the period in which Russia's general support for Spain in that country's struggle with its former American colonies was complicated by a Russian wish to maintain the United States as a counterweight to Great Britain, while still seeking to keep out American interlopers in Alaska. The formulation of the Monroe Doctrine was as much an outgrowth of the situation in the Pacific Northwest (where the United States, by the Treaty of 1819, had acquired Spain's claims to any territories north of the present northern boundary of California) as it was of concern over the Caribbean and the Atlantic shores of Latin America. (See also Dr. Bolkhovitinov's earlier volume, described in the next entry below). The good doctor is currently engaged in preparing a further work to cover the years 1832–1867, which unfortunately was not available for the writing of the present survey.

Bolkhovitinov, Nikolai N.

Stanovlenie russko-amerikanskikh otnoshenii, 1775–1815. [The establishment of Russo-American relations, 1775–1815]. Moscow, Izdatel'stvo "Nauka," 1966. 639 p.   E183.8.R9B6

This work has been translated as *The Beginnings of Russo-American Relations, 1775–1815* (Cambridge, Mass., Harvard University Press, 1975. 484 p.

E183.8.R9B613)

This was the first major work by Dr. Bolkhovitinov.

Borodin, Nikolai A.

Amerikantsy i amerikanskaia kul'tura [Americans and American culture]. Petrograd, "obshchestvennaia pol'za," 1915. 40 p.

microfilm 84/2662(E)

N. A. Borodin first visited the United States in 1893 as one of the Russian specialists sent to the World's Columbian Exposition in Chicago. His field of specialization was cold storage installations, in which he took particular note of American methods, and he again visited the United States sometime during the five years or so before 1914. This article of 1915 summarized some of the material he included in his *Sievero-Amerikanskie Soedinennye Shtaty i Rossiia* (Petrograd, 1915. 324 p.), a copy of which is available on microfilm in the Library of Congress (Microfilm 84/2657 (H)). During the period 1915–1917 Borodin was vice-president of the *Obshchestvo sblizhenii mezhdu Rossiei i Amerikoi* [Society for rapprochement between Russia and America]. Only one number of this organization's interesting *Izviestiia* is available in the Library of Congress (DK265.A203), but other numbers are reported held by the Hoover Institution on War, Revolution and Peace at Stanford University. Borodin emigrated to the United States after the October Revolution.

Buchanan, James

Works of James Buchanan, comprising his speeches, state papers, and private correspondence. Philadelphia, J. B. Lippincott Company, 1909–1911, 12 v.   E337.B9

Buchanan's papers include extensive material on his service as minister to Russia, with details on the negotiation of a trade treaty and reports of Russian attitudes toward America, including the fact that the Russian authorities opened and read mail addressed to the legation so boldly that they did not even trouble to provide convincing copies of American seals.

Buchhandlung von Carl Ricker in St. Petersburg

Unpaged announcement leaflet bound in with the Library of Congress copy of *Viestnik Evropy,* December 1878. AP50.V5

The firm of Carl Ricker offers in this leaflet to place subscriptions to a large number of foreign journals, including many immediately identifiable as American publications, ranging from the *Official Gazette of the United States Patent Office* to the *Phrenological Journal* of New York. A very short time spent with this announcement and any list of American periodicals of 1878 would add many other titles.

Bunge, Nikolai Kh.

Bumazhnye den'gi i bankovaia sistema Sievero-Amerikanskikh Soedinennykh Shtatov [Paper money and the banking system of the North American United States]. Russkii viestnik, 1867, no. 8: 311–77. AP50.R83

This is basically a reivew-survey of Karl F. von Hock's *Die Finanzen und Finanzgeschichte der Vereinigten Staaten von Amerika* (Stuttgart, J. G. Cotta, 1867. 811 p.) Bunge was particularly interested in the use of a paper currency in America during the Civil War and in the means by which it was proposed to bring this currency into parity with gold. As the minister of finance from 1881 to 1887, Bunge had to cope with a Russian paper currency that had been inflated by the stresses of the Russo-Turkish War of 1877–78 and, though it was not until 1897 that a later minister brought about the stabilization of the ruble, some of the methods suggested in Russia were similar to those applied in America.

Bunge, Nikolai Kh.

Teoriia kredita [The theory of credit]. Kiev, V universitetskoi tipografii, 1852. 310, (2) p. HG3701.B8

Written when the author was a professor at Kiev University, this work contains a number of references to the American situation and to the views of Henry Charles Carey of Philadelphia, the leading American writer on economic policy. A number of later works by Bunge continue their use of Carey's writings, and draw also on American public documents and the works of European economists analyzing the situation in America. In 1881 Bunge was appointed to the ministry of finance, serving until 1887. Like his predecessor M. Kh. Reitern, he had to deal with economic problems of foreign trade and tariff policies, currency stabilization, and rail and industrial expansion that paralleled those facing the United States. While there is no marked evidence that Bunge continued to pay attention to American economic theory while he was in office, he did have a rather marked record of writings that reflected a knowledge of American practices.

Channing, William Ellery

"Vill'iam Channing o trezvosti" [William Channing on temperance]. Russkii viestnik, April 1859, kn. 1: 474–507. AP50.R803

A Russian translation of one of Channing's sermons on temperance. It is the article that immediately follows the first part of Tolstoi's "Semeinoe schast'ex" [Family happiness]. While one cannot actually state that Tolstoi read Channing's work, there is a possibility that he did so, and it is of interest to note that at this time Tolstoi was undergoing a period of religious searching that brought him to a point of view not unlike that of the American Unitarian leader.

Chernyshevskii, Nikolai G.

Review of: Hawthorne, Nathaniel. Sobranie chudes, poviesti zaimstvovannye iz mifologii [Russian translation of A Wonder-Book for Girls and Boys]. St. Petersburg, 1860. 492 p. In: Sovremennik, 1860, no. 6, otd. III: 230–246.   AP50.S695

A good example of how in a review of a seemingly innocuous book, particularly one of foreign origin, the reviewer might in fact criticize Russian situations in a way that would be forbidden if done openly. Chernyshevski was a decided opponent of the Russian establishment and in his review of Hawthorne's book for children he actually aims blows at Russian writers who treat Russian adult readers condescendingly. "Our writers treat us as Hawthorne does children. They hide the truth of life from us in order not to tempt or pervert us. Others occupy us with empty wordiness as if we, like children, found it pleasant to listen to chattering." Chernyshevskii was considered so dangerous that a few years later he was exiled from St. Petersburg for practically the rest of his life. His almost unreadable novel *Chto dielat'?* [What is to be done?] became an inevitable part of the reading of all opponents of the state, even being used as a title of one of Lenin's writings.

Chukovskii, Kornei

Sobranie sochinenii [Collected works]. v. 6. Moscow, Izdatel'stvo k "Khudozhestvennaia literatura," 1969.   PG3476.C491965

This is the most readily available text of Chukovskii's worried essay on the baleful effects on young Russian minds of the flood of six-kopeck (ca. 3-cent) editions of stories about "Nik Karter—korol' syshchikov" [Nick Carter—king of detectives] or the even more popular Nat Pinkerton. Extrapolating from the fact that in May of 1908 622,300 copies of such detective stories were issued in St. Petersburg, Chukovskii foresees an absolute doom and decay of all culture, and the replacement of the noble heroes of the past by the apostles of gun, bludgeon, and electric chair. Chukovskii was then a young man and tended to see things in absolute tones of good and bad. His essay was, it appears, one of the last published works upon which Tolstoi commented before his death at Astapovo Station in 1910.

Chukovskii, it should be noted, was in later life the major Russian commentator on the work of Walt Whitman, a fine writer for children, and, given Soviet circumstances, a bold critic of the vulgarization of the Russian language by the leaden cliches of party jargon.

Cooper, James Fenimore

Shpion. Novyi roman, soderzhashchii v sebie podrobnosti amerikanskoi voiny s opisaniem nravov i obychaev sei strany [The spy. A new novel, containing the details of the American war, with a description of the mores and customs of that country] Moscow, Tip. S. Selivanovskago, 1825. 3 pts.

Microfilm 86/2078 (P)

The first Russian publication of a novel by an American author. This edition was translated from a French version. Pages 283–89 of the third part list the Russian subscribers to this work. Microfilm of the book has been supplied to the Library of Congress by a Soviet exchange partner.

Dixon, William Hebworth

Dukhovnyia zheny [Spiritual wives]. St. Petersburg, Tipografiia N. Tiblena i Ko. 1869. 380 p.

A translation (not available in the Library of Congress) of the author's *Spiritual Wives* London, Hurst and Blackett, 1868. 2 v. (2d ed./HQ961.D62)

The general tenor of Dixon's approach is that of examining the subject of "free love," although the American section is actually largely an examination of the quite celibate community of the Shakers. Dixon's book was accused by a leading London newspaper of indecency; a suit resulted in a verdict in favor of Dixon, who, however, was awarded only one farthing in damages.

Review-summary of: Dixon, William Hebworth

New America. London, Hurst and Blackett, 1867. 2 v. In: Otechestvennyia zapiski, 1867, v. 172: 82–116, 295–332, 522–64; 702–44; v. 173: 317–359.   AP50.O85

This article is practically an abridgement of Dixon's text, and gives much attention to such American phenomena as the Mormons and the Oneida Colony of John Humphrey Noyes. It was evidently a stimulus to the appearance in 1867 and 1869 of what seem to have been two differing translations, as well as providing the basis for a four-part essay on North American communal sects by the retired colonel-turned-dissident Petr L. Lavrov. It may possibly have formed part of the factors that impelled William Frey (pseud. of Vladimir K. Geins) to migrate to America to make repeated efforts to establish communes there, ones that, though they failed, influenced people who had in turn an influence on L. N. Tolstoi in his later years of seeking for a just way of life.

Dixon, William Hebworth

Novaia Amerika [New America]. St. Petersburg, "Russkaia knizhnaia torgovlia," 1867. 413 p.

This is the Russian translation (unavailable in the Library of Congress) of the author's *New America* (London, Hurst and Blackett, 1867. 2 v. [E168.D63]). The book was, it appears, of such interest to the Russian reader that a second edition, possibly a different translation, appeared in 1868, as translated by V. V. Butuzov. The work is full of lively and possibly somewhat inaccurate detail about such topics as the Mormons and the startling aspects of American life.

Dukh zhurnalov

[The spirit of the journals]. 1815–   AP50.D83

This serial was apparently intended to be a sort of summary or review of other serials, especially those of Western Europe. Many of the articles about the United States seem to have been taken from the German journal *Amerika, dargestellt durch sich selbst* published in Leipzig from 1818 to 1820 by Georg Joachim Goschen [E11.A51], whose other publications included many of the works of Goethe.

Evans, Frederick William

Autobiography of a Shaker. New York, American News Company, 1888. 271 p.   BX9793.E8A3 1888

Elder Evans was probably the most widely known leader of the Shakers in the post-Civil War period, and his autobiography was of interest to many people. Lev Tolstoi read this work and was in correspondence with Evans and other Shakers. The influence of this is evident in Tolstoi's views of marriage and celibacy set forth in the novel *Kreutzer Sonata*. One of the drafts of that work directly refers to the Shakers.

Evans, Warren Felt

The divine law of cure. Boston, H. H. Carter and Co., 1884. 302 p.
                                                                    RZ401.E86

L. N. Tolstoi read this work in the mid-1880s, and expressed a certain sympathy with the ideas of faith healing which W. F. Evans, influenced by some of the ideas of Phineas Parker Quimby, set forth. The editors of Tolstoi's "Iubileinoe izdanie"—the name usually given to the most complete collection of Tolstoi's writings—have managed to confuse W. F. Evans with F. W. Evans, the Shaker leader, and care must be used to separate the two quite different men, both of whom, however, found an interested reader in the Russian author.

Faresov, A.

Odin iz "semidesiatnikov" [One of the "men of the 1870s"]. In: Viestnik Evropy, 1904, no. 9:   AP50.V5

This article is an account of the spiritual pilgrimage of Aleksandr K. Malikov who, having come to the conclusion that all persons embodied the enigma and the strength of the Creator, decided to join William Frey in his Kansas commune. Arriving after Machtet had already left, Malikov and his followers appear to have met more or less similar conditions in their struggle to apply their doctrine to the American frontier.

Frey, William

(pseud. of Vladimir K. Geins)

Amerikanskaia zhizn'; pis'mo pervoe [American life; first letter]. In: Otechestvennyia zapiski, 1870, no. 1: 215–263.   AP50.O85

The article is a survey of the presidential campaign of 1868, based on the author's observations of the Democratic convention in New York in the summer of the year and electoral activities in the fall in St. Louis, Missouri. In its large details, it is an accurate account and reveals an analytical and critical mind, shaded by a number of preconceptions about American life that were to be more tellingly shown in Frey's later participation in several attempts to set up communes for Russian immigrants to the United States. Both

Frey and some of the other participants in his efforts were to have influence on the outlook of L. N. Tolstoi during the later years of his life and probably stimulated Tolstoi's marked interest in the so-called unorthodox movements in American religion. Although noted as "first letter," there appear to have been no other contributions in the series.

Gusev, Nikolai N.

Lev Nikolaevich Tolstoi; materialy k biografii s 1881 po 1885 [Lev Nikolaevich Tolstoi; materials for a biography from 1881 to 1885]. Moscow, Izdatel'stvo "Nauka," 1970.   PG3385.G825

This work is a day-by-day chronicle of the life of Tolstoi, indicating his place of residence, the people whom he saw, the books he read, and the names of his correspondents. It is extremely useful to anyone seeking to trace Tolstoi's personal and intellectual contacts, although it is not a work of narrative or analysis. Through this one can often discover possible sources of influences on Tolstoi's thought not otherwise recorded. This volume, one of several by Gusev that cover Tolstoi's life, is, for example, a record of the time and nature of Tolstoi's meeting with William Frey, and with others who took part in Frey's commune in Kansas.

Hapgood, Isabel

Review of: Tolstoi, L. N. The Kreutzer Sonata. In: The Nation, April 17, 1890: 313–315.   AP2.N2

Miss Hapgood had visited Tolstoi and had corresponded with him. She was, however, quite shocked by the boldness of The Kreutzer Sonata and by its thesis that sex in marriage without the intention of children was as sinful as prostitution. While she felt that it would be impossible to translate the novel in full, there appear to have been four differing translations available in the United States in 1890–1891, a period which antedated a change in American copyright laws that would give foreign authors some protection against pirate publication.

Ianzhul, Ivan and Ekaterina N. Ianzhul

Edem truzhenits (Amerikanskie statistiki ob amerikanskikh rabotnitsakh) [An Eden for working women (American statistics about American woman workers)]. Sievernyi viestnik, 1890, no. 5: 76–96.   AP50.S57

Basing their article on an official American statistical survey, the authors speak of the good conditions of American woman workers, being particularly impressed by the level of wages, then averaging $5.20 per week for women. Despite the seeming absurdity of this conclusion, Ivan Ianzhul was no fool, being a well-trained and sober economist who had been part of the first contingent of factory inspectors in Russia appointed under a ground-breaking, if rather weak, enactment in the 1880s, and was therefore fully aware of the truly horrible conditions that prevailed in many Russian factories of the time. His wife was a specialist on education, whose writings in the field were to be published even after the October Revolution. Thus, if these two honest and dedicated people called America a paradise, it may indeed have been considered one by ordinary Russian workers.

Ianzhul, Ivan I., ed.

Ekonomicheskaia otsienka narodnago obrazovaniia [The economic evaluation of public education]. Moscow, Tipografiia I. N. Skorokhodova, 1896. 87 p.   LC67.R9I16

A collection of articles by Ianzhul, his wife Ekaterina, A. I. Chuprov, and others, examining the effect on the economy of expenditures on public education. Relying chiefly on American material, the authors state that it is the high level of education among Americans that accounts for the skilled and efficient work force upon which industry has been able to rely to reach such a high level of productivity. Ianzhul and his wife had visited Chicago at the time of the Exposition in 1893, and both had written other articles for the Russian press on their experiences. In this work it is said that Americans realize "that each extra kopeck spent for education inevitably brings whole rubles back to the nation in the future." "And, if Russia is *educated,* she will be *rich.*" All this in spite of the fact that Chuprov notes that the average monthly pay of an American male teacher at the time was $42.00, and of a woman, $34.00. A second edition of this little volume, almost doubled in size, is reported to have appeared in 1899, one that is not, however, available in the Library of Congress.

Ianzhul, Ivan I.

Promyslovye sindikaty ili predprinimatel'skie soiuzy dlia reguliriovaniia proizvodstva preimushchestvenno v Soedinennykh Shtatakh Sievernoi Ameriki [Industrial syndicates, or entrepreneurial associations, for the regulation of production, primarily in the United States of North America.] St. Petersburg, Tip. M. M. Stasiulevicha, 1895. 459 p. (At head of title page: Ministerstvo finansov. Departament torgovli i manufaktur [Ministry of Finance. Department of Trade and Manufactures]).   HD2791.I2

Ianzhul's investigations were made in his capacity as an official delegate to the Columbian Exposition in Chicago. It is also clear that he had a good knowledge of the American literature on the problem of industrial trusts and of the major points of law concerning them. He also wrote other articles for the general press about his voyage and his impressions of America, while his wife Ekaterina, who accompanied him, studied the American educational system. Some of her writings on American schools appeared even after the 1917 revolution.

Iubileinoe izdanie

see Tolstoi, Lev Nikolaevich, Polnoe sobranie sochinenii.

Kachenovskii, Dmitrii I.

Review of: Works of Daniel Webster. Boston, 1853. 6 v. Russkii viestnik [Russian herald] 1856, v. 3: 385–416; v. 4: 239–278.   AP50.R83

This article is considerably more than the mere review of the *Works of Daniel Webster* that it purports to be. The author, a professor at Khar'kov University, has drawn upon other writings about Webster, and about Webster's opponents, including an edition of Calhoun's *Disquisition on Government, and on the Constitution of the United States* published in Columbia, South Carolina that apparently is not entered in the National Union Catalog. Kachenovskii notes that there are many misconceptions about the American governmental system, but says that it is actually "a quite complicated one of checks and balances, that it has its own history, institutions, traditions, prejudices, unevenness, and that in it is embodied the organic product of the life of the people." Webster, Kachenovskii writes, "clearly expressed the best traits of the American character, he fully understood the requirements of the age . . ." The essay also appeared in French, as "Amérique et ses hommes d'état. Daniel Webster. Étude biographique (Bruxelles, F. Claassen, 1858. 142 p.). One of Kachenovskii's students, Maksim M. Kovalevskii, also wrote about the United States, contributing prefaces to two translations of works by Woodrow Wilson.

Kareisha, Sergiei D.
Sievero-Amerikanskiia zhelieznyia dorogi [North American railroads]. Moscow, S. Kareisha, 1896. 774 p.   Microfilm 84/6001(T)
The author, in connection with his official mission to the World's Columbian Exposition in Chicago in 1893, had the opportunity of traveling more than 7,000 miles on American railroads and of inspecting equipment factories, grain elevators, and port facilities as well as rail installations. The resulting book is crammed with details, from the forms for bills of lading to the construction of outhouses at rural stations. While there are no precise specifications for rolling stock, almost all the other elements necessary for operating a railroad system are there and the man who mastered this book could truly be called an expert.

Kenig, Ivan F.
Statisticheskiia dannyia o zemledielii i torgovlie produktami sel'skago khoziaistva v Sievero-Amerikanskikh Soedinennykh Shtatakh i Rossii [Statistical data on agriculture and the trade in agricultural products in the North American United States and in Russia]. St. Petersburg, Tip. V. Kirshbauma, 1880. 1 v.   HD1765.1878.K45
Kenig was a major official of the Nikolaevskaia railroad, the line joining St. Petersburg and Moscow, which was a principal carrier of grain for export. This volume, the only one to be issued before Kenig's death, is a compendium of materials dealing with American agriculture, largely translated from English. Introductory material shows how seriously the factor of American competition was taken by a leading Russian economic administrator.

Kol', A.
Niekotoryia dannyia ob amerikanskikh parovykh i gazolinovykh traktorakh i ob odnoi molotylkie (Otvet na voprosakh iz Novorossii) [Some data about American steam and gasoline tractors and about one threshing machine (From an answer to inquiries from Novorossiia)]
Khoziaistvo, 1911, no. 10: 305–311; no. 11: 336–341; no. 12: 370–375.
                                                                S13.K36
Kol', identified as the Assistant Russian Agricultural Agent in the United States, provides detailed information on the use of tractors in America and

gives advice on the models most likely to be of value in Russia, with prices and addresses of suppliers in the United States.

Komsha, A. G. and L. P. Sokal'skii

Ob uchrezhdenii russkoi sel'sko-khoziaistvennoi agentury v Soed. Shtatakh Sievernoi Ameriki: doklad Imperatorskomu obshchestvu sel'skago khoziaistva iuzhnoi Rossii [Concerning the establishment of an agricultural agency in the United States of North America: report to the Imperial Society of Agriculture of Southern Russia]. Odessa, "Slavianskaia" tipographiia, 1906. 41 p.   European Div. Pamphlet File—Box S–1

Report of a meeting held on August 23, 1905 (O.S.), to propose that there be established in Topeka, Kansas, an official Russian agency to gather agricultural information, acquire machines and seeds, and foster Russia's own exports.

An active participant at this session was F. F. Kryshtofovich, who had been resident in the United States for some fifteen years, and whose views formed the major points of discussion. The Library of Congress copy of this pamphlet bears his signature, and he was, in 1909, the first American agent of the Imperial Ministry of Agriculture—located in St. Louis, however, rather than in Topeka.

Kovalevskii, Evgraf P.

Narodnoe obrazovanie i tserkovnoe dostoianie v III–i Gosudarstvennoi Dumie [Public Education and church property in the Third State Duma]. St. Petersburg, 1912. 2 v. in 1.   KR631.K6

Kovalevskii was a Russian delegate to the World's Columbian Exposition in Chicago in 1893, editing and writing a large part of the report of the Russian specialists in education who visited America in that year (see entry in this bibliography). When Russia was granted a quasi-parliament in 1905, he became a member, and in the present work his speeches to that body on the topic of education and the management of church property are collected. He was a member of the Octobrist Party, a largely conservative group that accepted the parliamentary structure granted by the emperor without calling for any great reforms and that is, therefore, roundly criticized by Soviet historians as being nothing more than a band of hopeless reactionaries. Examination of these speeches, however, shows that Kovalevskii at least was truly devoted to furthering education and to vigilant defense of every advance. While one finds only two or three direct references to the United States in the present work, there are some statements that echo Kovlevskii's earlier volume, drawing upon his experiences in Chicago in 1893 and repeating some of the outlook that he had then credited to an "American professor," a man who just might have been the American educator and diplomat Andrew D. White, the first president of Cornell University and, in 1892–1894, our Minister to Russia. Thus, while no great space is given to America in Kovalevskii's publication of 1912, it seems quite clear that he still remained influenced by the American system to which he gave such detailed attention in 1893.

Kovalevskii, Evgraf P.

Narodnoe obrazovanie v Soedinennykh Shtatakh Sievernoi Ameriki (vysshee, srednee, nizshee) [Public education in the United States of North America (higher, intermediate, elementary)]. St. Petersburg, Tipografiia V. S. Balasheva i Ko., 1895. 592 p.   LA210.K67

This work was one of the Russian publications that resulted from the visits of official delegations to the World's Columbian Exposition in Chicago in 1893. It includes sections by persons other than Kovalevskii, such as Pavel G. Mizhuev (see entry for him in this bibliography), and it is a most detailed survey of the American educational system, with copious references to sources such as the school legislation of Indiana, James Bryce's *The American Commonwealth* and the Harvard catalog. The most striking feature of all, however, is probably the original paper cover, included by great good fortune with the Library of Congress copy of this work. On the left, the Statue of Liberty, with torch lifted high and with between its rays the figure $200,000,000, on the right a portrait of Horace Mann, founder of American pedagogical methods, and below the title a box reading "23% of the population in educ(ational) insti(tutions)." There are numerous illustrations, strikingly more than was common for Russian books of the period. In some sections it is evident that Kovalevskii is making a careful use of selected American examples in order to indicate a deep criticism of Russian educational practices and to point out how American schools have served to unify the country. "Only by means of the school, open equally to all children of school age, ... is it possible, *as the experience of other countries shows* [Kovalevskii's italics], to unite students differing from one another in language, faith, and customs." Kovalevskii continued his interest in education for many years thereafter, issuing in 1912 a collection of speeches he had made on the subject in the State Duma, the quasi-parliament granted by Nicholas II (see entry for this work elsewhere in this bibliography).

Krichevskii, G. G.

"Konstitutsionnyi proekt" Nikity Murav'eva i amerikanskie konstitutsii ["The constitutional project" of Nikita Murav'ev and American constitutions]. In: Akademii nauk SSSR. Izvestiia, seriia istorii i filosofii. 1945, no. 6:   AS262.A6247

This article, a product of the somewhat kindlier intellectual view of the United States expressed in the Soviet Union during the war years, is an important examination of the way in which the Russian dissidents drew upon the constitutions of the United States and of several individual states to propose a plan of reform. Their attempt to use the confusion that followed the death of Alexander I and the lack of certainty as to whether the crown would go to Alexander's second brother, the unloved and unloveable Constantine, or to the third, the rigid and awesome Nicholas, failed. Nicholas, who had all the qualities of an excellent boot camp drill instructor, became emperor and spent his thirty-year reign in seeing to it that no such dangerous American precedents were ever brought up for public discussion.

Kuropiatnik, Gennadii P.
Rossiia i SShA; ekonomicheskie, kul'turnye i diplomaticheskie sviazi, 1867—1881 [Russia and the USA; economic, cultural and diplomatic relations, 1867–1881]. Moscow, Izdatel'stvo "Nauka," 1981. 373 p.
                                                           E183.8.S65K87
Issued under the auspices of the Institute of World History of the Academy of Sciences of the USSR, this is a richly documented study of fourteen years, from the American acquisition of Alaska to the assassination of Alexander II. It is particularly useful for the subject of the visit of the Russian fleet immediately before the Russo-Turkish War of 1877–78 and the voyage of the *Cimbria* and the Russian acquisition in America of ships to be fitted out as auxiliary cruisers in the war's immediate aftermath. The author has used American archives as well as what are clearly the very extensive materials of the imperial foreign office and navy. The book is among the best examples of Soviet historical research on American problems.

Lakier, Aleksandr B.
Puteshestvie po Sievero-Amerikanskim Shtatam, Kanadie, i ostrovu Kubie [Travels in the North American States, Canada, and the Island of Cuba]. St. Petersburg, Tip. K. Vul'fa, 1859. 2 v.   E166.L23
One of the earliest book-length works in Russian on travel in the United States. An English abridgement appeared as *A Russian Looks at America* (Chicago, University of Chicago Press, 1979. 272 p. E166.L2313). Although Lakier is of interest, the writings of Eduard R. Tsimmerman (*q.v.*) are of more value.

Lavrov, Petr L
Sievero-Amerikanskoe sektatorstvo [North American sectarianism]. In: Otechestvennyia zapiski, v. 177: 403–470; v. 178: 273–336; v. 179: 269–318, 324–354.   AP50.O85
Lavrov, a retired colonel-turned-radical, was one of the leading exponents of dissident thought in the 1860s and 1870s. This work, largely based on the *New America* of the British writer William Hebworth Dixon, tends to emphasize the utopian communal side of American radicalism and includes much about the position of women in the United States. Part of one article is an extended survey of the thought of the American Unitarian leader William Ellery Channing.

Ley, Francis
La Russie, Paul de Krüdener, et les soulèvements nationaux, 1814–1858 ... Paris, Hachette, 1971. 312 p.   DK190.2.K73L48
Krüdener, son of the Baroness Krüdener, who allegedly gave its name to the Holy Alliance, was Russian minister to the United States in the period from 1827 to 1837. His comments on the United States are pungent ones.

Libman, Valentina
Amerikanskaia literatura v russkikh perevodakh i kritike; bibliografiia 1776–1975 [American literature in Russian translations and criticism; bibli-

ography, 1776–1975]. Moscow Izdatel'stvo "Nauka," 1977. 451 p.

Z1231.T7L53

This is a magisterial work, showing great diligence in the compilation of information, and no one studying the reception of American literature in Russia can fail to use it. However, it omits the important element of Russian attention to works of American popular literature, including now-forgotten authors such as John Habberton, Kate Douglas Wiggin, and Edward Noyes Westcott, not to mention the totally unknown Etta W. Pierce, four of whose works appeared in Russian in the latter part of the last century, but about whom nothing can be found in standard American reference works. As parts of this survey show, it was this type of literature that had as wide a Russian readership as the more "respectable" writings of the authors studied in courses on literary history. Nor can one omit the Russian translations of books by such non-American writers as Mayne Reid and Gustave Aimard, who drew on their short stays in America to write copiously about adventures on the frontier. The Anglo-Irish Reid and the French Aimard filled a role for Russians that for Germans was held by the flamboyant—and usually erroneous— Karl May, of whose writings there appear to be no Russian versions.

Loubat, Joseph Florimond, duc de

Narrative of the mission to Russia, in 1866, of the Hon. Gustavus Vasa Fox, Assistant Secretary of the Navy. New York, D. Appleton and Co., 1873. 444 p.

DK26.L88

The visit of the American monitor *Miantonomoh*, carrying the former assistant secretary of the navy Gustavus Fox with a message of congratulation to Emperor Alexander II for having escaped assassination, is told in almost excruciating detail in this work. While the book does not say so directly, it is clear from the circumstances of the period that the United States was not loath to show to England and France the might of the American navy as a possible factor in some of the controversies resulting from the Civil War. After *The Times* of London had noted that there was "not one of them [ships of the Royal Navy] that the foreigner could not have sent to the bottom in five minutes" and after the high command of the French navy had been given a tour of the monitor, the rest of the journey was almost a pleasure excursion, but filled with indications of Russian appreciation of the value of America as a possible friend. The menus, the toasts, and the balls in St. Petersburg are excellent evidences of the ability, still retained by the Soviets, to give a visitor an overwhelming reception.

Machtet, Grigorii A.

Polnoe sobranie sochinenii [Complete collected works]. v. 1 & 2: Iz amerikanskoi zhizni [From American life] St. Petersburg, Knigoizd. t-va "Prosvieshchenie," 1911.

Microfilm 84/2501 (P)

Machtet was a popular, but unskilled, writer, noted for his very heroic heroes and his vile villains. As a young man of about twenty he had participated in one of William Frey's communes in Kansas. These two volumes of his works contain a number of short stories and articles on American themes, such as life on an emigrant steamer, small prairie towns, or American courts of law. On the last subject, drawing on a real episode, he tells of the fear of a group of Russian emigrants when one of them was accidentally shot and killed by another member. However, American justice was swift and the man was quickly released, particularly when it turned out that the jury and all the members of the court were well aware of the great unreliability of the revolver in the case. Machtet's writings are especially useful for their accounts of Frey's commune, showing the character of a would-be charismatic of a type who has frequently been found in similar groups in more recent times.

Mak-Gakhan [Mac Gahan], Varvara.
Pis'ma iz Ameriki [Letters from America]. Sievernyi viestnik.

AP50.S57

Letter no. 13. June 1891: 150–161 (second pagination).
Letter no. 20. January 1892: 103–114 (second pagination).
Letter no. 26. July 1892: 71–83 (second pagination).
Letter no. 31. December 1892: 52–60 (second pagination).
Letter no. 32. January 1893: 76–87 (second pagination).
Letter no. 37. May 1893 (second pagination).
Letter no. 38. June 1893: 64–78 (second pagination)
Letter no. 39. July 1893: 58–67 (second pagination).
Letter no. 40. August 1893: 45–56 (second pagination)
Letter no. 41. October 1893: 46–57 (second pagination)
Letter no. 42. November 1893: 62–75 (second pagination)
Letter no. 43. December 1893: 70–77 (second pagination).
Letter no. 44. January 1894: 33–46 (second pagination)
Letter no. 45. February 1894: 36–53 (second pagination).

Varvara MacGahan, the Russian-born widow of an American correspondent, lived in the United States from the early 1880s and wrote copiously for the Russian press. To *Sievernyi viestnik* she contributed a long series of letters from America; the ones cited above are concerned with the preparations for the World's Columbian Exposition in Chicago, its proceedings, and an analysis of its results. Mrs. MacGahan was a typical woman of the Russian intelligentsia, which is reflected in her choice of topics and in her verdicts on events, and she also appears to have had an eye for the telling detail. This gives her articles a value that compensates for some of her limitations of understanding, while her long experience in writing for the Russian press about America seems to have given her a continuity of experience that some other Russian commentators lacked. There were, however, also writers such as Peter A. Demens (born Petr A. Dement'ev, and using the pseudonym P. A. Tverskoi in his Russian articles) and P. I. Popov, with equally long records of writing American letters for the Russian press, who seem to have had comparable qualifications, and who may have been more influential, since they wrote principally for the more widely read *Viestnik Evropy* and *Novoe vremia* rather than the less circulated *Sievernyi viestnik*. Still, Varvara MacGahan must have helped form many Russians' ideas of America and its ways.

Markov, Evgenii L'vovich
Khoziaistvennaia politika [Economic Policy]. Russkaia riech', 1881, no. 3: 216–245.

AP50.R814

Neither the author nor the journal was an outstanding factor in Russian journalism of the time, but that is in itself a testimony to the way in which even the general run of literate Russians were aware of—and concerned by—the competition of the era between Russian and American exports of grain to Western Europe. During most of the era from 1865 to 1914 half of Russia's export was grain, a situation that gave the country during most years a favorable balance of trade, allowing the payment of foreign debts, the stabilization (after 1897) of the ruble on a gold basis, and the maintenance of a position among the great powers. However, the competing flow of grain from America was always a destabilizing element, and Russian economists and many journalists maintained an awareness of the resulting uncertainties. Although Markov does not give a fully developed analysis of this situation, he does serve to show how deep was the concern of thinking Russians.

Mel'nikov, P. I.
Nachalo zheleznodorozhnogo stroitel'stva v Rossii [The beginning of railroad construction in Russia]. In: Krasnyi arkhiv, v. 99 (1940):   DK1.K7
Describes the activities of Pavel Petrovich Mel'nikov, one of two Russian engineers sent to the United States in 1839–40 to study American railroads, and a member of the supervisory committee for the construction of the St. Petersburg–Moscow line, the first major rail project in Russia. This article contains references to Mel'nikov's American experience.

Mendeleev, Dmitrii I.
Neftianaia promyshlennost' v Sievero-Amerikanskom shtatie Pensil'vanii i na Kavkazie [The petroleum industry in the North American state of Pennsylvania and in the Caucasus]. St. Petersburg, Tip. T-va "Obshchestvennaia pol'za," 1877. 304 p.   HD9567.P4M4
The great chemist Mendeleev came to America at the time of the Centennial Exposition in 1876, spending much time in a detailed survey of Pennsylvania's oil regions. This work is largely technical, but there are a number of sharp remarks about the fact that the United States was no utopia.

Michael, Louis Guy
More corn for Bessarabia: Russian experience 1910–1917. Lansing, Michigan State University Press, 1983. 245 p.   HD9049.C8S74 1983
The author was hired in 1910 by the Bessarabian Province Zemstvo (local government board) as a specialist in the effort to improve corn growing in the region, the principal area for the crop in the Russian Empire. He found it difficult at times to deal with Russian bureaucratic delays and with the complications of the ethnic mix of Bessarabia's population, but his efforts to reach the region's "dirt farmers" appear to have had some success, while the American consul in Odessa reports a subsequent increase in Russian imports of American implements for the cultivation of corn, including tractors and other power tools.

Mizhuev, Pavel G.
Sovremennaia shkola v Evropie i Amerikie [The contemporary school in Europe and America]. Moscow, Knigoizdatel'stvo "Pol'za," 1912. 247 p.
LA621.8.M59

Mizhuev had been part of the Russian delegation of educational special-ists that visited the Columbian Exposition in Chicago in 1893, writing the section on secondary education in America for the extensive report that ap-peared in 1895 (see the work of that date by E. P. Kovalevskii listed in this bibliography). This did not exhaust Mizhuev's interest in America, for he wrote several works on American topics, including what seems to have been the most extensive Russian discussion of American Blacks to have appeared before 1917 (see Mizhuev's *Sotsiologicheskiia etiudy* [Sociological studies]. St. Petersburg, Tipografiia Ts. Kraiz, 1904. 343 p. H33.M53). In this work on the school Mizhuev has high praise for the ability of Americans to use orga-nized private initiative to attain goals apparently unreachable by European society, and his views of American secondary education are clearly based upon the thoughts he expressed in Kovalevskii's 1895 study noted elsewhere in this bibliography. While the date of publication removed it from the list of materials consulted for the present survey of pre-1917 Russian attitudes to-ward the United States, it should be noted that as late as 1925 Mizhuev pub-lished a work in the Soviet Union on American secondary education. Other writings by him, not mentioned in this study, that appeared before 1917, dealt with American literature, American history, and the women's movement in the United States. Mizhuev was most certainly one of the more productive authors of seriously intended works on American social topics in pre-1917 Russia.

Mizhuev, Pavel G.
Velikii raskol anglo-saksonskoi rasy. Amerikanskaia revoliutsii (prei-mushchestvenno s tochki zrieniia literaturnykh faktorov [The great schism of the Anglo-Saxon race. The American Revolution (primarily from the point of view of literary factors)]. St. Petersburg, 1901. 252 p.   E209.M58
First published as a series of articles in *Russkoe bogatstvo* (1900, no. 5: 65–102; no. 6: 51–88; no. 7: 25–62; no. 8: 82–116), this is actually an abridged version of Moses Coit Tyler's *Literary History of the American Revolution* (New York and London, G. P. Putnam's Sons, 1897. 2 v. PS185.T2) and is princi-pally of importance because of Mizhuev's other writings about the United States, including his analysis of American secondary ecucation based upon his visit to the World's Columbian Exposition in Chicago in 1893 (see the work on education in America edited by E. P. Kovalevskii) and his later dis-cussions of American schools.

Molinari, Gustave de
Ekonomicheskaia korrespondentsiia [Economic correspondence]. *In:* Russkii viestnik, 1870, no. 5: 61–103.   AP50.R83
The author was a Belgian-born economist whose contributions were prominent in the French press in the mid-nineteenth century. This article refers to America's increasing production of grain and to the fact that it would be a topic of interest to Russians concerned with their own export trade.

Morskoi sbornik
[Naval miscellany], St. Petersburg, 1848—   V5.M8
This is the major professional journal of the Russian navy, and one of

the two principal technical serials to have continued publication after 1917. In the years from 1850 to 1870 there were frequent items drawing on American experience, including reports on the construction in the United States of several vessels for the Imperial fleet. In the era of Captain Mahan, the Spanish-American War, and the rise of the United States as a naval power, there were further indications of interest in American experience and thought.

Moskovskiia viedomosti

[Moscow news]. 1756–1917   Newspaper
This was one of the oldest newspapers in the Russian Empire. From 1863 to his death in 1887 it was edited by the strongly conservative Mikhail N. Katkov who gave a great deal of attention in the early 1880s to the problem of Russia's foreign trade in grain, with many remarks about American competition and about the advisability of constructing elevators on the American model. Many of these editorials are reprinted in *Russkii viestnik* for 1884 and others may be found in *Sobranie peredovykh Statei Moskovskikh Viedomostei* [Collection of editorial articles in *Moskovskiia Viedomosti*] Moscow, 1897–1898. 25V. AC65.K3.

Moskovskoe obshchestvo sel'skago khoziaistva

Russkoe sel'skoe khoziaistvo [Russian agriculture]   S13.M25
The Imperial Moscow Agricultural Society was one of the leading associations in the field. Its journal, while it apparently did not have a wide circulation, was influential. During the 1870s, at least, it had a number of articles reflecting concern with the competition between Russia and the United States in the international grain trade.

Moskovskoe obshchestvo sel'skago khoziaistva

Trudy [Transactions], 1885, vyp. XVII. 141 p.
This issue of the Transactions of the Imperial Moscow Agricultural Society contains the "Stenographic Report of the Joint Sessions of 6 Scholarly Associations on the Question of the Construction of Elevators," a detailed examination of the place that grain elevators might have in the Russian economy. While the conclusions of the sessions were generally favorable to elevator construction, it was not until almost 25 years later that, under the auspices of the State Bank, a broad program of building elevators was undertaken. In 1914, at the outbreak of the First World War there were still fewer than 100 operating elevators in the Empire, and the Russian grain trade continued to labor under the handicaps of unclassified grain and the need for much hand labor in moving cargoes to export points. Issue no. XVIII of this serial contains the recommendations resulting from the session.

Nikoliukin, A. N.

Literaturnye sviazi Rossii i SShA; stanovlenie literaturnykh kontaktov [Literary relations between Russia and the U.S.A.; the origins of literary contacts]. Moscow, Izdatel'stvo "Nauka," 1981. 406 p.   PG2981.A45N5
The author has written a number of other works on Russo-American cultural relations. This book, issued by the publishing house of the Academy of Sciences, is a significant contribution to Soviet American studies.

Noyes, John Humphrey
History of American socialism. Philadelphia, J. B. Lippincott and Co.
1870. 678 p.   HX83.N9
One of the major works of a leader of American utopian thought, whose
Oneida Colony attained considerable economic success as well as great noto-
riety for its sexual theories and practices. L. N. Tolstoi read this work and
from it acquired some of his views of the Shakers, with whom he was later in
direct touch and whose views on celibacy affected his outlook, as reflected in
his novel *The Kreutzer Sonata.*

O dietskikh knigakh
[On children's books]. Moscow, Tipo-lit. T-va. I. N. Kushnereva i Ko.,
1908. 831 p.   Z1037.6.T84
This guide to Russian-language books for children is extremely useful as
an indication of what works were actively suggested to young readers. Among
them are many books by American authors, or on American themes, including twenty-one titles by the Anglo-Canadian-American E. Thompson Seton,
twelve Russian editions of *Uncle Tom's Cabin,* and four different translations
of *Little Lord Fauntleroy* by Frances Hodgson Burnett (though she was of English birth, her novel has a partial American setting and two Americans provide the deus ex machina). One of the translations even has the illustrations
by Reginald Burch of little Cedric done up in lace and velvet that inspired
proud mothers to imitation and impatient small boys to rebellion.

Orbinskii, Robert Vasil'evich
Ekonomicheskoe polozhenie Odessy v nastoiashchem i budushchem
[The economic position of Odessa at present and in the future] Russkii viestnik, 1883, no. 6: 257–276.   AP50.R83
This article extends Orbinskii's earlier evaluation (*see next entry*) of Russia's situation in the world grain market, particularly as it affected the chief
grain port of Odessa, after four more years in which the United States had
become an overwhelming competitor.

Orbinskii, Robert Vasil'evich
O khliebnoi torgovlie Soedinennykh Shtatov Sievernoi Ameriki [Con-
cerning the grain trade of the United States of North America]. St. Petersburg, Tip. Trenke i Fusno, 1880. 447 p.   HD9035.O7
A report on a study visit made by the author in 1879 at the orders of the
Imperial Ministry of Finance. It is a work of singular importance, undertaken
by a professor at the Novorossiiskii universitet in Odessa, who was also secretary of both the Odessa Committee for Trade and Manufactures and the
Odessa Exchange Committee. He had already written a number of statements on the rising American export trade in grain, a subject of great importance to Odessa, which was then Russia's chief port for the export of grain.
The book is comprehensive in its coverage, including American agricultural
methods as well as the organization of grain elevators, railroads, and credit
services that allowed the United States to become a major factor in the world
market. Orbinskii is not, however, antagonistic to America, saying in a letter
to a St. Louis newspaper that he had "never met a competitor so gentlemanlike and noble as your country."

Otchet General'nago Kommisara russkago otdiela Vsemirnoi Kolumbovoi Vystavki v Chikago Kamergera Vysochaishago Dvora P. I. Glukhovskago

[Report of the General Commissar of the Russian section of the World's Columbian Exposition in Chicago, Gentleman of the Imperial Court P. I. Glukhovskii]. St. Petersburg, Tipografiia V. Kirshbauma, 1895. 210 p.

T500.G1R88 (Russian Imperial Coll).

The volume is filled with illustrations of the fair, particularly of the Russian exhibits, and there are names of many Russians who came both officially and as private visitors, to view the exposition. The report notes (p. 150) that Russian visitors also had the opportunity of seeing many American industrial plants, for America, according to the report, lacks the practice of "factory secrets." This was particularly true, since, "between the two distant countries there can be no sort of mutual rivalry through trickery." Many of the Russians listed in this volume wrote about the Exposition or about individual branches of American industry for both technical and general publications in Russia. Some of these works are important and detailed analyses of American practices.

Otechestvennyia zapiski

[Fatherland notes].   AP50.O85

The first journal issued under this title was begun by Pavel Svin'in in 1818 and continued until 1830. In 1839, with Svin'in's permission and with some participation by him, another serial was begun, which continued until 1884. This series was generally regarded by the authorities as having questionable, and almost impermissible, tendencies, and in 1884, during the reaction that followed the assassination of Alexander II, it ceased publication (see also Syn otechestva, listed below).

Petrov, Grigorii Spiridonovich

Lampa Aladina [Aladdin's lamp]. 2. izd. St. Petersburg, Tipografiia P. F. Voshchinskoi, 1905. p. 24–46: Skazochnaia strana [A fabulous country].

AC65.P43 1905

The author (1868–1927) was a Russian Orthodox clergyman, represented in the Library of Congress catalog by 19 entries, largely on specific religious topics. This selection, however, deals with the United States, discussing the wealth not only of J. P. Morgan and Andrew Carnegie, but also that of the ordinary working man who has, Petrov writes, a house of such size and furnishings that, from the Russian point of view, it is entirely an unrealizable dream. America's prosperity, Petrov says, is based on the leading factor of American education, and the reader can easily infer that he felt that Russia could reach a comparable level only by developing the mind of the nation. "Look on the people not only as a crude labor force, but as a mental power capable of constant and endless development and perfection."

Pliskii, Nikolai N.

Podrobnyi putevoditel' na Vsemirnuiu Kolumbovuiu Vystavku v Chikago 1893 goda [Detailed guide to the World's Columbian Exposition in Chicago in 1893]. St. Petersburg, Tipo-lit. "Stefanov i Kachka," 1893. 125 p.

Yudin T600.P7

A small guidebook, almost awestruck in places by the energy and prosperity of Chicago, and filled with useful details about routes from Russia to America, the peculiarities of American railroads, the gaiety and variety of Chicago saloons, and yet—since it was prepared before the Exposition opened—relatively general in its description of the main event. A short phonetic guide to English is given for benefit of the Russian visitor, taking up such matters as "tu uash e shert" (to wash a shirt). Pliskii also wrote a small pamphlet with the long title *Prichiny bystrago obogashcheniia amerikantsev i prevoskhodstva amerikanskikh millionerov nad evropeiskimi* [Causes of the rapid enrichment of the Americans and of the superiority of American millionaires over the European ones] (St. Petersburg, Tipo-lit. Stefanova i Kachka, 1893. 27 p.) as well as *Reklama* [Advertising] (St. Petersburg, Izd. F. V. Shchepanskago, 1894. 175 p.) with much about American practices.

Poletika, Petr Ivanovich

Aperçu de la situation intérieure des États-Unis d'Amérique et de leurs rapports avec l'Europe. Londres, Chez J. Both, Duke Street, Portland Place, 1826. 164 p.   JK411.P78

The original title page indicates only "par un russe" as identification of the author, but it quickly became known that Petr Poletika, Russian minister to the United States in the early 1820s, had written it. An American edition appeared as *A Sketch of the Internal Conditions of the United States of America and of their Political Relations with Europe* (Baltimore, E. J. Coale, 1826. 163 p. JK411.P8). It is not distinguished by any great spark of style or anecdote, although Poletika does see that, while the United States may at times find itself in a position sympathetic to Russia, the whole ties of history, culture, and economics bring it closer to Great Britain.

Popov, V.

Russkoe slovo, 1861, no. 8, "Inostrannaia literatura:" 1–11.

AP50.R87

Popov is not otherwise known to history, and apparently with good reason, for his is of the opinion that French literature in 1860–61 was at so low a state that the blood-and-thunder writer of absurd tales about the American frontier Gustave Aimard was one of the few stars of the first order in the literature of a country concerned only with the outward side of life. Popov also uses this review to aim blows at an America in which "gold is everything" to its inhabitants.

Popytki konkurirovat' s Amerikoi i polozhenie nashei khliebnoi torgovli

[Efforts to compete with America and the situation of our grain trade]. Otechestvennye zapiski, 1881, no. 6 (Sovremennoe obozrienie): 239–266.

AP50.O85

This is essentially a review of Orbinskii's book, but indicates some of the politico-philosophical outlook of the reviewer. A Soviet guide to the anonymous and pseudonymous contents of this journal shows that it was written by Mikhail Evgrafovich Saltykov, who wrote bitter satires on Russian ills under the pseudonym of Shchedrin. In Soviet literary history he is one of the cultural heroes of the nineteenth century, and it is, therefore, interesting to note

(p. 245) his prediction that Russia may one day have to buy grain from America in place of forcing the export, as was then the case, of grain actually needed for domestic consumption.

Prugavin, Aleksandr S.

Nepriemlushchie mira: ocherki religioznykh iskanii [Those who do not accept the world: essays on religious strivings]. Moscow, Zadruga, 1918. 45–76.

                                                                 BR936.P72

This is a further account of Aleksandr K. Malikov's adventures in Frey's commune in Kansas. Some of the edged tone may be based on the fact that Prugavin was Malikov's brother-in-law. Certainly Prugavin tends to emphasize the commune's lack of competence—cow sheds built of such small logs that when a cow attempted to scratch herself the building fell.

Radishchev, Aleksandr I.

Puteshestvie iz Peterburga v Moskvu [A trip from Petersburg to Moscow]. 1790. 453 p.   HN525.R3 1790 (Rare BK Coll)

This scathing attack on serfdom and repression was so frightening to the authorities, especially to Catherine II, that all discoverable copies were confiscated and its author was condemned to death, by rather questionable legal procedures, a penalty later commuted to exile to Siberia. Not until 1906 was it possible to publish this book for general circulation. Original copies are great rarities. One of them is in the collection of the Library of Congress.

Rakov, V. A.

Lokomotivy zheleznykh dorog Sovetskogo Soiuza ot pervykh parovozov do sovremennykh lokomotivov [The locomotives of the railroads of the Soviet Union from the first steam engines to contemporary locomotives]. Moscow, Gosudarstvennoe transportnoe i zheleznodorozhnoe izdatel'stvo, 1955. 455 p.   TJ603.R34

The early Russian steam engines illustrated in this work have clear relationships to American machines of the time, which can be explained by the fact that the Baltimore firm headed by Ross Winans and other American builders participated in the management of Russia's locomotive factory.

Ral'f Val'do Emmerson, amerikanskii poet i filosof

[Ralph Waldo Emerson, American poet and philosopher]. Biblioteka dlia chteniia, 1847, t. 85, otd. VII: 36–69.   AP50.B5

The earliest extensive discussion of an American author in Russian to have come to light thus far. The anonymous author had a good knowledge of Emerson's work, and also of the work of some of those around him, and there is an emphasis on the factors in American life that made for stability and order that is in striking contrast to general European assumptions of the era that the United States was filled with turmoil and lack of consistency.

Reid, Mayne

The headless horseman. New York, G. W. Dillingham, 1892. 406 p.

                                                             PZ7.R273He2

Comment on Reid's novel in this work is based on this edition. The book had actually appeared more than thirty years earlier and there had been other publications in the meantime, including translations into several European languages. Reid is not so absurd as Aimard—he has no ostriches on the Upper Missouri—but his plots could only be called wildly comic: three times in a single morning the hero's neck is placed in a noose and three individual spoilsports turn up to interrupt. Several Russian journals for young people offered sets of Reid's novels as subscription premiums in the period before 1917, and the Christmas announcement journal of a major publisher emphasized Reid's volumes in its 1913 issue. Soviet editions of *The Headless Horseman* have appeared as recently as the 1980s. While the Library of Congress has a copy of *Vsadnik bez golovy* [The headless horseman] from 1943 (PR2519.R25H44 1943), there was not time in the preparation of this survey to examine it to determine how Reid's strong anti-Indian statements were handled.

Reitern, Mikhail Kh.

Vliianie ekonomicheskago kharaktera naroda na obrazovanii kapitalov [The influence of the economic character of a people on capital formation]. Morskoi sbornik, 1860, no. 5, unofficial section: 55–72.   V5.M8

Reitern, then a rising young official in the naval ministry, was sent abroad to study accounting methods and pension plans, and his trip included a visit to the United States. This article is in large part an analysis of the American spirit of enterprise, a spirit which he also finds among the Russians but which, he clearly indicates, is hampered by artificial barriers imposed from above. By reference to the bad effects of slavery on the economy of the American South, Reitern is able to make a strong criticism of Russian serfdom. The article is in essence a plea for a less regulated economy, strengthened by pointed citations of the American example. In 1862 Reitern was appointed Minister of Finance, holding that post until 1878. There is little direct evidence of any further use by him of American concepts, although in his term of office he did have to contend with problems of currency stabilization, tariff policy, and rail and industrial construction that were much like those of the United States of the time.

Rossiiski-Amerikanskaia kompaniia

Otchet . . . za 1851 g. [Report . . . for the year 1851]. St. Petersburg, Pechatano v tipografii Shtaba Inspektora po inzhenernoi chasti, 1852.
F907.R83

This includes as a supplement an unattributed Russian copy of a map by the American naval officer and pioneer oceanographer Matthew F. Maury showing the seas of the world divided into quadrangles of latitude and longitude, with symbols of the presence and seasonal frequency of several major species of whales. The Russian-American Company was interested in fostering whaling in the North Pacific, hiring American harpooners to teach their skills. It is not known what connection there may have been between this interest and the publication in Moskvitianin [The Muscovite] (1853, t. IV, no. 15, otd. VIII: 99–125) of the whaling chapter from *Moby Dick*, its apparent first appearance in another language.

Rozen, I. B.

Eshche nieskol'ko slov ob amerikanskikh traktorakh [A few additional words about American tractors]. *In:* Khoziaistvo, 1911, no. 39: 1247–1248.

S13.K36

Rozen was the American agent of the Ekaterinoslav province local government board. The article is a further consideration of the possibilities for the application of mechanization to Russian agriculture.

Rubinow, Isaac M.

Russia's wheat trade. Washington, Government Printing Office, 1908. 77 p. (U. S. Department of Agriculture. Bureau of Statistics, Bulletin 65)

HD9049.W5R98

The author, who was of Russian origin, came to the United States as a young man and was a frequent contributor to Russian journals of articles on American economic and social topics. During a period of employment in the statistical branch of the Department of Agriculture he wrote this and two other works, *Russia's Wheat Surplus* (Washington, Government Printing Office, 1906. 103 p. HD9001.A5(no.42)), and *Russian Wheat and Wheat Flour in European Markets* (Washington, Government Printing Office, 1908. 99 p. HD9049.W5R982), which are the chief American studies of the international role of Russia's grain. On page 10 of *Russia's Wheat Trade* is a telling anecdote of Russian peasants arriving at a grain shipping point with the question "How much was wheat in America yesterday?" as an indication of what they might expect to receive, being immediately able to translate cents per bushel into kopecks per pood.

Rubakin, N. A.

Etiudy o russkoi chitaiushchei publikie; fakty, tsifry i nabliudeniia [Studies of the Russian reading public; facts, figures and observations]. St. Petersburg, 1895. 246 p.

Z1003.R88

N. A. Rubakin was one of the originators of the study of the reading habits of the general public on the basis of what they actually read rather than upon assumptions as to cultural values and esthetic criteria. While library statistics are notoriously vague, Rubakin's conclusions that, at least in Nizhnyi Novgorod in 1883, Gustave Aimard was more popular than Gogol', Pushkin, or Lermontov, to mention but three of the most noteworthy Russian authors of the nineteenth century, provide some basis for the view that the public preferred gaudy adventure tales to the subtler forms of literature. When one notes in addition that such now obscure non-Russian writers as Ponçon-du-Terrail, Montepin, and Marlitt also outstripped some of the Russian classics, the level of readers' interests is clear.

Russia. Glavnoe upravlenie po dielam pechati

Ukazatel' po dielam pechati [Index to press affairs] 9.1–7; 1 sent. 1872–15dek.1878. St. Petersburg.

Z2491.R9

The monthly journal of the censorship authorities. It was issued to, among others, the customs officers at border crossing points as a guide to what publications might be admitted to the Empire and what must be excluded or, if admitted, what sections should be excised. Although the number of titles of foreign works included in this series suggests that French and German works predominated, there was a substantial flow of material in English, including many American books. Although an entry cannot be taken as showing that there was anything more than a single attempt to import a foreign work, there is a certain amount of evidence to be derived from the mere citation of an item.

Russia. Glavnoe upravlenie zemledieliia i zemleustroistva
Izviestiia [News] The principal official publication of the central agricultural authorities of the Russian Empire.   Microfilm 85196

Russia. Glavnoe upravlenie zemledieliia i zemleustroistva
Biuro po sel' sko-khoziaistvennoi mekhanikie. Izviestiia [News]. 1909–1916.   Microfilm 83/5231, no. 102, reels 24, 25
The publication of the Bureau of Agricultural Mechanization of the Chief Administration of Agriculture and Land Reclamation (one of the variant titles of the chief agricultural agency of the Empire). It contains many articles on American agricultural implements, including tests of tractors. The Library of Congress holds an incomplete, but important, run of this publication.

Russia. Ministerstvo inostrannykh del
Vneshniaia politika Rossii deviatnadtsatogo i nachala dvadtsatogo veka; dokumenty rossiiskago ministerstva inostrannykh del [The foreign policy of Russia of the nineteenth and beginning of the twentieth centuries; documents of the Imperial Russian ministry of foreign affairs]. Moscow, Gosudarstvennoe izdatel'stvo politicheskoi literatury, 1960–   DK65.A5
This is an important series of documents chosen from the archives of the Russian Empire, providing the original text, usually in French—since that language was used by Russia's diplomats through most of the nineteenth century—as well as a Russian translation. There are substantial annotations and references to other materials of relevance. While Russia was chiefly preoccupied with European affairs, there are numbers of documents relating to the United States. One may, for example, trace Russia's part in the events that brought about the formulation of the Monroe Doctrine, and there are some startling references to Russian hopes that the United States might join the so-called Holy Alliance. The latter subject was evidently not given much consideration by John Quincy Adams, either as secretary of state from 1817 to 1825 or as president from 1825 to 1829, as he does not mention it in his diary. The reader is also left with the impression that most of the Russian envoys to America were not extremely perceptive, although one of them did undertake his own intelligence gathering by visiting an American naval vessel about to set out for the West Coast to discover if it was planned to establish a base in the Oregon Country, which might cause complications in Russia's occupation of Alaska.

Russia. Ministerstvo putei soobshchenii Zhurnal [Journal]

The official organ of the ministry responsible for Russia's roads and waterways and, after 1840, railroads. There are numbers of articles reporting on American rail and water transport. The Library of Congress has received a substantial microfilm copy of this journal.

Salov, Vladimir Viktorovich

Zemledielie—glavnaia osnova blagosostoianiia Rossii. Sravnitel'nyi ocherk sostoianiia zemledieliia v Soedinennykh Shtatakh Sievernoi Ameriki i v Rossii po novieishim dannym. Miery k podniatiiu v Rossii sel'skokhoziaistvennoi promyshlennosti i sviazannykh s nieiu otraslei narodnago truda [Agriculture—the chief basis of the well-being of Russia. Comparative survey of the position of agriculture in the United States of North America and in Russia according to recent data. Measures for the improvement in Russia of agricultural production and of the related branches of the economy]. St. Petersburg, Tipografiia Ministerstva putei soobshcheniia, 1909. 143 p.

Microfilm 87/6240(H)

A comparison of the flourishing state of American agriculture with the ill-coordinated situation in Russia. America is seen as a source of fruitful, if not totally applicable, suggestions of benefit to Russia. The publishing house, that of the Ministry of Transport, indicates official backing for this work.

Scherr, Johannes.

Angliia i Sievernaia Amerika [England and North America]. *In:* Vseobshchaia istoriia literatury [History of world literature]. 3d ed. v. 2, pt. 3, chapter 1. St. Petersburg, 1880: 3–125.

A Russian translation, unavailable in the U.S., of Scherr's *Allgemeine Geschichte der Literatur* (several editions). To judge from the German original, this is largely a historical rather than critical work. Those interested in the scope of the unavailable Russian translation may wish to consult the 5th German ed.: 5. ergäntzte Aufl. Stuttgart, C. Conradi. 1875 2v. in 1.

PN553.S28 1875

S"ezd khlopkovodov, Tashkend, 1912

Trudy [Transactions]. v. 1.Tashkent, Tipografiia pri Kantseliarii Turkestanskago general-gubernatorstva, 1913.   SB251.R9S47 1912

The Library of Congress has only this first volume of the proceedings of the convention of cotton growers held in Tashkent in November 1912. This volume shows how much Russia, in its desire to free itself from dependence on imports of cotton from the United States, still rested upon the American example in its effort to improve Russian methods.

Shirokikh, Ivan O.

Ocherki mirovogo proizvodstva pshenitsy [Survey of the world production of wheat] *In:* Novo-Aleksandriiskii institut sel'skago khoziaistva i liesovodstva. Trudy [Transactions]. v. 22, vyp. 2. St. Petersburg, 1909. p. 1–45.

S13.N5

Neither Shirokikh nor the institute that published his article appear to have been major factors in Russian agricultural science, but the text, a lecture read at the institute on April 11, 1909, begins with a reference to Longfellow's description of Hiawatha bringing the gift of grain to man and contains references to Frank Norris's novel *The Octopus* and its description of grain growing in California. Russia will, he says, have to do all that is possible to increase production and the impression is left that the American model would be of great importance.

Skal'kovskii, Konstantin A.

V strane iga i svobody; putevyia vpechatleniia [In the country of the yoke and of freedom; travel impressions]. St. Petersburg, Tip. T-va "Obshchestvennaia pol'za," 1877. 415 p.   Microfilm 84/6011(G)

The author visited the United States in 1876 as an observer of the Centennial Exposition in Philadelphia. He also wrote a short treatise on American mining law and administration. His larger work is a compilation of his contributions to the conservative St. Petersburg newspaper *Novoe vremia*, and his verdict is in general an unfavorable one.

Slavinskii, Nikolai Evstaf'evich

Pis'ma ob Amerikie i russkikh pereselentsakh [Letters about America and the Russian emigrants]. St. Petersburg, Tip. P. P. Merkuleva, 1873. 303 p.   Microfilm 84/6002(E)

In addition to the description of William Frey's commune in Kansas which is drawn on in this survey, the book has a great deal of detail on the then small group of Russian immigrants to be found in New York City. The account of the adventures of a Russian operatic entrepreneur is worthy of the attention of such Russian authors as Leskov or Saltykov-Shchedrin.

Solov'eva, Aida M.

Zheleznodorozhnyi transport Rossii vo vtoroi polovine XIX v. [Railroad transport of Russia in the second half of the 19th century]. Moscow, Izdatel'stvo "Nauka," 1975. 315 p.   HE3137.S64

The major Russian car and locomotive plant produced between 1844 and 1856 196 locomotives, 253 passenger cars, and 2,600 freight cars. The plant was managed by an American firm in which the Baltimore locomotive builder Ross Winans had a leading role. Though the Soviet author speaks of him as an exploiter she also says that in the mid-nineteenth century the St. Petersburg-Moscow line rightfully held first place among the railroads of all countries of the world, which would seem to show that Winans was in fact a beneficial element in Russian development.

Sovremennik

[The contemporary] St. Petersburg, 1836–1866   AP50.S695

The first editor of this journal was Aleksandr Pushkin, and the most outstanding American item of the period is Pushkin's own review of John Tanner's *A Narrative of the Captivity and Adventures of John Tanner* . . . , an account of life among the Indians of the Upper Great Lakes. Vladimir Nabokov's copious annotations to Pushkin's great poem *Evgenii Onegin* make it clear that the writer's knowledge of English was not actually strong and it seems that the review was largely based on a French translation of Tanner's work. In the late 1850s and the 1860s there were numbers of American-related items, expressing a generally liberal outlook.

Stal'noe zhalo
[The steel sting]. Petrograd, Izdatel'stvo "Razvlechenie," 1916. 32 p.
Microfilm 85/2012(P)
Microfilm of this late example of the many translations of the adventures of Nat Pinkerton was supplied to the Library of Congress by a Soviet library in the early 1980s. The original edition was passed by the Military Censorship on November 18, 1916 (O.S.), scarcely three months before the abdication of the emperor. The action deals with a series of mysterious murders in New York, ending with a "triumph of justice" through the agency of the brave Nat Pinkerton. Russian liking for such bold tales did not disappear with the Revolution, for there was a current of what was called Soviet Pinkertonism, to the point that the greatest box office success of any Soviet film of 1927 was that of *Miss Mend,* a thriller in the Pinkerton tradition.

Stowe, Harriet Beecher
Khizhina diadi Toma; poviest' dlia dietei [Uncle Tom's cabin; a tale for children]. Moscow, Tip. A. A. Kartseva, 1887. 256 p.   Yudin PZ63.S89K45
It was not until 1857, five years after its completion, that *Uncle Tom's Cabin* appeared in Russian. The similarities between American slavery and Russian serfdom were such that discussions were considered impermissible by the authorities. Finally, the conservative publisher Mikhail Katkov included it as a supplement to his *Russkii viestnik,* issuing it also in separate form. The next year there were two other translations, one by five different translators. After that it was almost continuously in print. There were also stage versions, the only one of which available in the Library of Congress leaves Uncle Tom alive at the curtain. The edition cited here is the earliest of the four Russian ones entered in the Library of Congress catalog. As the Kushnerev firm's *O dietskikh knigakh* (listed by title in this bibliography) shows, there appear to have been twelve Russian editions available in 1908. Years of misunderstanding have clouded in American minds the skill and force of Mrs. Stowe's work, one in which Uncle Tom consciously accepts death rather than betray two women fellow slaves, and, apparently, the Russian reader did not fall prey to such an outlook. The book is still published in the Soviet Union and perhaps carries a message that Americans no longer seem to receive.

Suvorovskii, A.
Nat Pinkerton v dietskom ponimanii [Nat Pinkerton as understood by children]. Viestnik vospitanii, 1909, no. 1: 159–163.   LP51.V416
While Suvorovskii questioned only seventy students aged fourteen and fifteen equally divided between boys and girls, he concludes that the cultural effects of the Nat Pinkerton-Nick Carter literature were not so upsetting as they seemed to Chukovskii. Students were seeking examples of energetic and strong personalities, which these American heroes provided, and they found

compensation for the lack, in Russian literature for young people, of writings about struggle and activity.

Sviatlovskii, Vladimir V.
    V stranie dollarov [In the country of dollars].   Newspaper

Novoe vremia, 1893	28 July/9 August: 2
1/13 April: 3	2/14 August: 1
12/24 April: 1–2	12/24 August: 1–2
3/15 May: 2	13/25 August: 1
20 May/1 June: 2–3	19/31 August: 2
25 May/ 6 June: 2	26 August/7 September: 2
12/24 June 1893: 2	29 August/10 September: 3
17/29 June: 1	2/14 September: 3
18/30 June: 1–1	5/17 September: 3
21 July/2 August: 2	6/18 September: 1–2
23 July/4 August: 1	10/22 September: 2
27 July/8 August: 1–2	13/25 September: 1–2

    These letters to the major St. Petersburg newspaper *Novoe vremia*, a quite conservative journal that, at least typographically, modeled itself somewhat after *The Times* of London—classified advertisements on the first page in some periods—are in general quick to note America's flaws, and it appears that Sviatlovskii did not have the background knowledge that, for example, Varvara MacGahan had acquired over the years. *Novoe vremia* included other items about the Chicago Exposition, some from its long-time resident correspondent P. I. Popov, and there were advertisements such as [In English]: "English woman, experienced traveler, who has been in America offers services to those families or ladies wishing to visit Chicago" (19 April/1 May 1893: 3) or [in Russian]. "F. A. Hill of the New York (Insurance) Company can supply steamer tickets, etc. for visitors to the Chicago fair." Sviatlovskii appears to have published some of his material as articles in *Russkoe obozrienie*, April 1893: 845–64; June 1893: 784–817; August 1893: 831–42; September 1893: 327–38; October 1893: 887–909; and November 1893: 317–45. In 1896, following the All-Russian Exposition held that year in Nizhnyi Novgorod, he published "Iz zamietkok o vystavkie v Chikago" [From notes about the Exposition in Chicago] in *Russkoe obozrienie* of August, September, and October of 1896. The list of Sviatlovskii's articles in *Novoe vremia* may be incomplete, as searching the small and blurry type of the microfilms of this newspaper is rather difficult, and headline type was not generously sized. It also appears that there was no dispatch in this paper about the tragic end of the Exposition after the shooting of the Chicago Mayor and the consequent cancelling of a triumphal close.

Syn otechestva
    [Son of the Fatherland]. St. Petersburg, 1812–1844, 1847–1852.
                                                                AP50.S8
    This was a leading journal among the rather sparse group of Russian periodicals of its time. There was a marked American component in its contents, particularly in the form of contributions by the diplomat/writer/artist

Pavel Svin'in. It should be noted, in dealing with Russian serials of the nineteenth century, that many included more than one pagination in their issues. This poses bibliographic problems that can often only be resolved by careful examination of the individual numbers.

Tanner, John
A narrative of the captivity and adventures of John Tanner, (U. S. interpreter at the Saut de Ste. Marie,) during thirty years residence among the Indians in the interior of North America. New York, G. & C. & H. Carvill, 1830. 426 p. E87.T15 (Rare BK Coll)

Aleksandr Pushkin's review of this work in *Sovremennik*, 1836, no. 3: 207–256 is the Russian writer's most substantial reference to the United States. As Vladimir Nabokov's notes to Pushkin's *Evgenii Onegin* make clear, the review was actually based upon a French translation that had appeared in Paris in 1835—perhaps *Mémoires de John Tanner* (Paris, A. Bertrand, 1835. 2v. E87.T153)—since Pushkin's competence in English was not strong. While current Soviet analyses present this review as criticism of American policy from the a liberal point of view, it is in fact a strongly conservative piece of writing, repeating many of the themes used by those of monarchical convictions, and it is not particularly original in its thought.

Tolstoi, Lev Nikolaevich
Journaux et carnets. Edited and annotated by Gustave Aucouturier. Paris, Gallimard, 1979–1985. 3v. PG3377.F5A9

The notes of this edition, as well as the texts of Tolstoi's journals and notebooks, combine information about his view of America that is not available in the more extensive—but in some ways less knowledgeable—ninety volumes in Russian of his complete writings. There are also reflections of Tolstoi's religious searchings that may have some similarities with the outlook of the American Unitarian clergyman William Ellery Channing (see the entry for the Russian translation of a Channing essay and for a biographical sketch that may have been known to Tolstoi).

Tolstoi, Lev Nikolaevich
Polnoe sobranie sochinenii [Complete collected works]. Moscow, Leningrad, Gosudarstvennoe izdatel'stvo khudozhestvennoi literatury, 1928–1958. 90 v. PG3365.A1 1928

This is the edition conventionally known as "iubileinoe izdanie, "since it was issued to mark the centenary of Tolstoi's birth. It contains all his writings, including drafts, notes, letters, and diaries. However, the volumes offering works considered unsuitable for broad distribution in the Soviet Union were issued in restricted numbers in comparison to volumes with the approved classics. The series lacks a subject index and the reader must often resort to seeking in the name index those people who might have engendered correspondence or Tolstoi's remarks in order to determine the topics discussed. Often this method leads to startling results. There are, for example, some ninety-five references to Henry D. Thoreau and his writings—and Thoreau's influence on Tolstoi has been much discussed. However, the obscure American spiritualist writer Lucy Mallory and her journal *World Advance Thought* appear a total of 120 times. In other instances (see entries in this bibliography for F. W. Evans and W. F. Evans) people are confounded with one another. The most extensive reference to any American is the 300 some entries for the economist and reformer Henry George.

Trent, William P. and John Erskine
Velikie amerikanskie pisateli [Great American writers]. St. Petersburg, P. I. Pevin, 1914. 144 p.
A Russian translation, unavailable in the U.S., of *Great American Writers* (New York, H. Holt and Co., 1912. 256 p. PS92.T75), this work deals with a number of individual writers, from Franklin, Brockden Brown and Irving to Whitman, Bret Harte and Mark Twain, and is not, therefore, an analysis of the general nature of our literature. However, it appears to have been the most extensive treatment in the Russian language to have been published before 1917.

Tsimmerman, Eduard R.
Puteshestvie po Amerikie [Travels in America]. Russkii viestnik [Russian herald], No. I. February 1859: 404–434; No. II. March 1895: 23–60; no. III. June 1859: 582–612.   AP50.R83
Tsimmerman first visited the United States in 1857–58, and was to return at least twice thereafter, in 1869–70, and some time during the 1880s. All his visits were subject for books and articles in the Russian press, and he wrote about topics such as American education, land policies, and agriculture. His last work, issued the year he died, in 1903, was about the Trans-Siberian Railroad and included comments about contrasts between Russian and American methods. Tsimmerman's article on Chicago in *Russkii viestnik,* December 1858: 462–473 should also be noted.

Tsimmerman, Eduard R.
Soedinennye Shtaty Sievernoi Ameriki [The United States of North America]. Moscow, Izd. K. T. Soldatenkova, 1873. 2 v. in 1.
E168.T85 Rare BK Coll.
This work includes much of Tsimmerman's articles of 1859 describing his visit to America in 1857–1858, with further material on a second journey in 1869–1870. There is a certain breadth of view because of this historical perspective that is not common to most of the European travelers of the time. Tsimmerman was to visit this country at least one further time (in the 1880s) and to make additional contributions to the Russian press on American themes, including in his last published work—a discussion of the Trans-Siberian Railroad—comparisons between Russian and American rail policies.

Tur, Evgeniia
(pseud. of Elizaveta V. Salias de Turnemir). Uil'iam Channing [William Channing]. Russkii viestnik, 1858, t. 14: 445–512.   AP50.R83
Evgeniia Tur, an earnest, prolific, and not especially talented writer, has apparently drawn on at least one quite detailed biography of Channing and, it seems, other works about America in writing a survey that, according to an

obituary article for her in 1892, had not lost its importance. Although there is no direct evidence, it is possible that L. N. Tolstoi was aware of this article, for in the following year he was to write for *Russkii viestnik,* and one of his works appeared in immediate proximity to a translation from one of Channing's sermons. Furthermore, some of Tolstoi's religious searchings at this time are remarkably similar to elements in Channing's outlook.

Turkestanskoe sel'skoe khoziaistvo
[Turkestan agriculture]. Taskkent, 1906–1916.   S13.T85

This was the organ of the Turkestan Agricultural Society, a leading figure of which was the agronomist Rikhard Rikhardovich Shreder. Cotton was a major crop of the area, and the journal contains many references to American methods in that branch of agriculture, as well as advertisements of American machines. Many other articles deal with American implements in such fields as fruit growing, fodder crops, and cold storage installations. One area of particular interest was "dry farming," which includes procedures for making the best possible use of soil moisture in areas of low rainfall, a field in which American experience was a world leader at the time. The Library of Congress set, though not complete, is a substantial one, with many reflections of the American example.

Tverskoi, P. A.
(pseud. of Peter A. Demens, born Petr A. Dement'ev)

Sovremennaia belletristika v amerikanskoi periodicheskoi pechati [Contemporary literature in the American periodical press]. Viestnik Evropy, 1895, no. 8: 515–543   AP50.V5

Novoe techenie v amerikanskoi belletristikie [A new tendency in American literature]. Viestnik Evropy, 1909, no. 8: 671–678.

"P. A. Tverskoi"/Peter A. Demens/Petr A. Dement'ev resided in the United States from 1881 until his death in 1919. He was a railroad promoter in Florida, a citrus grower, steam laundry owner, banker, secretary of a company that made shaving soap in California, and a copious contributor to the Russian press of articles on American affairs. Many of his writings appeared in *Viestnik Evropy,* a serious journal that "everybody" read, including Tolstoi, Nicholas II, and—to judge by a quotation, albeit at second hand—Lenin. These articles on literature are the views of an alert and intelligent man, but not those of one with any great familiarity with American literature, although, while still in Russia he had been the first to translate Longfellow's "The Wreck of the Hesperus." His other writings on the United States must, nevertheless, have had considerable influence in forming Russian opinions.

U. S. Department of Commerce and Labor
Daily consular and trade reports. Washington, Government Printing Office, 1910–1940. 99v.   HC1.R98

Selections from the dispatches of American representatives in foreign countries. The information provided is often rather unexpected, such as reports of promising success with the export of American shoes to Russia, the clash between American agricultural implement makers and those of other nations, and the varying analyses of the possibilities for success of American motion pictures in pre-1914 Russia.

United States. Department of State
Commercial relations of the United States with foreign countries. Washington, Government Printing Office, 1855/56–1902.   HF105.B3

This annual compilation of selected reports from American consular and diplomatic officials frequently contains reflections on attitudes of foreign countries that cannot be found in other sources. The dispatches from Russia are often of great interest as testimony of the depth of Russian concern with American competition in the international grain trade.

U. S. Library of Congress. Manuscript Division. Foreign Copying Project
The materials of this project include: Russia. Ministry of Foreign Affairs. Principal Archives of the Ministry of Foreign Affairs. v. 49: Dispatches of Stoeckl, Russian Minister in Washington, to Gorchakov, Minister of Foreign Affairs, 1860–1865. Containers 2 & 3.

These reports of Éduard A. Stoeckl, the quite conservative and not too perceptive Russian envoy, reflect the events of the American Civil War and show something of the Russian wish to maintain an undivided United States as a useful counterweight to Britain and France with whom, in the summer of 1863, there was a controversy over the Polish question that seemed to provide a possible cause for war. Russia's need for America remained an element in relations between the two countries for at least fifteen years after the end of the Civil War, until growing disagreements over Russian treatment of naturalized Americans of Russo-Jewish background and a growing commercial rivalry in the North Pacific brought heightened differences between the two nations.

Vengerova, Zinaida.
Amerikanskaia literatura [American literature]. In: Batiushkov, F. D., ed. Istoriia zapadnoi literatury [History of Western literature]. v. 3. Moscow, 1914: 288–327.   PN583.B3

In fewer than forty pages Vengerova manages to include nineteen American writers, from Cotton Mather and Franklin to Holmes and Stowe. While she must be given credit for having noted the Southern writer W. G. Sims and having made one of the very few Russian references to John Greenleaf Whittier, she is but a pedestrian writer, on the level of a junior college textbook.

Veniukov, M. I.
Illinois i Chikago [Illinois and Chicago]. Nabliudatel', 1893, no. 5: 113–21.   AP50.N33

The writer is not a person of any great prominence, and the journal is a rather unattractive organ of a strong anti-Semitic outlook. This article, however, testifies to the way in which Russians looked upon the World's Columbian Exposition in Chicago in 1893, and it contains the phrase, startling to present-day American ears, that Russia would have forty commissars in Chicago to study the fair. By the usage of the time, however, commissar meant only delegate or official representative. By actual tally of those listed in the report of the head of the Russian delegation, there were at least 58 persons with official status, not counting others in government positions who came as private visitors.

Verigin, N.
Literatura syska v otsienkie uchenikov srednikh klassov gimnazii [Detective literature as evaluated by students of the intermediate classes of secondary schools] Pedagogicheskii sbornik, 1909, no. 10: 288–302.   L51.V416
The author is by no means so depressed by the flood of Russian translations of American dime novels about the detectives Nick Carter and Nat Pinkerton as was Kornei Chukovskii. Young people, so Verigin wrote, found in these publications compensation for the dullness of daily life and, in some degree, examples of bravery, self-sacrifice, and presence of mind.

Veshniakov, Vladimir I.
Departament zemledieliia v Soedinennykh Shtatakh [The Department of Agriculture in the United States]. In: Russkii viestnik, 1869, no. 1: 252–264.
AP50.R83
In large part a history of the establishment of the United States Department of Agriculture, but the last pages cast an eye on the way in which America's export of grain may be of concern to Russia.

White, Andrew D.
A statesman of Russia. Century magazine, May 1898: 110–18.
AP2.C4
White was the first president of Cornell University, the author of a number of works in defense of intellectual freedom, and America's envoy to both Germany and Russia. In the latter post he had met the Ober-Prokuror of the Most Holy Synod, the chief lay official in control of the Russian Orthodox Church, the eminent legal scholar, rigid conservative, and tutor in their earlier years of both Alexander III and Nicholas II, Konstantin P. Pobedonostsev. Somehow, within this pinched and deadened man, there was a surprising interest in at least one American writer, Ralph Waldo Emerson. White's article notes this factor as one of the touches that gives a somewhat more humane view of Pobedonostsev than newspaper clichés of the time suggested. And yet, given Pobedonostsev's uncredited use of an essay by Emerson in his *Moskovskii sbornik* (Moscow, Sinodal'naia tipografiia, 1896) and his further unattributed translation of an official American census of religious denominations, the question of possible hypocrisy remains open. He is the subject of a cutting sketch for a formal painting of a major governmental assembly by the noted artist Il'ia Repin, a sketch in which he resembles a barely animate mummy.

Yarmolinsky, Avrahm
A Russian's American dream: a memoir on William Frey. Lawrence, Kansas, University of Kansas Press, 1965. 147 p.   HX653.Y3
This work is based on a collection of Frey's papers, held by the New York Public Library. It should, however, be supplemented by reference to works

by Machtet, Slavinskii, Faresov, Hirsch, and Prugavin that are also listed in this bibliography.

Zavalishin, Dmitrii I.

Primiery bystrago razvitiia gorodov v Soedinennykh Shtatakh. I. Chikago [Examples of the rapid development of cities in the United States. I. Chicago]. Moscow, V universitetskoi tipografii, 1868. 34 p.   F548.42.Z3

The author was one of the last surviving members of the Decembrists, the conspirators who sought to bring about a constitutionalist uprising during the confusion that followed the death of Alexander I. This work indicates that, more than forty years after the failure of that attempt, the interest in the United States remained strong. It is not apparent where Zavalishin found his information, but the tone is in general laudatory, reading almost as if the Chicago Board of Trade had compiled it.

Zotov, Vladimir R.

Velikobritaniia i Sievero-Amerikanskie Shtaty. Angliiskaia literatura [Great Britain and the North American States. English literature]. *In:* Zotov, V. R. Istoriia vsemirnoi literatury [History of world literature]. v. 4. St. Petersburg, Moscow, 1882: 349–638.

This appears, from the entries in Valentina Libman's bibliography, to have been the only study of any length by a Russian author to have appeared between 1865 and 1917. It is, however, not available in any reporting library in the country, so that its actual contents cannot be determined. However, Zotov's short obituary article on Walt Whitman (Nabliudatel', 1892, no. 6: 15–16) is not without its interest.

Name Index